P9-DXL-799

Busy Executive! Harried Parent! Gourmet Chef!

Here is an invitation to enjoy to the fullest

The Pleasures of Your Food Processor

At last, in one comb-bound cookbook you find:
- 700 quick, easy, delectable recipes for your processor
- Hundreds of practical hints, shortcuts, money-savers
- Processor operating do's and don'ts that can save you and your machine.
- Daily Food Use Guide for quick and easy processing
- Processor-to-wok cooking
- Ethnic dishes adapted for the processor
- How to adapt cake recipes for the processor
- A chart of baking problems—the trouble-shooter's guide
- A guide to baking temperatures, times, and pan size
- Tips for freezing
- A special section of holiday recipes
- Every section separately indexed for efficiency

Begin your one-volume course now in cooking the easy, processor way!

Fort Nelson Public Library
Box 330
Fort Nelson, BC
V0C-1R0

JUN − − 2006

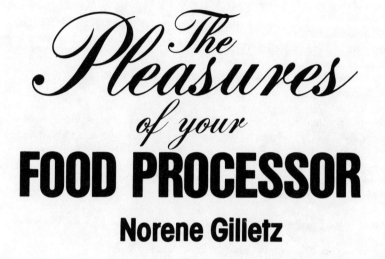

The *Pleasures*
of your
FOOD PROCESSOR
Norene Gilletz

WARNER BOOKS

A Warner Communications Company

Fort Nelson Public Library
Box 330
Fort Nelson, BC
V0C-1R0

Revised edition
Cover design by Barbara Buck
Cover photographs by Daniel Wagner

Warner Books Edition
Copyright © 1982 by Norene Gilletz
All rights reserved.
This Warner Books edition is published by arrangement with
J & N Publishing Ltd.

This book contains every word from the deluxe hardcover edition, with its easel
binder that forms its own cookbook stand, as published by J & N Publishing
Ltd., 141 Avenue Labrosse, Pointe Claire, Quebec, Canada H9R 1A3.

Warner Books, Inc., 666 Fifth Avenue, New York, NY 10103
A Warner Communications Company

Printed in the United States of America

First Warner Printing: June, 1984

10 9 8 7 6 5 4

Library of Congress Cataloging in Publication Data

Gilletz, Norene.
    The pleasures of your food processor.

    Includes index.
    1. Food processor cookery.   I. Title.
TX840.F6G55   1984   641.5'89   83–23542
ISBN 0-446-38373-2   (U.S.A.)
    0-446-38374-0   (Canada)

ATTENTION: SCHOOLS AND CORPORATIONS

Warner books are available at quantity discounts with bulk purchase for educational,
business, or sales promotional use. For information, please write to: **Special Sales
Department, Warner Books, 666 Fifth Avenue, New York, NY 10103.**

**ARE THERE WARNER BOOKS YOU WANT
BUT CANNOT FIND IN YOUR LOCAL STORES?**

You can get any **Warner Books** title in print. Simply send title and retail price, plus 75¢
per order and 50¢ per copy to cover mailing and handling costs for each book desired.
New York State and California residents, add applicable sales tax. Enclose check or
money order—no cash, please—to: **Warner Books, PO Box 690, New York, NY 10019.
Or send for our complete catalog of Warner Books.**

Norene Gilletz received her initial culinary training in her mother's kitchen, where she was taught the art of recycling leftovers! She moved from Winnipeg to Montreal in the sixties and quickly became involved in helping to create and publish *SECOND HELPINGS PLEASE!* which sold over 100,000 copies because of its delicious, down-to-earth recipes.

Numerous requests for another book led her to create *THE PLEASURES OF YOUR PROCESSOR,* which is often referred to as "the processor Bible". Its practical design, delicious recipes and handy hints have quickly made it a Canadian best-seller.

She began a combination cooking school and kitchen shop called *NORENE'S CUISINE* in 1975 in her home. In March 1980 she moved to larger quarters in a shopping centre in suburban Montreal. She has made guest appearances on radio and television, is a cooking consultant and has given numerous cooking lectures and demonstrations both at home and away. She is the mother of three, a daughter and two sons.

Norene constantly strives to broaden her knowledge about food and is an avid cookbook collector. She has studied with such experts as Jacques Pepin and Ann Willan. Norene is a member of the International Association of Cooking Schools.

Her love of good food, her belief that cooking doesn't have to be gourmet to be great and strong encouragement from her students, friends and family have inspired her to compile this book. Norene's recipes are quick and easy to follow, but most important of all, they work!

WELCOME TO THE PLEASURES OF YOUR PROCESSOR!

No, it is not a gadget! The food processor is probably the best investment you will make in your kitchen, and once you familiarize yourself with it, you will wonder how you ever managed without one.

Food processors can't do everything. They won't work in a power failure, they won't wash and dry themselves, and there are times when it **is** faster or easier to use a knife ....but then, nothing is perfect! It is the best friend you can have in your kitchen, that extra pair of hands you always wanted — and it won't talk back or tell you what to do. Its speed and versatility are sure to delight anyone who has to work with food.

My purpose in writing this book is to provide you with a repetoire of simple and delicious recipes for your processor, to encourage you to use it to its maximum potential, to adapt family favorites with ease, and perhaps even to experiment and create new culinary delights on your own!

I have compiled a collection of recipes from many ethnic cultures, recipes with universal appeal guaranteed to tempt the most discriminating palate. They can be enjoyed equally by thinnies, fatties or just-in-betweens. It doesn't matter if you are a swinging single or a harried housewife. My book will get the "I hate to cook" person out of the kitchen quickly and will open the doorway to a new world of cooking pleasures for both the novice and gourmet cook.

Because of my own particular culinary background, I have included many traditional Jewish favorites which are a snap to prepare with the aid of the food processor. I hope that they will become favorites of yours! The ingredients called for in my recipes are easily found on most supermarket shelves. Those who observe the Jewish dietary laws will find that availability of products with the Kosher seal of approval may vary from area to area.

Be a "Processor Planner" — that is, think ahead and plan how to use your machine to its maximum capabilities with minimum clean-ups. After a while, you will develop many shortcuts and tricks of your own. I try to do as many tasks as possible in advance, and store extra ingredients which I have processed in my refrigerator or freezer, ready to be used at a moment's notice.

All recipes in this book were tested on a standard-sized food processor with a direct drive motor, but most can be used on any brand of food processor. However, I suggest you carefully read the manufacturer's instructions **at least twice** to familiarize yourself with any do's and don't's for your particular machine. And practice, practice, practice!

Sincere thanks to my many friends and students who have shared their favorite recipes and tricks with me, and have offered excellent suggestions to make this book practical, informative and explicit. I would also like to thank a special few for their moral support and great assistance in making "The Pleasures of your Processor" become a reality. I will not name anyone specifically, but you know who you are, and I am forever grateful. A special thank you to my "tasters" for their honesty in rating my recipes. I'm glad you survived!

My biggest thank you must go to my family, who helped me in so many ways that I could not possibly list them. They encouraged me, helped clean up all those mountains of pots and pans, put up with my moods through thick and thin, and suffered through feast and famine! This book is dedicated to them.

You don't have to be a gourmet to use your processor, but you may become one once you enter the wonderful world of processing.

Happy Cooking! *Norene Gilletz*

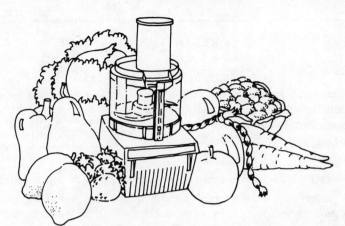

General Information

PARTS OF THE PROCESSOR

All processors have the same basic parts:—

a) A **base** to house the motor. Processor motors are either direct drive or belt driven. Direct drive machines have a temperature controlled circuit breaker so that the motor won't burn out when working with heavy batters. They also run more quietly.

b) A **bowl** that fits onto the base. There is usually a centre post at the bottom of the bowl which fits onto the motor shaft.

c) A **cover** which contains a vertical **feed tube.** Food is usually added through the tube.

d) A **pusher** to guide food through the feed tube, and also to prevent splashing when working with liquids. Never push foods through the feed tube with your fingers!

e) An S-shaped **Steel Knife** which performs about 95% of the tasks, perhaps a **Plastic Knife,** a **Slicer** and a **Grater** (Shredder).

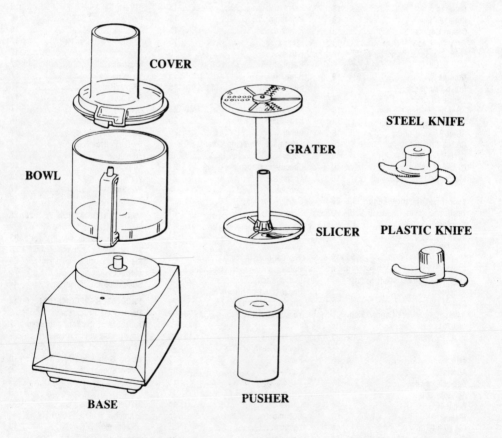

COVER

GRATER

STEEL KNIFE

BOWL

SLICER   PLASTIC KNIFE

BASE   PUSHER

FUNCTIONS OF THE FOOD PROCESSOR

Although a food processor takes up less than a square foot on your countertop, this little kitchen magician will replace the following equipment in your kitchen:- mixer, blender, ice crusher, meat grinder, garlic press, chef's knife, grater, whisk, slicer, pastry blender, parsley mill, peanut butter maker, food mill, nut chopper, cheese mill. There is almost no maintenance; blades can be changed in a snap, and they stay sharp indefinitely.

It is a time-saver, but only if you know how to use it properly. Take the time to read your instruction manual carefully before attempting to use the machine. **THE HINTS AND TIPS GIVEN HERE ARE NOT INTENDED TO REPLACE YOUR MANUAL.**

Ask yourself, "Can I use my processor to do this recipe or task?" The answer will probably be "Yes." Be a Processor Planner!

HOW TO USE YOUR PROCESSOR SAFELY

To use the processor, just lock the bowl onto the base, slip in a blade (making sure that it is all the way down on the motor shaft before turning on the machine), fit the cover onto the bowl, and give the cover a twist in one direction to start the blades spinning, then twist in the opposite direction to stop. **Wait until the blades stop spinning before you remove the cover.** Some processors are equipped with a pulse action button that turns the machine on and off quickly as you touch, then release, the button.

If the cover does not turn easily, rub a little cooking oil around the rim of the cover and the bowl. To prevent the bowl from developing an odor, don't store the pusher in the feed tube when the machine is not in use.

Keep your processor handy on the counter, ready to use. Don't hide it away in a cupboard! Blades should be stored in a special blade holder away from the reach of young children, on a magnetic knife rack, or in a large box or bowl. Don't store blades in a drawer where you may reach in blindly and perhaps cut yourself.

Remember that the blades are very sharp. Treat them with respect.

Don't leave the cord hanging over the edge of a counter where it can be pulled down accidentally by a young child. Don't let the cord dangle across or near a stove element.

Don't store the machine with the cover locked in the ON position. This could wear out the spring.

Never attempt to stop the blades from spinning with a spatula or any other kitchen utensil.

BLADES AND HOW TO USE THEM

Steel Knife:

This is the most important blade that comes with your processor. I call it the "Do-Almost-Everything" blade. The general rule of thumb is "If you are not slicing or shredding, then you are probably using the Steel Knife."

This blade is used to chop (use quick on/off turns), mince, grind, purée, mix, blend, knead, beat (although it doesn't incorporate air in the same way as an electric mixer). Use it for cake batters, pastry, yeast and other doughs, crepes, cookies, crushing ice, grinding raw or cooked meat, fish or poultry, salad dressings, mayonnaise, crushing garlic, making peanut butter, smooth sauces, grating Parmesan cheese, chopping and mincing vegetables, whipping cream, puréeing baby food.

The food to be processed may be added either directly into the processor bowl or through the feed tube. Small things or very hard foods (e.g. garlic, ice cubes) are dropped in through the feed tube while the machine is running and are drawn into the centrifuge produced by the whirling blades. The food is then flung outwards once it has been processed. Very hard foods such as chocolate and ice cubes make a loud noise at first, so don't be alarmed.

The Steel Knife can be used anywhere you use the Plastic Knife, but quick on/off turns should be used to avoid overprocessing. It is very easy to overprocess foods when using the Steel Knife because of its phenomenal speed. The most important technique you must learn is the **on/off technique.** This is done by giving a **quick twist of the wrist** when you turn the machine on, then immediately turn it off. It is important to practice this trick until you have perfected it. Practice with no food in the processor bowl. You will become adept at this technique very quickly. You should hear a quick double click for the on/off turn, not one click as the machine is turned on, then another as it is turned off.

There is no harm in stopping and starting the machine as often as is necessary to achieve the desired texture. There is absolutely no time where it will affect your recipe to stop and look, look, look. Better to be safe than sorry.

The on/off technique is used to chop (dice) foods. However, it is impossible to achieve neat little squares of dice as you would when using a sharp knife. (Refer to notes on French Fry Blade, p. 10). **For uniform chopping,** it is important to cut the foods being processed into the **same sized chunks.** About 1" to 1½" is a good size. Instead of using a ruler, **make a circle** with your thumb and index finger, or thumb and middle finger. This is a quick way of measuring. The food should not be larger in diameter than the circle you make with your fingers. Food should be evenly distributed in the processor bowl. About 1 cup at a time gives best results when chopping. Bowl, blade and food should be dry for chopping or mincing.

Since few tasks take more than a few seconds, it is easy enough to process a food, empty the bowl, then repeat with remaining batches. If you try to take shortcuts and overload the processor bowl, you will probably end up with mush. (e.g. Chop one or two onions which have been cut in chunks at a time. If you have three onions to chop, do them in two batches.)

Let your eye be your guide. Times given for processing are only estimates, and each person counts differently, or turns the machine on and off at a different rate. Time may also vary according to the texture, temperature and starting size of the food being processed. Don't hesitate to stop and check several times, until the desired texture is reached.

Should a piece of food accidentally become wedged between the bowl and the blade, turn machine off **immediately** and carefully remove the blade and the trapped food.

Even though you may often use the on/off method, you may also let the machine run. However, since most tasks are completed very quickly, don't walk away from your processor to do something else. Mincing is done in about 6 to 8 seconds of letting the machine run, creaming of cake batters will take about 1½ to 2 minutes, yeast doughs will be fully kneaded in less than a minute. You may have to stop the processor once or twice to scrape down the sides of the bowl with a rubber spatula.

Plastic Knife:

Use for light mixing and blending of foods, generally where a change of texture is not desired. Ideal for dips and spreads, flaked tuna and salmon mixtures, mashed potatoes, combining store-ground hamburger meat with other ingredients. May be used to coarsely chop mushrooms and nuts. Will whip cream (with some splashing), make mayonnaise, and will coarsely grind graham wafer and cracker crumbs. There is more chance of leakage when processing liquids on the Plastic Knife than on the Steel Knife.

Grater (also known as the Medium Shredding Disk):

Use to grate cheese into long, fine shreds, for coconut, potatoes, carrots and other vegetables. Make sure that the blade is pushed **all the way down** on the motor shaft. Arrange the food in the feed tube, either horizontally or vertically, to within ½'' from the top. Use the pusher to guide the food through the tube. **Begin the pressure on the pusher at the exact same time you turn the machine on,** or the food you are processing may become shredded unevenly, with some pieces being too coarse, and other pieces being too fine. Keep the palm of your hand flat on the top of the pusher in order to give you maximum control.

The harder you press, the coarser the grate; the lighter you press, the finer the grate. Adjust pressure according to the texture of the food being processed. Use light pressure for soft foods, medium to firm pressure for hard foods. Empty bowl as often as necessary.

For short shreds, arrange food in an upright position in the feed tube; for long shreds, arrange food crosswise. When grating foods that are very hard, you might try a bouncing action with the pusher to prevent jamming, or to avoid bending the blade. You may prefer to use the Steel Knife to ''grate'' foods where appearance is not important (e.g. Cheddar cheese for sauces, vegetables for soups).

For very fine shreds, let foods almost ''self-feed''; that is, use almost no pressure with the pusher. Always wait for the blades to stop turning before removing cover.

Slicer (also known as the Medium Serrated Slicer):

Use to slice vegetables, fruits, meats, cheeses, etc. Make sure that blade is pushed **all the way down** on the motor shaft. Place food in the feed tube either vertically or horizontally to within ½'' from the top. Pack feed tube snugly to prevent food from tipping over, which would result in slanted rather than round slices. If appearance is important, feed tube must be packed carefully. If appearance is not important, food may be arranged in feed tube at random. For a perfect slice, cut flat ends on the food to be processed, then insert food through the bottom of the feed tube. Empty bowl as often as necessary.

Use the pusher to guide the food through the tube. **Begin the pressure on the pusher at the exact same time you turn the machine on,** or the food you are slicing may be sliced unevenly, with some pieces being too thick, and others being too thin. Keep the palm of your hand flat on the top of the pusher in order to give you maximum control.

The harder you press, the thicker the slice; the lighter you press, the thinner the slice. Adjust pressure according to the texture of the food being processed. Use light pressure for soft foods such as strawberries and bananas, medium pressure for apples, firm pressure for carrots. Hard foods can be processed with light, medium or firm pressure, whereas you must be more careful with soft foods. For garnishing food, you may prefer to slice by hand.

Foods should be as large as possible before placing them in the feed tube. Measure the food to be processed against the length and width of the pusher as a guide to size. Foods that are often too large to fit in through the top of the feed tube may fit if inserted through the **bottom** of the tube, which has a slightly larger opening. You may combine foods if you don't have enough of one, thus getting a tighter fit (e.g. pack green onions in the indentation of celery stalks).

For very thin slices, let food almost ''self-feed''; that is, use almost no pressure with the pusher. This is excellent for cabbage to make cole slaw.

Chinese (Diagonal) Slice: This is the slice you are probably getting now! It occurs when food is not packed tightly into the feed tube. Place only one or two lengths of a food (e.g. celery) so that they are on an angle, rather than upright. Slice. Always wait for blades to stop turning before removing cover.

Optional Blades:

There are thinner and thicker slicers available for some processors. The **Non-Serrated Slicer** is excellent for mushrooms and other soft vegetables. It avoids ragged edges on carrots, and is excellent for slicing peeled apples for flans. Do not use for meats or cheese. The **Thin Serrated Slicer** produces slices half the thickness of the slicing disc which comes with the machine. It is excellent for pepperoni, vegetables and fruits, great for cabbage for cole slaw. There is also a **Thick Slicer** available, which makes slices approximately ¼'' thick. There is a **Fine Grater** available, as well as a **Julienne Blade.** A plastic **Dough Blade** is preferred by some cooks for making yeast doughs as it increases the capacity of the bowl to hold more flour. You alone can determine whether you need additional blades, for only you know what your needs are.

The French Fry Blade: This blade makes curved sticks about 2'' long and ¼'' wide. Use with firm pressure on potatoes, eggplant, zucchini, cucumber. This is an excellent blade for salads and also ideal to coarsely shred cheese. My son Doug loves apples done on this blade, and calls them apple french fries. It will also give an elongated diced effect to vegetables by placing one inch chunks of food in the feed tube and pushing them through with almost no pressure. This trick is ideal when ''dicing'' a large quantity of onions.

HOW MUCH FOOD CAN I PROCESS AT A TIME?
(CAPACITY OF STANDARD-SIZE MACHINES)

Quantities will vary according to the texture of the ingredient being processed and the task you are performing. **When slicing or grating,** food is added through the feed tube, which holds approximately one cup. The pusher (if it is hollow) will also hold one cup. The bowl will hold approximately 6 to 7 cups. Large processors will hold about 1½ - 2 times the amount of the small processor. Refer to your instruction manual for the exact capacity your particular processor will hold. Empty the processor bowl when it is filled with slices or shreds.

When using the Steel Knife; the usual capacity is as follows:-

Chopping nuts and vegetables: 1 to 1½ cups at a time.

Meat: ½ lb. (1 cup) at a time.

Thin-textured mixtures (e.g. thin soups and liquids): 2 to 2½ cups. (One milkshake at a time).

Thick mixtures (e.g. thick soups, crêpe batters): about 3½ cups.

Breads: one loaf at a time (no more than 3 to 3¼ cups of flour).

Pastry: one 2-crust pie (not more than 2 cups of flour).

Cakes: recipes generally not exceeding 2 to 2½ cups flour. Refer to hints in cake section for more specific information.

Puréeing soups: about 3½ cups vegetables at a time. Strain vegetables from the liquid and purée the solids only in batches.

The general rule is: the thicker the liquid, the larger the quantity that the machine can handle. Large processors will handle 1½ to 2 times the amounts listed above when using the **Steel Knife.** Refer to your manual for exact quantities.

I find that I can add extra liquid to the processor bowl without leakage by adding it through the feed tube while the machine is running. I then remove the bowl **immediately** from the base as soon as I shut the machine off, causing the Steel Knife (or Plastic Knife) to fall down around the central opening and form a temporary seal.

It may be necessary to empty the contents of the processor bowl into another mixing bowl from time to time.

QUICK CLEAN-UPS

Refer to your instruction manual as to whether the parts of your particular brand of processor are dishwasher-safe. Organize your thinking before beginning any recipe and work in a manner to keep clean-ups to a minimum. You will soon become adept at saving yourself unnecessary work.

Process dry foods first (e.g. chopping nuts, parsley; grating chocolate, cheese; making bread or cracker crumbs), then proceed with the recipe. Use paper towelling to wipe out the bowl quickly if you are in a hurry.

To avoid "ring around the counter", turn the work bowl cover upside-down before placing it on your countertop!

Rinse the bowl and blades quickly. There is no need to be too thorough. A bristle brush will come in handy and prevent unwanted nicks and cuts. Never let the blades soak in soapy water where you can accidentally cut yourself by reaching in blindly. Wipe up spills on the base or cord quickly with a damp cloth.

A Q-tip is excellent to remove excess dough which becomes stuck in the hole on the underside of the Steel Knife when making sticky bread dough.

At the end of the day, when I am hopefully finished with my processing tasks, I put the bowl and blades into the dishwasher for a thorough cleaning. (And many is the time that I rescue them in the middle of a cycle because I need my processor once again!)

TIPS, TRICKS & TECHNIQUES

- **Master** the on/off technique (refer to notes on **Steel Knife,** p. 8). This technique is only used with the Steel or Plastic Knife, never with the Slicer or Grater.

- **Assemble** and pre-measure ingredients in advance. Cut in chunks if necessary. The processor is so fast that it will do jobs in seconds that used to take minutes.

- **If** you are puréeing or mincing, foods may be cut in larger chunks than if you want uniform chopping.

- **Process** harder ingredients first, then softer ingredients (e.g. chop onions, then add eggs and mayonnaise for egg salad mixture).

- **Instead** of measuring onions, cut small onions in half, larger onions in quarters.

- **You** may combine ingredients of the same texture to save unnecessary steps. If foods are of different textures, process separately.

- **Learn** to count seconds accurately in order to avoid overprocessing food. Remember to stop the machine often and check.

- **Leave** bowl uncovered exposed to the air after washing if you have processed ''smelly'' foods such as garlic or onions.

- **If** you ever hear the motor laboring, turn the machine off right away.

- **Put** a towel, potholder or small mat underneath the base of your processor for ease in moving it around on the counter.

- **Purées** are smoother when fruits or vegetables are processed without the liquids.

- **Butter,** cheese, etc. can be used directly from the refrigerator. There is no need to soften them first. Just cut in chunks and scrape down the sides of the bowl if necessary.

- **To** knead yeast doughs, refer to yeast section for specific directions. Some processors are not equipped to handle heavy bread doughs. Refer to your instruction booklet.

- **When** adding flour to cakes, etc., blend in with on/off turns **just** until the flour disappears. Overprocessing results in poor volume and tough cakes. Refer to cake section for additional hints.

- **To** hold the **Steel Knife** in place when it is covered by cake batter, insert your middle finger in the hole in the bottom of the blade and press firmly against the centre post underneath the processor bowl. Tip bowl to empty. This is my favorite trick!

- **Another** method is to hold the blade in place with a rubber spatula while you are emptying the bowl. Be careful not to drop blade into food (or onto your foot) when emptying the bowl as it is not attached.

- **Process** a larger amount of food than you need (e.g. grated chocolate, cheese, nuts, crumbs, onions, parsley, pepperoni slices) and store them in the refrigerator or freezer for future use.

- **Shop** with the size of the feed tube in mind. If food doesn't fit through the top of the tube (e.g. cucumbers) try fitting them through the bottom, which is larger.

- **When** slicing foods that have peel on one side (e.g. apple wedges), place in feed tube so that the peel is facing the centre of the processor bowl. This minimizes the chances of the peel catching.

- **Always** wait for the blades to stop spinning before you remove the cover. The 3 or 4 seconds it takes is much shorter than the wait you will have in the emergency room at the hospital!

- **Handles** are available with some brands of processors.

- **There** is no danger in processing hot foods. The bowl may also be placed in the refrigerator or freezer unless otherwise directed in your instruction manual.

- **Sometimes** a small amount of food will not pass through the **Slicer** or **Grater.** Usually the next food being sliced or shredded will force it through, or else use this tidbit as a snack for the cook!

- **Most** of your favorite recipes can be adapted to the processor. All slicing, grating, chopping and mincing can be done in the processor using the appropriate blade. Analyse the recipe and organize the order of processing for maximum efficiency. Practice makes perfect! Just be careful to avoid overprocessing.

- **Be** familiar with the do's and don't's of your particular machine.

- **Slicing small items:** Since it is difficult to arrange small foods (e.g. mushrooms, strawberries, radishes, etc.) carefully in the feed tube for neat slicing, here is an easy trick to try:- Cut flat ends on a couple of the small foods and place cut-side down directly on the **Slicer.** The area that they cover should be the size of the opening of the feed tube. Replace the cover. The food should be just at the bottom of the feed tube. Stack the remaining pieces with ease through the top of the tube!

- **Julienne Sticks:** It is possible to julienne foods without a Julienne or French Fry Blade, but a "double processing" technique is required. Insert **Slicer.** Cut food in largest possible size to fit through bottom of the feed tube. Slice, using appropriate pressure. Remove blade from bowl.
Hold the processor cover on its side by the feed tube, with the pusher inserted. Withdraw the pusher partways. Fit re-assembled slices snugly into the bottom of the feed tube so that they will be **vertical** once the cover is replaced on the bowl. Re-insert **Slicer,** replace cover and slice once again.

- **The French Fry Blade** can be used for "dicing". Place 1" chunks of vegetables in the feed tube (e.g. celery, onions, peppers, tomatoes). Use very light pressure with pusher. Saves emptying bowl when processing several different vegetables.

- **Leftover vegetables** may be used to thicken gravies, sauces and soups with a minimum of calories! Purée on **Steel Knife** until smooth.

- **When recipes** call for 1 cup of a food (e.g. mushrooms, celery), fill the feed tube full. It will hold one cup. The pusher may be used as a 1 cup measure on some processors.

- **When slicing,** to avoid slanted slices if only processing a small quantity (e.g. one stalk of celery, a piece of cucumber) place the food to be sliced in an upright position on the right side of the feed tube if your blade spins counter-clockwise, and on the left side if your blade spins clockwise. The **Slicer** will move against the food and help to keep it from tipping.

- **To reconstitute** frozen orange juice, place contents of can in processor bowl with **one** can of cold water. Make sure to insert pusher in feed tube to prevent splashing. Process on **Steel Knife** until blended. Transfer to a serving pitcher and add remaining water called for in instructions (usually another 2 cans of water). If you add all the water called for in the instructions, you will have orange juice leaking out of the processor bowl and in a trail down your kitchen counter and onto the floor. (This is the voice of experience speaking!)

- **Chocolate** will melt quickly if you "grate" it first on the **Steel Knife** until fine.

DAILY USE FOOD GUIDE

READ CAREFULLY:

- If using the **Slicer or Grater,** cut food in largest possible size to fit feed tube.
- Cut flat ends on food for perfect slices.
- Peel if desired or necessary. Core or pit if necessary.
- Use pusher as a guide to size to fit food into feed tube.
- Pack feed tube either vertically or horizontally, with cut ends down.
- If slicing, pack feed tube tightly to prevent diagonal slices.
- Insert food through the bottom of the feed tube if it doesn't fit through the top.
- Adjust pressure according to type of food being processed. Use harder pressure for hard foods, softer pressure for soft foods.
- Pressure is the key. The harder you press, the thicker the slice or the coarser the shred; the lighter you press, the thinner the slice or the finer the shred.
- If using the **Steel Knife** (chopping, mincing, puréeing), cut foods in 1'' to 1½'' chunks. The harder the food, the smaller the chunk should be.
- If chopping, process no more than 1 cup at a time. If mincing, grinding or puréeing, process up to 2 cups at a time.
- Use on/off turns to chop (coarsely or finely); **stop and check** often until desired texture is reached. Let machine run to grind, mince or purée.

FRUITS	BLADE	COMMENTS
Apples (1 medium yields about 3/4 cup)	Slicer or Grater	Medium to firm pressure.
	Steel Knife	On/off turns to chop, or let machine run to mince.
Applesauce	Steel or Plastic Knife	Process up to 2 cups peeled, cored, cooked apples at a time. (If using cooked unpeeled apples, use a food mill as processor does not do a good job on peel.)
Bananas (3 medium yields about 1 cup)	Slicer	Light pressure. Bananas should be firm.
	Steel Knife	Let machine run until smooth. The riper the bananas, the better. Any extra "rotten" bananas may be puréed and frozen. Thaw and use in your favorite recipe.
Dates, Candied Fruits, Maraschino or Glazed Cherries	Steel Knife	Add about 1/4 cup flour called for in recipe to help chop the fruit without sticking. On/off turns. (Maraschino cherries take about 2 quick on/off turns.) Subtract the flour from the remaining amount of flour called for in the recipe.
Oranges, Lemons	Slicer	Do not peel. Cut flat ends. Firm pressure.
	Steel Knife	Quarter and remove any seeds. Process until fine, just a few seconds for peeled fruits, about 20 to 30 seconds for unpeeled fruits.
Zest (Rind) from Oranges, Lemons (1 orange yields about 3 tbsp. grated rind) (1 lemon yields about 1½ tsp. grated rind)	Steel Knife	Use a potato peeler to remove colored portion only from fruit. Add part of the sugar called for in the recipe. On/off turns to start, then let machine run until finely minced, about 30 to 60 seconds. Refrigerate or freeze extra zest and use as needed.

FRUITS (Continued)	BLADE	COMMENTS
Pineapple (1 medium yields 3 to 4 cups)	Slicer	Medium pressure. Makes thin slices.
	Steel Knife	On/off turns. (If recipe calls for canned crushed pineapple and you have only slices or chunks, drain fruit and process 6 to 8 seconds.)
Pears, Peaches, Plums, Nectarines, Apricots	Slicer	Light pressure.
	Steel Knife	On/off turns.
Prunes, Raisins	Steel Knife	On/off turns to chop, or let machine run to grind. (Check packaged pitted prunes carefully for any pits!)
Rhubarb	Slicer	Peel with potato peeler. Medium pressure. Makes thin slices.
Strawberries	Slicer	Berries should be firm. Stack on their sides in feed tube. Light pressure. (Partially thaw frozen berries. Use medium pressure.)
Strawberries, Raspberries, Blueberries	Steel Knife	Use fresh or thawed and drained frozen berries. Let machine run until smooth. Strain to remove seeds, if desired.
VEGETABLES		
Beans (Green or Wax)	Slicer	**French Style:** Trim and cut raw beans in half to fit feed tube **crosswise.** Use firm pressure.
	Steel Knife	Process cooked beans until smooth. Use in soups, to make latkes (pancakes) etc.
Beets	Slicer or Grater	Use firm pressure, with bouncing motion on pusher, for raw beets. Use light pressure for cooked beets.
	Steel Knife	On/off turns to chop, or let machine run to mince.
Cabbage (1 medium cabbage, about 2 lb., yields about 8 cups)	Slicer	Young cabbages are best. Cut in wedges. Use light pressure. For cole slaw, let cabbage self-feed, with almost no pressure on pusher. Roll soft outer leaves like a jelly-roll and use light pressure.
	Grater	Medium pressure. Ideal for egg rolls and fine cole slaw.
	Steel Knife	On/off turns to chop, or let machine run to mince.
Carrots (1 lb. or about 6 medium yields about 3 cups) **Parsnips**	Slicer or Grater	Medium to firm pressure. If grating use bouncing motion with pusher. For slicing or grating, pack carrots either upright or crosswise in feed tube.
	Steel Knife	If long shreds are not required, you may "grate" on the Steel Knife by letting the machine run. To chop, use on/off turns.
Celery (2 large stalks yields about 1 cup)	Slicer	Peel with a potato peeler to remove strings. Medium pressure. Pat dry before using.
	Steel Knife	Use on/off turns, or let machine run to mince or grate. (French Fry Blade will give a "diced" effect if using light pressure on pusher.)
Cucumber	Slicer or Grater	Long, slim, firm cucumbers are best and have less seeds. Use light to medium pressure. Pat dry before using. (Remove seeds first if grating.)
	Steel Knife	Remove seeds. Use on/off turns. Drain.

VEGETABLES (Continued)	BLADE	COMMENTS
Eggplant	Slicer or Grater	Medium pressure. Makes thin slices. Will not make large slices or cubes used for most recipes. Good results with the French Fry Blade.
	Steel Knife	Use on/off turns to chop raw eggplant or to avoid overprocessing cooked eggplant which you are combining with other vegetables.
Garlic	Steel Knife	Not necessary to peel garlic before processing! Drop cloves through feed tube while machine is running and process until minced, about 8 seconds. Discard peel (pieces are easy to pick out). Don't bother if garlic is to be cooked; peel will disintegrate during cooking. Flavor is stronger, so reduce quantity if adapting regular non-processor recipes.
Leeks; Chives; Green Onions (also known as scallions, spring onions or shallots)	Slicer	Trim off most of green portion from leeks and green onions. Wash well, especially leeks. Pack vertically in feed tube. (If only slicing small quantities, combine with other foods; e.g. pack green onions in the hollow of celery stalks.) Use medium pressure. Some slivering will occur.
	Steel Knife	On/off turns, until fine; drop small quantities through feed tube while machine is running and let mince. Some slivering will occur.
Lettuce	Slicer	Use light pressure. Good for salad base, sandwiches, tacos. For tossed salads it is preferable to tear lettuce into pieces by hand.
Mushrooms	Slicer	Stack mushrooms on their sides for "hammerhead" slices, or remove stems and place mushrooms rounded-side down for round slices. If appearance is not important, stack feed tube at random. Use light to medium pressure. (Non-Serrated Slicer, using firm pressure, reduces crumbling.) Mushrooms should be very firm for best results.
	Grater	Medium pressure.
	Steel or Plastic Knife	Use on/off turns. If overprocessed, refer to recipe for Duxelles, (p. 161) or use to make quiches.
Onions (1 medium yields about ½ cup)	Slicer or Grater	As onions have to be cut to fit feed tube, it is difficult to get round rings unless using very small onions. Use light to medium pressure. Some catching takes place when grating, so it is preferable to use the Steel Knife.
	Steel Knife	Cut small onions in halves, larger onions in quarters. Use on/off turns to chop. (One onion will take 2 to 3 quick on/off turns, two onions will take 3 to 4 on/off turns.) **Do not overprocess,** or onions will be too fine. To mince or grate, let machine run. French Fry blade "dices" well.
Parsley	Steel Knife	Discard tough stems. Bowl, parsley and blade should be dry. You can process a whole bowlful at a time. Use on/off turns, or let machine run until minced. Store in a plastic bag in the fridge for about 10 days. May also be dried.

VEGETABLES (Continued)	BLADE	COMMENTS
Peppers, Green or Red (1 medium yields about ½ to ¾ cup)	Slicer	Remove stems and seeds. Use medium pressure. For long slices, cut in widest possible width to fit feed tube. For narrow slices, arrange long strips vertically (upright) in feed tube. For rings, use small peppers that will fit through the bottom of the feed tube. Remove core and cut flat ends on pepper. Firm pressure with pusher. Pat dry.
	Steel Knife	Peppers are very watery, so take care. Quick on/off turns; do not overprocess. Pat dry. (Good results with French Fry Blade and very light pressure, or refer to comments on narrow slices, above.) Let machine run to mince or grate.
Pickles, Olives; Radishes; Water Chestnuts	Slicer	Pickles should be firm. Arrange pickles in feed tube either vertically or horizontally; olives should be arranged with flat ends down. Medium pressure for pickles, olives. Firm pressure for radishes and water chestnuts.
	Steel Knife	On/off turns to chop; let machine run to mince.
Potatoes; Sweet Potatoes	Slicer	Use medium pressure for raw potatoes. Cooked potatoes usually have a tendency to crumble when sliced.
	Grater	Light to medium pressure, depending on texture desired. Makes long shreds. (Store grated or sliced raw potatoes in cold water to prevent discoloration. Dry well before using.)
	Steel Knife	Use on/off turns to chop, let machine run to "grate" finely.
	Plastic Knife	Use for mashed potatoes. (See p. 163). Be careful not to overprocess, and do not use Steel Knife, or you will produce glue!
	French Fry Blade	Makes short shoestring fries.
Shallots These are a cross between garlic and onions. Do not confuse with green onions (scallions).	Steel Knife	Use on/off turns to chop; let machine run to mince.
Spinach, Watercress	Steel Knife	Discard tough stalks. Use on/off turns to chop; let machine run to mince. Cooked spinach should be squeezed dry before processing.
Tomatoes	Slicer	Should be firm. Cut in half, cut flat ends, use firm pressure (but do not squash!). Drain well. For salads it is preferable to slice tomatoes by hand. (French Fry Blade will give diced effect, but draining is necessary.)
	Steel Knife	Cut in quarters. Peeling is not necessary if you are cooking tomatoes as the blade does an excellent job on the skins. Use on/off turns to chop or mince. (Squeeze out seeds and juice before processing, if desired.)
		Canned Tomatoes: Drain before processing.
Turnips; Black Radish; Winter Squash (Acorn, Butternut, Hubbard)	Slicer or Grater	Use firm pressure, with bouncing motion on pusher.
	Steel Knife	On/off turns to chop; let machine run to mince or "grate" finely.

VEGETABLES (Continued)	BLADE	COMMENTS
Zucchini, Summer Squash (1 lb. yields about 3 cups)	Slicer or Grater	Peel if desired. Use medium pressure.
	Steel Knife	On/off turns to chop; let run to "grate" finely.

CHEESES

Hard Cheeses (e.g. Parmesan, Romano) (¼ lb. yields about 1 cup grated)	Steel Knife	Cheese should be at room temperature. Break into small chunks with a blunt knife or chisel. Process no more than 1 cup at a time. Let machine run until desired fineness is reached, about 20 to 30 seconds. Store in refrigerator in a tightly closed jar and use as needed.
Firm Cheeses (e.g. Mozzarella, Cheddar, Swiss) (¼ lb. yields about 1 cup grated)	Grater	Cheese should be chilled for best results. Light pressure results in fine shreds, medium pressure gives coarser shreds. Grate extra cheese to use in salads, for pizzas, etc. Store in freezer or refrigerator in a plastic bag. (French Fry Blade gives nice texture to use in salads.)
	Slicer	Use firm pressure.
	Steel Knife	Use on/off turns to chop. Use in cooking where appearance is not important (e.g. sauces, casseroles).
Cream Cheese	Steel Knife	May be used directly from refrigerator. Cut into chunks and process until smooth. Scrape down as necessary.
Cottage Cheese	Steel Knife	Process no more than 2 cups at a time, until smooth, scraping down bowl as necessary. For crepes or blintz filling, use less eggs in cheese mixture as processor makes cheese very creamy.

CRUMBS

Soft Bread Crumbs (1 slice yields ½ cup crumbs)	Steel Knife	Use fairly fresh bread or rolls. Tear into chunks and process up to 4 slices at a time. For larger quantities, add additional chunks through feed tube while machine is running. Must be stored in freezer or will mold.
		Buttered Crumbs: Once crumbs have been formed, blend in 1 tbsp. of butter for each slice of bread, using on/off turns.
Dry or Toasted Crumbs (1 slice yields ¼ c. crumbs)	Steel Knife	Keep a plastic bag in the freezer and gather all scraps of bread, rolls, bagels, etc. Place in a single layer on a cookie sheet. Bake at 300°F for one hour. (May also be dried thoroughly at room temperature.) Process chunks until fine. May be stored at room temperature.
		Italian Seasoned Crumbs: To each cup of crumbs, add ½ tsp. salt, a dash each of pepper, oregano, and basil, and ¼ c. grated Parmesan cheese (optional). Process a few seconds.

CRUMBS (Continued)	BLADE	COMMENTS
Cookie Crumbs; **Cracker Crumbs** Any of the following will yield **one cup crumbs:** 18 chocolate wafers 22-26 vanilla wafers 15 ginger snaps 12-14 graham wafer squares 28 Saltines	Steel or Plastic Knife	Break in chunks. (You may also use a combination of any leftover or broken cookies or crackers.) Place in bowl or drop through feed tube while machine is running. Process until fine. (Plastic Knife will give coarser texture.) Nuts may be processed with cookie crumbs for an interesting taste.
Corn Flake Crumbs (1 cup yields ¼ cup crumbs)	Steel Knife	Process up to 4 cups for 30-60 seconds, until desired fineness is reached.
Matzo Meal (3 matzos or 2 cups matzo farfel yields 1 cup.)	Steel Knife	Break matzos into chunks. Process matzos or farfel until fine, about 45-60 seconds.

FISH, MEAT, POULTRY, EGGS

	BLADE	COMMENTS
Fish, Raw (1 lb. yields 2 cups)	Steel Knife	Remove any skin and bones. Fish can be ground in batches of 1 pound (2 cups) at a time. Let machine run until smooth, about 15 to 20 seconds.
Fish, Cooked or Canned	Steel or Plastic Knife	Use on/off turns. Do not overprocess. Process no more than 1½ cups (about 2 - 7 oz. cans, well-drained) at a time. Any vegetables should be chopped or minced first, then add the fish, mayonnaise and seasonings. For flaked tuna or salmon use the Plastic Knife.
Raw Meat (Beef, Veal, Lamb, Chicken, etc.) (1 lb. yields 2 cups)	Slicer	Cut the meat in the largest possible size to fit through the bottom of the feed tube. Freeze meat until quite stiff, about 2 hours. You should **just** be able to insert the **point** of a knife into the meat. Use very firm pressure. (If meat is too solidly frozen, you can damage the blade. If meat is too soft, it will jam in the blade.) Chicken breasts should be boned and skinned. Use for Chinese stir-fry cooking.
	Steel Knife	Remove bones, excess fat, gristle from meat. Cut into 1½'' chunks. Process no more than ½ to ¾ lb. (1 to 1½ cups) at a time. Use several on/off turns, or else process about 8 seconds, until desired texture is reached. Do not overprocess or meat will become tough. **Cholesterol-watchers:** Trim away all excess fat from beef or veal and replace with 2 tbsp. oil or margarine for each cup of meat cubes. Without fat, meat will be dry and flavorless.
	Steel or Plastic Knife	**Combining Ground Meat with other ingredients: Never** more than 1 pound of meat at a time. Use on/off turns, **just** until mixture is blended. Do not overprocess or meat will become tough and look whitish.

FISH, MEAT, POULTRY, EGGS (Continued) BLADE		COMMENTS
Cooked Meat (Beef, Veal, Lamb, Chicken, Salami, Pepperoni) (1 lb. yields about 2 to 2½ cups)	Slicer	Remove casing from pepperoni. Trim fat, gristle and bones from meat. Discard skin from chicken. Place with flat ends down in feed tube. Use very firm pressure. (Harder meats such as salami and pepperoni can take light or medium pressure also. Salami should be halved lengthwise to fit feed tube.) The firmer the meat, the better it slices. Chicken will come out in chunks and is ideal for chicken salad. Roast slices will be narrow and you may prefer to slice by hand, but I suggest you try your processor at least once.
	Steel Knife	Trim fat, gristle and bones from meat. Discard skin from chicken. Cut in chunks. Process ½ to ¾ lb. (1 to 1½ cups) at a time. Use on/off turns to chop coarsely, or let machine run about 8 to 10 seconds, or until finely chopped. Blend in additional ingredients (e.g. eggs, chopped vegetables, seasonings) with quick on/off turns. For chopped liver, up to 1 lb. at a time can be processed.
Eggs	Grater	**Hard-Cooked:** Use light pressure. It is preferable to use the Steel Knife. For slices, results are unsatisfactory and it is better to slice by hand.
	Steel or Plastic Knife	**Hard-Cooked:** Up to 1 dozen at a time. Use on/off turns. Any vegetables should be chopped or minced first, then add the eggs, mayonnaise and seasonings. **Raw:** Process for 2 or 3 seconds, just until lightly beaten. For omelettes, scrambled eggs, etc. the processor is faster than a fork and bowl, and rinses out quickly. Up to 8 eggs at a time.
Egg Whites	Plastic Knife	Not recommended as volume is poor. If necessary, use at least 4 egg whites plus ¼ tsp. cream of tartar or ½ tsp. lemon juice. Remove the pusher to incorporate more air. Make sure that the bowl and blade are dry and free from grease. Egg whites should be at room temperature. Process until firm. (An electric mixer or whisk is preferable.)
MISCELLANEOUS		
Baby Food	Steel Knife	Cook or steam desired food until tender. Process until smooth. For smoother texture, process solids first, then add liquids. (Freeze extras in ice cube trays. They will defrost quickly.)
Butter; Margarine (¼ lb. or 1 stick yields ½ cup)	Slicer	Butter must be cold, but **not frozen.** Use medium to firm pressure. Makes nice slices. Some margarines may be too soft.
	Steel Knife	Always cut butter into chunks. There is no need to soften before using. For baking, use directly from the fridge. For pastry, always use frozen butter. To make sweet butter, refer to notes on Whipping Cream (p. 22).
Cakes, Cookies, Yeast Doughs, Pastry	Steel Knife	Refer to specific sections for full information.

MISCELLANEOUS (Continued)	BLADE	COMMENTS
Chocolate (1 oz. square yields ¼ cup grated)	Grater	Chocolate should be at room temperature. Use medium to firm pressure. It will be extremely noisy! (The processor will not make chocolate curls; they must be done by hand with a potato peeler.) I usually grate several squares at a time and store the extra in a container in the fridge. If recipe calls for melting chocolate, use ¼ cup grated. It will melt in moments! Grating may also be done on the Steel Knife (see below).
Chocolate, Chocolate Chips	Steel Knife	Cut chocolate squares in half. Use on/off turns to start, then let machine run until desired fineness is reached, usually 20 to 30 seconds. Texture will be more "pebbly" rather than grated, but is good to use in cakes, etc. where appearance is not important. Otherwise use Grater if chocolate is needed for garnishing.
Coconut (1 coconut yields about 2½ cups. Very economical.)	Steel Knife or Grater	Pierce the eyes and drain out the liquid from coconut. Place in a 400°F oven for about 20 minutes. Remove from oven and crack shell with a hammer. Peel off inner brown skin with a potato peeler or a sharp knife. Use firm pressure with Grater (to make long shreds) or if using Steel Knife, process 1 cup at a time until desired fineness. May be frozen and used as needed.
Hard Candy (e.g. peppermint sticks, cinnamon candy, toffee bars, etc.)	Steel Knife	Drop chunks through feed tube while the machine is running, keeping your hand on top to prevent pieces from flying out. Process until fine.
Ice	Steel Knife	**N.B.** Not all processors can chop ice. Refer to manufacturer's booklet. If machine is capable, add quickly through feed tube while machine is running. Will be extremely noisy. Work quickly to avoid overprocessing.
Milkshakes	Steel or Plastic Knife	Not more than one milkshake at a time or you may get leakage from the bottom of the bowl. Process until blended. **Lo-Cal Milkshakes** may be made with skim milk, 2 to 4 ice cubes, sweetener, fruit and/or various extracts. If you use frozen strawberries or raspberries, you will end up with mock soft ice cream!
Nuts (¼ lb. or 4 oz. yields 1 cup)	Steel Knife (Plastic Knife may be used with soft nuts such as walnuts, pecans, etc.)	6 to 8 on/off turns to chop, or let machine run for about 6 to 8 seconds. Timing will depend on hardness of nuts used and degree of fineness desired. Up to 1½ cups at one time. Do not overprocess or you will have nut butter! Freeze or refrigerate extras.
	Grater or Slicer	The Grater will produce a fine texture; the Slicer will produce a coarser texture. Use medium pressure.
Sugar	Steel Knife	**Fruit Sugar:** Process white sugar for 15 to 20 seconds, until fine. Measure after processing. **Brown Sugar:** To remove lumps, process 15 to 20 seconds. If very hard, soften by placing ½ apple cut-side up in bag. Discard apple the next day.

MISCELLANEOUS (Continued) BLADE		COMMENTS
Whipping Cream (35%) **Dessert Topping**	Steel Knife for Dessert Topping; Steel or Plastic Knife for Whipping Cream.	Will increase only 1½ times the volume instead of double. Will be firmer. Good for garnishing.
		Method: Place a heavy book under back part of base so machine is tipped forward. Do not insert pusher in feed tube. Whip until texture of sour cream, about 35 to 40 seconds for cream. (Dessert Topping requires about 2 minutes of processing.) Add sugar and process just until firm.
		To make butter: Process up to 2 cups whipping cream at a time. Let machine run for about 2 minutes, until cream separates and forms butter. Add a little salt if desired. Remove from liquid; pat dry. Refrigerate or freeze. Excellent way to use up leftover whipping cream.

SOME METRIC COMPARISONS

The following approximate comparisons should help you in visualizing metric measures:-

1 L (litre)	—	35.2 fluid ounces (about 4½ cups), about 1 quart
5 mL (millilitres)	—	1 teaspoon
15 mL (millilitres)	—	1 tablespoon
25 mL (millilitres)	—	1 coffee measure
125 mL (millilitres)	—	generous ½ cup
250 mL (millilitres)	—	1 generous cup
500 mL (millilitres)	—	2 generous cups
28.4 mL (millilitres)	—	1 fluid ounce (volume)
28.35 g (grams)	—	1 ounce (weight)
100 g (grams)	—	3½ ounces (slightly less than ¼ lb.)
125 g (grams)	—	Slightly more than ¼ lb.
250 g (grams)	—	Slightly more than ½ pound
500 g (grams)	—	1 generous pound (1.1 lb.)
1 kg (kilogram)	—	2 generous pounds (2.2 lb.)
2.5 cm (centimetres)	—	1 inch
5 cm (centimetres)	—	2 inches
1 mm (millimetre)	—	about the thickness of a dime
100° C (Celsius)	—	water boils
0° C (Celsius)	—	water freezes
160° C (Celsius)	—	oven temperature for roasting

METRIC MEASURES FOR BAKING PANS & CASSEROLES

With the advent of the Metric system, new baking pans becoming available on the market are indicated by the capacity or volume they contain (e.g. litres) as well as by measurement (e.g. centimetres).

Listed below are some of the more common pans used for the recipes in this book, and the new pan sizes replacing them. There may be slight differences in capacity, but this chart should give you an adequate guideline.

Remember that one inch equals 2.5 cm (centimetres), every 5 cm is 2 inches, and 30 cm is 1 foot (12 inches).

One litre = 1000 millilitres (mL) or 35.2 fluid ounces. This is midway between the U.S. quart (32 ounces or 4 cups) and the Canadian quart (40 ounces or 5 cups). A happy compromise!

	New Metric Measure	Metric Capacity
8'' square pan x 2'' deep	20 x 5 cm	2 litres
9'' square pan x 2'' deep	22 x 5 cm	2.5 litres
8'' x 4'' x 3'' loaf pan	20 x 10 x 7 cm	1.5 litres
9'' x 5'' x 3'' loaf pan	22 x 12 x 7 cm	2 litres
9'' tube pan x 4'' deep	22 x 10 cm	3 litres
10'' Bundt pan	25 x 10 cm	3 litres
10'' tube pan x 4'' deep	25 x 10 cm	4 litres
8'' round layer pan x 1¾'' deep	20 x 4 cm	1.3 litres
9'' round layer pan x 1¾'' deep	22 x 4 cm	1.5 litres
7'' x 11'' or 8'' x 12'' oblong pan	30 x 20 x 5 cm	3 litres
9'' x 13'' oblong pan	33 x 22 x 5 cm	3.5 litres
9'' pie plate	22 x 4 cm	1 litre
10'' x 15'' cookie sheet	40 x 30 cm	—
8'' spring form pan	20 cm	—
9'' spring form pan	22 cm	—
10'' spring form pan	24 or 26 cm	—

Casseroles will be available in the following sizes:- 1 litre, 1.5 litres, 2 litres, 2.5 litres, 3 litres and 4 litres. These will replace the 1 quart, 1½ quart, 2 quart, 2½ quart, 3 quart and 4 quart casseroles.

METRIC BAKING TEMPERATURES

A good rule of thumb is to halve the Fahrenheit temperature to find the approximate degree in Celsius for baking and cooking. For example, 400°F becomes 200°C. Most cakes are baked at 350°F (180°C).

Celsius temperatures will appear in multiples of 10°C. Fahrenheit temperatures will not be converted, but will be replaced on the temperature dial as follows:-

70°C	—	150°F	190°C	—	375°F
80°C	—	170°F	200°C	—	400°F
100°C	—	200°F	220°C	—	425°F
120°C	—	250°F	230°C	—	450°F
140°C	—	275°F	240°C	—	475°F
150°C	—	300°F	260°C	—	500°F
160°C	—	325°F	270°C	—	525°F
180°C	—	350°F	290°C	—	550°F

When baking in glass or dark baking pans, lower temperature by 25°F (10°C).

METRIC MEASURING EQUIPMENT

Don't bother trying to convert metric recipes to use with your regular (Imperial) measuring cups and spoons. The best thing to remember is:-

USE METRIC MEASURES FOR METRIC RECIPES, AND USE YOUR REGULAR MEASURING UTENSILS FOR REGULAR RECIPES.

The investment is small, and is well worth it to save the headache of trying to convert millilitres (mL) to cups and spoons. Metric measures for dry ingredients come in a set of three sizes:- 250 millilitres (mL), 125 mL and 50 mL. To measure small quantities of dry or liquid ingredients, the set includes five sizes:- 1 mL, 2 mL, 5 mL, 15 mL and 25 mL. They are available in either plastic or metal.

The following will give you an idea how metric measures compare to regular (Imperial) measuring cups and spoons.

Imperial Measuring Cups (Dry)
(Set of 4)

¼ cup	⅓ cup	½ cup	1 cup
(4 tbsp.)			(8 ounces)
(60 mL)	(78 mL)	(114 mL)	(227 mL)

Metric Measures (Dry)
(Set of 3)

50 mL	125 mL	250 mL
(less than ¼ cup)	(a little more than than ½ cup)	(replaces the standard 1 cup measure - about 10% larger)

Standard Measuring Spoons
(Set of 4)

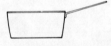

1 tbsp.	1 tsp.	½ tsp.	¼ tsp.
(15 mL)	(5 mL)		

Small Metric Measures
(Set of 5)

25 mL	15 mL	5 mL	2 mL	1 mL
	(1 tbsp.)	(1 tsp.)		

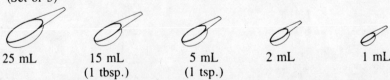

TO MEASURE LIQUIDS: Use a transparent (e.g. Pyrex) measure with a pouring spout. They are available to the consumer in three sizes:- 250 mL (which replaces the Imperial 1 cup measure and is about 10% larger), 500 mL and 1000 mL. Either the 250 or 500 mL size is most convenient.

METRIC PACKAGING

QUICK CONVERSION TO MILLILITRES & GRAMS (APPROXIMATE): It is impossible to list conversions for every ingredient in my book. If the size you want is not on this list, multiply the number of ounces times 30 and you will have an approximate metric size.

Example: 1 oz. is about 30 millilitres or grams (actual 28.4 mL or 28.35 g)

             10 oz. is about 300 millilitres or grams (actual 284 mL or 283 g)

QUICK CONVERSION TO OUNCES (APPROXIMATE): Drop the last digit from the number of millilitres or grams and divide by 3.

Example: 156 mL is about 5 oz. (15 ÷ 3 = 5).Exact conversion is 5½ oz.
             250 g is about 8 oz. (25 ÷ 3 = 8⅓). Exact conversion is 8.8 oz.

CANS, JARS & BOTTLED PRODUCTS

(Fruits, vegetables, soups, sauces, salad dressings, ketchup, olives, pickles, pie fillings, sweetened condensed milk, tomato sauce, tomato paste)

		15 oz.	— 426 mL
5½ oz.	— 156 mL	16 oz.	— 454 mL
7½ oz.	— 213 mL	17.6 oz.	— 500 mL
8 oz.	— 227 mL	19 oz.	— 540 mL
8.8 oz.	— 250 mL	24 oz.	— 682 mL
10 oz.	— 284 mL	26.4 oz.	— 750 mL
11 oz.	— 313 mL	28 oz.	— 796 mL
12 oz.	— 341 mL	32 oz.	— 909 mL
13.2 oz.	— 375 mL	35.2 oz.	— 1 litre (1000 mL)
14 oz.	— 398 mL	48 oz.	— 1.36 litres

BAKING PRODUCTS

Butter, Margarine, Shortening:
114 g	— ¼ lb. (1 stick) ½ cup
454 g	— 1 lb. (4 sticks) 2 cups

Cake Mixes:
520 g	— 19 oz. pkg. (2 layer size)

Chocolate, Chocolate Chips:
28 g	— 1 oz. (1 square baking chocolate)
175 g	— 6 oz. pkg. (1 cup chocolate chips)
350 g	— 12 oz. pkg. (2 cups chocolate chips)

Chocolate, Vanilla & Graham Wafers:
200 g	— scant ½ lb. (replaces 8 oz. pkg.)
400 g	— 14 oz. pkg.

Gelatins and Puddings: (Size varies according to flavor & brand.)
85 g	— 3 oz. pkg. (4 servings)
92 g	— 3¼ oz. pkg. (4 servings)
113 g	— 4 oz. pkg. (4 servings)
170 g	— 6 oz. pkg. (6 servings)

Jams & Jellies:
250 mL	— replaces 8 or 9 oz. jar (about 1 cup)

Nuts:
60 g	— 2 generous ounces (about ⅓ cup nuts)
100 g	— 3½ oz. (about ¾ cup nuts)
200 g	— 7 oz. (about 1½ cups nuts)

Sugar, Icing Sugar, Brown Sugar, Flour:
500 g	— 1 generous lb.
1 kg	— 2.2 lb. (replaces 2 lb. pkg.)
2 kg	— 4.4 lb. (replaces 5 lb. pkg.)
2.5 kg	— 5.5 lb. (replaces 5 lb. pkg.)
4 kg	— 8.8 lb. (replaces 10 lb. pkg.)
5 kg	— 11 lb. (replaces 10 lb. pkg.)

DAIRY PRODUCTS

Cheeses (Hard):
227- 250 g	— about 8 oz. or ½ lb. (about 2 cups grated)
454 - 500 g	— about 16 oz. or 1 lb. (about 4 - 4½ cups grated)

Cottage Cheese, Ricotta Cheese:
250 g	— about 8 oz. (1 generous cup)
454 g	— 1 lb. (2 cups)
475 - 500 g	— 1 generous lb. (2 generous cups)

Cream Cheese:
125 g	— about 4 oz. or ¼ lb. (½ cup)
250 g	— about 8 oz. or ½ lb. (1 cup)

For 1 lb. cream cheese, use two 250 g pkgs.

Cream, Milk:
200 mL	— scant ½ pint (7 oz. or 1 scant cup)
250 mL	— generous ½ pint (8.8 oz. or 1 generous cup)
500 mL	— 1 generous pint (2 generous cups)
1 L	— about 1 quart (4½ cups)

Remember that whipping cream (35%) doubles in volume when whipped on the electric mixer. When whipped on the processor, it produces 1½ times the volume.

Ice Cream:
½ litre	— about 1 pint
1 litre	— about 1 quart
2 litres	— about 1 gallon

Sour Cream:
250 mL	— generous ½ pint (1 generous cup)
500 mL	— 1 generous pint (2 generous cups)

Yoghurt:
175 g	— ¾ cup (6 oz. container)
250 g	— 1 generous cup
500 g	— 2 generous cups

MEAT, FISH, POULTRY, PASTA, VEGETABLES, FRUITS

Meat, Fish, Poultry:
250 g	— about ½ lb.
500 g	— 1 generous lb. (1.1 lb.)
1 kg	— 2 generous lb. (2.2 lb.)
1.5 kg	— 3½ lb. (an average chicken)

Pasta:
250 g	— replaces the 8 oz. pkg.
375 g	— replaces the 12 oz. pkg.
500 g	— 1 generous lb. (replaces the 16 oz. pkg.)
1 kg	— 2 generous lb.

Salmon, Tuna (Canned):
106 g	— 3¾ oz.
184 g	— 6½ oz.
198 g	— 7 oz.
220 g	— 7¾ oz.

Vegetables & Fruits (Fresh):
500 g	— 1 generous lb.
1 kg	— 2 generous lb.
227 g	— replaces 1 pint or ½ lb. fresh mushrooms (2 cups)

Vegetables & Fruits (Frozen):
170 g	— 6 oz. pkg. (pea pods)
283 g	— 10 oz. pkg. (broccoli, spinach)
340 g	— 12 oz. pkg. (peas)
425 g	— 15 oz. pkg. (strawberries)
907 g	— 2 lb. pkg. (assorted frozen veggies)
178 mL	— 6.25 fluid ounces (orange juice)

Appetizers, Dips & Spreads

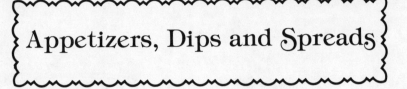

Appetizers, Dips and Spreads

- **Included in this section** are an assortment of dips and spreads, party pick-me-ups and sandwich fillings. Your processor will save you much time in preparing for family and friends, making any time party time!

- **Use the Slicer** from your processor to cut many of the vegetables you wish to serve with dips. Carrots, zucchini and celery may be cut to fit crosswise in the feed tube, rather than upright. Use fairly firm pressure or slices may be too thin.

- **Green pepper** should be cored, halved and seeded. For long strips, you might wish to try this trick:- Cut pepper open down one side. Remove seeds and core. Insert pepper through the bottom of the feed tube, overlapping the cut ends slightly so that the pepper is compressed and will fit. Slice with firm pressure.

- **Zucchini and cucumbers** may be sliced in rounds. Insert through the bottom of the feed tube to prevent unnecessary trimming. Peeling is not necessary. A decorative effect can be achieved by running the tines of a fork down the length of the vegetable. Slice with medium to firm pressure. Pat dry on paper towelling.

- **Some vegetables** may be too thin if sliced on the processor, so some hand slicing may be necessary (e.g. cauliflower or broccoli flowerettes; tomato wedges).

- **Dips** can be thinned with a little milk and used as interesting salad dressings.

- **Interesting containers** for dips and spreads can be made from any of the following:- hollowed out green peppers; scooped out tomatoes; grapefruit, melon or avocado shells. Cut flat bottoms so they will be able to stand properly. Try cutting the top off an unsliced bread, scooping out the soft bread (use to make croutons), making sure to leave a half inch wall all around. Fill as desired.

- **Many appetizers** may be served as a main dish, or vice versa. A main dish which serves 4 people will serve 6 to 8 as an appetizer.

- **Pastry canapés:** Roll out leftover pastry scraps and cut in small rounds. Bake at 400°F on an ungreased cookie sheet for a few minutes, until lightly browned. Then top with a little grated cheese, minced onion &/or mushrooms &/or green pepper. Place under the broiler for a few minutes, until cheese is melted and bubbling.

- **Easy Sandwich Hors D'Oeuvres:** Cut small dinner rolls in half. Top with assorted sandwich spreads (e.g. salmon, tuna, egg, chicken salad, etc.). Garnish with sliced olives, minced green onions or chives, pimento strips, paprika, etc. Arrange sandwiches attractively on a large platter and chill.

- **Interesting Miniatures:** Make Fish Patties (p. 81), Salmon Patties (p. 81), Potato Latkes (p. 166) or Carrot Latkes (p. 158), dropping mixture from a small spoon into hot oil. Brown on both sides and drain on paper towelling.

- **Miniature Kreplach** (p. 177) are delicious when filled with Corned Beef Filling (p. 176). Either boil or deep-fry.

- **Miniature Cream Puffs** (p. 316) may be filled with sautéed vegetables or seafood.

- **Cut Gefilte Fish** (p. 71) in 1'' cubes. Spear on toothpicks and serve with red horseradish.

- **Try Breaded Zucchini** (p. 170) or Crispy Fried Zucchini (p. 170).
- **Cut potato or noodle kugel** into small squares. Serve piping hot.
- **Saucy Dogs:** Combine ¾ cup mustard with a 10 oz. jar of grape or red currant jelly (or 1¼ cups jellied cranberry sauce) in a saucepan. Bring to a boil. Add 2 packages of cocktail hot dogs and simmer for about 10 minutes.
- **Water Chestnut Tid-Bites:** Drain canned water chestnuts and cut in half. Wrap either in beef fry (Kosher "bacon"), thinly sliced smoked meat or corned beef. Roll lightly in either brown sugar, bottled sparerib sauce or Honey Garlic Sparerib Sauce (p. 122). Broil for a few minutes, until piping hot. Serve immediately.
- **Hot Dog Tid-Bites:** Prepare as for Water Chestnut Tid-Bites (above), but use cocktail hot dogs instead of water chestnuts.

★★★★★★★★★★★★★★★★★

ANTIPASTO SPREAD

2 - 7 oz. tins tuna, drained	10 oz. can mushrooms, drained
24 oz. jar sweet mixed pickles, drained	1 onion, cut in chunks
	2 carrots, cut in chunks
12 oz. jar cocktail onions, drained, (if desired)	11 oz. bottle ketchup
	10 oz. bottle chili sauce
12 oz. jar stuffed olives, drained	1 tbsp. Worcestershire sauce
	2 tbsp. lemon juice

Steel Knife: Process tuna with 2 or 3 quick on/off turns, **just** until flaked. Do not overprocess. Empty into a large bowl. Process sweet mixed pickles with 3 or 4 quick on/off turns. Empty bowl. Repeat with cocktail onions, then stuffed olives, then mushrooms, then onions, then carrots, emptying bowl each time. These ingredients must be processed separately with quick on/off turns to avoid overprocessing.

Combine all ingredients in mixing bowl and mix well. Store in tightly closed jars in refrigerator. Mixture will keep up to 6 weeks.

Yield: about 2 quarts. Do not freeze. Serve on lettuce leaves as an appetizer or as a spread with assorted crackers.

CHICKEN SALAD SPREAD ✓

4 radishes, trimmed	2 c. cooked chicken (discard skin and bones)
1 stalk celery, cut in 2" chunks	⅓ c. mayonnaise or salad dressing
½ onion	salt and pepper to taste

Steel Knife: Process radishes, celery and onion until minced, about 6 to 8 seconds. Add remaining ingredients and process with several quick on/off turns, scraping down bowl once or twice. Do not overprocess.

Yield: 4 to 6 servings. Ideal as a sandwich spread. Do not freeze. Vegetables may be omitted for fussy children.

PECAN CHEESE SPREAD
(The pineapple gives it a tangy and delicious
touch without sweetening. Well worth trying!)

½ c. pecans
¼ green pepper
¼ small onion
8 oz. pkg. cream cheese

½ tsp. seasoning salt (or to
taste)
½ - 10 oz. can crushed
pineapple, well-drained

Steel Knife: Process nuts until coarsely chopped, about 8 to 10 seconds. Empty bowl. Process green pepper and onion with 2 quick on/off turns. Add cheese and seasoning salt and process until well creamed, about 20 seconds. Add pineapple and nuts. Process with several quick on/off turns to mix. Place in an attractive serving bowl and chill 2 to 3 hours to blend flavors. Serve with assorted crackers, melba toast, or rye or pumpernickel bread.

Yield: about 1¼ cups. May be frozen. Recipe may be doubled, if desired.

Note: May be served as a chip dip, but chop nuts very finely. Cottage cheese may be substituted for the cream cheese to trim calories, if desired.

CHOPPED CHICKEN AND EGG APPETIZER ✓
(Great as an appetizer, sandwich filling or as a spread
for crackers. The perfect way to use up leftover cooked chicken.)

1 onion, halved
1 stalk celery, cut in 2"
chunks
2 c. cooked chicken (discard
skin and bones)
4 hard-cooked eggs, halved

½ c. salad dressing or
mayonnaise
salt and pepper, to taste
1 tbsp. steak sauce (A-1 or
HP sauce)

Steel Knife: Process onion and celery until minced about 8 seconds. Add chicken and process 6 seconds more. Drop eggs through feed tube quickly while machine is running. Add remaining ingredients and process a few seconds longer to mix, scraping down bowl once or twice. Chill.

Yield: 8 servings. Do not freeze.

Serve on lettuce leaves, or stuff hollowed-out green pepper halves or tomatoes.

CHOPPED EGG SPREAD ✓

½ small onion (or 2 green
onions) cut in 3" lengths
6 hard-cooked eggs
3 tbsp. mayonnaise (about)

salt & pepper, to taste
dash Dijon mustard, if
desired

Steel Knife: Drop onion through feed tube while machine is running. Process until minced. Add remaining ingredients and process with 3 or 4 on/off turns, until desired texture is reached. Scrape down bowl once or twice.

Yield: filling for 6 sandwiches (or 3 lengthwise slices of bread for cheese loaves.) Do not freeze.

Note: Up to 1 dozen eggs may be processed in one batch. Allow about ½ tbsp. mayonnaise for each egg.

Calorie Counter's Version
Substitute 3 tbsp. low-fat creamed cottage cheese for the mayonnaise.

Yield: 6 servings of approximately 96 calories each.

EGGPLANT SPREAD #1

1 onion, halved	1 small clove garlic
1 tbsp. oil	salt & pepper, to taste
1½ lb. eggplant, peeled	juice of ½ lemon
water to cover	1 tomato, cut in chunks

Steel Knife: Process onion with 2 or 3 quick on/off turns, until coarsely chopped. Sauté in oil until golden, about 5 minutes.

Slicer: Cut eggplant to fit feed tube. Slice, using medium pressure. Place in a saucepan and add just enough water to cover. Cook covered until tender, about 10 to 15 minutes. Drain well.

Steel Knife: Drop garlic through feed tube while machine is running. Process until minced. Scrape down sides of bowl. Add remaining ingredients and process with several quick on/off turns, just until blended. Serve as a spread with assorted crackers. May be frozen.

Yield: about 1½ cups. Contains about 13 calories per tablespoon.

Variation: A hard-boiled egg may be added, if desired. Cut in half and process together with remaining ingredients. Do not freeze egg.

EGGPLANT SPREAD #2

2 eggplants (about 1¼ lb. each)	½ stalk celery, cut in chunks
1 onion or 6 green onions (scallions)	1 tomato, quartered
	salt & pepper, to taste
2 cloves garlic	1 tbsp. oil (or to taste)
1 green pepper, seeded & cut in chunks	1 tbsp. vinegar or lemon juice
	½ tsp. sugar

Cut eggplants in half lengthwise and place cut side down on a broiling rack. Preheat broiler. Broil eggplant about 4'' from heat for 15 minutes. Do not turn. (This gives the eggplant a charred flavor.) Let cool.

Steel Knife: Process onion with garlic until minced, about 6 to 8 seconds. Add green pepper and celery and process with 2 or 3 quick on/off turns, until coarsely chopped. Remove eggplant pulp from skin with a spoon and add with remaining ingredients to processor bowl. Process with 3 or 4 quick on/off turns, just until mixed. Adjust seasonings to taste. Refrigerate or freeze.

Yield: about 3 cups.

Note: I use very little oil in this recipe to reduce the calories. You may add more if you wish. Contains about 10 calories per tbsp., or 80 calories per half cup serving.

HERRING AND SOUR CREAM

2 - 16 oz. jars herring	¼ c. sugar
2 Bermuda onions	2 c. sour cream
¼ c. lemon juice	

Discard onion and juice from herring. Insert **Slicer** in processor. Cut onions to fit feed tube. Slice, using medium pressure. Mix herring with Bermuda onions, lemon juice, sugar and sour cream. Refrigerate for 24 hours. Ideal for brunch or as an appetizer.

Yield: 10 to 12 servings.

CHOPPED HERRING

6 oz. jar marinated herring   1 slice Challah or white bread
   fillets   2 hard-cooked eggs, halved
1 apple, cored (peel if desired)   1 tsp. sugar

Empty contents of herring jar into a colander. Discard any pickling spices. Rinse herring and onions under cold running water.

Steel Knife: Cut apple in quarters. Process until minced, about 10 seconds. Scrape down sides of bowl. Moisten bread with a little water, and squeeze out excess. Add bread, herring and onions to processor bowl. Process until coarsely chopped, about 8 seconds. Add eggs and sugar and process about 6 to 8 seconds longer, until finely chopped.

Yield: about 2 cups. Use as a sandwich filling, or serve as a spread with crackers or thinly sliced pumpernickel bread. Do not freeze. Keeps about 10 days to 2 weeks in the refrigerator. Contains about 17 calories per tbsp., or about 138 calories per half-cup serving.

MOCK CHOPPED HERRING
(Sardine Spread)

1 onion, halved   1 slice bread
1 apple, peeled, cored &   3 hard-cooked eggs, halved
   quartered   3 to 4 tbsp. vinegar (to taste)
2 -3¼ oz. tins sardines,   1 tsp. sugar
   drained   dash salt

Steel Knife: Process onion and apple until finely minced, about 6 to 8 seconds. Scrape down sides of bowl. Add sardines. Process about 6 seconds longer. Moisten bread with cold water and squeeze out excess moisture. Add chunks of bread along with remaining ingredients. Process about 8 to 10 seconds longer, until blended. Refrigerate. Serve as an appetizer, or with assorted crackers and breads as a spread. Do not freeze.

Yield: about 6 servings, or 2½ cups if used as a spread. Contains about 150 calories per serving.

HUMMOUS
(Chick Pea Spread)

¼ c. loosely packed parsley   6 tbsp. fresh lemon juice
2 cloves garlic   1 tsp. salt
19 oz. can chick peas, drained   freshly ground pepper
   & rinsed   ½ tsp. cumin (or to taste)
⅔ c. olive oil   3 tbsp. additional olive oil, to
½ c. Tahini (sesame seed   garnish
   butter or paste) available in   paprika and olives, to garnish
   Middle Eastern food markets   (optional)
   or specialty stores

Steel Knife: Make sure that parsley and processor bowl are dry. Process parsley until minced. Set aside. Drop garlic through feed tube while machine is running. Process until minced. Add chick peas, ⅔ c. olive oil, Tahini, lemon juice, salt, pepper and cumin. Process until smooth.

Spread mixture on a large flat serving plate. Drizzle with remaining oil and sprinkle with reserved parsley. May be garnished with paprika and olives. Serve chilled or at room temperature with pita bread. (If desired, split and cut in triangles; toast lightly). Also good with assorted vegetables or crackers.

CHOPPED LIVER

1 lb. beef or calves liver	2 or 3 tbsp. chicken broth
3 or 4 onions, quartered	(approximately)
¼ c. oil (approximately)	1 tbsp. mayonnaise, if desired
3 hard-boiled eggs, halved	salt & pepper, to taste

Liver may either be broiled or sautéed in oil on both sides. Do not overcook. Cool completely. (May be prepared in advance and refrigerated until needed.) Cut in 1½" chunks.

Steel Knife: Place half the onions in the processor bowl. Process with 3 or 4 quick on/off turns, until coarsely chopped. Empty bowl and repeat with remaining onions. Sauté in oil until golden, adding more oil if necessary.

Steel Knife: Process liver until minced, about 15 to 20 seconds. Add remaining ingredients and process until blended, about 10 to 15 seconds longer, scraping down sides of bowl as necessary. Mixture should be moist rather than dry, as it will firm up when refrigerated. The mayonnaise will give a "schmaltzy" delicious flavor. Try it, you'll like it!

Yield: 6 to 8 servings as an appetizer. Also delicious as a sandwich filling, or as a spread with crackers.

Note: If liver is hot when it is chopped, the resulting texture will be more like a pâté. Chicken livers may be substituted, if desired, but processing time will be slightly less, about 10 to 12 seconds instead of 15 to 20 seconds.

Calorie Counter's Version

Broil liver instead of sautéeing. Eliminate oil and mayonnaise; use a teflon frypan to sauté onions. Increase the amount of chicken broth, using enough to make liver moist. Contains 8 servings of about 125 calories each.

MOCK CHOPPED LIVER
(Calorie- Counter's Version)

½ lb. green or yellow beans	3 hard-cooked eggs, halved
(see Note)	2 tsp. mayonnaise
4 green onions, cut in 3"	salt and pepper, to taste
lengths	

Trim ends off beans and cook in boiling salted water until tender, about 10 to 15 minutes. Drain well.

Steel Knife: Drop onions through feed tube while machine is running. Process until minced. Add remaining ingredients and process 6 to 8 seconds longer. Chill.

Yield: 4 servings of about 89 calories each. Do not freeze.

Note: If desired, 14 oz. can green or wax beans, well-drained, may be substituted for fresh beans.

MOCK LOX SPREAD
(Salmon Pâté)

½ small onion or 3 green
onions, cut in 2" pieces
¼ lb. cream cheese or cottage
cheese
7¾ oz. can salmon, drained
½ tsp. horseradish

½ tbsp. lemon juice
dash pepper
¼ tsp. liquid smoke, if
available
½ tsp. Worcestershire sauce

Steel Knife: Process onion until minced, about 5 seconds. Add remaining ingredients and blend with quick on/off turns. Then let run until smooth. Scrape down bowl as necessary. Chill and serve as a spread with crackers, fresh rolls or bagel, or raw vegetables. If desired, garnish with minced parsley. Do not freeze.

Yield: 1 cup. Contains approximately 46 calories per tbsp. if made with cream cheese, 30 calories per tbsp. if made with cottage cheese.

LOX & CHEESE SPREAD

3 or 4 green onions, cut in 2"
lengths
½ lb. cream cheese or cottage
cheese

1 - 2 tbsp. milk or sour cream
(if cheese mixture is too
thick)
¼ lb. lox (lightly salted is best)

Steel Knife: Drop green onions through feed tube while machine is running. Process until minced. Add cream cheese or cottage cheese in chunks. Process until smooth. If necessary, add milk or sour cream to soften. Add lox and process with on/off turns, until mixed into cheese. (Or let machine run to blend thoroughly, making the cheese mixture a pale salmon color.) Chill and serve with bagels or pumpernickel bread or assorted crackers.

Yield: about 1¼ cups.

To Garnish: Spread narrow strips of lox with a little of the cheese and lox mixture. Roll up jelly roll style. Stand on end and insert a sprig of parsley in the centre of each roll as if they were little flower pots.

SALMON SPREAD √

½ stalk celery, cut in 2"
lengths
2 green onions (scallions), cut
in 2" lengths
7¾ oz. tin salmon, drained
(discard bones)

1 or 2 tbsp. mayonnaise
dash pepper & lemon juice
2 tbsp. relish, if desired

Steel Knife: Process celery and green onions until minced, about 6 to 8 seconds. Add remaining ingredients and process with 3 or 4 quick on/off turns, **just** until mixed. If necessary, scrape down sides of bowl once or twice. Do not overprocess, or you will have mush!

Yield: for 2 lengthwise slices of bread for cheese loaves, or 4 regular sandwiches. About ¾ cup filling. Do not freeze.

Note: If you are not experienced with your processor, I suggest using the **Plastic Knife** once the vegetables have been minced, in order to prevent overprocessing.

TUNA SPREAD✓

½ stalk celery, cut in 2"   7 oz. tin solid white tuna,
  lengths   drained (See Note)
3 radishes, trimmed   2 to 3 tbsp. mayonnaise
                                   dash salt & pepper

Steel Knife: Process celery and radishes until minced, about 6 to 8 seconds. Add remaining ingredients. Process with 3 or 4 on/off turns, **just** until mixed. Stop machine once or twice to scrape down sides of bowl with a rubber spatula. **Do not overprocess,** or tuna will have a very gritty texture.

Yield: for 4 sandwiches, or 2 lengthwise slices of bread for cheese loaves. Do not freeze.

Note: If you are using flaked tuna, I recommend changing to the **Plastic Knife** once the vegetables have been minced, in order to avoid overprocessing.

TUNA-EGG SPREAD✓

(Delicious served on lettuce leaves with tomato and cucumber
slices. Serve with fresh crusty rolls. Also excellent to
fill hollowed-out tomatoes.)

½ onion   2 hard-cooked eggs, halved
½ stalk celery, cut in 2"   ¼ c. mayonnaise
  lengths   (approximately)
3 or 4 radishes, trimmed   salt & pepper, to taste
7 oz. tin solid white tuna,
  drained (see Note)

Steel Knife: Process onion, celery and radishes until minced, about 6 to 8 seconds. Add remaining ingredients and process with 4 or 5 on/off turns, **just** until mixed. Do not overprocess. If necessary, scrape down once or twice.

Yield: for 6 sandwiches or 3 lengthwise slices of bread for cheese loaves. Do not freeze.

Note: If you are using flaked tuna, I recommend using the **Plastic Knife** once the vegetables have been minced, in order to avoid overprocessing.

HOME-MADE PEANUT BUTTER ✓

2 c. salted peanuts   2 - 3 tbsp. oil, if desired

Steel Knife: Place peanuts in processor bowl. Process for approximately 2½ minutes, stopping machine several times to scrape down sides of bowl. If you wish a smoother texture, add oil.

Yield: About 1 cup. Store in refrigerator.

CHUNKY PEANUT BUTTER: Add ½ cup peanuts to peanut butter. Process 6 to 8 seconds longer.

CHOCOLATE PEANUT BUTTER: Use 1½ cups peanuts and ½ cup semi-sweet chocolate chips. Do not add oil. Process as for peanut butter. Guaranteed to please your kids!

Note: You may use any nuts you wish instead of peanuts. For a real delicacy, try cashews. Do not use dry roasted peanuts.

GARLIC BUTTER

2 cloves garlic   ½ c. butter or margarine, cut in
3 sprigs parsley   1" chunks

Steel Knife: Process garlic and parsley until finely minced, about 10 seconds. Add butter and process until well blended, scraping down sides of bowl as necessary.

Yield: about ½ cup. May be frozen. Recipe may be doubled successfully. Butter will cream easily if slightly softened. Chives may be added, if desired.

DILL BUTTER

2 tbsp. fresh dill (discard   ½ c. butter or margarine, cut in
    stems)   1" chunks

Steel Knife: Process dill until chopped, about 8 seconds. Add butter and process until well blended, scraping down sides of bowl as necessary.

Yield: about ½ cup. Serve with salmon steaks, or your favorite fish, or to garnish baked potatoes.

LOW-CAL BUTTER OR MARGARINE

1 c. butter or margarine, cut in   ½ c. cold water
    chunks (slightly softened)

Steel Knife: Process butter or margarine until blended. Gradually add water through the feed tube while the machine is running. Process until butter is light and well whipped, about 2 minutes, stopping machine often to scrape down sides of bowl. Refrigerate. Contains about 50 calories per tbsp., compared to 100 calories per tbsp. in regular butter. Use as a spread, to make garlic butter, or for sautéeing. Do not use in baking cakes and cookies.

CURRY DIP

½ c. mayonnaise   3 to 4 drops Tabasco sauce
½ c. sour cream   salt & pepper, to taste
1 tsp. curry powder   dash of garlic powder
1 tbsp. chili sauce or ketchup

Steel Knife: Process all ingredients together until smooth, about 8 to 10 seconds. Chill. Serve with assorted raw vegetables, or as a chip dip.

Yield: about 1 cup. Do not freeze.

Calorie Counter's Version: Substitute ½ cup creamed cottage cheese and ½ cup natural yoghurt for the mayonnaise and sour cream. Increase processing time to about 45 seconds. Contains about 12 calories per tbsp.

GUACAMOLE DIP

1 small onion, halved   ¼ c. mayonnaise
½ green pepper or chili pepper   1 tbsp. lemon juice or vinegar
1 tomato, quartered   salt and pepper, to taste
1 avocado, peeled, pitted &   2 or 3 drops Tabasco sauce
    cut in chunks

Steel Knife: Process onion and green (or chili) pepper until minced, about 6 seconds. Add tomato and process a few seconds longer. Add remaining ingredients and process until smooth, about 20 to 30 seconds, scraping down bowl as necessary.

Yield: 2 cups. Do not freeze. Serve as a dip with vegetables, crackers or corn chips.

GARLIC CHEESE DIP

1 clove garlic	dash salt & pepper
¼ small onion	⅛ tsp. basil
½ c. creamed cottage cheese	⅛ tsp. oregano
½ c. mayonnaise	⅛ tsp. dill weed, if desired
1 tsp. Worcestershire sauce	

Steel Knife: Drop garlic and onion through feed tube while machine is running. Process until minced. Scrape down sides of bowl. Add cottage cheese and process until fairly well creamed, about 30 to 40 seconds, scraping down bowl once or twice. Add remaining ingredients and process about 8 to 10 seconds longer to blend. Chill.

Yield: about 1 cup. Do not freeze. Serve with raw vegetables, crackers or potato chips. If desired, thin with a little milk and use as a delicious dressing over your salads.

Note: Freshly snipped chives may be used instead of the onion, if desired.

PARMESAN DIP

1 oz. Parmesan cheese (about	1 tbsp. Worcestershire sauce
¼ c. grated)	dash of salt
½ c. mayonnaise	dash of white pepper
½ c. sour cream	

Cheese should be at room temperature. If cheese is not already grated, break into 1'' chunks. (A chisel is ideal.) Process on **Steel Knife** until finely grated. Add remaining ingredients and process until well blended, about 20 seconds. Refrigerate for several hours to blend flavors.

Yield: about 1 cup. Do not freeze. Serve with assorted raw vegetables or as a chip dip.

VEGETABLE DIP

1 clove garlic, peeled	1 c. mayonnaise
2 green onions or ½ small	1 tbsp. Worcestershire sauce
onion	dash of salt & pepper
2 sprigs parsley	dash of oregano and basil
1 c. sour cream	

Steel Knife: With machine running, drop garlic, onions and parsley through feed tube. Process until minced. Add remaining ingredients, scrape down sides of bowl and process just until blended, about 6 to 8 seconds.

Yield: 2 cups. Chill and serve with assorted crisp raw vegetables. Do not freeze.

Variation: Eliminate Worcestershire sauce, oregano and basil. Add any of the following:- 2 or 3 tbsp. grated cucumber; 1 tbsp. horseradish; 2 or 3 tbsp. anchovy paste; 2 or 3 tbsp. chili sauce or bottled barbecue sauce.

Calorie Counter's Version: Substitute low-fat plain yoghurt for sour cream and cottage cheese for mayonnaise. Increase processing time when combining all ingredients to about 45 seconds, or until smooth and creamy. Contains about 17 calories per tbsp.

YOGHURT CHEESE DIP
(Farmer's Dressing)

⅔ c. creamed cottage cheese   ¼ tsp. dill weed
¾ c. plain yoghurt   few drops Worcestershire
salt & pepper, to taste   sauce
¼ tsp. onion powder

Steel Knife: Process cheese until smooth, about 45 seconds. Scrape down sides of bowl once or twice. Add remaining ingredients and process a few seconds longer to blend. Chill and serve with assorted raw vegetables as a dip, or serve as a dressing over tossed salad. Thin with a few drops of milk, if necessary.

Yield: about 1½ cups. Do not freeze. Delicious, yet low in calories. Contains about 11 calories per tbsp.

Note: To add fresh garlic, drop a small clove through the feed tube while the machine is running. Process until minced. Then process remaining ingredients in order given.

SESAME CHEESE STRAWS

¼ lb. Cheddar cheese (about 1   ⅓ c. chilled butter or
c. grated)   margarine
1 c. flour   ½ tsp. Worcestershire sauce
½ tsp. salt   2 to 3 tbsp. cold water
¼ tsp. paprika   ¼ c. sesame seeds

Grater: Cheese should be cold for best results. Grate, using light pressure. Empty bowl.

Steel Knife: Place flour, salt, paprika and butter which has been cut into 1'' chunks into the processor. Process about 8 to 10 seconds, until particles are the size of small peas. Add cheese, Worcestershire sauce, water and sesame seeds. Process **just** until dough begins to gather in a ball around the blades, about 12 to 15 seconds. Use minimum amount of water, adding the extra tbsp. if dough seems too dry. Do not overprocess.

To shape: Divide mixture in half. Roll out each part into an 8'' x 12'' rectangle about ⅛'' thick. Using a sharp knife or pastry wheel, cut strips about 3'' by ½''. Bake on ungreased cookie sheets which have been lined with foil at 400°F for 10 to 12 minutes, until golden.

Yield: about 7 to 8 dozen. May be frozen baked or unbaked. It is not necessary to thaw them before baking.

Alternate shaping: Cut dough in strips about 6'' x ½''. Twist carefully and place on baking sheets. Bake as directed.

Yield: about 4 dozen.

SESAME CHEESE STICKS

Make dough for Sesame Cheese Straws (above).

To shape: Break off marble-sized pieces of dough and roll between your palms into pencil-thin sticks about ¼'' thick and 3 to 4 inches long. Roll in additional sesame seeds (about ¾ to 1 cup). Place on ungreased cookie sheets which have been lined with tinfoil. Bake at 400°F for about 15 minutes, until golden brown and crispy. Sticks should be turned after 10 minutes for even browning on both sides.

Yield: about 4 dozen. May be frozen baked or unbaked. It is not necessary to thaw before baking. Delicious served slightly warm with assorted raw vegetables and dip.

FROSTED CHEESE LOAF

2 loaves white or whole wheat bread, sliced lengthwise (or 1 loaf of each)
Mayonnaise (p. 65)
Chopped Egg Spread (p. 30)
Salmon Spread (p. 34)

Tuna Spread (p. 35) or Tuna-Egg Spread (p. 35)
Tomato &/or cucumber slices
Cheese Frosting (below), double recipe

Trim all crusts from bread and reserve to make your own bread crumbs. (Or use to make Stuffing Casserole (p. 178). You need 5 slices for each cheese loaf. Spread bread slices with mayonnaise on both sides (bottom and top slices should be spread with mayonnaise on one side only). Spread with filling.

Slicer: Cut cucumbers and tomatoes to fit feed tube. (Long, slim cucumbers are best, and have less seeds. Tomatoes should be very firm; cut lengthwise to fit feed tube.) Slice, using very light pressure. Salt lightly, then place between layers of paper towelling to remove excess liquid. Pat dry. I like to use the tomatoes and cucumbers as my middle layer of filling. Assemble loaves.

Ice with Cheese Frosting, and garnish with any of the following:- radish roses, carrot flowers, chopped parsley, gherkins, cucumber slices, corn niblets arranged into flower petals with a piece of pimento in the centre, etc. You may also tint part of the cheese frosting with a little food coloring and decorate the loaves with a cake decorating set.

Yield: 2 loaves, each serving 8 to 10 people. Do not freeze. May be made a day in advance. Will keep about 2 to 3 days in the fridge.

Note: Extra slices of bread and filling may be used to make party sandwiches.

CHEESE FROSTING

1 lb. cream cheese, cut in chunks plus ½ c. milk, yoghurt or sour cream

(or 2 c. creamed cottage cheese)

Steel Knife: Process cream cheese with milk, yoghurt or sour cream until very smooth and creamy, about 20 to 30 seconds. Scrape down sides of bowl once or twice. (If you are a calorie watcher and wish to use creamed cottage cheese, processing time will be slightly longer, about 45 seconds to one minute. It will not be necessary to add any other ingredients to the cottage cheese, and it will be very creamy. Cottage cheese contains about ¼ of the calories of cream cheese.)

Yield: To frost a 24 oz. loaf.

ALMOND CHEESE APPETIZERS

12 slices white bread
8 oz. Gouda cheese
10 oz. tin cream of mushroom
    soup

1 c. potato chips
½ c. slivered almonds
strips of pimento for garnishing

Trim crusts from bread. Toast and cut each slice into four squares. Cut cheese in half to fit feed tube. Discard waxy coating. Using **Slicer,** slice cheese using firm pressure. (Cheese should be chilled for best results.) Empty bowl.

Plastic Knife: Blend mushroom soup, potato chips and almonds with several quick on/off turns, just until combined.

Place one teaspoon of mixture on each toast square. Top with cheese and garnish with pimento. (May be prepared to this stage and refrigerated or frozen. Do not thaw before broiling.) Broil about 4'' from heat until golden.

Yield: 48.

ASPARAGUS CHEESE ROLLS

(Prepare in advance and freeze. Then pop under
the broiler when your company arrives.)

thinly sliced white bread, all
    crusts removed
½ lb. Cheddar cheese (2 c.
    grated)
½ c. soft butter, cut in chunks

2 tsp. prepared mustard
1 tsp. Worcestershire sauce
canned asparagus tips,
    well-drained

Place trimmed bread slices on a damp towel for a few minutes to make pliable, or flatten lightly with a rolling pin.

Grater: Grate cheese, using medium pressure. Remove grater and insert **Steel Knife,** making sure to push the blade all the way down. Add butter, mustard and Worcestershire sauce. Process just until mixed, scraping down bowl if necessary. Spread evenly on bread slices.

Place asparagus tips along one edge of bread slices. Roll up. Cut in half. Place seam-side down in a single layer on a cookie sheet and refrigerate or freeze until needed. Broil until golden. Serve hot.

Note: Leftover cheese is delicious served as a spread with crackers.

CHICKEN TIDBITS

Prepare Chicken Guy Kew as directed on p. 138. Serve piping hot with Chinese Sweet & Sour Sauce (p. 66).

Yield: 8 to 10 servings. May be frozen.

CHICKEN WINGS

Make any of the following as an appetizer or hors d'oeuvres. Allow 2 or 3 per person. If serving as finger food, it is preferable to split the wings in half and discard the wing tips.

Chinese Chicken Wings
    (p. 146)
Honey Glazed Chicken
    Wings (p. 145)

Honey Glazed Baby Drums
    (p. 145)
Sticky Chicky (p. 144) using
    chicken wings instead of
    chicken pieces

SESAME WINGS

4 lb. chicken wings, halved
(discard wing tips or save to
make soup)
salt, pepper, paprika &
garlic powder

32 crackers (or about 1¼ c.
toasted bread crumbs)
⅓ c. sesame seeds
2 eggs
1 tbsp. water

Prepare chicken wings and sprinkle lightly with seasonings.

Steel Knife: Process crackers to make fine crumbs. Add seasonings to taste, as well as sesame seeds. Process with several on/off turns to mix. Transfer to a plastic bag. Process eggs with water for 2 or 3 seconds to blend.

Dip wings first in egg mixture, then shake in crumbs. Arrange on lightly greased foil-lined cookie sheets. Bake at 400°F for 35 to 40 minutes, or until crisp and nicely browned. May be frozen, but I prefer to bake the wings for about 25 minutes, cool and refrigerate until needed. Then I pop them into a hot oven and bake about 20 minutes longer, giving them that "just-made" taste. Delicious!

EGG ROLLS

Dough:
2¼ c. flour
½ tsp. salt
2 large eggs
¼ c. warm water (approximately)

Egg Roll Filling (p. 42)
1 egg, lightly beaten
oil for deep frying (about 2
cups)

Steel Knife: Process flour, salt, eggs and water until dough forms a ball on the blade and is well kneaded, about 25 to 30 seconds. Remove from bowl, cover and let stand for 15 minutes. Prepare filling as directed and let cool.

Divide dough in half. Roll each portion into a large rectangle. Dough should be very thin. Cut in 4" squares for large egg rolls, or into 2" x 4" rectangles for miniatures. Brush edges of squares or rectangles with beaten egg. Place a spoonful of filling along the lower edge of dough. Roll up and press edges to seal. Repeat until all dough and filling are used.

Heat oil to 375°F in a deep-fryer or large deep saucepan. Fry egg rolls until golden. Drain on paper towelling. (May be frozen at this point. Thaw before reheating.) To reheat, place in a single layer on a foil-lined cookie sheet and heat at 350°F until piping hot and crisp. Do not cover. Serve with bottled plum sauce.

Yield: about 30 large or 60 small egg rolls.

Note: If you do not wish to make your own egg roll skins, you may buy them in the frozen food section of most supermarkets, or in Chinatown. Assemble and fry as directed above.

EGG ROLL FILLING

2 medium onions, quartered
2 stalks celery, cut in chunks
1 green pepper, cut in chunks
1 c. mushrooms
3 tbsp. oil
1 lb. fresh bean sprouts (or 28
   oz. can, rinsed under cold
   water and well-drained)

1 or 2 cloves garlic
2 tbsp. soya sauce
dash of pepper
dash of Accent, if desired

Steel Knife: Process onions with 3 or 4 quick on/off turns, until coarsely chopped. Empty bowl. Repeat with celery, green pepper and mushrooms, emptying bowl each time. Quickly brown onions, celery, green pepper and mushrooms in hot oil in a large skillet on high heat. Add beans sprouts and cook until moisture has evaporated and mixture is fairly dry.

Steel Knife: Drop garlic through feed tube while machine is running. Process until minced. Add to skillet along with soya sauce, pepper and Accent. Mix well.

Yield: filling for about 16 to 20 crêpes, or 24 to 30 egg rolls.

Note: About ½ medium cabbage may be substituted for the bean sprouts. Process on **Grater,** using firm pressure. Measure approximately 3 cups.

FELAFEL
(Chick Pea Balls)

14 oz. pkg. dried chick peas
   (See Note)
4 to 6 cloves garlic
2 large onions, quartered
½ c. loosely packed parsley
1½ tsp. salt (or to taste)
freshly ground pepper

1 tsp. cumin (or to taste)
dash cayenne pepper or
   coriander
6 tbsp. toasted bread crumbs
2 eggs
½ tsp. baking powder

Soak chick peas overnight in cold water. Drain thoroughly. **Divide all ingredients in half and process in two batches.**

Steel Knife: Drop garlic through feed tube while machine is running. Process until minced. Discard peel. Add onion and parsley; process until minced. Add remaining ingredients and process until finely ground and smooth, about 20 to 30 seconds, scraping down bowl as necessary. Transfer to a mixing bowl and repeat with second batch of ingredients.

Form into 1'' balls. Deep fry in hot oil until golden. Serve with toothpicks as an hors d'oeuvre, or in pita bread or rolls with assorted chopped salad vegetables (e.g. cucumbers, tomatoes, peppers, onions, lettuce) and Tachina, a mayonnaise-like dressing (p. 43).

Yield: about 100 balls. May be frozen.

Note: If desired, substitute 3 cups drained canned chick peas for the dried chick peas. Soaking is then not necessary.

TACHINA DRESSING
(To be served with Felafel)

1 clove garlic
½ c. Tahini (sesame seed butter or paste which is available in Middle Eastern food markets or specialty stores)
⅓ c. water
2 tbsp. lemon juice
½ tsp. salt (or to taste)
pepper to taste
dash of cumin, if desired

Steel Knife: Drop garlic through feed tube while machine is running. Process until minced. Add remaining ingredients and process until smooth, about 10 to 15 seconds. Consistency should be like mayonnaise.

Yield: about ¾ cup. Recipe may be doubled successfully.

FILO HORS D'OEUVRES

Filo dough is available in Greek pastry shops or in the frozen food section of many supermarkets or gourmet food shops. Keep dough covered with a damp cloth or plastic wrap as it is very fragile and dries out quickly. Work with one sheet at a time.

Place one sheet of filo on countertop so that the longer edge of the dough is parallel to the edge of the counter. Brush with melted butter, margarine or vegetable oil. (You will need about ½ cup for 1 lb. of filo dough.) Cover with a second sheet of dough and brush once again with fat. Cut dough into 6 strips about 2'' wide. Place about 1 rounded teaspoon filling 1'' from the bottom of each strip. Fold upwards once to cover filling.

Bring right bottom corner of dough upwards to meet the left edge, making a triangle. Continue folding from side to side until the strip is completely folded. Repeat with remaining dough and filling. Place triangles seam-side down on a lightly greased baking pan and brush with additional melted butter or margarine. (May be frozen at this point.)

Bake at 350°F for about 20 minutes, or until golden. One pound of dough will make about 100 hors d'oeuvres. Freezes well. To reheat, bake uncovered at 300°F for about 10 minutes, or until heated through.

Suggested Fillings: Cheese Filling (p. 104); Spinach or Broccoli Filling (below); double recipe of filling for Mushroom Pinwheels (p. 45); Meat or Chicken Filling (p. 175), using oil to brush filo dough.

SPINACH OR BROCCOLI FILLING

2 - 10 oz. pkgs. frozen spinach or broccoli
1 onion, quartered
2 tbsp. butter or margarine
¼ c. grated Parmesan cheese
½ lb. dry cottage or Ricotta cheese
1 or 2 eggs
salt & pepper, to taste
¼ tsp. nutmeg

Cook spinach or broccoli according to package directions. Drain well. Squeeze out all moisture from spinach.

Steel Knife: Process onion with 2 or 3 quick on/off turns, till coarsely chopped. Sauté in melted butter for 5 minutes. Process spinach or broccoli until finely chopped, about 8 to 10 seconds. Add remaining ingredients and process just until mixed. (Add second egg only if mixture seems dry.) Use as a filling for Filo Hors D'Oeuvres, or as an alternative filling for Cheese Turnovers (p. 95).

HOT DOGS IN BLANKETS

Flaky Ginger Ale Pastry (p. 305) 2 pkgs. cocktail hot dogs
2 eggs, lightly beaten

Prepare pastry as directed. Chill if possible. Roll out thinly into a large rectangle and cut in small rectangles about 2'' x 3''. Brush edges with beaten egg. Place hot dogs on dough and roll up. Place seam-side down on a foil-lined cookie sheet. Brush with remaining egg. (May be frozen at this point.) Bake at 375°F about 15 minutes, or until golden brown. Serve hot with mustard. If freezing after baking, it is best to underbake slightly.

MOCK KISHKA HORS D'OEUVRES

Follow directions for Mock Kishka (p. 158). Bake as directed. Slice in ½'' slices. Serve hot on toothpicks.

Yield: about 4 to 5 dozen. Freezes well.

MINIATURE KNISHES

Knishes are ideal when made in miniature as hors d'oeuvres. Follow recipe for your favorite knishes and roll dough into a rectangle about 18'' x 6''. Place a narrow band of filling about 1'' wide along the longer side of the rectangle, about 1'' from the edge. Roll up into a long, narrow roll. Cut with the edge of your hand into 1'' pieces. Seal ends.

Bake at 375°F for 20 to 25 minutes, until golden brown. The recipe for Warm Water Knish Dough (p. 174) will yield about 5 to 6 dozen knishes. Best if frozen unbaked for maximum flavor. Bake frozen knishes at 375°F about 30 minutes.

MEAT BALL KNISHES

Prepare dough and filling for Crusty Meat Loaf (p. 132) and roll dough as thin as possible into a rectangle about 8'' x 15''. Place meat in a narrow band along one edge of dough, about 1'' from edges. Roll up. Using the edge of your hand, press down on roll, and with a sawing motion, cut through. Repeat about every inch. Turn knishes on end, pressing ends in slightly. Bake at 350°F about 25 to 30 minutes.

Yield: about 2 dozen miniature knishes. Freeze unbaked. Thaw completely before baking.

Note: The dough and meat do not adhere to each other when baked, giving the effect of a meatball wrapped in dough.

MEATBALLS

Any of the meatball recipes may be used as an hors d'oeuvre or appetizer. Form into tiny balls and cook as directed.

Saucy Meatballs (p. 127)
Hawaiian Meatballs (p. 129)
MMM- Good Meatballs (p. 130)
Meatballs in Pineapple Plum Sauce (p. 126)

Pineapple Chicken Meatballs (p. 146)
Cranberry Chicken or Meat Balls (p. 145)

SPARE RIBS

Make Honey Glazed Spare Ribs (p. 123) or Honey Garlic Ribs (p. 123).

PARTY MEATBALL DISH

1 clove garlic
1 small onion, halved
2 lb. ground beef (or 2 lb. lean
   beef, cut in 1½" chunks)
1 egg
2 tbsp. bread or cracker
   crumbs

1½ tsp. salt
dash pepper
9 oz. jar grape jelly
11 oz. jar chili sauce or 1½ c.
   bottled barbecue sauce
2 tbsp. lemon juice
½ tsp. garlic powder

Steel Knife: Process garlic and onion until minced. If meat is not already ground, add about ⅓ of the beef chunks to the processor bowl. Process until finely chopped, about 8 seconds. Transfer to a large mixing bowl. Repeat twice more with remaining beef chunks, adding each in turn to the mixing bowl. Add egg, crumbs and seasonings and mix lightly to blend.

Steel Knife: Combine jelly, chili or barbecue sauce, lemon juice and garlic powder in processor bowl. Process until mixed, about 6 to 8 seconds. Transfer to a large saucepan. Bring to a boil. (If desired, mix about 2 or 3 tbsp. of the sauce into the ground beef.)

Drop walnut-sized meatballs into simmering sauce. Cover partially and simmer for about one hour. If desired, add 2 lb. hotdogs, cut on the diagonal into ½" slices. Simmer for 5 minutes to heat through. Freezes well. Reheat in oven at 300°F until piping hot. Excellent for the buffet table!

Yield: about 50 meatballs and 50 hot dogs slices.

MUSHROOM PINWHEELS

Flaky Ginger Ale Pastry
   (p. 305)
2 onions, halved
2 tbsp. butter or margarine

1 pint mushrooms
⅓ c. sweet red wine
salt and pepper, to taste
pinch nutmeg, if desired

Prepare dough as directed and chill.

Steel Knife: Chop onions with 3 or 4 quick on/off turns, until coarsely chopped. Sauté gently in butter, but do not brown. Process mushrooms with about 4 or 5 on/off turns, until finely chopped. Add to onions and sauté until mixture is quite dry, about 7 to 8 minutes. Add wine and cook on high heat until moisture is evaporated. Add seasonings and let cool.

Roll out one portion of dough on a pastry cloth or floured board into a 10" x 12" rectangle. Spread half of filling over dough to within ½" of edges. Roll up, sealing edge with a little oil, if necessary. Repeat with remaining dough and filling. Bake on a lightly greased baking sheet at 350°F about 35 minutes, brushing with melted margarine or oil once or twice during baking. Cut while warm in ½" slices, using a sharp knife.

Yield: about 4 dozen. Lay flat and reheat at 350°F for a few minutes before serving.

To Freeze: Bake and slice as directed. Freeze until needed. Thaw and reheat uncovered at 350°F on a cookie sheet about 10 to 12 minutes, until heated through.

STUFFED ITALIAN MUSHROOMS
(Ideal as an appetizer or a side dish)

1 doz. very large mushrooms (or 2 doz. medium)	½ green pepper
1 clove garlic	⅓ c. toasted bread crumbs
5 tbsp. margarine	salt and pepper, to taste
1 small onion	⅛ tsp. oregano
1 stalk celery, cut in chunks	2 oz. Mozzerella cheese (½ c. grated), if desired

Wash mushrooms and pat dry with paper towelling. Remove stems and set aside.

Steel Knife: Drop garlic through feed tube while machine is running. Process until minced. Add mushroom stems and process until finely chopped, about 6 to 8 seconds. Melt 3 tbsp. margarine in a skillet. Add minced mushrooms and garlic. Process onion, celery and green pepper until minced, about 6 to 8 seconds. Add to skillet. Sauté all vegetables except mushrooms caps about 5 minutes. Stir in bread crumbs and seasonings.

Melt remaining margarine in a baking dish. Stuff mushroom caps.

Grater: Grate cheese, using medium pressure. Top mushrooms with cheese. Place in baking dish and bake at 350°F for 20 minutes.

Yield: 3 to 4 servings.

Note: May be prepared in advance but do not bake. Refrigerate until needed, then bake at serving time.

To Freeze: Bake for 10 minutes at 350°F. Cool and freeze. Bake frozen mushrooms covered at 350°F for 15 minutes, then uncover and broil until golden brown.

Variation: Eliminate celery, green pepper and cheese. Process ¼ cup almonds on the **Steel Knife** for 12 to 15 seconds, or until coarsely chopped. Add with bread crumbs to sautéed stems. Add a little lemon juice if desired. Stuffed mushrooms may either be drizzled with melted butter or margarine, or sprinkled with a little grated Parmesan cheese.

PIZZA TARTS

Sour Cream Pastry (p. 305) or Cream Cheese Pastry (p. 303)	5½ oz. tin tomato paste
1 clove garlic	2 tbsp. water
1 onion, quartered	¼ tsp. salt
½ green pepper, seeded	dash pepper, oregano & basil
10 oz. can sliced mushrooms (or 1 pint fresh mushrooms)	2 or 3 tbsp. Bac-O's if desired
2 tbsp. oil	½ lb. Mozzerella cheese (2 c. grated)

Prepare pastry as directed. Roll out and cut 3½'' circles. Line 24 muffin cups with dough.

Steel Knife: Drop garlic through feed tube while machine is running. Process until minced. Add onion and process with 2 or 3 quick on/off turns, until coarsely chopped.

Slicer: Slice green pepper (and mushrooms if using fresh), using light pressure. (I have even sliced whole canned mushrooms on the processor most successfully.) Brown vegetables lightly in oil for about 5 minutes. Stir in tomato paste, water and seasonings. Simmer for 3 or 4 minutes.

Grater: Grate cheese, using medium pressure.

Place about 1 tbsp. vegetable mixture in each tart shell. Top with grated cheese and Bac-O's. Bake at 400°F about 20 minutes, until golden.

Yield: 2 dozen. Freezes well. Sure to please!

MAKE-AND-BAKE PIZZA

Warning: Once you try this recipe, your family may never let you order from the local pizzeria again! Pizzas may be assembled and frozen unbaked. Just pop frozen pizza into the oven and bake. Increase baking time by about 5 minutes. Pizzas may also be frozen after baking.

Dough:
1 pkg. dry yeast
¼ c. warm water (105°F-115°F)
2¾ c. flour
1 tbsp. sugar
1 tsp. salt
1 tbsp. shortening or oil
1 c. lukewarm water

Topping:
2 tsp. oil
1 c. tomato or pizza sauce
dash oregano, garlic powder & basil (omit if using spicy pizza sauce)
1 c. mushrooms
1 green pepper, halved & seeded
½ lb. pepperoni, if desired (See Note)*
½ lb. Mozzerella cheese (2 c. grated)

Sprinkle yeast over ¼ c. warm water and let stand for 8 to 10 minutes. Stir to dissolve.

Steel Knife: Place flour, sugar and salt in food processor. Process 6 seconds. Add yeast. Process 10 seconds longer. Combine oil and water, and pour through the feed tube while the machine is running. Process until dough forms a ball on the blades. (Keep a reserve of ¼ c. flour in case the machine slows down or the dough does not form a ball; then dump, if necessary, through the feed tube.) Once the dough has formed a ball around the blades, process 30 to 40 seconds longer.

Divide dough in two. Knead into smooth balls. Flatten and roll into 2 twelve inch circles (or make 12 smaller circles). Place on greased pizza pans or baking sheets. Turn edges to raise slightly. Let rise 10 to 15 minutes in pan while you prepare topping. Brush dough with oil. Spread with sauce and sprinkle with seasonings.

Slicer: Slice mushrooms and green pepper, using light pressure. Spread over sauce. Cut pepperoni to fit feed tube. Slice, using firm pressure. Spread over mushrooms and green pepper.

Grater: Grate cheese, using medium pressure. Top pizzas. Bake on lowest rack at 425°F — 450°F for 20 minutes. Freezes well.

Yield: 2 large or 12 miniature pizzas.

*Note: If you observe the Jewish dietary laws and do not wish to use pepperoni with the cheese, you may substitute 2 - 7 oz. tins tuna, flaked and drained, or ½ c. Bac-O's (Artificial bacon-flavored bits) which are pareve. You may make your own Pizza Sauce (see recipe on p. 65).

QUICHELETTES

Follow recipe for your favourite quiche (refer to "Fish Eggs & Cheese" section for specific recipes), but use Cream Cheese Pastry (p. 303) instead of an unbaked pie shell. Divide dough into 20 to 24 walnut-sized balls. Press into the bottom and slightly up the sides of lightly greased muffin cups. (Dough may also be rolled, giving you 24 tarts.)

Fill and bake at 375°F about 20 minutes, until golden brown.

Yield: about 20 to 24. Freezes well.

LOW-CAL QUICHELETTES

...pare Zucchini (p. 107) or Mushroom Quiche (p. 108) as directed. Grease 12 muffin cups. Fill and bake at 350°F about 20 minutes.

Yield: 12. Ideal to serve as hors d'oeuvres. Zucchini Quichelettes contain about 94 calories each. Mushroom contain about 84 calories each. May be frozen.

TERIYAKI KABOBS

Cut lean steak into bite-sized pieces. Marinate in Chinese, Cantonese or Piquante Marinade (p. 114-115), or in the marinade for Teriyaki Steak (p. 115). Let marinate at room temperature for 1 hour or in the refrigerator up to 24 hours. Drain well.

Arrange on aluminum foil in a single layer. Broil on both sides very briefly. Thread onto wooden skewers along with green pepper chunks, drained cocktail onions and bits of pimento. Liver may be substituted for steak.

LIVER TURNOVERS

Flaky Ginger Ale Pastry (p. 305)   **1 egg, lightly beaten**
Chopped Liver (p. 33)

Prepare pastry as directed. Roll out into a large rectangle. Cut in 2'' circles. Prepare liver as directed and place a teaspoon of liver on the lower half of each circle. Fold over and press to seal with the tines of a fork. Brush with beaten egg.

Bake on a lightly greased baking sheet at 375°F for about 20 minutes, until golden.

Yield: about 24 to 30. May be frozen.

Variations: Fill with Meat or Chicken Filling (p. 175) or Corned Beef Filling (p. 176).

CHEESE TURNOVERS

See recipe for Cheese Turnovers (p. 95), but cut circles only 2'' in diameter. Fill and bake as directed. May be frozen.

Yield: 24 to 30.

Additional Recipes

Soups, Sauces & Miscellaneous

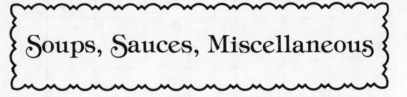

Soups, Sauces, Miscellaneous

- **Soups** do not need exact measures. You may thin soups by adding a little extra liquid, or cook down a watery soup by cooking uncovered to allow some of the liquid to evaporate. Otherwise, cook covered for maximum flavor.

- **To thicken** soups, purée some of the vegetables. With a processor, the most successful way is to strain out the solids and place them in the processor bowl. Purée on the **Steel Knife** until smooth, about 10 seconds. Do not add the cooking liquid as this will limit the quantity you can purée at one time. **Thick purées** (vegetables only): 3 to 3½ cups at a time. **Thin purées** (vegetables **and** liquid): only 2½ cups at a time.

- **Save** the raw skin and bones from chicken breasts when your recipe calls for boneless breasts. Store skin and bones in the freezer in a plastic bag until you have enough to make a soup. See recipe on p. 54. The carcass from roasted turkey is also ideal to use in soups.

- **Leftover rice,** noodles, macaroni or mashed potatoes may be added to soups. Keep a box of instant mashed potatoes on your pantry shelf to quickly thicken a puréed soup made from cooked leftover vegetables. This is a good way to ''stretch'' soups. A minute or two of cooking is all that is necessary.

- **Leftover salad** may be placed in a strainer and rinsed under cold water to remove salad dressing. Then chop finely on the **Steel Knife** and add to vegetable soups. (An emergency gazpacho may be made by adding leftover salad to a combination of tomato juice and bouillon. Season to taste.)

- **Save liquids** from canned vegetables, as well as the cooking liquid from fresh vegetables. They impart a nice flavor to soups, as well as retaining vitamins.

- **Celery tops** do not have to be discarded. Chop finely on the **Steel Knife** and add to soups for a delicious fresh flavor.

- **Save** any cooked leftover vegetables (e.g. cauliflower, carrots, spinach, peas, broccoli spears) and add them to your vegetable soups. They may be puréed on the **Steel Knife** before adding them to the liquid. They will act as low-calorie thickeners. Canned or frozen vegetables may also be used.

- **Adding meat** to soups gives a heartier flavor. Place in a large soup pot with cold salted water to cover. Bring to a boil, remove any scum, add your choice of vegetables and seasonings and simmer until the meat is tender. Barley, beans, lentils, peas may be added.

- **Vegetables** for soups may be cooked in water, or add bouillon cubes or instant soup mix for additional flavor. Canned broth may also be used, or if you have home-made, that is ideal.

- **An easy way** to remove fat from soup is to refrigerate it. Discard congealed fat and say goodbye to unwanted calories and cholesterol.

- **To freeze soups:** Leave 2'' on the top of the container to allow for expansion during freezing. Plastic ice cream containers or Tupperware are ideal. Jars sometimes become brittle when frozen and could crack, and frozen soup is difficult to remove. Immerse container in warm water for a minute or so to loosen the soup from the edges. Then dump frozen soup into a saucepan. Heat on low heat, turning often.

- **Sauces** are smooth and lump-free when made in the processor. To make a wh[...] there is no need to cook the butter/flour mixture first. There are several exc[...] easy recipes in this section using this new method of making sauces (e.g. [...] Sauce, Mushroom Sauce, Bechamel (White) Sauce).

- **If cooked sauces** have lumps, you can make them smooth as silk by processing them for a few seconds on the **Steel Knife.**

- **Use leftover cooked vegetables** (especially potatoes) to thicken sauces and gravies. Purée vegetables, then add hot liquid through feed tube until desired texture is reached. Season to taste. Liquid may be hot broth or pan juices.

★★★★★★★★★★★★★★★★★

DAIRY BEET BORSCHT

2½ lb. beets, peeled	3 pieces of sour salt or 2
1 onion	tbsp. lemon juice
2 quarts cold water	1 c. sugar
19 oz. can tomato juice	2 tsp. salt
	few sprigs fresh dill

Grater: Cut beets to fit feed tube. Grate, using fairly firm pressure. (A slight bouncing motion with the pusher is best.) Grate onion. Combine in a large saucepan with water. Bring to a boil, reduce heat to simmer and add remaining ingredients.

Simmer for 1 hour partially covered. Taste to adjust seasonings. Refrigerate. Serve chilled with sour cream. Will keep for 2 to 3 weeks in the refrigerator in a tightly closed jar.

CABBAGE SOUP WITH MEAT BALLS ✓

2½ quarts boiling water	2 tbsp. bread crumbs
28 oz. canned tomatoes	¼ tsp. garlic powder
5½ oz. tin tomato paste	1 onion, quartered lengthwise
8 oz. tin tomato sauce	½ head cabbage
1 lb. ground beef (or 1 lb. lean beef, cut in 1½" chunks)	½ c. brown or white sugar (or to taste)
¾ tsp. salt	2 tbsp. lemon juice
freshly ground pepper	salt & pepper, to taste
1 egg	½ c. rice, if desired

Combine water, canned tomatoes, tomato paste and tomato sauce in a large soup pot and bring to a boil.

Steel Knife: If meat is not already ground, put half of the beef chunks in the processor bowl and process until coarsely chopped, about 6 seconds. Empty bowl and repeat with remaining beef chunks. Return first batch of meat to processor along with salt, pepper, egg, crumbs and garlic powder. Process with quick on/off turns to mix. Do not overprocess. Shape into tiny meatballs and add to soup pot.

Slicer: Slice onion, using light pressure. Cut cabbage in wedges to fit feed tube. Discard core. Slice, using very light pressure. Add onion and cabbage to soup along with remaining ingredients except rice. Cover and simmer for about 2½ hours. Add rice and simmer 25 minutes longer. Adjust seasonings to taste.

Yield: 12 to 16 hearty servings. If soup is too thick, a little additional water may be added. May be frozen.

Note: If desired, make double the amount of meatballs, but do not mix together on the processor. Combine ground meat with remaining ingredients for meatballs in a large mixing bowl.

LOW CALORIE CABBAGE SOUP ✓

3 tbsp. fresh parsley, if
   desired
½ medium cabbage
48 oz. can tomato juice
4½ c. water
4 tsp. instant chicken or beef
   soup mix
2 tbsp. lemon juice

1 tbsp. salt
½ tsp. pepper
1 tsp. Accent, if desired
½ tsp. garlic powder
1 tbsp. dried vegetable flakes
1 tsp. onion flakes
sweetener to equal 4 tbsp.
   sugar (or to taste)

Steel Knife: Process parsley until minced. Insert **Grater.** Cut cabbage to fit feed tube. Grate, using medium pressure. Combine all ingredients except sweetener in a large pot. Bring to a boil. Cover and simmer 30 to 40 minutes. Add sweetener.

Yield: 12 - 8 oz. servings of 39 calories each. 1 serving equals ½ cup of tomato juice. Freezes well.

Meatier Version: Place 1 or 2 lbs. lean beef or veal in soup pot. Add tomato juice and water and bring to a boil. Remove scum. Add remaining ingredients, omitting instant soup mix. Cover and simmer for about 3 hours. (You may use 1 large onion, chopped, instead of the onion flakes.) Serve meat in soup as a one-dish meal.

FREE CHICKEN SOUP
(This recipe is an ideal way to use up the leftover skin
and bones from chicken breasts used in recipes calling
for boneless breasts.)

skin and bones from 8
   whole chicken breasts
8 c. cold water
3 to 4 tsp. salt (to taste)
¼ tsp. pepper

4 to 6 carrots, scraped &
   trimmed
3 stalks celery
1 onion
2 sprigs dill

Combine bones, skin and cold water in a large pot. Add salt and bring to a boil. Skim. Add remaining ingredients, cover and simmer for about 2 hours. Strain and refrigerate. Remove the fat which congeals on top and discard. Serve soup with Matzo Balls (p. 60), Kreplach (p. 177), noodles or rice.

Yield: 8 servings. Freezes well.

FLANKEN AND BARLEY SOUP

6 or 8 strips short ribs
   (flanken)
3 qts. cold water
1 tbsp. salt
2 onions, quartered
3 stalks celery, cut in 2"
   chunks

½ turnip, cut in 1" chunks
3 carrots, scraped and cut in
   1" chunks
1¼ c. barley
¼ tsp. pepper
½ tsp. Accent, if desired

Place short ribs in a large soup pot. Add cold water and salt. Bring to a boil and skim well.

Steel Knife: Process onions and celery until finely minced, about 6 to 8 seconds. Add to soup. Repeat with turnip and carrots. Add remaining ingredients to soup. Cover and simmer slowly for 3 hours. Taste to correct seasonings.

Yield: 10 to 12 hearty servings. May be frozen. Thin soup with a little water if necessary when reheating.

GAZPACHO

(Sometimes known as salad soup)

1 large cucumber, peeled	¼ c. olive or corn oil
1 green pepper, seeded	½ tsp. each chili powder &
1 onion	basil
6 tomatoes, peeled	1 tbsp. salt
4 cloves garlic	19 oz. can tomato juice
juice of ½ lemon	

Cut cucumber, green pepper, onion and tomatoes into chunks.

Steel Knife: Process cucumber with 4 or 5 on/off turns, until finely chopped. Transfer to a large bowl. Repeat with green pepper, then onion, then tomatoes, adding each in turn to the mixing bowl. Drop garlic through feed tube while machine is running. Process until minced. Discard garlic peel. Add lemon juice, oil, chili powder, basil, salt and **half** of the tomato juice. Process until smooth. Add to chopped vegetables along with remaining tomato juice. Adjust seasonings to taste. Chill for several hours in order to blend flavors. This will keep very well in the refrigerator in a tightly closed jar. Serve with croutons and additional chopped vegetables if desired. Contains 6 servings of approximately 130 calories each.

Note: Vegetables may be processed on the French-Fry Blade, if desired. Cut into 1'' chunks and process, using very light pressure. This will give a coarser texture to the Gazpacho. If desired, you may substitute up to 2 cups of consommé for part of the tomato juice and reduce oil to 2 tbsp. Approximately 90 calories per serving.

MANHATTAN FISH CHOWDER

1 clove garlic	19 oz. canned tomatoes
2 medium onions, cut in	¼ c. ketchup
chunks	1½ lb. fillets of sole, cut in large
1 green pepper, cut in chunks	chunks
2 stalks celery, cut in chunks	6 c. water
1 c. mushrooms	1 tbsp. salt (or to taste)
3 tbsp. butter or margarine	¼ tsp. pepper
3 carrots, scraped & trimmed	1 bay leaf, crumbled
3 medium potatoes, pared	½ tsp. thyme

Steel Knife: Drop garlic through feed tube while machine is running. Process until minced. Discard peel.

Either: Process onions with 3 or 4 quick on/off turns, until coarsely chopped. Empty bowl and repeat with green pepper, then with celery, emptying bowl each time.

Or: Insert **French Fry Blade.** Add onions, pepper and celery through the feed tube, using almost no pressure. This will give a coarse ''dice''.

Slicer: Slice mushrooms, using medium pressure. Sauté onions, pepper, celery and mushrooms in butter or margarine in a large soup pot for about 10 minutes, stirring occasionally. Cut carrots and potatoes to fit feed tube. Slice, using fairly firm pressure. Add with remaining ingredients to soup pot and bring to a boil. Reduce heat to simmer and cook, covered, about 30 minutes, or until vegetables are tender.

Yield: 8 hearty servings. Serve with crusty rolls as a light ''meal-in-one''.

MINESTRONE SOUP ✓

3 onions
2 carrots
2 stalks celery
4 medium potatoes, peeled
¼ head cabbage (2 c. sliced)
2 medium zucchini
¼ c. olive or vegetable oil
2 cloves garlic
½ lb. fresh green beans,
  halved

28 oz. can tomatoes (or 2 lb.
  ripe tomatoes)
8 c. water
3 tbsp. instant beef soup mix
salt & pepper, to taste
1 tsp. oregano
½ tsp. basil
2 c. spaghetti, broken into 1"
  pieces
grated Parmesan cheese, to
  garnish

Cut onions, carrots, celery and potatoes into chunks. Cut cabbage and zucchini to fit feed tube.

Steel Knife: Process onions with 3 or 4 on/off turns, until coarsely chopped. Heat oil in a large soup pot. Add onions and sauté until golden, about 5 minutes. Process garlic until minced. Add carrots and process with on/off turns, until coarsely chopped. Empty bowl. Repeat with celery and potatoes.

Slicer: Slice cabbage and zucchini, using medium pressure. Add with remaining ingredients except spaghetti and Parmesan cheese to soup pot. (If using fresh tomatoes, purée them on the **Steel Knife** before adding to soup.) Cover and simmer slowly for 2 to 2½ hours. Add spaghetti and cook about 8 minutes longer. Serve with a bowl of grated Parmesan cheese.

Yield: 12 servings. Freezes well.

Note: If desired, add a 19 oz. can of drained Canellini beans (white lima beans) 15 minutes before soup is completed.

PHONY MINESTRONE ✓
(My kids call this spaghetti soup)

2 chicken breasts
6 c. cold water
1 tbsp. salt
3 to 4 cloves garlic
1 large onion, cut in chunks
2 carrots, cut in chunks
2 stalks celery, cut in chunks
½ c. green split peas
¼ c. barley
5½ oz. can tomato paste
28 oz. canned tomatoes
2 bay leaves

freshly ground pepper
1 tsp. Italian seasoning (or ½
  tsp. each basil and oregano)
¼ tsp. each rosemary and
  thyme
1 c. fresh green beans, if desired
2 additional carrots
1 c. canned baked beans
14 oz. can green peas
1½ - 2 c. spaghetti, broken into
  2" pieces

Place chicken in cold salted water in a large soup pot. Bring to a boil. Skim.

Steel Knife: Drop garlic through feed tube while machine is running. Process until minced. Discard peel. Add onion, 2 carrots and celery and process until fine. Add to soup. Add split peas, barley, tomato paste and juice from canned tomatoes. Process drained tomatoes on **Steel Knife** until puréed, about 6 seconds. Add to soup. Season, cover and simmer for 2 hours.

Slicer: Cut green beans to fit crosswise in feed tube. Slice, using firm pressure. Slice carrots, using firm pressure. Add all remaining ingredients to soup. Simmer about 25 minutes longer, stirring occasionally. Adjust seasonings.

Yield: 12 hearty servings. May be frozen.

ONION SOUP AU GRATIN ✓

6 medium onions, halved	¼ tsp. basil
3 tbsp. butter or margarine	¼ tsp. nutmeg
½ tsp. sugar	salt & pepper, to taste
2 tbsp. flour	8 slices French bread, 1"
8 c. hot broth (use	thick
consommé or	¼ lb. Mozzerella cheese
pareve onion soup mix)	¼ lb. Swiss cheese
½ c. red wine or sherry	¼ c. grated Parmesan cheese
1 bay leaf	

Slicer: Slice onions, using medium pressure. Melt margarine or butter on low heat in a heavy 4 quart saucepan. Stir in onions. Cook uncovered on low heat for 25 to 30 minutes, until deep golden brown, stirring often. Stir in sugar and flour and cook for 2 minutes. Add broth, wine and seasonings. Cover and simmer about 20 to 25 minutes. (Soup may be prepared to this point and refrigerated or frozen.)

Dry bread slices at 325°F for about ½ hour.

Grater: Grate Mozzerella and Swiss cheeses, using medium pressure. Mix lightly.

Ladle soup into individual ovenproof bowls. Top each bowl with a bread slice. Sprinkle with combined Mozzerella and Swiss cheeses. Top with a little Parmesan cheese. Bake at 350°F for about 20 minutes, then broil lightly to brown cheeses. (If soup is already hot when you ladle it into the bowls, you may eliminate baking and just broil for 4 to 5 minutes, until bubbly and golden.)

Yield: 8 servings.

Hint: Place onion soup bowls on a baking sheet which has been lined with foil to catch any drips.

MOCK POTATO SOUP

10 oz. pkg. frozen cauliflower	1 tbsp. chives
1½ c. boiling salted water	salt and pepper, to taste
¼ tsp. onion powder	½ c. skim milk

Cook cauliflower in boiling salted water in a covered saucepan for 12 to 15 minutes, until tender.

Steel Knife: Place all ingredients in processor and process until smooth, about 10 to 15 seconds.

Yield: 2 generous servings. Freezes well. About 40 calories per serving.

POTATO MUSHROOM SOUP
(An old European recipe.)

2 onions, quartered	1 pint mushrooms
2 tbsp. butter or margarine	5 c. boiling water
4 or 5 medium potatoes,	1 tsp. salt
pared	freshly ground pepper

Steel Knife: Process onions with 3 or 4 quick on/off turns, until coarsely chopped. Melt margarine in a heavy 3 quart saucepan. Sauté onions for 5 minutes on medium heat.

Slicer: Cut potatoes to fit feed tube. Slice, using medium pressure. (If you have a **French Fry Blade,** process with light pressure.) Use either blade for the mushrooms, using medium pressure. Add all ingredients to saucepan, cover and simmer for 20 to 25 minutes, until tender.

Yield: 4 to 6 servings. May be frozen.

PARMENTIER SOUP

(Potato-Leek Soup)

¼ c. parsley
2 large leeks (or a
   combination of leeks &
   onions, about 3 c. sliced)
3 tbsp. butter or margarine
3 tbsp. flour
6 c. water

4 medium potatoes, peeled &
   cut in chunks
salt & pepper, to taste
2 c. milk
2 tbsp. additional butter, if
   desired

Steel Knife: Process parsley until minced. Set aside.

Slicer: Wash leeks well. Cut to fit feed tube, discarding most of green part. Slice, using firm pressure.

Melt butter or margarine in a heavy saucepan. Add leeks and/or onions, cover pan and cook for 5 minutes over low heat without browning. Then blend in the flour and cook for 1 minute without browning. Add water very gradually, blending with a whisk.

Steel Knife: Chop potatoes in 2 batches with on/off turns, until coarsely chopped. Add with seasonings to saucepan; bring to a boil, and simmer, covered, for 30 to 35 minutes. Add milk and butter and garnish with parsley. Correct seasonings, if necessary.

Yield: 6 servings. Freezes well.

LEEK & BROCCOLI SOUP

Prepare as for Parmentier Soup (above), but substitute 1 package frozen chopped broccoli for the potatoes. Delicious, and with less calories than Parmentier Soup. Freezes well.

VICHYSSOISE

Prepare as for Parmentier Soup (above), but strain vegetables through a sieve over another saucepan. Purée half the vegetables at a time on the **Steel Knife.** Return to cooking liquid. Stir in milk plus ½ cup heavy cream (35% cream). Omit additional butter. Cover and refrigerate. Garnish with parsley at serving time. May be frozen.

DIET MOCK PEA SOUP

14 oz. can green beans
14 oz. can wax beans
 2 stalks celery, cut in 2"
   pieces
 1 tbsp. instant chicken soup
   mix

4 c. boiling water
1 tbsp. dried onion flakes
1 tbsp. dried vegetable flakes,
   if desired
1 bay leaf
salt and pepper, to taste

Steel Knife: Place beans, bean liquid, celery, soup mix, and **1 cup** boiling water in food processor. Purée until smooth. Combine with remaining ingredients in a large saucepan and bring to a boil. Simmer partially covered for 20 minutes.

Yield: about 8 cups. Freezes well. Each 8 oz. serving contains about 12 calories.

QUICK POTATO SOUP

3 medium potatoes, peeled	3 c. boiling water
1 onion	2 tsp. salt
1 large carrot, scraped	¼ tsp. pepper
1 stalk celery	1½ c. milk

Steel Knife: Cut potatoes in chunks. Process until minced, about 8 to 10 seconds. Transfer to a 3 qt. saucepan. Cut onion, carrot and celery in chunks. Process until minced. Add to potatoes with boiling water and seasoning. Cover and simmer for 15 to 20 minutes, until vegetables are tender. Add milk and heat just to boiling.

Yield: 4 to 6 servings. An excellent lunch for the kids. Freezes well.

SWISS-STYLE POTATO SOUP

Prepare Quick Potato Soup as directed above. Grate ¼ lb. Swiss cheese, using medium pressure. Stir into soup. Adjust seasonings to taste. If too thick, add more water or milk. Serve with crusty fresh rolls. May be frozen, but add cheese when reheating.

CREAM OF SPINACH SOUP

10 oz. pkg. fresh or frozen spinach	5 c. chicken stock (made from boiling water and pareve chicken soup mix)
1 onion, quartered	salt & pepper, to taste
¼ c. butter or margarine	
¼ c. flour	3 c. light cream (15%) or milk

Cook frozen spinach according to package directions. Fresh spinach should be washed well and cooked for 3 or 4 minutes in the water clinging to the leaves in a tightly covered saucepan. Drain well. Squeeze out all moisture thoroughly.

Steel Knife: Chop onion, using 2 or 3 quick on/off turns. Sauté for 5 minutes in butter. Add spinach and cook for 2 minutes longer. Stir in flour and cook for 1 minute, stirring. Add stock gradually. Season. Simmer uncovered for 20 to 25 minutes.

Purée soup in batches of not more than 2 cups at a time on the **Steel Knife**. Return to saucepan and add cream or milk. Heat. Adjust seasonings to taste.

Yield: 8 servings. May be frozen.

CREAM OF ASPARAGUS SOUP: Substitute 1 bunch cooked fresh asparagus or 2 - 14 oz. cans asparagus pieces for the spinach. If using canned asparagus, measure the liquid and substitute for part of the chicken stock.

VEGETABLE AND DUMPLINGS SOUP

Follow directions for Mom's Vegetable Soup (p. 60), but omit barley and green peas. Cook for about 40 to 45 minutes. Instead of serving with Matzo Balls, prepare Soup Dumplings as directed below and drop into simmering soup. Cook 5 minutes longer.

Yield: 8 hearty servings. May be frozen.

SOUP DUMPLINGS

1 egg	½ tsp. salt
½ c. water	½ tsp. baking powder
1 c. flour	

Steel Knife: Process all ingredients just until smooth, about 6 to 8 seconds. Drop from a tablespoon into simmering soup.

AS-YOU-LIKE-IT VEGETABLE SOUP √
(Low-Cal)

3 tomatoes, quartered	1 c. green beans
2 medium onions, halved	salt and pepper, to taste
2 medium carrots, cut in 2" chunks	3 c. water
	1 tbsp. instant chicken soup mix, if desired
3 stalks celery, cut in 2" chunks	½ tsp. dill weed

Steel Knife: Process tomatoes until puréed. Add to saucepan along with remaining ingredients. Simmer covered until all vegetables are tender, about 40 minutes. Remove vegetables from liquid with slotted spoon and place in processor bowl. Process on **Steel Knife** until puréed. Return to saucepan and adjust seasonings to taste.

Yield: 6 servings of about 45 calories each, depending on vegetables used. May be frozen.

Note: Any combination of raw or leftover cooked vegetables may be added to this soup. Two cups of skim milk plus 1 tsp. butter may be added for a creamier soup, making 8 servings of 59 calories each.

MOM'S VEGETABLE SOUP √

3 stalks celery	salt & pepper, to taste
1 large potato, peeled	(seasoning salt may be
2 - 3 carrots, scraped & trimmed	used, if desired)
	1 tsp. monosodium glutamate
1 large onion	14 oz. can green peas, with
2 quarts water	liquid
½ c. barley	2 tbsp. margarine
	Matzo Balls (below)

Grater: Cut vegetables to fit feed tube. Grate, using medium pressure. Place in a large saucepan with remaining ingredients except margarine and Matzo Balls. Bring to a boil, reduce heat and simmer partially covered for about 2 hours. Adjust seasonings to taste, add margarine and Matzo Balls.

Yield: 8 hearty servings. May be frozen.

Variation: Omit Matzo Balls and add 1 cup elbow macaroni to soup during last 15 minutes of cooking.

MOM'S MATZO BALLS

(Baking powder makes them light like a cloud. Omit during Passover!)

4 eggs	½ tsp. salt
½ c. oil	½ tsp. baking powder
1 c. matzo meal	

Steel Knife: Process all ingredients just until smooth, about 10 seconds. Place in refrigerator for 1 hour, or in freezer for 20 minutes, until thickened.

Shape into small balls. Drop into boiling salted water in a large pot and cook partially covered for about 40 minutes.

Yield: about 14 to 16. May be frozen in soup. Delicious in chicken soup, consommé or Mom's Vegetable Soup (above).

FROZEN MIXED VEGETABLE SOUP

1 onion
1 stalk celery
2 lb. frozen mixed vegetables
(broccoli, cauliflower,
carrots or any assortment
you wish)

2 quarts boiling water
2 tbsp. instant chicken soup
mix
¼ tsp. pepper
2 tsp. salt (or to taste)
½ tsp. dillweed, if desired

Steel Knife: Cut onion and celery in chunks. Process with on/off turns, until finely chopped. Place in a saucepan with frozen vegetables. Add water, soup mix and seasonings, cover and bring to a boil. Simmer for 15 minutes.

Place a strainer over a large bowl or saucepan. Strain soup. Purée solids in two batches on the **Steel Knife** until smooth. Stir puréed vegetables into cooking liquid. Adjust seasonings to taste.

Yield: 8 servings of approximately 65 calories each. May be frozen.

Note: If you use a vegetable mixture which contains lima beans, the calorie count will be slightly higher.

GARDEN VEGETABLE SOUP ✓

3 onions, quartered
1 green pepper, cut in 1"
chunks
½ small cabbage (about 3
cups grated)
3 stalks celery
3 carrots, scraped & trimmed

2 potatoes, peeled
3 tbsp. margarine
2 tbsp. flour
2 quarts boiling water (or
chicken broth)
salt & pepper, to taste

Steel Knife: (See **Note***). Add half of onions and process with 3 or 4 quick on/off turns. Empty bowl and repeat with remaining onions. Empty bowl and repeat with green pepper.

Slicer: (See **Note***). Cut cabbage, celery, carrots and potatoes to fit feed tube. Slice, emptying bowl if necessary.

Melt margarine in a 4 quart saucepan. Add vegetables and cook on medium heat for 6 to 8 minutes, stirring occasionally. Sprinkle flour over and cook 1 minute longer, stirring. Add boiling water (or broth) and seasonings. Cover and bring to a boil. Reduce heat and simmer covered for about 1 hour.

Yield: 8 servings. May be frozen.

Variations: 1) Omit potatoes and add 1 cup fine noodles or ⅓ cup raw rice to soup 20 minutes before done. Add a little extra water and seasonings if soup is too thick.

2) **Steel Knife:** Process separately with on/off turns to chop coarsely:- 1 c. green beans, 1 c. wax beans, 2 stalks broccoli. Add to soup along with ½ small head cauliflower which you have broken into small flowerettes, plus a 28 oz. can of tomatoes. Use a Dutch oven or large soup pot.

*Note: If you have a French Fry Blade, cut all vegetables in chunks and add through the feed tube, using fairly light pressure. Empty bowl as necessary. This avoids having to process vegetables separately and emptying the processor bowl each time.

CREAM OF ZUCCHINI SOUP

1 large onion, quartered
¼ c. butter or margarine
4 sprigs parsley
1 carrot, scraped & trimmed
3 or 4 medium zucchini
3 tbsp. flour
6 c. boiling water

½ tsp. tarragon
4 tbsp. instant chicken soup
mix
1 c. light cream or milk
(approximately)
salt & pepper, to taste

Steel Knife: Process onion with 2 or 3 quick on/off turns, until coarsely chopped. Melt butter in a 3 quart saucepan. Add onion and sauté on medium heat for 5 minutes. Place parsley and 1½'' chunks of carrot in processor bowl. Process until minced. Add to saucepan.

Slicer: Cut off ends of zucchini, but do not peel. Cut to fit feed tube. Slice, using medium pressure. Add to saucepan. Stir and cook for 1 minute. Sprinkle with flour.

Add remaining ingredients except cream; partially cover and simmer for ½ hour. Strain out the vegetables and place in the processor with the **Steel Knife.** Process until smooth and puréed, about 10 seconds. Stir puréed vegetables back into the cooking liquid. Correct seasonings, and thin with a little cream. Do not boil. Delicious!

Yield: 6 to 8 servings. May be frozen.

ZUCCHINI NOODLE SOUP

3 sprigs parsley
2 onions, quartered
3 tbsp. butter or margarine
2 tbsp. flour
4 zucchini, unpeeled (about
1½ lb.)
3 carrots, scraped

6 c. boiling water
6 tsp. instant chicken soup mix
salt & pepper, to taste
½ tsp. tarragon, if desired
1 c. noodles
2 c. milk or water
1 tsp. butter

Steel Knife: Process parsley until minced. Empty bowl. Process onions with 3 or 4 quick on/off turns, until coarsely chopped. Melt butter in a heavy bottomed saucepan. Add onions and sauté for 7 or 8 minutes, until golden. Stir in flour and cook 1 to 2 minutes longer, stirring. Do not brown. Remove from heat.

Grater: Cut zucchini and carrots to fit feed tube. Grate zucchini, using medium pressure. Grate carrots, using firm pressure. Add zucchini, carrots, water, soup mix and seasonings to saucepan along with parsley. Cover and simmer for ½ hour. Add noodles and cook 15 minutes longer, stirring occasionally.

Thin soup with milk or water. Add butter and adjust seasonings.

Yield: 8 servings. May be frozen.

VEGETABLE CHEESE CHOWDER

2 large potatoes, peeled & cut in chunks
1 large onion, quartered
2 stalks celery, cut in chunks
6 medium tomatoes, quartered (peel if desired)
2½ c. boiling water
2 tsp. salt
¼ tsp. pepper
¼ tsp. oregano

3 tbsp. butter or margarine
¼ c. flour
1½ tsp. salt
¼ tsp. pepper
½ tsp. dry mustard
2 c. hot milk
1 tsp. Worcestershire sauce
6 oz. Cheddar cheese (1½ c. grated)
1 tbsp. parsley

If you have a **French-Fry Blade,** you will find it very handy to "dice" the vegetables. Use very light pressure with the pusher. The smaller you wish to dice the vegetables, the smaller the chunks should be. Otherwise use the **Steel Knife.** Process each vegetable separately, using on/off turns. About 4 or 5 quick on/offs will suffice for each vegetable. Process tomatoes in 2 batches. Empty bowl each time. Place all vegetables in a large saucepan with boiling water, salt, pepper and oregano. Bring to a boil, cover and simmer for about 15 minutes, until vegetables are tender.

Steel Knife: Process butter with flour, salt, pepper and mustard for 5 or 6 seconds. Add hot milk and Worcestershire sauce through the feed tube while the machine is running. Process until blended. Place in another saucepan and heat over medium heat, stirring, until thickened.

Grater: Grate cheese, using medium pressure. Stir into sauce and cook until melted, stirring. Add to vegetables along with parsley. Bring to a boil.

Yield: 6 generous servings. May be frozen.

BECHAMEL (WHITE) SAUCE

(The processor makes a smooth, creamy sauce with no precooking of the butter-flour mixture.)

2 tbsp. butter or margarine
2 tbsp. flour
¼ tsp. salt

dash of white pepper
1 c. hot milk

Steel Knife: Process butter with flour until blended, about 5 seconds. Add seasonings. Pour hot milk through feed tube while machine is running. Process until smooth.

Transfer sauce to a heavy bottomed saucepan and cook over medium heat, stirring constantly, until bubbly and thickened.

Yield: 1 cup sauce. May be frozen. Thaw before reheating. To prevent scorching, use the top of a double boiler.

Note: Recipe may be doubled successfully in processor. For a thinner sauce, use only 1 tbsp. butter and 1 tbsp. flour to each cup of milk. For a thicker sauce, use 3 tbsp. butter and 3 tbsp. flour for each cup of milk.

SAUCE VELOUTÉ

Follow recipe for Bechamel (White) Sauce above, but substitute chicken stock for milk and use margarine instead of butter.

CHEESE SAUCE

¼ c. butter or margarine	½ tsp. salt
¼ c. flour	⅛ tsp. white pepper
¼ lb. Cheddar cheese, cut in	½ tsp. dry mustard
2" chunks	1 tsp. Worcestershire sauce, if
2 c. hot milk	desired

Steel Knife: Process butter with flour and cheese until blended, about 15 to 20 seconds. Pour hot milk through feed tube while machine is running. Add seasonings and process a few seconds longer, until smooth.

Transfer sauce to a heavy saucepan and cook on medium heat, stirring, until bubbling and thick.

Yield: about 2 cups sauce. Recipe may be halved, if desired. May be frozen. Thaw before reheating. To prevent scorching, reheat in the top of a double boiler.

MUSHROOM SAUCE

1 c. mushrooms	¾ tsp. salt
5 tbsp. butter (or margarine)	¼ tsp. white pepper
3 tbsp. flour	dash of nutmeg
1½ c. hot milk (or broth)	

Slicer: Slice mushrooms, using light pressure. Melt 2 tbsp. butter in a skillet. Add mushrooms and sauté until golden.

Steel Knife: Process remaining 3 tbsp. butter with flour until blended, about 5 seconds. Pour hot liquid through feed tube while machine is running. Add seasonings. Process until smooth.

Transfer sauce to a heavy bottomed saucepan and cook over medium heat, stirring constantly, until bubbly and thick. Stir in mushrooms.

Yield: about 1¾ cups sauce. May be frozen. Thaw before reheating. To prevent scorching, reheat in the top of a double boiler.

HOLLANDAISE SAUCE

(This gourmet sauce is ever so easy with the processor!)

½ c. butter	dash of salt
3 egg yolks	¼ tsp. pepper
2 tbsp. lemon juice	

Melt butter and heat until bubbling. Butter must be very hot or sauce will not thicken in the processor. See **Note** below.

Steel Knife: Process yolks with lemon juice and seasonings for about 5 seconds. Pour hot butter through feed tube in a thin but steady stream while the machine is running. Process about 10 seconds longer. Serve immediately.

Yield: about ¾ cup sauce. May be doubled successfully. Do not freeze. Delicious with fish or vegetables. May be held over hot water in the top of a double boiler until serving time.

Note: If sauce is not thick enough, transfer it to the top of a double boiler. Heat over hot, not boiling water, whisking until thick and creamy. Serve immediately or hold over hot water until serving time. If sauce curdles while standing, or separates, whisk in 1 or 2 tbsp. hot water.

MAYONNAISE

(Try it — you'll like it!)

1 **egg (at room temperature)**
or 2 egg yolks
2 **tbsp. fresh or bottled lemon**
juice (or vinegar)
1 **tsp. prepared mustard (such**
as Dijon) or ½ tsp. dry
mustard

¼ **tsp. salt**
dash white pepper
1 **c. vegetable or corn oil**

Steel Knife: Place all ingredients except oil in food processor. Process for 5 seconds. While machine is running, add oil in a very slow, steady stream through the feed tube. You may increase the speed towards the end. Process until thickened. Total time is approximately 45 seconds.

Yield: about 1 cup. Will keep about 2 weeks in a tightly covered container or Tupperware bowl in the refrigerator. May be used for Passover, but eliminate mustard. Do not freeze.

TARTAR SAUCE

2 **small dill or sweet pickles**
¼ **small onion (or 2 green**
onions (shallots))

2 **sprigs parsley**
¼ **tsp. dry mustard**
1 **c. Mayonnaise (above)**

Steel Knife: Process pickle with onion and parsley until minced, about 6 to 8 seconds. Add mustard and mayonnaise and process a few seconds longer, until blended.

Yield: about 1 cup. Do not freeze. Delicious with fish.

HOME-MADE PIZZA SAUCE ✓

3 **large cloves garlic**
2 **large onions, cut in 2"**
chunks
28 **oz. can tomatoes**
2 **- 5½ oz. cans thick tomato**
paste
1 **tsp. sugar**
1 **tsp. salt**
freshly ground pepper

½ **tsp. each basil & oregano**
¼ **tsp. thyme**
2 **tsp. Worcestershire sauce**
3 **or 4 drops Tabasco sauce**
2 **tbsp. dry red wine**
1 **tbsp. oil**

Steel Knife: Add garlic through feed tube while machine is running. Process until minced. Add onions and process with 3 or 4 quick on/off turns, until coarsely chopped.

Combine all ingredients except oil in a large saucepan. Simmer uncovered for 45 minutes to 1 hour, stirring occasionally. Cool and transfer to a large glass jar. Add oil on top but do not stir. Will keep 2 weeks in refrigerator, or may be frozen.

Yield: about 4 cups pizza sauce, or the equivalent of four 8 oz. cans. Use for pizza or lasagna.

VEGETARIAN SPAGHETTI SAUCE

(Nutritious, yet low in calories.)

2 or 3 cloves garlic
2 medium onions, quartered
1 green pepper, cut in 2"
  chunks
3 tbsp. oil
1 c. mushrooms
1 eggplant (about 1¼ lb.),
  peeled
1 medium zucchini, peeled

19 oz. can tomatoes
2 - 5½ oz. tins tomato paste
¼ c. dry red wine or sherry, if
  desired
salt & pepper, to taste
¼ tsp. each oregano, basil &
  chili powder
pinch of cloves
1 bay leaf

Steel Knife: Drop garlic through feed tube while machine is running. Process until minced. Add onions and process with 3 or 4 quick on/off turns, until coarsely chopped. Empty bowl and repeat with green pepper. Heat oil in a Dutch oven. Add garlic, onions and green pepper. Sauté for 5 minutes on medium heat.

Slicer: Slice mushrooms, using light pressure. Add to pan and cook 2 minutes longer.

Grater: Cut eggplant to fit feed tube. Grate, using medium pressure. Repeat with zucchini. Add to pan and cook 5 minutes longer. Stir in remaining ingredients, cover and simmer about 45 minutes to 1 hour, stirring occasionally. Taste and adjust seasonings.

Yield: 6 to 8 servings. Freezes well. Delicious.

EASY BARBECUE SAUCE ✓

1 clove garlic
½ c. brown sugar, packed

½ c. bottled barbecue sauce
½ c. apple sauce

Steel Knife: Drop garlic through feed tube while machine is running. Process until minced, about 8 seconds. Scrape down sides of bowl. Add remaining ingredients and process with several quick on/off turns, just until blended.

Use as a marinade for spare ribs, London broil, chicken wings or parts, etc. Marinate overnight. Brush additional sauce on meat during cooking.

Yield: about 1½ cups sauce.

CHINESE SWEET & SOUR SAUCE ✓

½ c. ketchup
½ c. vinegar
¾ c. cold water
2 tbsp. lemon juice
1¼ c. white sugar

½ c. brown sugar, lightly
  packed
3 tbsp. cornstarch
¼ c. cold water

Combine all ingredients except cornstarch and ¼ cup cold water in a saucepan and bring to a full boil. Simmer for 2 or 3 minutes. Dissolve cornstarch in cold water and stir into sauce. Simmer until thickened, stirring. Cool and store in refrigerator in a tightly closed jar. Delicious with Chicken Guy Kew (p. 138). This sauce keeps very well.

HORSERADISH

½ lb. fresh horseradish root   dash pepper
14 oz. can whole beets, drained   1 tbsp. sugar (or to taste)
2 to 3 tbsp. beet juice   ½ c. white vinegar (about)
¼ tsp. salt

Peel the horseradish and cut into 1'' chunks. Insert **Steel Knife** in processor. Process the horseradish until finely minced, about 30 seconds. Empty bowl. Process beets until fine. Return horseradish to processor bowl along with remaining ingredients. Process until quite fine and well blended, about 30 seconds. Taste to adjust seasonings. (Guaranteed to clear up your sinus problems!)

Store in the refrigerator in tightly closed jars. This will keep for months, but will lose strength gradually.

Yield: about 3 cups.

Note: For white horseradish, omit beets and beet juice. Serve with Gefilte Fish, boiled flanken, roast beef.

DEEP-FRY BEER BATTER

(For fried fish, onion rings, boneless breasts of chicken, etc.)

Use equal amounts of flour and beer. Process on **Steel Knife** until smooth, about 10 seconds. Let stand at least 4 hours either at room temperature or in the refrigerator. Dip onion rings etc. in batter and deep-fry in hot oil (375°F) until crisp and golden brown. Drain well. May be kept in a warm oven and will remain crisp. Freezes well.

QUICKY CHOCOLATE SAUCE

½ c. water   4 squares semi-sweet
1 tbsp. butter   chocolate
¼ c. sugar   ½ tsp. vanilla

Combine water, butter and sugar and boil for 1 to 2 minutes. Meanwhile, process chocolate with 7 or 8 quick on/off turns on the **Steel Knife,** then let machine run until chocolate is finely chopped, about 45 seconds. Pour boiling liquid through feed tube while machine is running. Add vanilla. Boiling liquid will melt chocolate instantly!

Yield: about ¾ cup sauce. Serve warm or chilled. Delicious on Cream Puffs (p. 316) which you have filled with ice cream, for milkshakes and sundaes, or over Ice Cream Crêpes (p. 235).

Variation: Substitute coffee for water. About 3 tbsp. Kahlua may be substituted for part of the water or coffee.

Fish, Eggs & Cheese

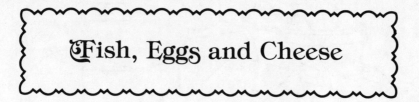

Fish, Eggs and Cheese

FISH
- **Fresh fish** should be cooked the same day it is purchased for maximum flavor. Otherwise, wash and dry it well, wrap in paper towels and place in the coldest part of the refrigerator for no longer than a day.

- **Frozen fish** should be solidly frozen when purchased. Put in your grocery cart just before going to the check-out counter, go straight home and place in the freezer immediately.

- **It is recommended** that frozen fish should not be stored longer than 1 month in the freezer section of your refrigerator as the temperature is likely to be between 10°F and 25°F. In a deep freezer, where the temperature is 0°F, store no longer than 3 months for maximum flavor.

- **Fish** can be refrozen safely as long as there are still a few ice crystals remaining. However, texture may be affected, so it is preferable to cook the fish and serve within a day.

- **To thaw** fillets completely, allow 18 to 24 hours in the refrigerator. Another method is to place the unopened package in a deep dish and cover with cold (not hot) water. Allow 1 to 3 hours. Complete thawing at room temperature is not recommended as fish will lose its juices. Cook fish as soon as possible after thawing.

- **Complete thawing** is not necessary unless you are rolling fish fillets. Let fish stand at room temperature for about 1 hour and then cut into serving size portions.

- **Thin fish fillets** do not need to be turned when broiling. They may break easily, so it is preferable to broil on one side only. Broil about 3'' from heat until browned. They will be cooked through.

- **Use the following rule** for cooking fish:- Allow 10 minutes cooking time per inch of thickness for fresh fish. Allow 20 minutes per inch of thickness for frozen fish. Fish should be measured at the thickest point. If fish is baked in sauce, increase cooking time by about 5 minutes per inch of thickness. Fish is cooked when it flakes easily when tested with a fork. It will take on a whitish tint. Do not overcook.

- **When frying** fish, use oil or a mixture of half oil and half butter or margarine to prevent burning. Fry 3 or 4 minutes on the first side, and 2 or 3 minutes on the second side.

EGGS
- **Pierce a hole** about ½'' deep in the large end of an egg before cooking it in its shell. Even if the egg is cracked, it won't leak.

- **When hard-boiled eggs** are cooked, place them under cold running water immediately to stop the cooking process.

- **Crack shells** easily by shaking pot of drained eggs rapidly back and forth. Then let eggs stand in cold water for 2 or 3 minutes. The cold water will work its way under the cracked shells causing the egg to shrink slightly and the shells to slip off easily.

CHEESE

- **Don't throw away** mouldy cheese; just cut away the mouldy parts and wrap the remaining cheese tightly in tinfoil. If desired, you may grate the cheese, then refrigerate or freeze it in a plastic bag. A great idea if you make a lot of pizzas!

- **Cheese** should be chilled for grating. If there is excess cheese on the Grater, it means that the cheese was either not chilled enough or that too soft a cheese was used. Don't attempt to grate cheeses that are softer than Mozzerella.

- **Parmesan** and Romano cheeses are "grated" on the **Steel Knife.** They should be at room temperature.

- **Cream cheese** may be replaced in many recipes by pot cheese or dry cottage cheese which is similar in texture to the cream cheese and comes in a block.

★★★★★★★★★

GEFILTE FISH

(Ground fish shaped into balls and poached)

(The ingredients given below may be processed in 1 batch. Should you wish to make a larger quantity, repeat the recipe in as many batches as necessary. I find a mixture of whitefish, doré (pickerel) and pike very tasty. You may use whatever fish you prefer, depending on what is available from your fish merchant.)

For 1 lb. fish fillets:
- 1 large onion
- 1 small carrot, scraped
- 1 lb. fish fillets (or ground fish)
- 2 eggs
- 1 tbsp. matzo meal
- ¼ c. cold water
- ¾ tsp. salt
- ¼ tsp. pepper
- ½ tsp. sugar (or to taste)

For 1½ lb. fish fillets:
- 2 medium onions
- 1 large carrot, scraped
- 1½ lb. fish fillets (or ground fish)
- 3 eggs
- 1½ tbsp. matzo meal
- 6 tbsp. cold water
- 1¼ tsp. salt
- ¼ tsp. pepper
- ¾ tsp. sugar (or to taste)

Cut onion, carrot and fish into 2" chunks. Insert **Steel Knife** in processor. Process onion and carrot until finely minced, about 10 seconds. Add fish chunks and process until very smooth, about 35 to 40 seconds. (If fish is already minced, reduce processing time to 20 seconds.) Add remaining ingredients and process about 15 seconds longer, until well mixed. Scrape down sides of bowl as necessary.

Fish Stock:
- head, skin and bones from fish (optional)
- 4 c. cold water (approximately)
- 2 onions
- 2 carrots, scraped
- 1 tsp. salt
- 1 tsp. sugar

Place head, skin and bones from fish in a large pot or fish poacher. Add enough cold water to barely cover.

Slicer: Slice onions and carrots, using very firm pressure. Add with seasonings to pot. Cover and simmer for ½ hour. (If you are not using trimmings from fish, just bring water, vegetables and seasonings to a boil before adding gefilte fish balls.) Discard trimmings from fish.

Moisten your hands with cold water to facilitate shaping of fish. Shape into balls and add to simmering liquid. Cover and simmer for 2 hours. Remove cover last ½ hour of cooking to reduce liquid. Cool. Carefully remove from broth and transfer to a large platter. Garnish with the cooked carrot slices. Serve hot or cold with horseradish. (If frozen, fish may become watery. Simmer thawed fish balls for about 15 minutes in water to cover. Drain well. It will taste freshly cooked.)

GEFILTE FISH RING

Prepare Gefilte Fish mixture (p. 71) as directed. Use 1½ lb. fish for a ring mold, or 2 lb. fish for a 12 cup Bundt pan, processing fish mixture in 2 batches. Do not make Fish Stock.

Oil pan very generously. Spread fish mixture evenly in pan. Bake at 325°F for 1 hour and 15 minutes, or until done. (Edges will be brown and if a knife is inserted into the fish, the knife will come out clean.) Covering the top of the pan loosely with tinfoil for the last half of the baking time will prevent the fish from being too dry. Cool.

Loosen with a long, narrow spatula and remove carefully from pan onto a serving plate. Chill or serve hot. Fill centre ring with horseradish and garnish serving plate with lettuce, tomatoes and cucumber. 1½ lb. fish will serve 8, and 2 lb. fish will serve about 12. If frozen, fish may become watery.

Note: Fish may also be shaped into a loaf.

MY FAVORITE GEFILTE FISH PATTIES

Prepare Gefilte Fish mixture   (p. 71) as directed, adding garlic powder and paprika to taste. Do not make Fish Stock. Shape into large, thick patties, wetting your hands to facilitate shaping.

Heat enough oil to cover the bottom of a large skillet. An electric frypan may also be used. Insert **Slicer** in processor. Slice a large onion, using firm pressure. Add fish patties and onion to skillet and brown on both sides. Cover and steam on low heat for about 1 hour. (If pan is too small, transfer patties to a large casserole, cover and bake at 300°F for 1 hour.) Patties will be light and puffy, as well as delicious. Serve hot or cold. Each pound of fish will yield about 4 to 6 patties, depending on size. May be frozen.

GEFILTE FISH LEFTOVERS

(This is the way my mother and grandmother always
disposed of the gefilte fish that nobody wanted.
A great way to entice youngsters to eat fish.)

Slice leftover fish into ½'' slices with a sharp knife. (If desired, dip into lightly beaten egg and seasoned bread crumbs or matzo meal. It depends on how hard you are trying to disguise the fish!)

Heat about 1 tbsp. oil and 1 tbsp. butter or margarine together in a skillet. Add fish slices and brown quickly on both sides, until golden and crisp. Serve immediately. Very quick and easy.

BREADED BAKED HALIBUT

4 halibut steaks   4 tsp. margarine
salt and pepper, to taste   paprika
4 tbsp. toasted bread crumbs

Place halibut on lightly greased foil. Season with salt and pepper. Sprinkle one tablespoon of crumbs on each portion of fish. Dot with margarine and sprinkle with paprika. Bake at 425°F for 20 minutes.

Yield: 4 servings. May be frozen, but best served immediately.

FISH SALAD: Combine leftover fish with minced onion, enough mayonnaise to moisten and salt and pepper to taste. Discard any skin and bones from fish. Process on **Steel Knife** with several quick on/off turns, just until mixed. Do not freeze.

BAKED HALIBUT PROVENCAL

4 tomatoes
4 onions
salt & pepper, to taste
garlic powder & basil, to
taste

4 halibut steaks (about ¾"
thick)
1 tbsp. lemon juice
2 - 3 tbsp. white wine

Slice tomatoes by hand into thick slices. Cut onions to fit feed tube. Slice on **Slicer,** using very light pressure. Place half the tomatoes and onions in a single layer in a greased 7" x 11" baking dish. Sprinkle lightly with seasonings. Season both sides of fish. Arrange in a single layer over vegetables. Top with remaining vegetables. Sprinkle with lemon juice and wine. Cover and bake at 375°F about 30 minutes, or until fish flakes with a fork.

Yield: 4 servings. May be frozen, but best served fresh.

Variation: Sprinkle 3 to 4 tbsp. grated Parmesan cheese over top layer of tomatoes and onions. Bake as directed. Place under broiler for 2 or 3 minutes to brown before serving.

BAKED HALIBUT AND POTATO CASSEROLE

4 large potatoes, peeled
salt, pepper & paprika, to
taste
4 halibut steaks (about ¾"
thick)

2 onions
1 tbsp. butter or margarine
1½ c. milk or tomato juice
(approximately)

Slicer: Cut potatoes to fit feed tube. Slice, using firm pressure. Arrange half of potatoes in a buttered 9" x 13" Pyrex baking dish. Sprinkle with seasonings. Season fish and arrange over potatoes. Cut onions to fit feed tube. Slice, using gentle pressure. Top fish with onions and remaining potatoes. Season again and dot with butter. Cover with milk or tomato juice. Bake uncovered at 350°F about 1 hour, until tender.

Yield: 4 servings. Do not freeze.

PICKLED SALMON

2 large yellow onions
2 c. water
½ tsp. salt
¼ tsp. pepper
3 to 4 lb. fresh salmon, sliced
in 1" thick steaks

1½ c. white vinegar
2 tsp. pickling spices
½ c. sugar
1 Spanish onion

Slicer: Cut yellow onions to fit feed tube. Slice, using medium pressure. Place in a dutch oven or fish poacher with water, salt and pepper. Bring to a boil. Let cook for 20 minutes. Add salmon steaks to boiling stock. Cover and simmer for 10 minutes. Remove fish from stock and place in a 9" x 13" Pyrex dish. Add vinegar, pickling spices and sugar to fish stock. Boil 5 minutes longer. Pour stock through sieve over fish.

Slicer: Slice Spanish onion, using light pressure. Add to fish. Cool fish and refrigerate 2 to 3 days before serving. An excellent summer meal.

Yield: allow 1 steak per person as a main course, or half a steak as an appetizer.

Note: Halibut or pike may be substituted for the salmon.

POACHED FISH

4 lb. whole fish, fish steaks or   ½ tsp. thyme
   fillets (salmon, halibut, sole,   1 bay leaf
   haddock, or any fish you   few sprigs of parsley
   like)   1 tbsp. butter or margarine, if
8 c. boiling water   desired
1 c. dry white wine   2 stalks celery, with tops
¼ c. lemon juice   1 lemon
1 tbsp. salt   1 or 2 onions, halved
8 peppercorns

If fish is whole, remove head and tail. Salt interior. Wrap fish carefully in several layers of cheesecloth.

Place boiling water, wine, lemon juice, salt, peppercorns, thyme, bay leaf, parsley and butter in a fish poacher or large roaster and bring to a boil.

Steel Knife: Cut celery into chunks. Process with quick on/off turns, until coarsely chopped.

Slicer: Slice lemon and onions, using medium pressure. Add celery, lemon and onions to poacher and simmer covered for 20 minutes. Lower fish carefully into poacher.

Once water returns to simmering, begin timing fish. Cook covered, allowing 10 minutes cooking time per inch of thickness of fish measured at the thickest point. If fish is frozen, allow 20 minutes for each inch of thickness.

Small fillets will take about 3 to 4 minutes.
Salmon or halibut steaks will take about 10 to 15 minutes.
Whole fish will take about 30 to 40 minutes, depending on thickness of fish.

If fish is large, it may have to be turned once during cooking. The cheesecloth will make it easier for you.

When done, lift fish from liquid and drain well. Fish should flake easily with a fork. Remove from cheesecloth. If desired, strip off the skin from whole fish, being careful not to tear the flesh. Transfer carefully to a large serving platter. Garnish with additional lemon slices, chopped parsley and strips of pimento. Serve hot or chilled. Delicious with Hollandaise Sauce (p. 64) or Dill Butter (p. 36).

Leftover fish may be used to make a delicious fresh fish salad. Mince onion and celery on the **Steel Knife.** Add fish, a little mayonnaise to moisten and salt and pepper to taste. Process with on/off turns, just until mixed. Serve chilled.

DIP 'N' CHIP FISH

1½ to 2 lb. fish fillets (sole,   3 c. potato chips (about)
   haddock, turbot)   ¼ lb. Cheddar cheese
Italian Salad Dressing (p. 186)

Dip fish on both sides in salad dressing. Place in a single layer on a greased 10" x 15" baking sheet.

Plastic Knife: Crush chips with quick on/off turns. Sprinkle over fish. (An easy way to "measure" the chips is to fill the processor bowl so that the top of the blade is covered. Exact measurements are not necessary).

Grater: Grate cheese, using medium pressure. Sprinkle over fish. Bake uncovered at 400°F for about 10 to 12 minutes.

Yield: 4 to 6 servings.

BAKED SALMON

4 to 5 lb. whole salmon, head
   removed
2 large onions, halved
1 tbsp. salt
freshly ground pepper
½ tsp. thyme
½ tsp. basil

½ tsp. oregano
1 tsp. garlic powder
1 tsp. dill weed
2 tsp. paprika
juice of ½ lemon
3 tbsp. oil

Wash salmon and pat dry. Scale if necessary, or ask your fish merchant to do it for you. Place in a well-greased large baking dish.

Slicer: Slice onions, using light pressure. Season fish inside and out with seasonings. Rub inside and out with lemon juice, oil and onions; arrange onions around fish. Cut slits in skin of fish on top side in 3 or 4 places. Stuff if desired with Mushroom Stuffing or Rice Stuffing (see below).

Bake uncovered at 450°F for about 30 minutes. An easy guide to timing is to measure the thickness of the fish at the thickest point and allow 10 minutes for each inch of thickness. If fish is frozen, allow 20 minutes per inch. Fish should flake easily at the thickest point, and the flesh should be opaque.

Garnish with lemon slices which have been dipped in chopped parsley. Serve with Hollandaise Sauce (p. 64) or Dill Butter (p. 36).

Yield: 6 to 8 servings.

Note: If fish is frozen, thaw before stuffing. You may substitute bass, Arctic char or any whole fish you like instead of salmon.

MUSHROOM STUFFING

¼ c. fresh parsley
2 shallots
¼ c. margarine or oil
2 c. mushrooms

½ c. dry bread crumbs
2 to 3 tbsp. dry white wine
salt & pepper, to taste

Steel Knife: Process parsley and shallots until minced. Empty bowl. Sauté in hot butter for about 2 minutes over medium heat. Chop mushrooms with several quick on/off turns. Add to skillet and cook 2 to 3 minutes longer. Add remaining ingredients, using just enough wine to moisten stuffing. Mix well. Stuff fish and fasten with skewers. Bake as directed above.

RICE STUFFING

Prepare as for Mushroom Stuffing (above), substituting 1 cup cooked rice for the bread crumbs. Omit wine and add 1 lightly beaten egg to bind the stuffing together.

BROILED CHEESY FILLETS

2 lb. fish fillets
3 tbsp. oil or melted butter
1 tsp. salt
dash each of pepper and
   thyme

4 or 5 sprigs of parsley
10 oz. can mushrooms,
   well-drained
¼ lb. Swiss cheese (1 c.
   grated)

Place fish on a well-greased broiler pan and brush on both sides with oil. Sprinkle with seasonings.

Steel Knife: Process parsley for a few seconds to mince. Add mushrooms and process with 3 or 4 quick on/off turns to chop fine. Empty bowl.

Grater: Grate cheese, using medium pressure. Mix together with mushrooms and parsley.

Broil fish about 3 inches from heat for 3 to 4 minutes. Turn carefully and broil 3 to 4 minutes longer, or until fish flakes with a fork. Spread cheese mixture on fillets and broil 2 to 3 minutes longer, or until light brown and cheese is melted.

Yield: 6 servings.

FILLETS OF SOLE BONNE FEMME

1 pint mushrooms
2 tbsp. butter or margarine
2 lb. sole fillets
salt & pepper
1¼ c. dry white wine or
   vermouth
   (part water may be used)

juice of ½ lemon
2 tbsp. butter
3 tbsp. flour
¾ c. heavy cream (35%) or
   evaporated milk (or
   evaporated skim milk)

Slicer: Slice mushrooms, using medium pressure. Sauté in hot butter in a large skillet for 2 or 3 minutes. Remove from heat. Roll up fillets, dark side out, and arrange in skillet. Season lightly. Add enough wine to barely cover fish. Add lemon juice. Cover with buttered wax paper or parchment paper. Bring to simmering. **Either** simmer on top of the stove for 3 to 4 minutes **or** place on bottom rack in a preheated 350°F oven for 8 to 10 minutes. Fish should be milky white. Do not overcook and do not boil fish. Water should be barely simmering. Drain off all liquid from fish into a saucepan. Boil liquid to reduce to about 1 cup.

Steel Knife: Process butter with flour for 4 or 5 seconds. Pour in fish stock and ½ c. cream through the feed tube while the machine is running. Process for a few seconds to blend. Return sauce to saucepan and bring to a boil, stirring constantly. Gradually stir in remaining cream until sauce coats the spoon nicely. Season to taste.

Arrange fish on a serving platter and spoon sauce over fish. Garnish with lemon wedges and parsley.

Yield: 4 to 6 servings.

Variation: Grate 2 oz (about ½ cup) Swiss cheese on the **Grater,** using medium pressure. Stir about half the cheese into the cooked sauce. Pour over the fish, top with remaining cheese and dot with about 1 tbsp. butter cut in bits.

Either broil for 2 to 3 minutes and serve immediately, or refrigerate, then bake at serving time at 400°F for about 25 minutes, until piping hot and cheese has melted slightly.

FISH ITALIAN STYLE

2 lb. fish fillets or 6 halibut
   steaks
salt & pepper, to taste
6 oz. Mozzerella cheese (1½ c.
   grated)
1 c. mushrooms
1 green pepper, seeded &
   halved
1 clove garlic

8 oz. can tomato sauce or
   pizza sauce
¼ c. chili sauce or ketchup
¼ tsp. oregano
¼ tsp. basil
   few drops Tabasco sauce, if
   desired
   dash of onion powder

Wash fish and pat dry with paper towelling. Sprinkle on both sides with a little salt and pepper. Place in a lightly greased oblong casserole.

Grater: Grate cheese, using medium pressure. Empty bowl and set aside.

Slicer: Slice mushrooms and green pepper, using medium pressure. Set aside.

Steel Knife: Drop garlic through feed tube while machine is running. Process until minced. Add tomato sauce, chili sauce, seasonings and Tabasco. Process for a few seconds to blend. Pour over fish. Sprinkle mushrooms and green pepper over fish. Top with cheese.

Bake uncovered at 375°F for 30 minutes, or until fish flakes with a fork. Halibut will take about 45 minutes, depending on thickness of steaks.

Yield: 6 servings.

OVEN FRIED FISH #1 ✓

1 c. bread crumbs
1 tsp. salt
dash pepper
dash garlic powder
1 egg

2 tbsp. water
1½ lb. sole fillets
⅓ c. melted butter or
   margarine

Steel Knife: Process crumbs with seasonings for 2 or 3 seconds to blend. Transfer to a flat dish. Process egg with water for 2 seconds to blend. Transfer to another flat dish. Dip fish fillets in egg, then in crumbs. Place on a greased cookie sheet in a single layer. Drizzle with melted butter. Bake at 450°F for 12 to 15 minutes, until crispy.

Yield: 4 servings. Best prepared when needed.

Note: If desired, add ⅓ cup grated Parmesan cheese to crumb mixture.

OVEN-FRIED FISH #2 ✓

Crackers or rusks to make
   about 1¼ c. crumbs
1 tsp. salt
¼ tsp. pepper

1½ lb. sole fillets
½ c. milk
3 tbsp. melted butter or oil

Steel Knife: Process crackers with salt and pepper until fine crumbs are formed. Transfer to a sheet of waxed paper. Dip fish first in milk, then coat with crumbs. Place in a single layer on a well-greased 10'' x 15'' cookie sheet. Drizzle with butter or oil. Bake uncovered at 500°F for about 12 to 15 minutes, until fish flakes easily when tested with a fork. If necessary, broil for a minute or two.

Yield: 4 servings.

Optional: Substitute ¼ c. sesame seeds for part of the crumbs.

BAKED FILLETS ALMONDINE IN GARLIC BUTTER

1 clove garlic, peeled	½ c. slivered almonds
2 sprigs parsley	1½ lb. fish fillets
⅓ c. butter or margarine	salt & pepper, to taste

Preheat oven to 375°F. Insert **Steel Knife** in processor. Drop garlic and parsley through feed tube while machine is running. Process until minced. Scrape down bowl and add butter. Process until blended, scraping down bowl if necessary. Place garlic butter in a 9" x 13" pyrex baking dish. Place in oven and heat until melted. Stir in almonds and bake 5 minutes, stirring occasionally. Remove almonds from pan and set aside.

Dip fish in garlic butter on both sides and arrange in a single layer in baking dish. Sprinkle with seasonings. Bake 15 to 20 minutes. Sprinkle with reserved almonds.

Yield: 4 servings.

SOLE OR DORÉ ALMONDINE

1½ - 2 lb. fillets of sole or doré (pickerel)	¼ tsp. paprika
salt & pepper	2 eggs + 2 tbsp. water
1¼ c. toasted bread crumbs	½ c. flour
1 tsp. salt	3 tbsp. butter or margarine
¼ tsp. pepper	½ c. slivered blanched
¼ tsp. thyme, if desired	almonds
	2 - 3 tbsp. oil

Sprinkle fish lightly with salt and pepper. Insert **Steel or Plastic Knife** in processor. Process crumbs with salt, pepper, thyme and paprika until blended, about 5 seconds. Spread on a large piece of wax paper. Process eggs with water to blend, about 2 seconds. Transfer to a pie plate. Spread another piece of wax paper with flour. Dip fish in flour, then in egg, then in crumbs. (May be prepared in advance up to this point and refrigerated.)

Melt 1 tbsp. butter or margarine in a large heavy skillet. Add almonds and sauté for 2 to 3 minutes. Remove from pan and reserve. Add remaining butter along with oil to skillet and heat. Pan-fry fish on medium high heat about 2 to 3 minutes per side, until golden brown and crispy. Drain on paper towelling. Arrange on a heated platter and top with reserved almonds. Serve with buttered green peas, whipped potatoes and crusty rolls.

Yield: 4 to 6 servings. May be frozen, but best prepared and served immediately.

BROCCOLI STUFFED SOLE WITH MUSHROOM SAUCE

10 oz. pkg. frozen chopped
    broccoli (or ½ bunch fresh
    broccoli)
2 tbsp. butter or margarine
1 small onion, halved

1 slice bread, quartered
salt & pepper, to taste
dash of thyme
2 lb. sole fillets (about 6)
Mushroom Sauce (p. 64)

Cook frozen broccoli according to package directions. Fresh broccoli should be cooked in boiling salted water until tender. Drain well. Melt butter in a large skillet and remove from heat.

Steel Knife: Process onion with 2 or 3 quick on/off turns, until coarsely chopped. Add to skillet, pushing onions to one side. Remove about 2 tsp. melted butter from skillet and add to processor along with bread. Whirl until fine crumbs are formed. Empty bowl.

Sauté onion briefly. If broccoli is not already chopped, process chunks of broccoli with quick on/off turns on the **Steel Knife,** until finely chopped. Add to skillet. Season to taste.

Season fillets on dark side; spread each fillet with about 3 tbsp. of the vegetable mixture and roll up. Place seam-side down in a buttered casserole. (Oven-to-table type is ideal.)

Prepare sauce as directed. Pour over fish. Sprinkle with reserved crumbs. (May be prepared in advance up until this point.) Bake at 375°F for 35 minutes.

Yield: 6 servings.

Variation: Grater: Grate 2 oz. Cheddar or Swiss cheese (½ c. grated). Add to sauce. Add ¼ tsp. dry mustard with Cheddar cheese or ⅛ tsp. nutmeg with Swiss cheese.

STUFFED FILLETS OF SOLE AU GRATIN

8 sole fillets
salt, pepper, paprika &
    garlic powder
dash thyme
1 large onion, quartered
2 stalks celery, cut in chunks

½ green pepper, cut in chunks
1 c. mushrooms
½ c. butter or margarine
8 slices white or whole wheat
    bread
⅓ c. grated Parmesan cheese

Sprinkle fish lightly on both sides with seasonings. Arrange half of fillets in a single laver in a greased oblong casserole.

Steel Knife: Process onion with 3 or 4 quick on/off turns, until coarsely chopped. Empty bowl and repeat with celery, then with green pepper, then with mushrooms. Melt butter in a large skillet. Remove about 3 tbsp. butter and set aside. Add vegetables to skillet and sauté for about 10 minutes, until fairly dry.

Steel Knife: Tear bread into chunks and drop through the feed tube while the machine is running. Process to make fine crumbs. Add to sautéed vegetables and mix well. Season to taste. Top each fillet with some of the stuffing. Place remaining fillets on top. Brush with reserved butter and sprinkle with Parmesan cheese.

Bake uncovered at 375°F for 30 to 35 minutes, or until fish flakes with a fork.

Yield: 4 servings.

Variation: Do not top fish with butter and Parmesan cheese. Instead, grate ¼ lb. Cheddar cheese on the grater, using medium pressure. Sprinkle over fish. Bake as directed above.

SOLE MORNAY

2 lb. fillets of sole (or any fish fillets)	¼ lb. Swiss cheese, cut in chunks
salt & pepper, to taste	¼ tsp. dry mustard
paprika	1½ c. hot milk
4 tbsp. butter or margarine, cut in chunks	½ c. toasted bread crumbs
4 tbsp. flour	2 tbsp. melted butter or margarine

Sprinkle fish lightly with salt, pepper and paprika. Roll up (or fold in half) and fasten with a toothpick. If desired, fish may be stuffed with Mushroom Duxelles (p. 161). Arrange seam-side down in a lightly buttered shallow baking dish.

Steel Knife: Process butter, flour and Swiss cheese until cheese is fine, about 15 to 20 seconds. Add mustard and a little salt and pepper. Pour hot milk through the feed tube while the machine is running. Transfer sauce to a heavy-bottomed saucepan and cook over medium heat, stirring, until bubbling and thick. Cool slightly.

Pour sauce over fish. Top with crumbs and drizzle with melted butter. Bake uncovered at 375°F for about 30 minutes, until fish flakes.

Yield: 6 servings.

HALIBUT MORNAY: Substitute 4 to 6 halibut steaks for sole fillets. Increase baking time to 35 or 40 minutes, depending on thickness of fish.

Yield: 4 to 6 servings.

SOLE THERMIDOR

Follow directions for Sole Mornay (above), but substitute Cheddar cheese for Swiss cheese.

FISH FILLETS AU GRATIN

2 lb. sole or whitefish fillets	½ c. dry white wine
salt & pepper	1 c. light cream or milk
1 stalk celery, cut in chunks	6 oz. Swiss cheese (1½ cups grated)
1 large onion, quartered	
4 tbsp. butter	¼ c. toasted bread crumbs
3 tbsp. flour	2 tbsp. melted butter

Sprinkle fish lightly with salt and pepper. Place in a buttered large shallow baking dish.

Steel Knife: Process celery and onion until minced, about 6 to 8 seconds. Melt butter in a saucepan. Add celery and onion and cook for 2 or 3 minutes. Stir in flour; cook for 1 minute. Add wine gradually and mix well. Whisk in cream and heat to simmering. Season with salt and pepper to taste. Cool slightly. Pour over fish.

Grater: Grate Swiss cheese, using medium pressure. Sprinkle over fish. Top with crumbs and drizzle with melted butter. (May be assembled to this point and refrigerated.)

Bake at 400°F for about 30 minutes, or until fish flakes with a fork and cheese is golden.

Yield: 6 servings.

Note: If desired, garnish with sliced mushrooms before baking.

EASY FISH BAKE

2 lb. fish fillets	½ c. toasted bread crumbs
Italian Salad Dressing	¼ c. grated Parmesan cheese
(p. 186) or Best Vinaigrette	dash of salt & pepper
Dressing (p. 187)	

Dip fish on both sides in desired salad dressing. Arrange in a single layer on a lightly greased foil-lined baking sheet.

Steel Knife: Process crumbs with cheese and seasonings for a few seconds to mix. Sprinkle over fish. Bake uncovered at 450°F for 10 to 12 minutes, or until fish flakes with a fork.

Yield: 6 servings.

Note: For lazy people, bottled salad dressing may be used.

FISH PATTIES

1 medium onion	1 tsp. salt
½ stalk celery	freshly ground pepper
2 eggs	½ c. bread crumbs
1 lb. fish fillets (sole, haddock	oil for frying
or perch)	

Steel Knife: Cut onion and celery in chunks. Process until minced, about 6 seconds. Add eggs and fish which has been cut in 2'' chunks. Process about 20 seconds, until fish is minced. Add crumbs and seasonings and process a few seconds longer to mix.

Moisten hands and form fish mixture into patties. Brown in hot oil on medium heat on both sides, until golden brown. Drain on paper towels.

Yield: 4 servings. Freezes well. To make small patties, drop mixture from a spoon into hot oil.

Note: To double recipe, process in 2 batches. For 6 servings, use 1½ lb. fish, 1 large onion, 1 stalk celery, 3 eggs, 1¼ tsp. salt, dash pepper and ¾ c. crumbs. This quantity may be processed in 1 batch. One carrot, cut in chunks, may be processed with the vegetables, if desired.

SALMON PATTIES

1 onion	4 eggs
1 carrot, if desired	dash salt & pepper
2 - 7¾ oz. tins salmon	oil for frying
2½ c. corn flakes (or ⅓ c.	
crumbs)	

Steel Knife: Cut onion and carrot in 1'' chunks. Process until minced, about 8 seconds. Add salmon (it is not necessary to remove the skin, bones and juice), corn flakes, eggs and seasonings. Process just until blended, about 6 to 8 seconds longer.

Heat about ⅛'' oil in a large skillet. Drop salmon mixture from a large spoon into hot oil. Flatten slightly with the back of the spoon. Brown over medium heat on both sides, until golden. Drain well on paper towelling.

Yield: 4 to 6 servings. Freezes well.

Note: Patties may be made in miniature and used as hors d'oeuvres. To reduce calories, omit oil and fry on a teflon frying pan.

SWEET & SOUR FISH PATTIES

Fish Patties (p. 81) or Tuna   1 c. mushrooms
  Patties (below) (use 1½ lb.   oil for frying (about 2 tbsp.)
  fish for Fish Patties)   Chinese Sweet & Sour Sauce
1 onion, halved   (p. 66) (See Note)
1 stalk celery, cut in 2"   2 c. tomato sauce
  chunks

Prepare and cook Tuna or Fish Patties as directed. Place in a large casserole.

Steel Knife: Process onion and celery with 3 or 4 quick on/off turns, until coarsely chopped.

Slicer: Slice mushrooms, using light pressure. Sauté vegetables in oil for about 5 minutes. Stir in sauces. Pour over patties. Bake uncovered at 325°F for 25 to 30 minutes. Serve on a bed of fluffy hot rice.

Yield: 6 servings. Freezes well. May be prepared in advance and baked at mealtime.

Note: A 14 oz. tin jellied cranberry sauce plus 2 tbsp. lemon juice may be used instead of Chinese Sweet & Sour Sauce.

TUNA PATTIES

1 medium onion, halved   ½ tsp. salt
2 - 7 oz. tins tuna, drained   ¼ tsp. pepper
4 eggs   ¼ tsp. garlic powder
¾ c. bread crumbs   oil for frying

Steel Knife: Process onion until minced, about 6 to 8 seconds. Add remaining ingredients except oil and process until mixed, about 10 seconds.

Shape into patties, or 1" balls. Heat oil to a depth of about ⅛" in a large skillet. Brown in hot oil on all sides over medium heat. Drain well on paper towelling.

Yield: 6 servings. Serve with Best-Ever Scalloped Potatoes (p. 165) and Peapods and Mushrooms (p. 160). Freezes well.

Calorie Trimmer's Version

Omit oil and use a teflon skillet to brown patties.

TUNA LOAF OR MUFFINS

Follow recipe for Tuna Patties (above), but reduce crumbs to ⅔ cup. Shape mixture into a free-form loaf on a greased cookie sheet and bake at 350°F for about 45 minutes, or until done.

Yield: 6 servings. Freezes well. May be sliced and used in sandwiches for your child's lunch.

Note: May be made in greased muffin tins and baked for about 25 minutes, until golden.

Yield: about 1 dozen.

TUNA PATTIES IN SPANISH SAUCE

Tuna Patties (p. 82)
2 stalks celery, cut in 2"
  chunks
1 green pepper, halved &
  seeded
1 onion, halved

2 tbsp. oil
2 - 8 oz. cans tomato sauce
14 oz. can peas & carrots,
  drained
salt & pepper, to taste
¼ tsp. basil

Prepare and fry Tuna Patties as directed. Place in a large casserole.

Steel Knife: Process celery with 3 or 4 quick on/off turns, until coarsely chopped. Empty bowl. Repeat with green pepper, then with onion.

Sauté in hot oil for about 5 minutes. Add sauce, peas & carrots and seasonings and mix well. Pour over patties. Bake uncovered at 350°F for 20 to 25 minutes.

Yield: 6 servings. Serve with rice. May be frozen, or prepared in advance and baked at mealtime.

Note: French Fry Blade may be used to "dice" vegetables. Use light pressure.

ORIENTAL TUNA BALLS

Tuna Patties (p. 82)
1 large onion, halved
1 large green pepper, halved
  & seeded
2 tbsp. oil
¾ c. mushrooms
14 oz. can pineapple chunks,
  drained (reserve ½ c. juice to
  use in sauce)

Sauce:
2 cloves garlic
½ c. brown sugar, packed
¼ c. soya sauce
2 tbsp. flour
¼ c. cold water

Prepare mixture for Tuna Patties as directed, shaping mixture into 1" balls. Brown on all sides in hot oil and drain well.

Slicer: Slice onion and green pepper, using light pressure. Brown quickly in hot oil. Slice mushrooms, using medium pressure. Add to onions and brown for 2 to 3 minutes. Add pineapple chunks and tuna balls. Set aside.

Steel Knife: Drop garlic through feed tube while machine is running. Process until minced. Add brown sugar, soya sauce and reserved ½ cup pineapple juice. Process for a few seconds to blend. Transfer to a small saucepan and bring to a boil, stirring. Dissolve flour in cold water. Stir into simmering sauce and cook, stirring constantly, until smooth and thickened, about 2 minutes. Pour over tuna balls and vegetables and mix thoroughly. Serve on a bed of fluffy hot rice.

Yield: 6 to 8 servings.

To freeze: Prepare tuna balls and freeze. Vegetables and pineapple should be added just before serving for a crisp rather than soggy texture.

CURRIED TUNA RICE CASSEROLE

1 onion	2 oz. Cheddar cheese (½ c.
½ green pepper	grated)
2 tbsp. butter or margarine	10 oz. can cream of mushroom
2 - 7 oz. tins flaked tuna,	or celery soup
drained	½ c. milk
3 c. cooked rice	1 tsp. curry powder
2 hard-boiled eggs	salt & pepper, to taste

Steel Knife: Cut onion and green pepper in chunks. Process with 3 or 4 quick on/off turns, until coarsely chopped. Sauté in melted butter in a large skillet for 5 minutes on medium heat. Stir in tuna and rice. Process egg whites on **Steel Knife** until minced, about 5 seconds. Add to tuna mixture. Process yolks until minced and set aside to use as a garnish.

Grater: Grate cheese, using light pressure. Combine in a small saucepan with soup, milk and curry powder. Cook just until mixture is heated through, stirring often. Add to tuna mixture. Season to taste with salt and pepper.

Pour mixture into a greased 7'' x 11'' pyrex baking dish. Sprinkle with reserved egg yolks. Bake uncovered at 350°F for 25 to 30 minutes.

Yield: 6 servings. Do not freeze.

TUNA CHOW MEIN CASSEROLE

1 onion, cut in chunks	7 oz. tin solid white tuna,
2 stalks celery, cut in chunks	drained
2 tbsp. butter or margarine	6 oz. pkg. frozen Chinese pea
10 oz. can cream of mushroom	pods
soup	14 oz. tin pineapple chunks,
¼ c. water	drained
5 oz. tin Chinese chow mein	
noodles	

Steel Knife: Process onion and celery with 3 or 4 quick on/off turns, until coarsely chopped. Sauté in margarine in a large skillet until golden. Stir in soup and water. Add ¾ of noodles. Process tuna on **Steel Knife** with 2 or 3 quick on/off turns, just until coarsely chunked. Add to skillet. Mix well.

Place mixture in a greased 1½ quart casserole. Top with remaining noodles. Bake uncovered at 350°F for 20 minutes. Meanwhile, cook pea pods according to package directions. Gently stir into casserole. Top with pineapple. Cover and heat about 5 minutes longer. Serve with salad and crusty rolls.

Yield: 4 to 6 servings. Do not freeze.

TUNA ROLL ✓

Dough:
½ c. margarine or butter, cut in
chunks
1 tbsp. sugar
1 egg
½ tsp. salt
2 tsp. baking powder
2 c. flour
½ c. sour cream or milk

Filling:
1 large onion, quartered
1 stalk celery, cut in 2"
chunks
2 tbsp. margarine or butter
½ green pepper, seeded & cut
in chunks
½ red pepper, seeded & cut in
chunks
1 c. mushrooms
1 egg
7 oz. tin tuna, drained &
flaked
1 tbsp. flour
salt & pepper, to taste

Steel Knife: Process butter, sugar and egg for 1 minute. Add remaining ingredients for dough and process until dough forms a ball on the blades, about 8 to 10 seconds. Divide into two equal pieces and flour lightly. Set aside. (May be prepared in advance and refrigerated or frozen until needed.)

Steel Knife: Process onion with celery until coarsely chopped, about 3 or 4 quick on/off turns. Sauté in margarine until golden, Meanwhile, process green & red peppers with 3 or 4 quick on/off turns, until coarsely chopped. Add to skillet. Process mushrooms with 3 or 4 quick on/off turns. Add to skillet. Process egg until blended, about 1 or 2 seconds. Add with remaining ingredients for filling to sautéed vegetables. Mix well. Let cool.

Roll half of dough into a rectangle on a floured board, or on a pastry cloth. (Either flour your rolling pin or use a stocking cover.) Spread half the filling to within 1" of the edges of the dough. Roll up jelly roll style, turning in ends to seal. Place seam-side down on a greased cookie sheet. Repeat with remaining dough and filling. Bake at 350°F for 45 to 50 minutes, until golden brown. Serve with Cheese Sauce (p. 64).

Yield: 8 to 10 servings. Freezes well, but underbake slightly.

Note: Vegetables may be "diced" using the **French Fry Blade** and very light pressure.

TUNA PINWHEELS

Follow recipe for Tuna Roll (above), but slice rolls into 1" slices. Place cut-side up on a greased cookie sheet. Bake at 350°F for 40 to 45 minutes.

Yield: 14 to 16 pinwheels. Serves 8.

TUNA STRUDEL

Flaky Ginger Ale Pastry (p. 305)
1 medium onion
1 green pepper, halved & seeded
2 tbsp. butter or margarine
2 oz. Parmesan cheese (½ c. grated)

½ c. bread or cracker crumbs
2 - 7 oz. tins tuna, drained & flaked
1 c. sour cream
1 tsp. dry mustard
dash salt & pepper
1 egg yolk plus 2 tsp. cold water

Prepare pastry as directed and chill.

Steel Knife: Cut onion and pepper in 1½'' chunks. Process with 3 or 4 quick on/off turns, until coarsely chopped. Sauté in butter until golden, about 5 minutes.

Steel Knife: If cheese is not already grated, break into small chunks with a chisel or blunt knife. Process until fine. Add crumbs and process 3 or 4 seconds longer. Remove about ¼ cup of the cheese/crumb mixture from the bowl and set aside.

Add tuna, sour cream, seasonings and sautéed vegetables to crumb mixture in processor bowl. Process with several quick on/off turns, **just** until mixed.

Roll out one portion of dough on a pastry cloth or lightly floured board to form a rectangle about 8'' x 10''. Sprinkle with half the reserved cheese/crumb mixture.

Spoon half of tuna mixture onto pastry along one long edge. Leave a 1'' border on all 3 sides. Roll up, turning in ends.

Steel Knife: Blend egg yolk with cold water for 1 or 2 seconds. Brush a little of the egg wash along the edge of the dough to help seal the roll. Transfer roll to a lightly greased cookie sheet, brush with egg wash and cut several slits on the top with the edge of the **Steel Knife.** Repeat with remaining dough and filling.

Bake at 375°F about 35 to 45 minutes, until golden brown.

Yield: 2 rolls of 3 to 4 servings each. Serve with soup and salad, as well as crusty rolls.

To Freeze: Prepare completely, but do not bake. May be frozen up to 1 month. Thaw and bring to room temperature before baking.

SALMON-TUNA PIE

1 onion
1 stalk celery
7¾ oz. tin salmon, drained
7 oz. tin tuna, drained
3 eggs

½ c. sour cream or yoghurt
salt & pepper, to taste
2¼ c. corn flakes
2 tbsp. butter or margarine

Steel Knife: Cut onion and celery in chunks. Process until minced, about 6 to 8 seconds. Add remaining ingredients except for ¼ cup corn flakes and the butter or margarine. Process just until blended, about 10 seconds. Place tuna-salmon mixture in a greased 9'' pie plate. Crush remaining corn flakes coarsely between your fingertips and sprinkle over mixture. Dot with butter. Bake at 350°F for 50 to 60 minutes, until golden brown.

Yield: 4 to 6 servings. May be frozen.

SWISS TUNA BAKE

(Easy, delicious and nutritious!)

2 - 6½ oz. cans tuna, drained
3 green onions (scallions), cut in chunks
1 c. mushrooms
¼ lb. Parmesan cheese (1 c. grated)
½ lb. Swiss cheese (2 c. grated)
½ tsp. dill weed

½ tsp. salt
6 slices bread (white or whole wheat)
4 eggs
½ tsp. dry mustard
1 tsp. Worcestershire sauce
3 or 4 drops Tabasco sauce
¼ tsp. additional salt
2 c. milk

Flake tuna into a large mixing bowl.

Steel Knife: Process onions and mushrooms with several on/off turns, until finely chopped. Add to tuna. Use a chisel or blunt knife to break Parmesan cheese into small chunks. Process until finely grated. Add **half** to tuna and reserve the remainder.

Grater: Grate Swiss cheese, using medium pressure. Add **half** to tuna. Add the remainder to the reserved Parmesan cheese. Add dill and salt to tuna.

Place bread slices in the bottom of a greased 7'' x 11'' Pyrex casserole, trimming slices to fit. Spread tuna mixture over bread.

Steel Knife: Process eggs with seasonings for 2 or 3 seconds. Add milk through feed tube while machine is running. Immediately pour over tuna mixture. Top with reserved cheeses. Cover and refrigerate at least 2 hours or overnight. Bake at 350°F covered for 30 minutes. Uncover and bake 30 minutes longer.

Yield: 6 servings. Do not freeze.

FAVORITE TUNA CASSEROLE

(My kids adore this!)

7¼ oz. pkg. macaroni & cheese dinner
1½ c. broad noodles
1½ c. macaroni shells
3 qts. boiling salted water
1 tbsp. oil
1 onion, halved
3 tbsp. butter or margarine

¼ lb. mild Cheddar cheese, chilled
¾ c. milk
10 oz. can cream of mushroom soup
2 - 7 oz. tins tuna, drained
salt & pepper, to taste

Cook the pastas together in boiling salted water in a large saucepan, adding oil to prevent boiling over. Drain and rinse well. Return noodles to saucepan.

Steel Knife: Process onion with 2 or 3 quick on/off turns, until coarsely chopped. Sauté in butter on medium heat for 5 minutes. Cut cheese into 1'' chunks. Process on **Steel Knife** until finely chopped, about 20 seconds. Add to noodles along with remaining ingredients. Mix well. Place in a greased 9'' x 13'' casserole or 2 smaller casseroles. (May be prepared in advance up to this point and refrigerated or frozen — see **Note** below.)

Bake uncovered at 350°F about 35 minutes.

Yield: 8 servings.

Note: If desired, freeze the casserole without baking. Remove frozen casserole from freezer. Do not thaw. Drizzle ½ cup milk over the top and bake uncovered at 350°F for 45 to 50 minutes.

SAUCY SALMON CASSEROLE

4 tbsp. butter or margarine,   ¼ tsp. dry mustard
   cut in chunks   1½ c. hot milk
¼ c. flour   10 oz. pkg. frozen green beans
¼ lb. Swiss or Cheddar   10 oz. pkg. frozen broccoli
   cheese, cut in chunks   spears
¼ tsp. salt   2 - 7¾ oz. tins salmon,
dash pepper   drained
                                    ½ - 3 oz. can onion rings

Steel Knife: Process butter, flour and cheese until cheese is finely chopped, about 15 to 20 seconds. Add seasonings. Pour hot milk through the feed tube while the machine is running. Process until blended, about 5 seconds. Transfer sauce to a heavy-bottomed saucepan and cook over medium heat, stirring, until thick and bubbly. Cool slightly.

Cook beans and broccoli according to package directions. Drain thoroughly. Combine with sauce and salmon and mix well. Taste to adjust seasonings. Place in a greased 2 quart shallow casserole. Top with onion rings.

Bake uncovered at 400°F for about 20 to 25 minutes, until piping hot.

Yield: 4 to 6 servings. Serve with tossed salad and fresh rolls.

Note: Tuna may be substituted for the salmon. You may use different combinations of fresh or frozen vegetables (e.g. cauliflower, peas and carrots).

BROCCOLI & TUNA CASSEROLE

(Canned salmon may be substituted)

2 - 10 oz. pkgs. frozen   1 c. mushrooms
   broccoli, partially thawed   2 stalks celery, cut to fit feed
2 - 7 oz. tins tuna, drained &   tube
   flaked   ¾ c. milk (approximately)
1 lb. Mozzerella cheese,   salt & pepper, to taste
   chilled
1 green pepper, halved &
   seeded

Lightly grease a 7'' x 11'' Pyrex dish. Arrange broccoli in a single layer on the bottom of the dish. Add tuna over broccoli.

Grater: Cut cheese to fit feed tube. Grate, using medium pressure. Sprinkle **half** the cheese over the tuna.

Slicer: Slice vegetables, using light pressure. Pour about ½ cup milk over the grated cheese, and then top with vegetables. Sprinkle with seasonings. Top with remaining cheese and then drizzle remaining milk over all.

Bake uncovered at 350°F for about 30 minutes, until bubbly and golden.

Yield: 4 to 6 servings. May be assembled in advance and baked at serving time.

TUNA & MUSHROOM LASAGNA

9 lasagna noodles (packaged or home-made, p. 172)
2 cloves garlic
2 onions, quartered
1 green pepper, cut in chunks
3 tbsp. butter or margarine
3 - 7 oz. tins tuna, drained & flaked
2 - 10 oz. tins cream of mushroom soup

salt & pepper, to taste
½ lb. Mozzerella cheese (2 c. grated)
1 oz. Parmesan cheese (¼ c. grated)
2 c. Ricotta or cottage cheese
1 or 2 eggs

Cook lasagna noodles according to package or recipe directions. Drain well.

Steel Knife: Drop garlic through feed tube while machine is running. Process until minced. Add onions. Process with 3 or 4 quick on/off turns, until coarsely chopped. Empty bowl. Repeat with green pepper. Sauté garlic, onions and green pepper in butter in a large skillet for 5 minutes, until golden. Add tuna, soup and seasonings. Mix well.

Grater: Grate Mozzerella cheese, using medium pressure. Empty bowl and set aside.

Steel Knife: If Parmesan cheese is not already grated, process until fine. Add Ricotta cheese and 1 egg; process until mixed, about 8 to 10 seconds. Add second egg if mixture seems very dry.

Arrange three lasagna noodles in the bottom of a greased 9'' x 13'' Pyrex baking dish. Spread with half of tuna mixture. Add another layer of noodles. Spread Ricotta cheese on top. Add remaining noodles, and then the remaining tuna mixture. Sprinkle with grated Mozzerella.

Bake at 350°F for 35 to 45 minutes.

Yield: 6 to 8 servings. Serve with tossed salad and garlic bread. May be frozen.

CHEDDAR CHEESE PUFF
(Great for Sunday Brunch - and so easy!)

½ lb. Cheddar cheese (2 c. grated)
6 slices white or whole wheat bread
3 tbsp. melted butter

3 eggs
1 tsp. salt
¼ tsp. pepper
¾ tsp. dry mustard
2 c. milk

Grater: Grate cheese, using light pressure. Empty into a greased 7'' x 11'' Pyrex baking dish. Insert **Steel Knife** in processor. Tear bread into chunks and drop through the feed tube while the machine is running. Process to make soft bread crumbs. Add to cheese and mix well. Spread evenly in baking dish. Drizzle melted butter over bread and cheese mixture. Still using **Steel Knife,** process eggs with seasonings and milk, using 2 or 3 quick on/off turns. Immediately pour over bread and cheese mixture. Cover with foil and refrigerate ½ hour, or up to 24 hours.

Bake covered at 350°F for 30 minutes. Uncover and bake 30 minutes longer, until nicely browned.

Yield: 6 to 8 servings. Do not freeze.

Note: If desired, bread may be cut by hand into 1'' squares instead of making soft bread crumbs.

LUSCIOUS LASAGNA ✓

Vegetarian Spaghetti Sauce (p. 66) (See Note)

9 lasagna noodles (packaged or home-made, p. 172)

3 oz. Parmesan cheese (¾ c. grated)

1 lb. Mozzerella cheese (4 c. grated)

1 green pepper, seeded & halved

1 c. mushrooms

3 c. Ricotta or creamed cottage cheese plus 1 large egg

Prepare sauce as directed. (Sauce may be prepared in advance and refrigerated or frozen until needed.)

Cook lasagna noodles according to package or recipe directions. Drain well.

Steel Knife: Parmesan cheese should be at room temperature. Break into small chunks with a chisel. Process until finely grated. Empty bowl.

Grater: Mozzerella cheese should be chilled. Cut to fit feed tube. Grate, using medium pressure. Empty bowl.

Slicer: Slice green pepper and mushrooms, using very light pressure. Empty bowl.

Steel Knife: Process the cheese with egg until blended, about 10 seconds.

To Assemble: Place about 1½ cups sauce in the bottom of a greased 9" x 13" baking dish. Arrange 3 lasagna noodles over sauce. Spread with half the Ricotta cheese. Sprinkle with half the Parmesan cheese, and about ⅓ of the Mozzerella cheese. Repeat with sauce, noodles and cheeses. Top with noodles, then sauce, then remaining Mozzerella cheese. Garnish with green peppers and mushrooms. (Freeze or refrigerate at this point, if desired. Thaw before baking.)

Bake at 375°F for about 45 minutes, until bubbling and cheese topping is golden. Serve to 8 hungry people with Caesar salad, garlic bread and Chianti wine. Enjoy!

Note: If you do not observe the Jewish dietary laws, substitute Super Spaghetti Sauce (p. 135) for the Vegetarian Spaghetti Sauce. Spinach lasagna noodles may be used.

GOLDEN CHEESE PUFF ✓

This is a simple and delicious recipe which can easily be prepared in advance and frozen until needed. I often prepare two, using about ½ lb. filo dough. It is available in Greek pastry shops, or in the freezer section of many chain supermarkets or gourmet food shops.

8 sheets filo or strudel dough

½ c. melted butter or margarine

1½ lb. dry cottage cheese or Ricotta cheese

2 eggs

¼ c. sugar

2 tbsp. lemon juice, if desired

Keep dough covered with plastic wrap and work with one sheet at a time as it is very fragile and dries out quickly. Line a buttered 7" x 11" Pyrex baking dish with 4 filo sheets, brushing each piece with melted butter as you place it in the pan. Let edges of dough hang over pan.

Steel Knife: Combine cheese, eggs, sugar and juice and process 20 seconds. Stop machine once or twice to scrape down sides. Spread evenly over dough.

Cover cheese with remaining 4 sheets of dough, once again brushing each layer with butter. Fold overhanging edges over the top, and brush with butter again. Refrigerate or freeze. Thaw before baking.

Bake at 350°F for 30 minutes, until puffed and golden. Serve immediately with sour cream and berries. (If reheated, it will not puff up.)

Yield: 8 servings.

SPINACH & CHEESE PUFF

8 sheets filo or strudel dough	2 tbsp. fresh dill
½ c. melted butter or margarine	2 oz. Parmesan cheese, cut in chunks (½ c. grated)
1 onion, halved	¾ lb. cottage cheese or Ricotta cheese
¼ c. butter or margarine	
10 oz. pkg. frozen chopped spinach, defrosted & drained (See Note)	3 eggs
	salt & pepper, to taste

Keep dough covered with plastic wrap and work with one sheet at a time as it is very fragile and dries out quickly. Line a buttered 7'' x 11'' Pyrex baking dish with 4 filo sheets, brushing each piece with melted butter as you place it in the pan. Let edges of dough hang over pan.

Steel Knife: Process onion with 2 or 3 quick on/off turns, until coarsely chopped. Sauté in butter for 5 minutes. Add spinach and cook until moisture has evaporated. Process dill with Parmesan cheese until fine. Add cottage cheese and eggs and process until well mixed. Add spinach and process with several on/off turns, just until mixed. Season to taste.

Spread filling over dough evenly. Cover with remaining 4 sheets of dough, once again brushing each layer with melted butter. Fold overhanging edges over the top, and brush with butter once again.

Bake at 350°F for 30 minutes, until puffed and golden. Serve immediately. If reheated, it will not puff up.

Yield: 8 servings. May be prepared in advance and refrigerated or frozen until needed. Thaw before baking.

Note: If desired, use fresh spinach. Wash and drain well. Chop in batches on **Steel Knife.** Sauté as directed above.

DIET ITALIAN CHEESE PUFF

2 slices bread, quartered	1 c. skim milk
2 oz. Mozzerella cheese, cut in chunks	¾ tsp. salt
1 tomato, quartered	dash pepper
½ green pepper, quartered and seeded	¼ tsp. oregano
2 eggs	¼ tsp. basil
	¼ tsp. onion powder

Steel Knife: Process bread with cheese for 5 to 6 seconds. Empty bowl. Process tomato with green pepper with 3 or 4 quick on/off turns.

Return bread and cheese to processor bowl along with remaining ingredients. Process with 2 or 3 quick on/off turns, to mix. Pour into 2 lightly greased onion soup bowls. Fill to within 1'' from the top.

Bake at 375°F for 25 to 30 minutes, until puffed and golden.

Yield: 2 servings. Serve with a tossed green salad to you and a dieting friend. Contains about 270 calories per serving.

Note: Tomato and/or green pepper may be omitted. Substitute 1 cup mushrooms and/or ½ small onion.

LUNCHEON PUFF

(Quick and easy to serve to an unexpected guest!)

½ c. flour
½ c. milk
2 eggs
dash of salt
½ tsp. cinnamon

dash of nutmeg
2 tbsp. butter or margarine
1 tbsp. lemon juice
2 tbsp. icing sugar

Preheat oven to 425°F.

Steel Knife: Process flour with milk, eggs, salt, cinnamon and nutmeg for 8 to 10 seconds. Melt butter in a shallow 1 quart casserole or two individual casseroles (about 1½ cup capacity). Pour in batter, but do not stir. Sprinkle with a little additional nutmeg and cinnamon.

Place immediately into oven and bake for 20 to 25 minutes, until browned on top. Sprinkle with lemon juice and icing sugar. Serve **immediately** with sour cream and berries or drained fruit cocktail.

Yield: 2 servings. Do not freeze.

EASY COTTAGE CHEESE PIE

Topping:
½ c. Corn Flake or bread crumbs
1 tbsp. sugar
¼ tsp. cinnamon

Dough:
½ c. butter or margarine, cut in chunks
½ c. sugar
1 egg
1 tsp. vanilla
1½ c. flour
½ tsp. baking powder
¼ tsp. salt
2 tbsp. sour cream

Filling:
1 lb. dry cottage cheese
2 eggs
¼ c. sugar
2 tsp. sour cream
dash salt
1 tsp. lemon juice

Steel Knife: Combine all ingredients for topping and process until fine. Set aside.

Steel Knife: Process butter, sugar, egg and vanilla for 2 minutes, scraping down sides of bowl once or twice. Add remaining ingredients for dough. Process with several on/off turns, just until mixed. Spread dough into bottom and up sides of a greased 9'' pie plate with a rubber spatula. Wash and dry bowl and blade.

Steel Knife: Combine all filling ingredients in processor bowl. Process until blended. Spread evenly over dough. (May be frozen at this point, if desired. Thaw before baking.) Sprinkle with topping.

Bake at 350°F for about 45 minutes. Serve with sour cream and berries.

Yield: 6 servings. May be frozen.

DIET CHEESE SOUFFLE

(An easy treat.)

1 slice cheese, quartered (See Note)
1 slice bread, quartered
1 egg
½ c. skim milk

salt and pepper, to taste
¼ tsp. nutmeg
⅛ tsp. paprika
¼ tsp. onion powder

Steel Knife: Process cheese with bread for 5 or 6 seconds. Add remaining ingredients and process with 2 or 3 quick on/off turns.

Bake in a lightly greased onion soup bowl at 375°F for 25 to 30 minutes, until golden and puffy. Filling, delicious and nutritious.

Yield: 1 serving containing 280 calories. May be doubled, if desired. Serve with a tossed salad.

Note: One ounce of Swiss, Colby, Cheddar or any of your favorite cheese may be used.

HOT CHEESE CAKE

(A specialty of my friend Rozie)

Topping:
1 c. corn flakes (or ¼ c. crumbs)
½ tsp. cinnamon
1 tbsp. brown sugar

Base:
¼ c. butter or margarine
2 tbsp. sugar
1 egg
1 c. flour
½ tsp. baking powder
½ tsp. cinnamon

Filling:
1 lb. dry cottage cheese
2 eggs
½ c. sugar
dash salt
2 tbsp. cornstarch
½ c. milk

The **Steel Knife** is used to process all the ingredients.

Topping: Process corn flakes with cinnamon and brown sugar until fine. Transfer to a small bowl.

Base: Process butter with sugar and egg for about 1 minute, scraping down sides of bowl as necessary. Add dry ingredients and process just until dough begins to form a ball around the blades, about 10 seconds. Pat into a greased 8'' square baking pan or 9'' pie plate.

Filling: Process cheese for 15 seconds. Add eggs, sugar and salt. Process 15 seconds longer. Dissolve cornstarch in milk and pour in through the feed tube while the machine is running. Process about 10 seconds longer, until well mixed. Pour over base and sprinkle with reserved topping.

Bake at 350°F for 1 hour. Serve hot with sour cream and fresh fruit salad or berries. Ideal to serve after a light dairy meal, or to Saturday night guests.

Yield: 8 servings. Freezes well. Recipe may be doubled and baked in a greased 9'' x 13'' baking pan, if desired. Also delicious made with a Graham Wafer Crust (p. 306).

LO-CAL CHEESE PUDDING

1½ lb. cottage cheese	½ c. buttermilk or sour milk
4 eggs	1 tbsp. lemon juice
artificial sweetener to equal	1 tsp. cinnamon
⅔ c. sugar	dash nutmeg

Steel Knife: Process all ingredients until smooth and well-blended, about 45 to 60 seconds, scraping down bowl as necessary.

Pour into a greased 7'' x 11'' pyrex casserole. Bake at 375°F for 35 to 40 minutes, until set. Serve hot.

Yield: 8 servings of about 120 calories each. Serve with fresh or frozen strawberries.

CHEESE KNISHES
(A cheese-filled crispy baked dumpling)

½ c. butter or margarine, cut in chunks	2 lb. dry cottage cheese
2 tbsp. sugar	1 egg
2 eggs	2 tbsp. lemon juice
2⅔ c. flour	¼ c. sugar
2 tsp. baking powder	½ c. well-drained crushed pineapple, if desired
½ c. milk	

Steel Knife: Process butter, sugar and eggs for 2 minutes, scraping down sides of bowl once or twice. Add flour, baking powder and milk and process about 8 to 10 seconds longer, **just** until mixed. Remove from bowl and wrap in plastic wrap to prevent dough from drying out.

Steel Knife: Process cheese, egg, lemon juice and sugar for 10 to 15 seconds, until blended. Add pineapple and mix in with 2 or 3 quick on/off turns.

Divide dough into 4 equal parts. Coat lightly with flour. Roll one portion of dough into a rectangle on a floured board or pastry cloth.

Place about ¼ of filling in a row along one edge, about 1'' from edges. Roll up. Using the edge of your hand, press down on roll, and with a sawing motion, cut through. Repeat about every 2''. Turn knishes on end, pressing ends in slightly. Repeat with remaining dough and filling.

Bake at 350°F on a lightly greased baking sheet for 35 minutes, until golden.

Yield: 24 to 30 knishes. May be frozen before or after baking. Serve with sour cream and strawberries.

EASY MOCK CHEESE KNISHES
(No dough to roll)

1 lb. dry cottage cheese	½ tsp. salt
3 eggs	¼ c. sugar
½ c. butter or margarine, melted	1½ c. flour
	2 tsp. baking powder

Steel Knife: Process all ingredients together until well mixed, about 20 seconds. Drop by heaping spoonfuls onto cookie sheets which have been lined with foil and well-greased. Bake on middle rack of oven at 350°F for 25 to 30 minutes, until golden brown. Serve hot with sour cream and berries.

Yield: 18 to 20 knishes. Freezes well.

CHEESE ROLL

Flaky Ginger Ale Pastry
(p. 305) or Cream Cheese
Pastry (p. 303)

Cheese Filling (p. 104)
1 egg yolk plus 2 tsp. cold
water

Prepare pastry and filling as directed. Roll one portion of dough on a pastry cloth or floured board into a rectangle about 8'' x 10''. Spread half of the cheese mixture onto pastry along one long edge. Leave a 1'' border on all 3 sides. Roll up, turning in ends. Repeat with remaining dough and filling. Place on a greased cookie sheet.

Steel Knife: Process egg yolk with cold water for 1 or 2 seconds to blend. Brush rolls with egg wash and cut several slits on the top with the edge of the **Steel Knife.**

Bake at 375°F for 35 to 45 minutes, until golden. Serve hot with sour cream.

Yield: 2 rolls. 6 to 8 servings. May be frozen.

CHEESE TURNOVERS

Follow directions for Cheese Roll (above), but roll dough as thin as possible into a large square. Cut dough into 3'' circles with a glass or cookie cutter. Place about 1 tbsp. or so of the cheese mixture on the lower half of each circle. Fold over and press to seal with a fork which you have dipped in flour. Brush with egg wash.

Bake on a lightly greased baking sheet at 375°F for about 20 minutes, until golden.

Yield: about 20. May be frozen.

Note: These are excellent as hors d'oeuvres. Cut dough in 2'' circles. An alternative filling is sautéed vegetables such as onions, celery, green pepper and mushrooms. Season to taste, and sprinkle with a little flour to absorb any excess moisture. Also excellent filled with Spinach or Broccoli Filling (p. 43).

EASY COTTAGE CHEESE PANCAKES

1 c. cottage cheese
¼ c. sour cream or yoghurt
2 eggs
1 tbsp. melted butter or
margarine
½ c. flour

¼ tsp. salt
½ tsp. baking powder
½ tsp. cinnamon
combination of ½ oil and ½
butter or margarine, for
frying

Steel Knife: Combine all ingredients in processor bowl and process until fairly smooth, about 20 to 25 seconds.

Melt about 2 tbsp. butter and 2 tbsp. oil in a large skillet. When bubbling, drop cheese mixture from a large spoon into skillet. Brown on medium heat on both sides until golden brown. Repeat with remaining cheese mixture, adding more butter and oil as necessary. Serve hot with sour cream or yoghurt.

Yield: about 15 pancakes. Freezes well.

BUTTERMILK PANCAKES ✓

1¼ c. flour	½ tsp. baking soda
1 tbsp. sugar	1¼ c. buttermilk or sour milk
½ tsp. salt	2 tbsp. oil or melted butter
1 tsp. baking powder	1 egg

Steel Knife: Combine dry ingredients in processor and process for 3 or 4 seconds. Add remaining ingredients and process about 6 to 8 seconds, until smooth, scraping down sides of bowl if necessary. Do not overprocess.

Pour onto a hot, slightly greased griddle or skillet and cook until bubbles appear on the top side. Turn over and brown on the other side.

Yield: about 14 four inch pancakes. Serve with maple syrup or honey.

Variation: Replace part of the all-purpose flour with wholewheat flour. A tablespoon or two of wheat germ may be added, if desired.

BLUEBERRY PANCAKES ✓

Follow recipe for Buttermilk Pancakes (above), but stir about ½ cup drained fresh or frozen blueberries into the batter.

CHOCOLATE PANCAKES ✓

Follow recipe for Buttermilk Pancakes (above), but increase sugar to 3 tbsp., milk to 1⅓ cups, and add 3 tbsp. cocoa with the dry ingredients. Serve with chocolate syrup.

CORNMEAL PANCAKES

1¼ c. cornmeal	1 c. buttermilk or sour milk
1 tsp. baking powder	¼ c. oil or melted butter
½ tsp. baking soda	2 eggs
½ tsp. salt	

Steel Knife: Combine dry ingredients in processor and process for 3 or 4 seconds. Add remaining ingredients and process for 8 to 10 seconds, until smooth.

Pour onto a hot, slightly greased griddle and cook on both sides until browned.

Yield: about 2 dozen small pancakes. May be frozen.

FETTUCINI ALFREDO

Home-Made Pasta (p. 172) or 12 oz. pkg. medium noodles	**1 oz. Parmesan cheese (¼ c. grated)**
	½ c. butter or margarine salt & pepper, to taste

Prepare pasta or noodles according to package or recipe directions. Cook in boiling salted water until done. Drain well. Return noodles to saucepan. If cheese is not already grated, process on **Steel Knife** until fine.

Add butter and cheese to noodles and mix well. Season to taste. Place in an oven-proof bowl in a hot oven (400°F) for 2 to 3 minutes. Serve immediately.

Yield: 4 servings. Do not freeze.

Variation: For an extra-creamy version, add 1 cup heated 15% cream to noodles, or else reduce butter to 2 tbsp. and stir 2 cups Bechamel (White) sauce (p. 63) into noodles along with cheese and seasonings.

NOODLE & CHEESE CASSEROLE

(Much tastier than the packaged mixes. The sauce takes only minutes to make, and you may use packaged noodles instead of making your own, although home-made are out of this world!)

Home Made Pasta (p. 172)   **2 c. Cheese Sauce (p. 64)**
or 12 oz. pkg. broad noodles   **¼ c. bread crumbs**
                                   1 tbsp. butter

Prepare pasta or noodles according to package or recipe directions. Drain and rinse well. Return to saucepan. Prepare sauce. Add to noodles and mix well.

Place noodles and cheese in a greased 2 quart casserole. Sprinkle with crumbs and dot with butter. (May be prepared in advance up to this point.)

Bake at 350°F for 20 to 25 minutes, until bubbly and hot.

Yield: 6 delicious servings. May be frozen.

Note: ½ lb. macaroni, cooked according to package directions, may be substituted for the noodles, if desired.

THREE CHEESE SWEET KUGEL (Noodle Pudding)

Home-Made Pasta (p. 172)   **1 c. sour cream**
or 12 oz. pkg. broad noodles   **½ c. sugar**
¼ lb. Cheddar cheese (1 c.   **½ c. cottage cheese**
grated)   **½ tsp. salt**
4 oz. pkg. cream cheese   **½ c. corn flake crumbs (See**
3 eggs   **Note)**
1½ c. milk   **cinnamon**
¼ c. soft butter or margarine

Prepare pasta or noodles according to package or recipe directions. Drain and rinse well. Return noodles to saucepan.

Grater: Grate Cheddar cheese, using medium pressure. Empty bowl.

Steel Knife: Process cream cheese with eggs until smooth, about 20 seconds, scraping down sides of bowl once or twice.

Add all ingredients except corn flake crumbs and cinnamon to noodles and mix well. Place in a well-greased 9" x 13" Pyrex baking dish. Sprinkle with reserved corn flake crumbs and cinnamon. Bake at 350°F for 1 hour, until golden brown. Serve hot with sour cream. Yummy!

Yield: 8 servings as a main course, 12 servings as a side dish. Freezes well.

Note: If you wish to make your own crumbs rather than using packaged crumbs, process 2 cups corn flakes on the **Steel Knife** about 25 to 30 seconds, until desired fineness is reached. To save unnecessary washing of the processor bowl, prepare crumbs before the other ingredients.

PINEAPPLE NOODLE KUGEL (Noodle Pudding)

Home-Made Pasta (p. 172)   **4 eggs**
or 12 oz. pkg. medium or   **¼ c. sugar (to taste)**
broad noodles   **½ c. raisins**
1 c. cottage cheese   **14 oz. can crushed pineapple,**
½ c. sour cream   **well-drained**

Prepare pasta or noodles according to recipe or package directions. Cook in boiling salted water until done. Drain well. Return to saucepan. Combine with remaining ingredients and mix well. Place in a well greased 7'' x 11'' Pyrex baking dish. Bake at 375°F for 45 minutes, or until golden brown. Serve hot with sour cream.

Yield: 8 servings. Freezes well.

PINEAPPLE UPSIDE-DOWN KUGEL (Noodle Pudding)

Prepare Pineapple Noodle Kugel as directed above, but eliminate crushed pineapple. Line a well-greased 7'' x 11'' Pyrex baking dish with 8 drained pineapple rings. Place a maraschino cherry in the centre of each ring. Arrange well-drained peach slices or mandarin oranges between pineapple rings. Bake at 375°F for 45 minutes, or until golden brown. Invert onto a heated oblong serving platter.

Yield: 8 servings. Do not freeze.

COOKIE'S HOT MILK CHEESE KUGEL (Noodle Pudding)

Home-Made Pasta (p. 172)   **3 tbsp. sugar (or to taste)**
or 12 oz. pkg. medium or   **½ c. sour cream**
broad noodles   **2 c. hot milk**
½ c. soft butter or margarine,   **2 tbsp. melted butter**
cut in chunks   **¼ c. cornflake or bread**
1½ c. creamed cottage cheese   **crumbs**
4 eggs   **½ tsp. cinnamon, if desired**

Prepare pasta or noodles according to package or recipe directions. Drain and rinse well. Return noodles to saucepan.

Steel Knife: Process softened butter with cheese, eggs, sugar and sour cream until well mixed, stopping machine once or twice to scrape down sides of bowl. Add to noodles. Add hot milk and mix well.

Grease a 9'' x 13'' Pyrex baking dish with the melted butter. Add noodle mixture and top with crumbs and cinnamon. Bake at 350° for 1 hour, until golden brown. Serve hot with sour cream and berries.

Yield: 10 to 12 servings. Freezes well. Light and delicious!

Note: To make crumbs, use either 1 cup cornflakes or 2 or 3 rusks, broken into chunks. Process on **Steel Knife** until fine. Packaged crumbs may be used, if desired.

BUTTERMILK NOODLE KUGEL (Noodle Pudding)
(Mock Cheese Kugel)

Home-Made Pasta (p. 172)
    or 12 oz. pkg. medium or
    broad noodles
4 eggs

3 tbsp. sugar, if desired
salt to taste
dash cinnamon, if desired
4 c. buttermilk

Prepare pasta or noodles according to package or recipe directions. Drain and rinse well. Return to saucepan.

Steel Knife: Process eggs for 2 to 3 seconds. Add with remaining ingredients to noodles and mix well. Pour into a greased 9'' x 13'' Pyrex baking dish. Bake at 375°F for 50 to 60 minutes, until golden brown. Serve hot with sour cream or yoghurt and berries.

Yield: 12 servings. Freezes well. Light and delicious, and not too fattening.

Note: Recipe may be halved and baked in a greased 8'' square Pyrex dish.

SPINACH SOUFFLE

1 c. milk
3 tbsp. butter
4 tbsp. flour
½ tsp. salt
dash pepper
dash nutmeg
5 egg yolks

10 oz. pkg. fresh or frozen
    spinach, cooked, drained
    and squeezed dry
2 tbsp. grated Parmesan
    cheese
7 egg whites
¼ tsp. cream of tartar

Heat milk in a heavy saucepan.

Steel Knife: Process butter, flour and seasonings for 5 or 6 seconds. Add hot milk through feed tube while machine is running. Add egg yolks and blend 5 seconds longer. Return mixture to saucepan and cook over medium heat, stirring constantly with a whisk or wooden spoon, until thick. Remove from heat. Do not boil.

Steel Knife: Process spinach until minced, about 10 to 12 seconds. Add spinach and Parmesan cheese to saucepan. (May be prepared in advance to this point, and the beaten egg whites can be folded in just before baking).

Beat egg whites with cream of tartar on electric mixer until stiff peaks form. Quickly stir about ¼ of egg whites into soufflé mixture. Then carefully fold in remaining whites.

Turn into a lightly buttered 8 cup soufflé dish. Bake at 375°F for about 25 to 30 minutes, until puffed and golden. Serve immediately.

Yield: 4 servings. Do not freeze.

BROCCOLI SOUFFLE

Follow recipe for Spinach Soufflé (above), but substitute 1½ cups cooked broccoli (10 oz. pkg. frozen broccoli) for spinach. Process broccoli on **Steel Knife** until minced, about 12 to 15 seconds.

Yield: 4 servings. Do not freeze.

MUSHROOM SOUFFLE

Follow recipe for Spinach Soufflé (above), but substitute 1 recipe Mushroom Duxelles (p. 161) for spinach.

Yield: 4 servings. Do not freeze.

FISH SOUFFLE

Follow recipe for Spinach Soufflé (p. 99), but substitute 1¼ cups cooked fish (e.g. sole, salmon, halibut, etc.) for spinach. Process fish on **Steel Knife** with quick on/off turns, until flaked. Do not overprocess.

Yield: 4 servings. Do not freeze.

ROULADE

(A Roulade is a Soufflé which is baked in a jelly roll pan and filled.)

Prepare Spinach, Broccoli or Mushroom Soufflé as directed (p. 99), but instead of using a soufflé dish, butter a large jelly roll pan, line it with waxed paper and then butter the paper generously. Spread soufflé mixture evenly in pan.

Bake at 400°F for about 15 minutes, or until set. Remove from oven and turn out onto a tea towel. Peel off waxed paper carefully.

Sprinkle with ¼ cup grated Parmesan cheese. (Use the **Steel Knife** to grate cheese. Break about 1 ounce of room temperature cheese into chunks. Process until finely grated.) Roll up roulade from the short side to form a jelly roll. Serve immediately or reheat. Delicious with a Mushroom or Cheese Sauce (p. 64). May be frozen.

Yield: 4 to 6 servings.

Variation: Fill with Mushroom Duxelles (p. 161).

LO-CAL CHEESE & SPINACH PIE
(Delicious and very filling.)

½ onion	¾ tsp. salt
10 oz. pkg. frozen spinach, cooked according to pkg. directions	dash pepper
	¼ tsp. dill weed or chervil
2 eggs	2 tbsp. grated Parmesan cheese
⅔ c. cottage cheese	

Steel Knife: Process onion until minced. Squeeze out all moisture from spinach. Place in processor with onion and process until finely chopped. Add remaining ingredients except Parmesan cheese and process until blended, about 10 to 15 seconds.

Place in a lightly greased 9'' pyrex pie plate. Sprinkle with Parmesan cheese. Bake at 350°F for about 30 minutes.

Yield: 2 large lunch servings of about 215 calories each. Serve with sliced tomatoes. May be frozen, but best prepared when needed. Reheats well.

NOTES ON CRÊPES

Crêpes are a perfect way to use up leftovers and make a main course dish. Fillings are varied; you might use creamed fish (or meat, making a pareve* crêpe and sauce). Vegetables make a tasty filling, and of course you can use a fruit filling to make dessert crêpes. Let your imagination be your guide!

*Pareve crêpes are made with water instead of milk. An excellent pareve sauce would be Sauce Velouté (p. 63).

Shaping: Crêpes are paper-thin pancakes, usually 6'' or 7'' in diameter for main-course crêpes, and 5'' in diameter for dessert crêpes. They may be shaped as follows:

1. Roll-ups (like a jelly roll).
2. Wedges or triangles (fold in half, then in half once again.)
3. Envelopes, usually used for blintzes (fold bottom edge up over filling, fold sides towards centre, and bring top flap down.)
4. Torte (layers of crêpes, with filling in between, and topped with a sauce).

Filling may be spread in a thin layer over the crêpe, or else you may place about 2 tbsp. filling on the lower ⅓ of the circle, and then roll up.

Sauces: These act as a binding for the filling, and also may be served over the crêpes. A quick substitute for White Sauce is canned Cream of Mushroom or Celery Soup, thinned with a little milk.

Crêpes Pans: The best type of pan to make crêpes is a cast-iron skillet, about 6'' to 7''in diameter. The sides should be sloped, and the longer the handle, the better. A non-stick skillet may also be used (with sloped sides).

To Season the Pan: Some pans require seasoning to make them non-stick. First scour the pan with a soap pad. Rinse and dry well. Grease the entire inside, both the bottom and sides, generously with solid vegetable shortening (e.g. Crisco). Place in a 250°F oven for two hours. Let cool. Wipe out excess shortening.

Do not wash your pan once it has been seasoned. Put it in a paper bag and hide it from the other cooks in your family, as well as the cleaning lady! After each use, wipe it out with paper towels. If the pan is accidentally washed, repeat the same seasoning process. Use pan only for crêpes and eggs.

Mixing: Your processor will make a smooth, lump-free batter in 10 to 15 seconds. Refrigerate for at least ½ hour. Letting batter stand before using allows the flour particles to swell and soften, resulting in a more tender crêpe.

Instant-Blending Flour: (e.g. Robin Hood brand in Canada, Wondra flour in U.S.A.) If you use Instantized flour, the batter is always smooth, and it is not necessary to let batter stand before using. Batter may be used immediately.

Frying: Grease pan lightly with a few drops of oil, or a little butter, applying it with waxed paper or paper towelling. Heat pan almost to smoking. Use a scant ¼ c. of batter, lift pan from heat, and pour batter into the centre of the pan quickly. Tilt pan in all directions to make a thin, even film of batter on the bottom. Pour out excess, and note correct amount for your next crêpe. Return pan to heat and fry 1 minute, or until the edges brown. Flip with a spatula and cook on the other side for about 30 seconds. (The 30 second side will be spotty rather than evenly browned; it will be on the inside of your folded or rolled crêpe). Grease pan inbetween crêpes only if they begin to stick.

Heating: Filled crêpes should be heated in a buttered casserole at 400°F for 15 minutes, uncovered. If topped with cheese, brown under the broiler an additional 2 to 3 minutes, until golden. Unfilled crêpes may be heated in tinfoil at 400°F for 15 minutes.

Storing and Freezing Crêpes: The batter may be kept in the fridge for 24 hours. It may be necessary to thin the batter with a little milk or water. It should be the consistency of heavy cream.

Cooked crêpes can be kept in the fridge wrapped in plastic wrap for 2 to 3 days. They may be frozen filled or unfilled for about one month. Thaw at room temperature, or place in a covered dish and thaw at 300°F.

BASIC CREPE BATTER✓

(Read Notes on Crêpes)

¾ c. flour (instant or all-purpose)
¼ tsp. salt
3 eggs
¼ c. vegetable oil

1 c. milk (or water for pareve crepes)
1 tbsp. sugar (optional for dessert crêpes)

Steel Knife: Process all ingredients for 10 to 15 seconds, until blended. Refrigerate for 1 hour if using all-purpose flour.

Fry crêpes 60 seconds on one side, until the edges brown, and 30 seconds on the other side in a lightly greased 6'' crêpe pan. (See notes on frying.)

Yield: 12 to 14 crêpes. Freezes well.

Note: Prepare no more than one batch of batter at a time in order to avoid leakage from bottom of processor bowl. Transfer batter to a mixing bowl and repeat as many times as necessary.

SALMON CREPES

Double recipe Bechamel (White) Sauce (p. 63) or 10 oz. can cream of mushroom soup + ½ can milk
1 small onion, halved
1 c. mushrooms

2 tbsp. butter or margarine
1 lb. tin Sockeye salmon, drained
2 oz. Swiss cheese (½ c. grated)
12 crêpes (above)

Prepare sauce as directed and set aside. (Or using the **Plastic Knife,** combine canned soup with milk for a few seconds, until blended.) Wash and dry bowl.

Steel Knife: Process onion and mushrooms with 3 or 4 quick on/off turns, until coarsely chopped. Sauté in melted butter on medium heat in a large skillet, until golden. Process salmon with 3 or 4 quick on/off turns, until flaked. Do not over-process. Add to skillet along with **half** of the Bechamel Sauce or soup.

Grater: Grate cheese, using medium pressure.

Place half the remaining sauce in the bottom of a buttered casserole large enough to hold the crêpes in a single layer. Spread each crêpe with 2 to 3 tbsp. salmon mixture. Roll up and arrange over sauce. Top with remaining sauce. Sprinkle with grated cheese. (May be prepared in advance up to this point and refrigerated.)

Bake at 400°F for 15 to 20 minutes, until bubbling hot and cheese has browned slightly.

Yield: 4 servings of 3 crêpes each. Serve with a tossed salad. May be frozen, but best prepared fresh.

Note: Tuna or any leftover cooked fish may be substituted for the salmon.

CREPES ITALIANO

Basic Crêpe Batter (p. 102)
8 oz. Mozzerella cheese
   (2 c. grated)
2 oz. Parmesan cheese (½ c.
   grated)
1 lb. dry cottage or Ricotta
   cheese

1 egg
salt and pepper
14 oz. tin tomato sauce
¼ tsp. garlic powder
¼ tsp. oregano

Prepare crêpes as directed.

Grater: Grate Mozzerella cheese, using medium pressure. Set aside.

Steel Knife: If Parmesan cheese is not already grated, break in small chunks with a chisel or blunt knife. Process until fine. Add cottage or Ricotta cheese, egg and a dash of salt and pepper. Process until mixed.

Place about 2 generous tbsp. cheese mixture on each crêpe, roll up and place in a greased 9'' x 13'' casserole. (You may freeze recipe at this stage. Thaw when needed, and continue with remaining ingredients.)

Combine sauce, salt, pepper, garlic powder and oregano. Pour over crêpes. Top with grated cheese. Bake at 350°F about 25 to 30 minutes, until bubbly and golden. Serves 4.

Note: I have used the crêpes directly from the freezer without thawing, topped them with sauce, and baked the crêpes at 350°F about 35 to 40 minutes.

TUNA BROCCOLI CREPES

16 crêpes (p. 102)
10 oz. pkg. frozen chopped
   broccoli or 1 bunch fresh
   broccoli
6 oz. Cheddar cheese (1½ c.
   grated)

2 - 7 oz. tins tuna, drained &
   flaked
2 - 10 oz. cans cream of
   mushroom soup
salt & pepper, to taste
¼ c. milk

Prepare crêpes as directed. (May be prepared in advance and refrigerated or frozen until needed.) Cook frozen broccoli according to package directions. Cook fresh broccoli in boiling salted water in a covered saucepan for 10 to 15 minutes, until tender. Drain and cut into chunks. Process on **Steel Knife** until minced, about 10 to 15 seconds. Transfer to a large mixing bowl.

Grater: Grate cheese, using medium pressure. Leave about ½ cup cheese in processor. Add remaining cheese to broccoli along with tuna, one can of soup and the seasoning.

Place about 3 tbsp. filling along the lower part of each crêpe, and roll up into a cylinder. Arrange in a single layer in a lightly greased 9'' x 13'' oblong casserole.

Insert **Plastic Knife** in processor. Add remaining can of soup and the milk to the cheese. Process for a few seconds, just until blended. Pour over crêpes. (May be refrigerated or frozen at this point. Thaw before baking.)

Bake uncovered at 400°F for about 20 minutes. Ideal for a luncheon, light supper or as a treat for Saturday night company. Serve with tossed salad and garlic bread.

Yield: 16 crêpes.

FLORENTINE CREPES

(This recipe seems complicated, but really isn't.
The results are well worth it!)

Basic Crêpe Batter (p. 102)
1 **dinner roll (or 2 slices French or white bread)**
2 **tbsp. melted butter**
2 **pkgs. frozen spinach (or 2-10 oz. pkgs. fresh spinach)**

3 **oz. Parmesan cheese (¾ c. grated)**
1 **egg**
½ **lb. dry cottage or Ricotta cheese**
salt and pepper, to taste
Double recipe of White (Bechamel) Sauce (p. 63)

Prepare crêpes as directed and set aside.

Steel Knife: Tear bread into 1'' chunks. Process until fine crumbs are formed. Add melted butter and process a few seconds longer. Empty bowl.

Cook frozen spinach according to package directions. (Fresh spinach should be washed well and cooked in the water clinging to the leaves.) Drain well and squeeze dry.

Steel Knife: If Parmesan cheese is not already grated, break into small chunks with a chisel or blunt knife. Process until fine. Empty bowl. Process spinach until fine, about 8 seconds. Add egg, cottage or Ricotta cheese, seasonings and **half** of Parmesan cheese. Process until mixed.

Place about 3 to 4 tbsp. spinach filling on the lower part of each crêpe and roll up. Place in a well-greased 9'' x 13'' casserole.

Prepare double recipe of sauce as directed. Stir reserved Parmesan cheese into bubbling sauce. Pour sauce over crêpes. Top with reserved crumbs. (May be frozen or refrigerated at this point, but sauce should be cooled before adding to crêpes.) Bake at 350°F about 20 to 25 minutes.

Yield: 6 to 8 servings.

Note: The easiest way to make this recipe is to make the crêpes one day and refrigerate or freeze them. The remaining steps may be done in stages, if desired.

BLINTZES
(Filled crepes folded like an envelope,
then fried in butter until golden brown.)

Basic Crêpe Batter (p. 102)   Desired Filling (See below)

Note: Blintzes are prepared in the same manner as crêpes, except the pancake is fried on **one side only,** just until no more moisture remains on the top of the pancake, 30 to 40 seconds. Place filling on browned side, and fold to seal like an envelope. Place seam-side down in skillet and brown on all sides in butter or margarine until golden. May be frozen about one month.

Fillings: Cheese, Potato, Blueberry or Cherry Pie Filling. Meat, Chicken or Liver (may be served with gravy.)

CHEESE FILLING
(For Blintzes & Kreplach)

1½ **lb. dry cottage cheese**
1 **egg yolk**

2 **to 3 tbsp. sugar**
1 **tbsp. lemon juice**

Steel Knife: Process all ingredients until smooth, about 10 seconds.

Yield: 3 c. filling. Makes 12 to 16 blintzes or 30 kreplach.

BLINTZ SOUFFLE

(Cheese crêpes are combined with a custardy orange mixture
and baked in a casserole. Great for company.)

Basic Crêpe Batter (p. 102)
- 3 tbsp. sugar
- 2" square orange rind
- 1½ lb. dry cottage cheese
- 1 egg yolk
- 3 tbsp. orange juice

Topping:
- 1½ c. sour cream (or plain yoghurt)
- 1 tsp. vanilla
- ½ c. sugar
- 4 eggs
- ½ c. orange juice

Prepare crêpes as directed, but brown on one side only.

Steel Knife: Place sugar in processor bowl. Drop orange rind through feed tube while machine is running. Process until minced, about 30 to 40 seconds. Add cottage cheese, yolk and 3 tbsp. orange juice. Process until mixed, about 10 seconds.

Place about 3 tbsp. cheese mixture on lower third of browned side of crêpe. Fold to seal like an envelope. Repeat with remaining cheese and crêpes. (May be prepared in advance to this stage and either refrigerated or frozen. It is not necessary to thaw before adding topping and baking.) Wash and dry bowl and blade.

Steel Knife: Process sour cream with vanilla and sugar for a few seconds. Add eggs and orange juice through feed tube while machine is running. Process until smooth and blended. Immediately remove bowl from base of machine and pour topping over blintzes. Bake at 350°F for 1 hour, until puffed and golden. Serve with sour cream and strawberries.

Yield: 4 to 6 servings.

Note: An easy way to freeze blintzes is to place them on a cookie sheet, freeze until firm, then store in plastic bags.

CATCH-ALL QUICHE

Follow recipe for Onion Cheese Quiche (p. 106), but use a combination of up to 2 cups raw vegetables or 1 cup cooked vegetables (e.g. onions, celery, green pepper, mushrooms, leeks, cooked green beans or broccoli or spinach.) Leftover cooked or canned fish may be substituted.

Process each vegetable until finely chopped, using on/off turns with the **Steel Knife.** Sauté vegetables in melted butter or margarine until golden.

Any gratable cheese may be substituted for the Swiss cheese (Cheddar, Mozzerella, Norwegian skim milk, etc.)

Some combinations are:-

VEGETABLE: Onions, celery, green pepper and/or mushrooms. Use 2 cups raw chopped vegetables.

LEEKS & MUSHROOMS: Use 2 medium leeks, sliced, plus 1 c. mushrooms, sliced.

MUSHROOM & ONIONS: Use 1 chopped onion and 1 to 2 cups chopped mushrooms.

SEAFOOD: Use 1 chopped onion plus ½ to 1 cup of any canned or leftover cooked fish.

SPINACH OR BROCCOLI: Use 1 chopped onion plus 1 pkg. fresh or frozen spinach or broccoli which has been cooked and well drained.

TUNA & MUSHROOM QUICHE: Use 1 chopped onion plus 1 tin flaked tuna and ¼ lb. grated Cheddar cheese.

ONION CHEESE QUICHE ✓
(Basic Quiche Recipe)

(My son Steven's favourite lunch. He used to wrap it in foil, bring it to school, and heat it on the radiator!

½ recipe Standard Butter Pastry (p. 304)	2 eggs
3 large onions, quartered	⅔ c. light cream or milk
3 tbsp. butter or margarine	1 tsp. salt
1 tbsp. flour	dash pepper
4 oz. Swiss Cheese (1 c. grated)	dash nutmeg

Prepare pastry as directed. Chill and roll out about 2'' larger than pie plate or quiche pan. (Use a 9'' or 10'' pie plate or ceramic quiche dish, or an 11'' metal quiche pan with a removable bottom.) Place pastry in pan. Line with aluminum foil and weigh it down with uncooked rice or dried beans. Bake at 400°F for 10 minutes, remove foil and beans or rice, and bake 5 minutes longer. Cool slightly.

Steel Knife: Process onions with 3 or 4 quick on/off turns, until coarsely chopped.

Sauté onions in melted butter about 10 minutes. Do not brown. Sprinkle in flour and mix well.

Grater: Grate cheese, using medium pressure. Remove from bowl and reserve.

Steel Knife: Process eggs, milk and seasonings for a few seconds. Add onions and **half** of cheese. Process with 2 or 3 quick on/off turns to blend. Place in partially baked pastry shell. (Fill no higher than ¼'' from top of shell as quiche will puff during baking and may run over.) Sprinkle with remaining cheese. Bake immediately at 375°F for 30 to 35 minutes, until golden, and a knife inserted in the centre comes out clean.

Yield: 6 to 8 servings. May be frozen. Serve with a dry white wine and a green salad.

Note: For that "just-baked" taste, prebake pastry shell, cool and freeze. Prepare filling up to 2 days in advance and refrigerate. About half an hour before serving, pour filling into frozen shell, pop the quiche in the oven and bake for 30 to 35 minutes. Serve to your hungry guests.

SOUR CREAM TUNA QUICHE
(This recipe does not require pre-baking of the crust.)

Pastry for 9'' pie crust	¾ tsp. salt
2 oz. Cheddar cheese (½ c. grated)	dash pepper
3 eggs	¼ tsp. Worcestershire sauce
1 c. sour cream	7 oz. tin tuna, drained
	3 oz. can onion rings

Prepare your favorite pastry and place in a 9'' Pyrex pie plate. Flute edges, but do not prick pastry.

Grater: Grate cheese, using medium pressure. Empty bowl and insert **Steel Knife.** Process eggs, sour cream, salt, pepper and Worcestershire sauce for a few seconds to blend. Add tuna and cheese. Process with 3 or 4 very quick on/off turns, just until mixed.

Place half the onion rings in a single layer in the pie shell. Add tuna mixture, and top with remaining onion rings. Bake immediately 350°F for about 45 minutes, until set and golden.

Yield: 6 to 8 delicious servings. May be frozen.

PAREVE* VEGETABLE QUICHE

(You can use any combination of vegetables you choose.)

Pareve Pie Crust or Egg Pastry (p. 304)
2 onions, quartered or 1 bunch green onions (shallots), cut in 2" lengths
2 stalks celery, cut in 2" lengths
1 c. mushrooms
3 tbsp. oil

3 tbsp. flour
2 eggs
1 tsp. pareve instant chicken soup mix
⅔ c. cold water
¼ tsp. each salt & pepper
⅛ tsp. each garlic powder & basil
paprika to garnish quiche

Prepare pastry as directed and reserve half to use another time. (It may be frozen, if you wish.) Roll out chilled dough to fit an 11'' quiche pan or 9'' pie plate. If you have time, refrigerate crust for at least ½ hour to minimize shrinkage. Line crust with tinfoil and fill with uncooked rice or dried beans. Bake at 400°F for about 12 minutes. Remove foil and rice or beans; bake 6 to 8 minutes longer, until golden. Cool slightly. (Baked crust may be frozen up to 2 months.)

Meanwhile, prepare filling. Insert **Steel Knife.** Process onions with 3 or 4 quick on/off turns, until coarsely chopped. Empty bowl. Repeat with celery, then with mushrooms, emptying bowl after you process each vegetable.

Heat oil in a large skillet. Add onions and celery and brown quickly. Add mushrooms and cook a few minutes longer, until mixture is fairly dry. Remove from heat and stir in flour.

Steel Knife: Process eggs with remaining ingredients except paprika for 3 or 4 seconds. Stir into vegetables. (May be prepared in advance up to this point.)

To assemble: Pour vegetable mixture into prebaked crust and garnish with paprika. Bake immediately at 375°F for 25 to 30 minutes, until set and golden.

Yield: 6 to 8 servings. May be prepared in advance and reheated, if desired. Freezes well.

Pareve means that no dairy or meat products are used in this recipe.

LOW-CAL ZUCCHINI QUICHE

3 medium zucchini, peeled
1 tsp. salt
½ lb. Swiss, Mozzerella or Cheddar cheese (2 c. grated)
½ onion

3 eggs
dash pepper
½ tsp. oregano
½ tsp. basil
3 tbsp. grated Parmesan cheese

Grater: Cut zucchini to fit feed tube. Grate, using firm pressure. Transfer to a strainer and sprinkle with salt. Let stand 10 minutes. Press out all liquid. Grate cheese and onion, using medium pressure. Do not empty bowl.

Remove Grater and insert **Plastic Knife.** Add remaining ingredients except Parmesan cheese to processor bowl. Process with 3 or 4 quick on/off turns, just until mixed. Place in a greased 9'' pie plate or ceramic quiche dish. Sprinkle with Parmesan cheese. Bake at 350°F for 35 to 40 minutes, until set and golden brown.

Yield: 8 servings of about 140 calories each. Freezes up to 1 month.

NO CRUST MUSHROOM QUICHE

(Much lower in calories than regular quiche.)

½ lb. Cheddar or Swiss cheese (2 c. grated)	2 tbsp. butter or margarine
2 onions, quartered	16 Ritz-type crackers
2 - 10 oz. cans sliced mushrooms. drained (see Note)	8 eggs
	salt & pepper, to taste
	dash of nutmeg

Grater: Grate cheese, using medium pressure. Empty bowl.

Steel Knife: Process onions with 3 or 4 quick on/off turns, until coarsely chopped. Sauté onions and mushrooms in butter or margarine for 5 minutes on medium heat.

Steel Knife: Process crackers until crushed, about 20 seconds. Add remaining ingredients except for mushrooms and onions. Process until mixed, about 10 to 15 seconds. Mix in mushrooms and onions with quick on/off turns.

Pour into two buttered 9'' pie plates, or fill muffin tins half full. Bake large quiches at 350°F for approximately 35 minutes, or 25 minutes for miniatures.

Yield: about 16 to 20 muffins, or 2 quiches. Freezes well.

Note: If you ever overprocess fresh mushrooms, they can be used successfully in this recipe. Just place the minced mushrooms into a tea towel and wring out mushrooms to remove excess moisture. Sauté with onions for about 10 minutes, until dry. About 2½ cups fresh mushrooms will be sufficient for this recipe.

NO CRUST SPINACH QUICHE

Follow recipe for No Crust Mushroom Quiche, but substitute a 10 oz. pkg. of frozen chopped spinach for the mushrooms and/or onions. Pour boiling water over spinach to thaw. Squeeze out excess moisture. Sauté in butter for 5 minutes. Mix into quiche mixture with 2 or 3 quick on/off turns. Bake as directed.

Yield: 16 to 20 muffins or 2 quiches. Freezes well.

LOW- CAL MUSHROOM QUICHE

½ lb. Swiss, Mozzerella or Cheddar cheese (2 c. grated)	½ tsp. salt
	dash pepper
	dash nutmeg
½ medium onion	3 tbsp. grated Parmesan cheese
1 pint mushrooms	
3 eggs	

Grater: Grate cheese and onion, using medium pressure. Empty bowl.

Plastic Knife: Process mushrooms until coarsely chopped, about 5 or 6 seconds. Add remaining ingredients except for Parmesan cheese and process with 3 or 4 quick on/off turns, just until mixed.

Place in a greased 9'' pie plate or ceramic quiche dish. Sprinkle with Parmesan cheese. Bake at 350°F for 35 to 40 minutes, until set and golden.

Yield: 8 servings of about 125 calories. May be frozen.

CHEESE FONDUE ✓

2 loaves French bread, cut in
  ½" thick slices
1½ lb. Swiss cheese
¼ c. flour
1 clove garlic, halved

3 c. dry white or red wine
  juice of ½ lemon
¼ c. Kirsch
  dash salt and nutmeg
  freshly ground pepper

Cut bread slices into bite-size chunks, each with some crust.

Grater: Cut cheese to fit feed tube. Grate, using medium pressure. Combine cheese with flour in a bag and shake well.

Rub bottom and sides of a ceramic fondue pot with cut clove of garlic. Add wine and lemon juice. Heat on stove over low heat just until bubbles begin to rise. Gradually add cheese, stirring constantly, until cheese melts. Add Kirsch and seasonings. Cook and stir about 2 minutes longer. Transfer to fondue burner.

Yield: 6 servings. Serve with tossed salad and a bottle of your favourite wine.

Additional Recipes

Meat & Poultry

Meat and Poultry

- **Store meat** in the coldest section of your refrigerator. The larger the cut, the longer you can store it. Ground meat should be used within 24 hours of purchase, and stewing meat, steaks, chicken and chops within 2 days. Roasts should be used within 3 days. Refrigerator temperature should be 40°F or less (5°C).

- **When freezing meat,** wrap well in freezer wrap and store at 0°F (-18°C). Ground meats will freeze for 2 to 3 months. Meat Loaves, Meat Balls, Hamburgers (cooked) will freeze for 1 to 2 months. Roasts and Steaks:- 8 to 12 months. Cooked Stews & Roasts:- 2 to 3 months. Chicken and Turkey (whole) will freeze for 8 to 10 months, but only 5 to 6 months if in pieces and for 2 to 3 months if cooked.

- **Meat and poultry** shrink during cooking. To provide a 3 to 4 oz. cooked serving, allow the following raw weights:-
Boneless:- ¼ to ⅓ lb. per serving. Small Bone:- ⅓ to 1 lb. per serving.
Large Bone:- ¾ to 1 lb. per serving. One Single Chicken Breast.

- **Poultry or roasts** that are to be stuffed may be prepared in advance, but do not insert the stuffing until you are ready to put the meat into the oven. Refrigerate prepared stuffing until cooking time, then stuff.

- **Stuffings may be frozen** after cooking, but they should be removed from the poultry or roast and cooled completely first.

- **For maximum flavor,** season poultry with desired spices and let stand at least 1 hour, or refrigerate overnight before completing recipe.

- **Brown meats** in hot oil a few pieces at a time to keep the temperature of the oil constant and to keep juices in meat. Do not let pieces of meat touch each other. Remove with a slotted spoon as they are browned.

- **To bread meat** or poultry, always dry well before dipping into egg or coating. Allowing breaded meat or poultry to stand at least 15 minutes will help set the crumbs.

- **Meats may be roasted** covered or uncovered. If covered, make certain not to cover too tightly or meat will not brown. Remove cover last half hour for extra browning and crispness. Thawing is not necessary before cooking. Just add 10 minutes per pound to the cooking time. Par-boiled potatoes may be added during the last ½ hour.

- **To prevent scorching** when cooking or reheating meatballs, spaghetti sauces, stews, etc reheat or cook in a 300°F oven. Stir occasionally. This method prevents pot-watching.

- **Your processor** is ideal to chop either raw or cooked meats and poultry. It is also excellent for thin slicing. Refer to method on p. 19-20. You can choose exactly what kind of meat your family is eating and the amount of fat content. Some of the cuts you might wish to try are:- boneless chuck, shoulder steak, lean brisket, veal shoulder or neck, boneless chicken breasts. Remember that the processor will not chop gristle, so trim and discard before processing. Ground veal may be substituted in any of the recipes calling for beef if you are watching your cholesterol.

- **If you do not have a scale,** remember that 2 cups meat cubes is equal to 1 pound. Always use the **Steel Knife** to mince meat. Do not process more than ½ to ¾ lb. at a time.

- **It is preferable** to combine minced meat with remaining ingredients in a large mixing bowl rather than in the processor for maximum tenderness. The **Plastic Blade** may be used to mix meat with remaining ingredients, but one pound is the maximum amount; blend together with no more than 6 or 8 quick on/off turns. Too large a quantity will not mix properly, causing the meat at the bottom of the processor bowl to become overprocessed and the meat at the top not to be mixed at all.

- **Garlic** does not need to be peeled before processing. Drop through feed tube while machine is running and let mince. Remove cover and pick out the few pieces of papery peel. Don't even bother to discard peel of garlic is being cooked in a sauce. It will disintegrate during cooking.

WOK-KING IS GOOD FOR YOU

The wok is the essential stir-fry cooking utensil in Chinese cuisine, although a large, heavy skillet may be successfully used. However, a wok uses less oil, so it is great for calorie counters. Foods cook quickly, and are both nutritious and tasty. High heat, constant stirring and short cooking time make for successful wok cooking.

A wok is a bowl-shaped utensil with handle(s). I prefer a carbon steel wok as it holds heat evenly and gives superior results in cooking. A copper-bottom, stainless steel wok is easier to clean, will not rust and you can serve directly from it at the table, but it does not cook as efficiently. A ring will prevent tipping, especially when deep-frying. I place the wok directly on the burner when I do stir-frying. Flat bottom woks are also excellent and do not require the use of a ring.

To season your wok, wash with soap and hot water, then rinse well. Dry thoroughly with a paper towel. Coat interior generously with vegetable or peanut oil and heat on low heat about 10 to 15 minutes. Wipe out excess oil. After you use your wok just wipe it out with a paper towel and put it away. If it is very dirty, use hot water and a bamboo brush to remove any burnt-on bits — no soap please! Immediately dry it thoroughly and coat interior lightly with oil to prevent rusting.

Recommended oils for frying are: peanut, soybean, sunflower seed, safflower seed, corn and rapeseed oils. These permit cooking at high temperatures and quickly seal in flavors. Do **not** use the following in a wok: olive oil, lard, chicken fat, butter, margarine, drippings, or any type of shortening.

All cutting of foods should be done in advance. Foods are all cut in bite-size pieces for rapid cooking. They may be sliced, chopped or shredded. Meats should be sliced paper-thin against the grain. Freezing meat just until it begins to firm up eases the cutting process (about 1 to 2 hours). Foods should be uniform in size. Your processor will save you a tremendous amount of time.

A tablespoon or two of oil is poured into the wok and brought to a very high heat. Oil should be almost smoking. Add 1 clove garlic (halved) and a dash of salt. Then add foods in order of length of cooking time. Foods are usually added one at a time. Stir constantly to coat foods lightly with oil and seal in juices. After a minute or two, the smoking of the oil will stop due to the moisture content of the vegetables. As soon as this happens, either remove the slightly crispy food from the wok, or push up the sides of the wok so that the oil drains back into the pan. Let oil return to high heat between addition of the various foods. Season as desired.

To make certain that vegetables are evenly cooked, add ¼ cup water (or broth) to wok, reduce heat to medium, and cover for 2 minutes. No peeking allowed! Then remove cover, and add any remaining ingredients (e.g. beef or chicken tidbits which were previously browned). Add 1 tbsp. cornstarch dissolved in 2 tbsp. cold water to centre of wok. Stir until it thickens. Serve immediately.

A few hints:

- Thinly sliced beef or chicken requires about 2 to 3 minutes cooking. Cook first. Then remove from pan and cook vegetables.

- Broccoli stems require slightly longer cooking than the tender flowers. Slice stems thinly, and stir fry about 1 minute. Then add cut-up flowers and cook 1 minute longer.

- Frozen vegetables such as peas, snow peas (also known as pea pods), broccoli, etc., may be quickly thawed by pouring boiling water over, and let stand 1 minute. Drain thoroughly.

- Thinly sliced cabbage can be substituted for bean sprouts.

- To restore crunchiness to canned bean sprouts, open can several hours before using, drain off liquid, rinse sprouts under cold water, then soak in cold water until needed. Drain thoroughly.

- About 2 tsp. soya sauce and ¼ tsp. Accent (and a pinch of sugar, if desired) is a good general guide for seasoning. Adjust to your own taste.

- Stir-frying is a great show-off talent in front of company. Always serve immediately.

Suggested recipes for the wok:

Stir-Fried Beef & Broccoli (p. 116)
Moo Goo Guy Pan (p. 137)
Mushroom Almond Chicken (p. 137)
Moo Goo Guy Kew (p. 138)
Chinese Sweet & Sour Chicken (p. 138)
Chicken Livers Chinese Style (p. 139)
Pea Pods, Peppers & Mushrooms, Chinese Style (p. 159)
Vegetable Chow Mein (p. 162)
Tuna Chow Mein (p. 162)
Chicken Chow Mein (p. 162)
Broccoli Chow Mein (p. 162)
Chinese Vegetables Almondine (p. 160)
Chinese Company Casserole (p. 159)
Chinese Fried Rice (p. 170)

CHINESE MARINADE
(Excellent on chicken, London Broil and chuck steak)

2 cloves garlic	2 tbsp. soya sauce
4 green onions (scallions)	2 tbsp. dry sherry or wine
1 tbsp. ketchup	2 tbsp. honey or corn syrup
1 tbsp. chili sauce	dash salt & pepper

Steel Knife: Drop garlic and green onions through feed tube while machine is running. Process until minced. Scrape down sides of bowl. Add remaining ingredients and process for a few seconds to blend.

Place meat or chicken in a single layer in a large pan. Pour marinade over and let stand at room temperature for 2 hours, turning meat over after 1 hour. (May also be marinated overnight in the refrigerator.)

Place chicken or meat on a broiling rack. Broil until done, brushing often with marinade. Chicken will take approximately 30 to 40 minutes, London Broil or chuck steak will take about 10 minutes for the first side and 7 to 8 minutes for the second side. Meat is best cooked medium-rare to medium.

Yield: enough marinade for about 3 lb. meat.

Note: Excellent on the outside barbecue. You may brush the meat with a little honey as well.

CANTONESE MARINADE

2 cloves garlic
¼ c. soya sauce
¼ c. honey

¼ c. apricot jam
¾ c. pineapple or orange juice
1 tsp. ginger

Steel Knife: Drop garlic through feed tube while machine is running. Process until minced. Add remaining ingredients and process a few seconds longer to blend. Delicious for spare ribs, chicken, London Broil, steak kabobs, etc.

Yield: 1½ cups.

PIQUANTE MARINADE

(For Shish Kebabs, Chicken, etc.)

2 cloves garlic, unpeeled
¼ c. soya sauce
½ c. oil
½ c. dry red wine
2 tbsp. ketchup

1 tbsp. curry powder
½ tsp. pepper (do not add any salt)
¼ tsp. ginger

Steel Knife: Drop garlic through feed tube while machine is running. Process until minced, about 8 seconds. Discard any pieces of peel. Add remaining ingredients and process a few seconds longer to blend. Marinate desired meat or poultry for at least 12 hours, and up to 2 days in advance. Refrigerate, turning meat once or twice for even marinating.

Yield: about 1¼ cups.

TERIYAKI STEAK ✓

2 cloves garlic
¼ c. soya sauce
¼ c. pineapple juice
2 tbsp. oil
1 tbsp. lemon juice or vinegar
2 - 3 tbsp. brown sugar

1 tbsp. ketchup, if desired
½ tsp. ginger
¼ tsp. paprika
2 lb. London Broil (flank steak)

Steel Knife: Drop garlic through feed tube while machine is running. Process until minced. Add remaining ingredients except meat and process 3 to 4 seconds longer.

Pour over meat. Marinate 1 to 2 hours at room temperature, turning meat once, or 1 to 3 days in refrigerator, covered. Remove meat from marinade and broil or barbecue 10 minutes on first side, and 7 minutes on second side. Brush meat with marinade during cooking. Slice meat across grain as for roast.

Yield: 4 servings. Leftover meat is also delicious cold in sandwiches. Slice very thin.

Note: This marinade is delicious on veal chops and chicken.

Variations: You may vary the flavour by using any of the following marinades:

Chinese Marinade (p. 114)
Cantonese Marinade (above)
Piquante Marinade (above)
Honey-Garlic Spare Rib Sauce (p. 122)
Italian Salad Dressing, homemade or bottled (p. 186)

STIR-FRIED BEEF & BROCCOLI

(Although there is much preparation to this recipe, final assembly
is quick and well worth the effort. Recipe may be done
easily in stages.)

1½ lb. lean boneless steak (spencer steak, flank steak, etc.)	2 large onions, quartered
2 cloves garlic	1 bunch fresh broccoli (or 2 - 10 oz. pkgs. frozen broccoli, thawed)
¼ c. soya sauce	oil for frying (about ⅓ c.)
1 tbsp. lemon juice	2 additional cloves garlic
1 tbsp. honey or maple syrup	2 tbsp. cornstarch dissolved in ¼ c. cold water
1 tbsp. ketchup	
1 pint mushrooms	

Cut meat in pieces to fit feed tube snugly. Trim away all fat. Wrap in plastic wrap and freeze until firm, about 2 hours. You should just be able to insert the point of a knife. If meat is too frozen, let stand for a few minutes until you can do the knife test.

Slicer: Slice meat, using very heavy pressure. Place in a large bowl or plastic bag.

Steel Knife: Drop 2 cloves garlic through feed tube. Process until minced. Add soya sauce, lemon juice, honey and ketchup and process a few seconds longer to blend. Pour over meat and marinate at least ½ hour at room temperature or overnight in the refrigerator. Wash and dry bowl.

Slicer: Slice mushrooms, using medium pressure. Empty bowl and place in a small pile on waxed paper. Repeat with onions. Cut flowers from broccoli and slice stems, using medium pressure. Arrange stems in one pile and flowers in another pile.

Heat about 2 tbsp. oil in a large skillet or wok. When nearly smoking, add onions and stir-fry for 1 minute. Empty into a large bowl. Stir-fry mushrooms for 30 seconds. Add to onions. Stir-fry broccoli stems for 1 minute. Add flowers and fry 1 minute longer. Add to onions.

Steel Knife: Drop garlic through feed tube while machine is running and process until minced. Remove with a rubber spatula and add to vegetables. Mix well.

Add about 3 tbsp. oil to wok or skillet and heat until nearly smoking. Remove meat from marinade with a slotted spoon and stir-fry about ⅓ of meat in hot oil for about 2 minutes. Sprinkle with a little cornstarch to prevent spattering. Remove meat and repeat twice more with remaining meat. (May be prepared in advance to this point.)

Combine all ingredients except cornstarch and water mixture in wok or skillet and toss to mix. Make a well in the centre and stir in cornstarch/water mixture. Cook, stirring, until thickened and smooth. Serve over hot fluffy rice.

Yield: 6 to 8 yummy servings.

To freeze: Cook meat as directed and freeze. Vegetables will lose their crispness if frozen, and are best added at serving time.

SHOULDER STEAK BAKE

4 shoulder steaks	3 tbsp. soya sauce
1 pkg. dry onion soup mix	1 tbsp. vinegar
2 cloves garlic	¼ tsp. ginger
3 tbsp. honey	¼ tsp. chili powder
3 tbsp. apple juice (or any fruit juice)	

Place meat in a single layer in a large roasting pan. Sprinkle with onion soup.

Steel Knife: Drop garlic through feed tube while machine is running. Process until minced, about 8 seconds. Add remaining ingredients and process for a few seconds, just until blended. Pour over meat. Cover and bake at 350°F for 2 hours, or until tender.

Yield: 4 servings. Freezes well. Serve with fried rice and Sautéed Garlic Mushrooms (p. 161).

MARINATED BRISKET

3 - 4 onions	1 tsp. dry mustard
4 - 5 lb. brisket	4 cloves garlic
2 tsp. salt	½ c. soya sauce
freshly ground pepper	2 - 3 tbsp. honey or maple
1 tbsp. paprika	syrup

Slicer: Cut onions to fit feed tube. Slice, using medium pressure. Place in the bottom of a large roasting pan. Rub brisket on all sides with salt, pepper, paprika and mustard. Place in pan.

Steel Knife: Drop garlic through feed tube while machine is running. Process until minced. Add soya sauce and honey; process 2 or 3 seconds longer. Pour mixture over brisket and rub into meat on all sides. Cover pan with tinfoil. Let marinate at least 1 hour at room temperature, or overnight in the refrigerator.

Bake covered at 325°F. Allow 45 minutes per pound, or until meat is fork tender. Uncover for the last hour and baste occasionally. Let stand for 20 to 30 minutes before slicing. Reheat for a few minutes in pan gravy.

Yield: 8 to 10 servings. Freezes well. May be prepared in advance. Mouthwatering!

SUPER ROAST BRISKET

5 - 6 lb. shelled brisket	¼ c. honey
2 or 3 garlic cloves	¼ c. coca cola
1 small onion, halved	3 tbsp. ketchup
2 tbsp. vinegar or lemon juice	1 tbsp. salt
¼ c. red wine	pepper (about ¼ tsp.)
½ c. oil	1 tsp. paprika

Place brisket in a large roasting pan.

Steel Knife: Process garlic and onion until minced. Add remaining ingredients and process a few seconds longer to blend. Pour over brisket, making sure to cover all surfaces. Let marinate at room temperature for 1 to 2 hours, or overnight in the refrigerator. Cover roasting pan well with foil. Cook at 300°F for 5 hours, until very tender. (About 1 hour per lb. is correct.) When cool, refrigerate. This will slice better the next day. (Remove the hardened fat and discard.)

Yield: 10 to 12 servings. Freezes well.

OVEN ROASTED PICKLED BRISKET
(Delicious either hot or cold)

4 - 5 lb. pickled brisket or top rib	**2 tsp. paprika**
	⅓ c. brown sugar, packed
2 tsp. dry mustard	**2 tbsp. honey**

Wash spices off meat. Dry well. Line a roasting pan with a double thickness of tinfoil large enough to wrap roast completely. Place meat on foil; sprinkle with seasonings and brown sugar on all sides. Drizzle honey over and rub into meat. Wrap tightly. Bake at 325°F about 3 hours, or until tender.

Yield: 8 servings.

Note: Leftover meat may be used to make filling for knishes, blintzes, kreplach, etc. See recipe for Corned Beef Filling (p. 176) or Corned Beef and Potato Filling (p. 176). May also be sliced and frozen for a future meal.

SAVORY BRISKET

3 large onions	**¼ c. ketchup**
3 - 4 cloves garlic	**¼ c. prepared mustard**
1 tsp. salt	**3 tbsp. brown sugar**
¼ tsp. pepper	**4 - 5 lb. brisket or top rib roast**

Slicer: Cut onions to fit feed tube. Slice, using medium pressure. Place in the bottom of a large roasting pan.

Steel Knife: Drop garlic through feed tube while machine is running. Process until minced, about 6 seconds. Scrape down sides of bowl. Add salt, pepper, ketchup, mustard and brown sugar. Process for a few seconds, just until blended. Spread this mixture over roast on all sides. Cover and cook at 325°F for 3½ hours, or until tender. If desired, uncover last half hour and baste with pan juices. (It should not be necessary to add any liquid as the roast will produce its own gravy.) Cool completely. Refrigerate overnight, or at least several hours. Discard fat which has congealed on the gravy. Slice and reheat in gravy in a covered casserole at 325°F about 20 to 25 minutes.

Yield: 8 to 10 servings. Freezes well.

TERIYAKI CHUCK ROAST

4 lb. boneless chuck roast
2 cloves garlic
¼ c. oil
½ c. orange juice
¼ c. sherry

¼ c. soya sauce
1 tbsp. brown sugar
½ tsp. ginger
1 large onion

Pierce roast deeply on both sides with a fork and place in a 9" x 13" Pyrex dish or roasting pan.

Steel Knife: Drop garlic through feed tube while machine is running. Process until minced. Add remaining ingredients except onion and process for a few seconds to blend. Pour over meat. Cover and marinate in refrigerator overnight, turning meat once. (Meat may also be marinated at room temperature for 3 hours.)

Slicer: Cut onion to fit feed tube. Slice, using medium pressure. (This may be done at the same time you prepare the marinade, while the processor bowl is already in use, to save cleanup the next day. Store sliced onions separately in a plastic bag in the refrigerator.)

Drain most of the marinade from the meat and refrigerate marinade until just before serving time. Add onion to meat, cover tightly and bake at 325°F for about 3 hours, or until tender. Let stand about 20 minutes before slicing.

Heat reserved marinade in a saucepan and serve over slices of roast.

Yield: 8 servings. May be frozen. Delicious with rice and broccoli.

OVERNIGHT ROAST

5 - 6 lb. brisket or top rib roast
2 tsp. salt
½ tsp. pepper
1 tbsp. paprika
½ tsp. basil, if desired
2 tbsp. Worcestershire or
   soya sauce

4 cloves garlic
3 onions, cut in chunks
3 stalks celery
4 carrots, scraped
¾ c. wine
¼ c. water (approximately)

Rub roast on all sides with seasonings and Worcestershire sauce. Insert **Steel Knife** in processor. Drop garlic through feed tube while machine is running. Process until minced, about 6 seconds. Place half the onions in the processor. Process with 3 or 4 quick on/off turns, just until coarsely chopped. Rub onion/garlic mixture over roast. Process remaining onions with quick on/off turns and arrange around the roast.

Slicer: Cut celery and carrots to fit feed tube. Slice, using medium pressure for the celery, and firm pressure for the carrots. Add to roasting pan. Add wine and water. Cover **tightly** and place in a 175°F - 200°F oven. Cook overnight about 7 to 8 hours. (I put the roast into the oven just before going to sleep, and remove it first thing in the morning.)

Uncover and cool. Refrigerate until suppertime; slice and reheat in gravy.

Yield: 10 to 12 servings. Freezes well.

Note: To remove unwanted calories, discard fat which congeals on top of gravy when refrigerated.

STUFFED VEAL BRISKET #1

5 to 6 lb. veal brisket (have
butcher make a pocket)
2 cloves garlic
salt, pepper & paprika, to
taste
1 tbsp. oil
Minced Veal Stuffing (p. 148)

1 large onion, halved
½ green pepper
½ pkg. dry onion soup mix
3 tbsp. ketchup
1 tsp. Kitchen Bouquet or
soya sauce
¼ c. water

Place roast in large roasting pan. Insert **Steel Knife** in processor. Drop garlic through feed tube while machine is running. Process until minced. Remove from processor bowl with a rubber spatula and spread over meat. Sprinkle lightly with salt and pepper, and very generously with paprika. Rub roast inside and out with garlic and seasonings. Rub with oil.

Prepare stuffing as directed. Stuff roast loosely.

Slicer: Slice onion and pepper, using medium pressure. Add to roasting pan. Add remaining ingredients. Cover tightly and bake at 350°F for 3 to 3½ hours, until very tender. Baste during last hour of cooking. Excellent! Using a meat stuffing for the veal compensates for the fact that there is a large proportion of bone and fat and a small amount of meat on a veal brisket.

Yield: 6 to 8 servings. Reheats well. May be frozen.

STUFFED VEAL BRISKET #2

5 to 6 lb. veal brisket or
shoulder (have butcher
make a pocket)
3 cloves garlic
2 tsp. salt
¼ tsp. pepper
1 tsp. dry mustard
2 tsp. paprika
½ tsp. thyme

Bread Stuffing (p. 147) or
your favorite stuffing recipe
(see Note)
2 onions
3 stalks celery
12 small whole carrots
½ c. chicken broth or water
¼ c. red wine

Place roast in a large roasting pan. Insert **Steel Knife** in processor. Drop garlic through feed tube while machine is running. Process until minced. Remove from processor bowl with a rubber spatula and spread over meat. Rub roast inside and out with garlic and seasonings. Stuff loosely with stuffing and fasten with skewers. (If roast is very lean, you may wish to rub the surface with 1 tbsp. oil.)

Slicer: Cut onions and celery to fit feed tube. Slice, using medium pressure. Add to roasting pan along with carrots, broth and wine. Cover and bake at 325°F for 3 hours. Baste occasionally. Uncover and bake ¾ hour longer, adding quartered potatoes if desired. Freezes well, but remove stuffing and freeze separately. Do not freeze potatoes.

Yield: 6 servings for a veal brisket, or 8 to 10 servings for a veal shoulder.

Note: A delicious stuffing may be made by making Stuffing Casserole (p. 178), but omit the baking powder. For calorie counters, you may wish to stuff the roast with Minced Veal Stuffing (p. 148).

VEAL CACCIATORRE √

2 lb. veal cutlets, pounded thin	½ tsp. basil
salt & pepper, to taste	½ tsp. oregano
3 large cloves garlic	1 tsp. sugar
¼ c. fresh parsley (or 1 tbsp.	¾ tsp. salt
dried)	¼ tsp. pepper
2 onions, cut in chunks	1 tbsp. oil
19 oz. can tomatoes	1 bay leaf
5½ oz. can tomato paste	¼ c. red wine

Sprinkle veal lightly on both sides with salt and pepper. Set aside. Insert **Steel Knife** in processor. Drop garlic through feed tube while machine is running. Process until minced. (It is not necessary to peel the garlic as it will dissolve during cooking.) Add parsley and onions. Process until minced. Empty into a large roasting pan.

Process half the canned tomatoes and half the tomato paste with the remaining ingredients until blended. Add to roasting pan. Repeat with remaining tomatoes and tomato paste. Add to roasting pan and stir to blend. Add meat. Spoon sauce over. Cover tightly and bake at 325°F for 2 hours. Uncover and bake about ½ hour longer, until meat is tender.

Yield: 4 to 6 servings. Freezes well.

Note: If desired, you may add 2 green peppers and 1 pint of mushrooms. Slice on **Slicer,** using light pressure. Sauté briefly in 2 tbsp. oil. Garnish veal. Serve with spaghetti or rice. Do not freeze vegetables, but add at serving time. I have also made this dish using veal chops, and it is equally delicious.

ITALIAN ROASTED VEAL

(The seasonings for this recipe may be used on any cut of veal (shoulder, breast, steaks, chops, etc.). If the roast is stuffed, allow an extra ½ hour cooking time. The low temperature is important. Allow 50 to 60 minutes cooking time per pound of meat, and cook until fork tender. Let roast stand for 20 minutes before slicing, or preferably, slice when cold and reheat in the pan gravy.)

4 to 5 lb. veal roast (or 6 veal	4 cloves garlic, cut in slivers
steaks or chops)	2 large onions
2 tsp. seasoning salt	4 large carrots
freshly ground pepper	½ c. tomato sauce or chicken
2 tsp. Italian seasoning (or 1	broth
tsp. each oregano and basil)	½ c. dry red wine
1 tsp. dry mustard	

Rub meat with seasonings. Cut several slits in meat and insert garlic slivers. Place in a large roasting pan.

Slicer: Cut onions and carrots to fit feed tube. Slice, using firm pressure. Add vegetables, tomato sauce or broth, and wine to roasting pan. Cover and bake at 300°F for about 3 hours for a roast and 1½ hours for steaks or chops. Uncover and roast ¾ to 1 hour longer, basting occasionally. If desired, sliced or quartered potatoes may be added when you uncover the meat.

Allow ½ lb. per person for boneless roasts, and up to 1 lb. per person if there is a large percentage of bone. Freezes well, but omit potatoes. Thinly sliced cold roast is delicious served on crusty rolls.

BAKED VEAL CHOPS

30 Ritz or soda crackers (or 1   2 tbsp. water
    c. bread crumbs)   1 egg
 1 tsp. salt   4 to 6 large veal chops
 ¼ tsp. pepper   oil for frying
 ¼ tsp. garlic powder   1 or 2 cloves garlic
 ½ tsp. paprika   15 oz. can tomato sauce
 ¼ tsp. oregano   1 green pepper, halved &
 ¼ tsp. basil   seeded
 dash of thyme   1 medium onion, halved

Steel Knife: Process crackers with seasonings until fine crumbs are formed, about 30 seconds. Transfer to a flat plate or plastic bag. Process water with egg for 2 or 3 seconds. Transfer to a pie plate.

Dip chops first in egg mixture, then in seasoned crumbs. Heat oil to a depth of ⅛ inch in a large skillet. Brown chops quickly on both sides, adding more oil if necessary. (Calorie watchers may use a teflon skillet and omit the oil.) Drain well on paper towels. Arrange in a single layer in a large casserole.

Steel Knife: Drop garlic through feed tube while machine is running. Process until minced. Add sauce and a little additional oregano, basil and thyme. Process for a few seconds to blend. Pour over chops.

Slicer: Slice vegetables, using medium pressure. Add to casserole. Cover and bake at 350°F for ½ hour. Uncover and bake ½ hour longer, or until tender. Serve with rice or potatoes.

Yield: 4 to 6 servings. May be frozen.

HONEY GARLIC SPARERIB SAUCE √

1 clove garlic   ¾ c. honey
½ small onion   ½ tsp. salt
1 tbsp. ketchup or chili sauce   ¼ tsp. each dry mustard,
1 tbsp. lemon juice or vinegar   ginger, chili powder and
2 tbsp. soya sauce   pepper

Steel Knife: Drop garlic through feed tube while machine is running. Process until minced. Add onion and process until minced. Scrape down sides of bowl. Add remaining ingredients and process for 3 or 4 seconds to blend.

Transfer mixture to a heavy bottomed saucepan and bring to a boil over medium heat. Boil for 30 to 40 seconds. Remove from heat and use in your favorite recipes.

Yield: 1 cup sauce. Recipe may be doubled successfully and extra sauce stored in a glass jar in the refrigerator for about 1 month. Delicious on spare ribs, chicken wings, chicken pieces or as a marinade for London Broil or brisket.

HONEY GLAZED SPARE RIBS ✓

3 lb. spare ribs   1 c. Honey Garlic Sparerib
                                          Sauce (p. 122)

Cut ribs into serving size pieces. Place in a saucepan with just enough water to cover. Simmer, covered, for ½ hour. Drain well.

Prepare sauce as directed. It is not necessary to cook the sauce first as it will cook with the ribs. Place ribs in a shallow baking dish and spoon about ⅔ of the sauce over. Mix well. Bake uncovered at 350°F for about 1 hour, basting ribs with reserved sauce from time to time.

Yield: 4 servings. Delicious served on a bed of fluffy white rice. Freezes well. May also be used as an appetizer (will serve 6 to 8).

HONEY GARLIC RIBS ✓

3 lb. spare ribs   1 c. brown sugar, packed (or honey)
salt and pepper, to taste   ¼ c. soya sauce
1 tsp. ginger   2 tsp. vinegar
2 or 3 cloves garlic   ½ c. water

Place ribs in a single layer on a broiling rack. Sprinkle with salt, pepper and ginger. Broil on both sides until brown. Drain on paper towelling. Cut up into individual ribs. Place in a 2-quart oven-proof casserole.

Steel Knife: Drop garlic through feed tube while machine is running. Process until minced. Add brown sugar, soya sauce, vinegar, and water. Process a few seconds, until mixed. Pour over ribs. Bake uncovered at 300°F for 1½ hours, basting every fifteen minutes. Serve over rice.

Yield: 4 servings. May be frozen.

SPICY SHORT RIBS

8 strips short ribs (flanken)   3 tbsp. soya sauce
3 cloves garlic   1 tbsp. Worcestershire sauce
14 oz. can peaches, well   ¼ c. brown sugar, packed
   drained (or 8 oz. jar baby   ¼ c. lemon juice or vinegar
   food peaches)   ½ tsp. dry mustard
½ c. ketchup or chili sauce

Arrange short ribs in a single layer in a 9" x 13" baking dish or large shallow roasting pan.

Steel Knife: Drop garlic through feed tube while machine is running. Process until minced. Add remaining ingredients and process until smooth. (No salt or pepper are necessary.) Pour over meat and marinate 1 to 2 hours at room temperature, or overnight in the refrigerator.

Bake covered at 325°F for 2½ hours. Uncover and bake ½ hour longer, or until very tender. Baste occasionally. Serve with rice or noodles.

Yield: 4 to 6 servings, depending on size of short rib strips. Freezes well.

CANTONESE SHORT RIBS

14 oz. can pineapple chunks, with juice
2 cloves garlic
¼ c. soya sauce
¼ c. honey
¼ c. apricot jam
1 tsp. ginger
4 lb. short ribs (flanken), cut in serving size pieces

1 green pepper, halved & seeded
1 onion, halved
19 oz. can bean sprouts (or 2 c. fresh)
1 pkg. frozen pea pods
10 oz. can whole mushrooms, drained

Drain juice from pineapple and measure liquid to equal ¾ cup. If necessary, add a little water.

Steel Knife: Drop garlic through feed tube while machine is running. Process until minced. Add pineapple juice, soya sauce, honey, jam and ginger. Process for a few seconds, until blended. Place short ribs in a 9'' x 13'' pyrex dish. Pour marinade over and let stand at room temperature for at least 3 to 4 hours, or refrigerate and marinate overnight. Meat should be turned several times.

Bake at 300°F for approximately 3 hours, or until tender, basting occasionally. If necessary, add a little extra pineapple juice or water.

Slicer: Slice pepper and onion, using medium pressure. Drain canned bean sprouts and rinse under cold water. (If using fresh sprouts, pour boiling water over to soften slightly.) Pour boiling water over pea pods to break apart. Add pineapple and vegetables to meat and cook about 10 minutes longer, or until heated through. Serve with rice.

Yield: 6 servings. If freezing, add pineapple and vegetables when reheating.

Note: Canned drained mandarin oranges may added along with the pineapple, if desired. Juice from oranges may be added to pan juices if necessary.

OVEN ROASTED SHORT RIBS (FLANKEN)

3 cloves garlic
6 to 8 strips short ribs (flanken)
salt, pepper & paprika, to taste
½ tsp. basil

½ tsp. oregano
¼ tsp. dill weed
3 onions, halved
½ c. water, red wine or tomato juice

Steel Knife: Drop garlic through feed tube while machine is running. Process until minced. Remove from processor bowl with a rubber spatula and spread over meat. Add seasonings and rub into meat on all sides. Place in a large roaster.

Slicer: Slice onions, using medium pressure. Add to roasting pan. Add desired liquid. Cover and bake at 325°F for 2 hours. Uncover and cook 1 hour longer, basting occasionally. Sliced potatoes may be added the last ½ hour, if desired.

Yield: 4 to 6 servings. May be frozen, but omit potatoes.

SPICY OVEN STEW

Follow recipe for Spicy Short Ribs (p. 123), but substitute 2½ lb. stewing beef for flanken.

3 large carrots, scraped & trimmed
2 onions

4 or 5 potatoes, peeled
3 stalks celery

Slicer: Cut vegetables to fit feed tube. Slice, using firm pressure. Add to stew during the last hour of cooking. Freezes well, but omit potatoes.

SHORT RIBS SURPRISE

(Your family will be surprised to learn this melt-in-your-mouth dish is made with short ribs rather than steak. The cooking liquid can be saved to make a quick and easy soup.)

6 to 8 strips lean short ribs (flanken)
4 bay leaves
½ tsp. salt
4 peppercorns
cold water
3 stalks celery

3 or 4 onions
2 green peppers
1 pint mushrooms
3 tbsp. oil
28 oz. can tomatoes
3 to 4 tbsp. soya sauce

Place short ribs, bay leaves, salt and peppercorns in a Dutch oven. Add cold water to cover. Bring to a boil; skim. Cover and simmer for 45 to 50 minutes. Remove meat from liquid and place on a cutting board. Let cool. Discard bay leaves and peppercorns from cooking liquid. Chill overnight. (See **Note**).

Trim bones and fat from meat. Using a sharp knife, cut meat on a 45 degree angle into slices ½'' thick.

Slicer: Cut vegetables to fit feed tube. Place 2 lengths of celery at a time in feed tube. Slice, using firm pressure. (This will give you diagonally-cut slices.) Slice onions, peppers and mushrooms, using medium pressure. Brown vegetables in hot oil in a large skillet. Transfer to a large ovenproof casserole. Add liquid from canned tomatoes.

Steel Knife: Process drained tomatoes for 3 or 4 seconds, until puréed. Add to casserole along with meat and soya sauce. Mix well. Cover and bake in oven at 350°F for 1 hour or until very tender. Serve meat and sauce on a bed of rice.

Yield: 6 servings. May be frozen.

Note: To make soup, discard congealed fat from cooking liquid. Bring to a boil.

2 carrots, scraped
2 stalks celery, with tops
1 onion

½ c. raw rice
salt & pepper, to taste

Steel Knife: Cut vegetables in 1½'' chunks. Process until minced, about 8 to 10 seconds. Add to cooking liquid along with rice and seasonings. Cover and simmer about ½ hour. May be frozen.

Yield: 6 servings.

HEARTY BEEF STEW IN WINE ✓

1 c. flour
1 tsp. salt
¼ tsp. pepper
¼ tsp. paprika
2 - 3 lb. stewing beef
½ c. oil (about)
½ c. dry red wine
1¼ c. chicken soup or
    consommé
    (if canned, do not dilute)

1 tbsp. soya sauce
1 tsp. HP steak sauce
4 carrots, scraped
4 potatoes, peeled
1 green pepper, halved &
    seeded
2 onions
3 stalks celery
2 zucchinis (do not peel)

Combine flour with salt, pepper and paprika in a plastic bag. Drop in stewing beef a few pieces at a time and shake to coat. Brown meat a few pieces at a time in oil in a large Dutch oven on medium heat. Remove as ready. To deglaze, add wine to pot and scrape up browned bits from the bottom of the pan using a wooden spoon. Add all ingredients except vegetables to pot. Cover and simmer 3 hours, stirring occasionally. Adjust seasonings to taste.

Slicer: Cut vegetables to fit feed tube. Slice, using firm pressure for carrots and potatoes, and medium pressure for remaining vegetables. Empty processor bowl as necessary. Add vegetables to meat and cook ½ hour longer, or until vegetables are tender.

Yield: 6 to 8 servings.

Note: This stew freezes well. However, for best results, reduce cooking time by ½ hour, and do not add potatoes until reheating (or omit potatoes and serve over hot fluffy rice or cooked noodles).

MEATBALLS IN PINEAPPLE PLUM SAUCE ✓

1 clove garlic
1½ lb. ground beef or veal (or
    1½ lb. lean beef or veal, cut
    in 1½" chunks)
1 egg
2 tbsp. water
1 tsp. salt
¼ tsp. pepper
½ tsp. dry mustard

2 tbsp. bread crumbs
2 tbsp. oil
10 oz. can crushed pineapple,
    with juice
½ c. Chinese plum sauce
¼ c. Chinese cherry sauce
1 tsp. monosodium glutamate,
    if desired

Steel Knife: Drop garlic through feed tube while machine is running. Process until minced. If meat is not already ground, put about ½ of the meat chunks into the processor bowl and process until finely chopped, about 8 seconds. Do not over-process, or meat will become tough. Transfer to a mixing bowl. Repeat with remaining meat.

Process egg with water and seasonings for 2 or 3 seconds. Add with crumbs to meat. Mix lightly to blend. Form into balls about 1 inch in diameter. Brown on all sides in hot oil. Drain off all fat from skillet, and add remaining ingredients. Cover and simmer about 20 minutes. Serve over boiled rice as a main course, or as an appetizer. Ideal for cocktail parties!

Yield: 4 servings as a main course and 6 to 8 servings as an appetizer. May be frozen.

BEEF STEW ITALIANO ✓

1 c. flour	salt & pepper, to taste
1 tsp. salt	1 tsp. basil
¼ tsp. pepper	1 tsp. oregano
½ tsp. paprika	1 bay leaf
2 - 2½ lb. stewing beef, cut in chunks	1 tbsp. brown sugar
3 cloves garlic	4 carrots, scraped & trimmed
2 onions, cut in chunks	4 potatoes, peeled and cut in chunks
oil for browning (about ¼ c.)	10 oz. pkg. frozen peas
½ c. red wine	10 oz. can whole mushrooms, drained
28 oz. can tomatoes	

Combine flour with salt, pepper and paprika in a plastic bag. Add meat a few pieces at a time and shake to coat well on all sides.

Steel Knife: Drop garlic through feed tube while machine is running. Process until minced. Scrape down sides of bowl. Add onions and process with 3 or 4 very quick on/off turns, until coarsely chopped.

Heat just enough oil to film the bottom of a Dutch oven. Add onions and garlic and brown over medium heat. Remove from pan. Add beef chunks a few at a time and brown on all sides. Remove from pan as ready. Add oil as needed. Add wine to pan and stir with a wooden spoon to scrape up any browned bits from the bottom of the pan. Add beef chunks, onions, garlic, liquid from tomatoes and seasonings. Place drained tomatoes in processor and purée on **Steel Knife** until smooth. Add to stew. Cover and simmer for approximately 2½ hours, until nearly tender. (If desired, stew may be baked at 300°F.)

Slicer: Cut carrots to fit feed tube. Slice, using firm pressure. Add with potatoes to stew and cook about 25 to 30 minutes longer. Add peas and mushrooms and cook 10 minutes more.

Yield: 4 to 6 servings. May be frozen, but do not add potatoes.

Variation: Omit potatoes. Serve over hot spaghetti or noodles.

SAUCY MEATBALLS ✓

(Sweet and Sour, without the addition of tomatoes.
Different and tasty.)

2 or 3 lbs. of your favorite recipe for hamburger or meatball mixture	1 tsp. salt
	½ c. sugar (or to taste)
3 large onions	1 tbsp. paprika
3 c. water	2 tbsp. vinegar or lemon juice
	½ tsp. garlic powder

Prepare your favorite recipe for meatball mixture. Insert **Slicer** in processor. Cut onions to fit feed tube. Slice, using medium pressure. Add to a large saucepan with remaining ingredients except meat and bring to a boil. Reduce heat to simmer.

Shape meat into small meatballs if using as an appetizer, or larger meatballs if using as a main course. Drop into simmering sauce. Cover partially and simmer for about 2 hours. Taste to adjust seasonings. Each pound of meat will serve 6 as an appetizer, or 3 as a main course. Freezes well.

TASTY MEATBALL STEW ✓

Meat Mixture:
- 2 cloves garlic
- ½ small onion
- 2 lb. ground beef or veal (or 2 lb. lean beef or veal, cut in 1½" chunks)
- 1½ tsp. salt
- ½ tsp. pepper
- 2 tsp. Worcestershire sauce
- 1 egg
- ¼ c. water
- ¼ c. bread crumbs

Sauce & Vegetables:
- 2 cloves garlic
- 5½ oz. tin tomato paste
- 2 c. water
- 1 tsp. salt (or to taste)
- freshly ground pepper
- ¼ tsp. oregano
- 1 bay leaf
- 4 medium potatoes, quartered
- 4 onions, quartered
- 4 carrots, scraped & cut in 2" chunks
- 2 stalks celery
- 1 green pepper

Steel Knife: Process garlic and onion until minced, about 6 to 8 seconds. Transfer to a large mixing bowl. If meat is not already ground, put about ¼ of the beef chunks in the processor bowl and process until finely chopped, about 8 seconds. Do not overprocess, or meat will become tough. Add to garlic/onion mixture. Repeat three more times with remaining beef chunks, adding each in turn to the mixing bowl. Add seasonings, Worcestershire sauce, egg, water and crumbs to meat. Mix lightly to blend.

Shape into 1'' balls, moistening your hands for easier handling. Place on a cookie sheet which has been lined with lightly greased tinfoil. Bake at 400°F for 20 to 25 minutes. Transfer to a Dutch oven.

Steel Knife: Drop garlic through feed tube while machine is running. Scrape down sides of bowl. Add tomato paste, water, salt, pepper and oregano and process for a few seconds, until mixed. Add with bay leaf to meatballs. Cover and simmer for 35 to 40 minutes. Add potatoes, onions and carrots.

Slicer: Cut celery and green pepper to fit feed tube. Slice, using light pressure. Add to meatballs. Simmer about 45 minutes longer, or until vegetables are tender. Add more water if necessary.

Yield: 6 to 8 servings. Freezes well, but do not add potatoes.

Note: This recipe is also delicious as a regular beef stew. Substitute 2 lb. stewing beef for the meatball mixture. Dip meat in flour which has been seasoned with salt, pepper and paprika. Brown pieces a few at a time in hot oil. Prepare sauce and vegetables and cook as directed, increasing cooking time to a total of about 3 hours, or until meat and vegetables are tender.

HAWAIIAN MEATBALLS

Meatballs:
- 2 lb. ground beef or veal (or 2 lb. lean beef or veal, cut in 1½" chunks)
- 1 clove garlic
- 1 small onion
- 1 egg
- 1½ tsp. salt
- ¼ tsp. pepper
- ¼ tsp. ginger
- 2 tbsp. bread crumbs

Sauce:
- 19 oz. tin pineapple chunks, drained (reserve ¾ c. juice)
- 2 tbsp. cornstarch
- ½ c. juice from canned peaches
- ¼ c. honey
- 2 tbsp. lemon juice or vinegar
- 1 tbsp. soya sauce
- ¼ tsp. ginger
- ¼ tsp. garlic powder

Steel Knife: If meat is not already ground, put about ¼ of the beef chunks in the processor bowl and process until finely chopped, about 8 seconds. Do not overprocess, or meat will become tough. Transfer to a large mixing bowl. Repeat 3 more times with remaining beef chunks, adding each in turn to the mixing bowl. Drop garlic and onion through feed tube while machine is running. Process until minced. Scrape down sides of bowl. Add egg and process until onion is puréed. Add with remaining meatball ingredients to mixing bowl. Mix lightly to blend.

Wet hands and form tiny meatballs as an appetizer or larger ones as a main course. Place on a foil-lined cookie sheet and bake at 400°F for 25 minutes. Transfer meatballs to an ovenproof casserole.

Add pineapple chunks to meatballs, reserving juice. Dissolve cornstarch in peach and pineapple juices in a small saucepan. Add remaining sauce ingredients. Bring to a boil, stirring constantly. Simmer for 2 minutes. Carefully pour over meatballs and mix gently. Cover and bake at 350°F for 45 minutes.

Yield: 8 to 10 servings as an appetizer, and 4 to 6 servings as a main course. Serve on a bed of fluffy hot rice. May be frozen, but add pineapple when reheating.

Note: If desired, add about ½ cup peach slices during last 10 minutes of cooking.

MMM-GOOD MEATBALLS √

Sauce:
9 oz. jar grape jelly
19 oz. tin tomato juice
2 - 28 oz. tins tomatoes
½ c. brown sugar or honey
2 tbsp. lemon juice
1 tsp. salt

Meatballs:
2 cloves garlic
4 lb. ground beef (or 4 lb. lean
   beef, cut in 1½" chunks)
(*See Note below)
4 slices bread, quartered
2 eggs
⅔ c. water
1 tbsp. salt
½ tsp. pepper

Combine ingredients for sauce in a heavy-bottomed Dutch oven. Heat slowly on low heat, stirring often to prevent jelly from scorching. Bring to simmering.

Steel Knife: Drop garlic through feed tube while machine is running. Process until minced. If meat is not already ground, put about 1½ cups of the beef chunks into the processor bowl and process until finely minced, about 8 seconds. Do not overprocess. Transfer to a large mixing bowl. Repeat with remaining meat, adding each batch in turn to mixing bowl. Process bread to make fine crumbs. Add to meat. Process eggs, water and seasonings for 2 or 3 seconds. Add to meat. Mix lightly to blend.

Form small meatballs about the size of a walnut. Drop into simmering sauce and cook partially covered for 2½ to 3 hours, stirring occasionally. (Meatballs may also be baked in the oven at 325°F.)

Yield: about 100 meatballs. Freezes well. Tastes even better reheated.

*Note: Recipe may be halved, if desired. Veal may be substituted for the beef.

OLD FASHIONED BREADED HAMBURGERS √

24 Ritz or soda crackers (or ¾
   c. cracker or bread crumbs)
1 lb. lean ground beef or veal
   (or 1 lb. beef or veal, cut in
   1½" chunks)
1 clove garlic

½ small onion
1 egg
¼ c. water
¾ tsp. salt
¼ tsp. pepper
oil for frying

Steel Knife: Process crackers until fine crumbs are formed, about 20 to 30 seconds. Transfer to a small bowl. If meat is not already ground, put about half the meat chunks into the processor bowl and process until finely chopped, about 8 seconds. Do not overprocess, or meat will become tough. Transfer to a large mixing bowl. Repeat with remaining meat and add to first batch.

Process garlic with onion until minced. Scrape down sides of bowl; add egg, water and seasoning and blend until onion is fairly fine, about 10 to 15 seconds. Add to meat along with ¼ cup of the cracker or bread crumbs. Mix lightly to blend. Do not overhandle, or hamburgers will be tough. (May also be mixed with on/off turns on the **Plastic Knife.** Do not overprocess.)

Wet hands and form meat into 5 or 6 patties. Coat on both sides in remaining crumbs. Brown on both sides on medium heat in hot oil. Drain well. Place in a baking dish and bake uncovered at 400°F for 20 minutes.

Yield: 5 to 6 hamburgers. Recipe may be doubled for a larger family. Freezes well.

Note: For onion lovers, slice 2 large onions on the **Slicer,** using medium pressure. Brown in hot oil and add to hamburgers. Bake as directed.

HAMBURGERS A LA DUTCH ✓

Meat Mixture:
2 cloves garlic
2 lb. ground beef or veal (or 2 lb. lean beef or veal, cut in 1½" chunks)
1½ tsp. salt
½ tsp. pepper
½ tsp. onion powder
6 tbsp. matzo meal or bread crumbs
⅓ c. water
oil for frying

Vegetable Mixture:
3 or 4 onions, halved
3 green peppers, halved & seeded
1 red pepper, halved & seeded
2 stalks celery, cut to fit feed tube
1 pint mushrooms
salt, pepper & paprika
½ c. dry red wine

Steel Knife: Drop garlic through feed tube while machine is running. Process until minced. If meat is not already ground, put about ⅓ of the meat chunks into the processor bowl. Process until finely chopped, about 8 seconds. Do not over-process or meat will become tough. Transfer to a large mixing bowl. Repeat twice more with remaining meat chunks, adding each in turn to the mixing bowl. Add seasonings, crumbs and water; mix lightly to blend.

Form into 9 or 10 patties about ½" thick. Brown in hot oil on medium heat in a large skillet or electric frypan for about 6 minutes on the first side, and about 4 minutes on the second side, until well browned. Cover and let steam on low heat for 10 minutes. Remove from pan. Add more oil if necessary.

Slicer: Slice vegetables, using medium pressure. Add to skillet and brown in pan juices, stirring often, about 3 to 4 minutes. Sprinkle with seasonings, being quite generous with the paprika (about 2 to 3 tsp). Add wine and hamburgers and cook 3 to 4 minutes longer.

Yield: 4 to 6 servings. Serve with rice or potatoes. Hamburgers may be frozen, but vegetables are best added at serving time.

CHILI ✓

1 large clove garlic
1½ lb. ground beef (or 1½ lb. lean beef, cut in 1½" chunks)
2 large onions, quartered
1 stalk celery, cut in chunks
10 oz. can condensed tomato soup
½ soup tin water

19 oz. can red kidney beans, with liquid
2 tbsp. chili powder (or to taste)
1 tsp. salt
½ tsp. pepper
½ tsp. cumin
few drops Tabasco sauce

Steel Knife: Drop garlic through feed tube while machine is running. Process until minced. If meat is not already ground, put about ½ of the beef chunks in the processor bowl and process until coarsely ground, about 6 seconds. Empty bowl and repeat with remaining beef chunks. Preheat a large Dutch oven and add ground meat and garlic. Process onions and celery with on/off turns, until finely chopped. Add to Dutch oven. Brown meat and vegetables over medium high heat, stirring often. Add remaining ingredients. Simmer uncovered for about 1 hour, stirring often. Taste and adjust seasonings.

Yield: 4 servings. May be frozen. Serve over spaghetti or noodles, or in a bowl along with crackers and garnished with chopped onions.

Note: If desired, increase meat to 2 lb.

CRUSTY MEAT LOAF ✓

½ recipe Warm Water Knish Dough (p. 174)
1 clove garlic
1½ lb. ground beef (or 1½ lb. lean beef, cut in 1½ chunks)
1 egg
1 tsp. salt
¼ tsp. pepper
3 tbsp. ketchup
½ c. bread or cracker crumbs
½ c. water
1 egg yolk plus 2 tsp. cold water

Prepare dough as directed. If necessary, add 1 or 2 tbsp. flour if dough seems a little sticky. Place on a floured board and cover to prevent drying.

Steel Knife: Drop garlic through feed tube while machine is running. Process until minced. If meat is not already ground, put half of the beef chunks into the processor bowl and process until finely chopped, about 8 seconds. Do not over-process. Transfer to a large mixing bowl. Repeat with remaining beef chunks and add to first batch of meat. Process egg with salt and pepper for 1 or 2 seconds. Add with ketchup, crumbs and water to ground meat. Mix lightly to blend ingredients.

Divide dough in half. Roll one portion into an 8" x 10" rectangle. Arrange half of meat on dough about 1" from edges in the shape of a loaf. Roll up, folding in edges. Repeat with remaining dough and filling. Place on a greased cookie sheet.

Steel Knife: Process egg yolk with 2 tsp. water for 1 or 2 seconds to blend. Brush dough with egg wash. Cut 3 or 4 slits along the top of each loaf with the **Steel Knife.** Bake at 350°F about 45 to 50 minutes, until nicely browned and crusty.

Yield: 6 servings. May be frozen, but reduce original baking time by 10 minutes. Reheat thawed loaves at 350°F for 20 to 25 minutes.

Variation: Refer to recipe for Meat Ball Knishes (p. 44). Excellent as an hors d'oeuvre.

POTATO KUGEL MEAT LOAF ✓
(Grated raw potatoes make an unusual topping for this version of Shepherd's Pie.)

Meat Mixture:
1 lb. ground beef or veal (or 1 lb. lean veal or beef, cut in 1½" chunks)
1 tbsp. oil
¾ tsp. salt
freshly ground pepper
dash of garlic powder
1 egg
2 tbsp. ketchup

Potato Mixture:
1 small onion, halved
3 medium potatoes, peeled and cut in chunks
2 eggs
¾ tsp. salt
pepper, to taste
3 tbsp. flour or potato starch
½ tsp. baking powder

Steel Knife: If meat is not already ground, put about half of the beef chunks into the processor bowl. Process until finely chopped, about 8 seconds. Empty bowl. Repeat with remaining meat.

Heat oil in a skillet. Add meat and cook over medium heat about 4 to 5 minutes, mashing it to keep it crumbly. When meat has lost its red colour, add seasoning, egg and ketchup. Mix well. Transfer to a well-greased 1 quart shallow casserole.

Steel Knife: Place onion, potatoes and eggs in processor bowl. Process until puréed, about 20 to 30 seconds. Add remaining ingredients and process a few seconds longer to blend into a smooth mixture. Spread over meat. Bake at 375°F until well-browned and crisp, about 1 hour.

Yield: 4 servings. May be frozen.

SHEPHERD'S PIE MEAT LOAF ✓

Prepare meat mixture as for Potato Kugel Meat Loaf (p. 132), but use the following potato topping:

3 potatoes, peeled & cut in 2" chunks	**2 tbsp. oil**
boiling salted water to cover	**salt & pepper, to taste**
1 onion, halved	**1 egg**
	½ tsp. baking powder

Cook potatoes in boiling salted water until tender. Drain well. Return pan to heat to remove excess moisture from potatoes. This will take about a minute or so.

Steel Knife: Process onion with 2 or 3 quick on/off turns, until coarsely chopped. Sauté in hot oil for 3 or 4 minutes, until nicely browned.

Plastic Knife: Process potatoes with several on/off turns. Add remaining ingredients and process for 10 or 15 seconds, until lump-free. Do not overprocess. It may be necessary to scrape down sides of bowl once or twice.

Spread sautéed meat mixture in a greased shallow 1 quart casserole. Top with potato mixture. If desired, make an attractive design with a fork and sprinkle with a little paprika.

Bake at 375°F for 45 minutes, or until golden brown and puffy.

Yield: 4 servings.

Variation: Top meat mixture with 1 tin drained corn niblets or peas and carrots before topping with potato mixture.

SHIPWRECK ✓
(A Version of Shepherd's Pie)

2 medium onions	**½ c. raw rice**
2 potatoes, peeled	**2 stalks celery**
salt, pepper, garlic powder and paprika, to taste	**3 or 4 medium carrots, scraped & trimmed**
1½ lb. ground beef (or 1½ lb. lean beef, cut in 1½" chunks)	**2½ c. chicken or beef broth (or 19 oz. can tomatoes)**

Slicer: Cut onions and potatoes to fit feed tube. Slice onions, using medium pressure. Place in a well-greased 2 qt. casserole. Slice potatoes, using medium pressure. Arrange in a layer over onions. Sprinkle lightly with seasonings.

Steel Knife: If meat is not already ground, put half of the beef chunks into the processor bowl and process until finely chopped, about 8 seconds. Do not overprocess. Empty bowl and repeat with remaining meat. Spread meat over potatoes and season lightly. Top with rice.

Slicer: Cut celery and carrots to fit feed tube. Slice celery using light pressure and carrots using heavy pressure. Arrange over rice. Season once again.

Pour broth over casserole. (If using canned tomatoes, process for a few seconds, until pureed, using **Steel Knife**.) Cover and bake at 250°F for 2½ to 3 hours. The long, slow cooking develops the delicious flavour.

Yield: 4 to 6 servings. Freezing is not recommended.

CHINESE SHIPWRECK

Follow recipe for Shipwreck (above) but omit potatoes and increase rice to 1 cup. Substitute 2 cups of bean sprouts for the carrots. Use chicken or beef broth as the liquid, adding 2 tbsp. soya sauce. Bake as directed.

MOIST & SPICY MEAT LOAF ✓

(A delicious way to stretch one pound of meat to serve a family. Chock full of vegetables and vitamins.)

- 1 lb. ground beef or veal (or 1 lb. lean beef or veal, cut in 1½" chunks)
- 1 clove garlic
- 1 onion, halved
- 3 green onions (shallots), cut in chunks
- ½ stalk celery, cut in chunks
- ½ green pepper, cut in chunks
- 4 slices bread (or 2 stale rolls)
- ½ c. mushrooms
- 10 oz. tin chicken broth or consommé
- 1 egg
- ¾ tsp. salt
- ¼ tsp. pepper
- ½ tsp. Italian seasoning
- ¼ tsp. allspice, if desired
- 1 or 2 tbsp. bread crumbs, if needed

Topping:

- 2 to 3 tbsp. H.P. steak sauce
- ½ green pepper
- ½ c. mushrooms
- 2 tbsp. bread crumbs

Steel Knife: If meat is not already ground, put half of the beef chunks into the processor bowl and process until finely chopped, about 8 seconds. Do not overprocess. Empty into a large mixing bowl. Repeat with remaining beef chunks. Add to bowl. Drop garlic through feed tube while machine is running. Process until minced. Add onion, shallots, celery and green pepper. Process until minced, about 6 seconds. Add to meat.

Break bread or rolls into chunks. Process until coarse crumbs are formed, about 10 seconds. Add to meat.

Slicer: Slice mushrooms, using light pressure. (If desired, mushrooms may be coarsely chopped with quick on/off turns on the **Steel Knife** instead of slicing them.) Add to meat.

Add remaining ingredients except those for the topping and mix to blend thoroughly. Place in a greased 9" x 5" loaf pan, packing mixture very lightly. Spread steak sauce over top.

Slicer: Slice green pepper and mushrooms for topping, using light pressure. Spread over meat loaf. Sprinkle with crumbs.

Bake at 350°F for 1 hour and 10 minutes.

Yield: 4 to 6 servings. May be frozen. Delicious with Scalloped Potatoes.

SUPER SPAGHETTI SAUCE ✓

3 cloves garlic	28 oz. can tomatoes
2 medium onions, quartered	2 - 5½ oz. tins tomato paste
3 tbsp. oil	¼ c. red wine
1 green pepper, halved & seeded	1 tbsp. salt
1 c. mushrooms, if desired	½ tsp. pepper
2 lb. ground beef (or 2 lb. lean beef, cut in 1½" chunks)	½ tsp. oregano
	¼ tsp. basil
¼ lb. salami or pepperoni (½ c. chopped)	½ tsp. sugar
	1 bay leaf

Steel Knife: Drop garlic through feed tube while machine is running. Process until minced. Add onions and process with 3 or 4 quick on/off turns, until coarsely chopped. Do not overprocess. Brown garlic and onions slowly in hot oil in Dutch oven for 5 minutes.

Slicer: Slice green pepper and mushrooms, using very light pressure. Add to Dutch oven and cook 2 minutes longer. Remove vegetables from pan.

Steel Knife: If meat is not already ground, put ¼ of the beef chunks (about 1 cup) into the processor bowl and process until finely chopped, about 8 seconds. Do not overprocess. Empty bowl and repeat three more times with remaining beef chunks. Empty bowl as each batch is minced. Cut salami or pepperoni into 2" chunks. Process with about 6 quick on/off turns, until coarsely chopped. Add salami and ground beef to pan and brown slowly for 10 minutes, until beef loses its red color. Stir often.

Add remaining ingredients to pan, stirring well to break up tomatoes. (Tomatoes may be broken up by processing them on the **Steel Knife** for a few seconds. Do not add the liquid or you will have leakage from the bottom of the processor bowl.) Cover and simmer gently for about 1½ to 2 hours. Taste to adjust seasonings.

Yield: 6 to 8 generous servings. Freezes well.

Note: This recipe may be halved, if desired.

SPAGHETTI SAUCE DELUXE ✓

Super Spaghetti Sauce (above)	2 green peppers, halved & seeded
½ lb. pepperoni	2 c. mushrooms
	2 tbsp. oil

Prepare and cook spaghetti sauce as directed. Insert **Slicer** in processor. Cut pepperoni to fit feed tube. (It is best to use pepperoni that is firm and dry rather than soft.) Slice, using light pressure. Slice peppers and mushrooms, using light pressure.

Heat oil in a large skillet. Add pepperoni and vegetables and fry on medium heat until browned, stirring occasionally. Pour spaghetti sauce over hot pasta and top with pepperoni and vegetables. Serve with a tossed salad and garlic bread.

Yield: 6 to 8 servings.

THE ANATOMY OF A CHICKEN

How to Cut Chicken into Parts:

1) Place the whole chicken with the breast facing upwards. Using a sharp knife, cut through the breastbone, opening the chicken completely. Then cut through the remaining bone (the backbone). You now have 2 halves.

2) Hold onto the drumstick, then wiggle it slightly to see where the thigh joint is. Cut through. You may separate the drumstick from the thigh by wiggling to find the joint, then cut through. Repeat with other drumstick-thigh portion.

3) Take hold of the wing and wiggle it to find the joint attaching it to the shoulder. Cut through. The wing tip may be cut off and used in making broth, if desired.

4) The wing may be cut in two, giving you a straight piece, and a "**miniature drumstick**". These little drumsticks are great as hors d'oeuvres at a cocktail party. Dip in beaten egg and seasoned crumbs, and baked at 400°F for about 40 to 45 minutes.

5) The backbone, wing tips, breastbone and skin, plus the giblets, can be used to make chicken broth. A good guide is 1 cup water to the bones of each pound of chicken. Refer to recipe for Free Chicken Soup (p. 54).

Boning Chicken Breasts:

1) Begin with split breasts from young broiler-fryers. Pull off the skin, then turn the breast over. With your fingers and a sharp knife, remove breastbone and smaller bones. Pull out white tendons. Don't worry if you can't do it perfectly. You will improve with practice. Use skin and bones for soup (see #5 above).

2) Boned chicken breasts freeze very well. Thaw before cooking. They cook very quickly and are ideal for a fast meal.

3) Boneless chicken breasts are excellent for Chinese stir-fry cooking. Roll chicken breasts to fit feed tube. Wrap in plastic wrap and freeze for about 2 hours, until very firm, but not completely frozen. You should just be able to insert the point of a knife. If chicken is not frozen firmly enough, it will not slice well. If frozen too firmly, let stand at room temperature until you are able to insert the point of a knife.

4) Use firm pressure and slice on the **Slicer.** You will have paper-thin slices. Chicken will cook in 2 to 3 minutes when stir-fried. Add to assorted stir-fried vegetables (e.g. mushrooms, onions, peppers, celery, water chestnuts, bamboo shoots) and season with a little soya sauce and garlic. Let your imagination be your guide. Easy, delicious and economical.

MOO GOO GUY PAN √

4 single chicken breasts, skinned and boned
½ tsp. salt
¼ tsp. pepper
2 tsp. cornstarch

1 green pepper, halved and seeded
1 pint mushrooms
2 tbsp. corn or peanut oil
1 clove garlic, peeled and halved

Wash and dry chicken thoroughly. Cut into 1'' squares with a sharp knife. Mix with ½ tsp. salt, ¼ tsp. pepper and cornstarch.

Slicer: Slice green pepper and mushrooms, using light pressure. Set on paper towelling to absorb excess moisture.

Heat oil in wok. Add garlic and brown for a minute or two. Discard garlic. Make sure oil is nearly smoking, then add chicken and stir constantly over high heat for 2 or 3 minutes, until pieces turn white. Push chicken up sides of wok. Add mushrooms and green pepper and stir-fry for 2 minutes. Adjust seasonings to taste and mix to combine all ingredients.

Yield: 4 servings. Do not freeze, or vegetables will lose their crispness.

Note: One large onion, sliced on the **Slicer** may be added just before the mushrooms and green pepper. Cook onion 1 minute. Best prepared in a wok, but a large skillet may be used.

MUSHROOM ALMOND CHICKEN

4 single chicken breasts, skinned & boned
1 pint mushrooms
1 onion, halved
2 tbsp. peanut or corn oil
1 c. frozen peas, thawed
¼ c. chicken broth

1 tbsp. soya sauce
1 tbsp. cornstarch
2 tbsp. cold water
salt & pepper, to taste
½ tsp. garlic powder
½ c. slivered blanched almonds

Cut chicken in pieces to fit feed tube snugly. Freeze chicken until quite stiff, about 2 hours. You should just be able to insert the point of a knife into the chicken.

Slicer: Slice chicken, using very heavy pressure. (If chicken is not frozen firmly enough, it will not slice easily. If chicken is fully frozen, partially thaw it **just until you can insert the point of a knife.**)

Slicer: Stack mushrooms on their sides in the feed tube. Slice, using light pressure. Slice onion, using medium pressure.

Heat oil in a wok. (A large skillet may be used instead.) Add chicken pieces when oil is nearly smoking; stir-fry over high heat for 2 minutes, until chicken is white. Add mushrooms and stir-fry for 1 minute. Add onion and peas and cook 1 minute longer.

Add broth and soya sauce. Cover and let simmer for 2 minutes. Dissolve cornstarch in cold water. Uncover wok and push chicken and vegetables up the sides. Stir cornstarch mixture into boiling liquid at the bottom of the wok. Cook just until thickened, stirring constantly. (If not thick enough, add 1 to 2 teaspoons cornstarch dissolved in a little water.)

Add seasonings and almonds and mix well. Serve immediately.

Yield: 4 servings. If frozen, vegetables will not be crispy.

CHICKEN GUY KEW

6 single chicken breasts,   1 tbsp. paprika
  skinned & boned   ½ c. water or beer
1 c. flour   2 tbsp. oil
½ tsp. baking powder   2 eggs
1 tsp. salt   oil for frying

Cut chicken into 1'' squares with a sharp knife. Set aside.

Steel Knife: Process remaining ingredients (except oil for frying) until smooth, about 10 to 15 seconds. Dip chicken pieces in batter. Fry in hot oil until brown on all sides, about 2 to 3 minutes. Drain well on paper towelling. Serve with Chinese Sweet & Sour Sauce (p. 66). Freezes well.

Yield: 8 to 10 servings as an hors d'oeuvre, and 6 servings as a main course. Allow for second helpings! Freezes well.

To reheat: Place thawed tidbits on a foil-lined cookie sheet and reheat uncovered at 450°F until hot and crispy, about 7 to 8 minutes.

MOO GOO GUY KEW

Chicken Guy Kew (above)   1 c. mushrooms
10 oz. pkg. frozen broccoli   8 oz. can water chestnuts,
  spears   drained
1 large onion, quartered   2 to 3 tbsp. oil
1 green pepper, halved &   2 cloves garlic, crushed
  seeded   2 tsp. soya sauce
1 stalk celery, cut in thirds

Prepare chicken as directed and drain well. Keep warm. (May be prepared in advance and reheated.) Pour boiling water over broccoli and separate spears. Pat dry.

Slicer: Slice remaining vegetables and place on paper towelling to absorb excess moisture. Use medium pressure for onion and pepper, light pressure for celery and mushrooms, firm pressure for water chestnuts. Pat each vegetable dry. Celery should be arranged on a slant in the feed tube to give diagonal slices.

Heat oil in a wok. Stir-fry onion for 1 minute. Push up sides of wok. Repeat with green pepper, then with celery, then with mushrooms. Stir in water chestnuts and broccoli. Add garlic and soya sauce and mix well. Cover and cook for 2 minutes. Add chicken and mix well. Serve with rice.

Yield: 6 servings. Do not freeze or vegetables will lose their crispness.

CHINESE SWEET & SOUR CHICKEN √

Chicken Guy Kew (above)   2 tbsp. oil
Chinese Sweet & Sour   6 oz. pkg. frozen pea pods,
  Sauce (p. 66)   thawed
1 pint mushrooms   14 oz. can pineapple chunks,
2 onions, quartered   well drained

Prepare chicken as directed and set aside. Prepare sauce.

Slicer: Slice mushrooms and onions, using medium pressure. Sauté briefly in hot oil in a wok or large skillet. Add pea pods; stir-fry about 1 minute longer. Add remaining ingredients and mix well.

Yield: 6 servings. If desired, sprinkle with ¼ cup lightly toasted sesame seeds before serving. Serve with rice.

CHICKEN LIVERS CHINESE STYLE

1 lb. chicken livers, halved
2 onions, quartered
2 green peppers, halved &
   seeded
1 pint fresh mushrooms
3 tbsp. oil
6 oz. pkg. frozen pea pods

2 tbsp. soya sauce
1 clove garlic, crushed
1 tbsp. brown sugar
½ tsp. ginger
2 tbsp. cornstarch dissolved
   in ¼ c. cold water
freshly ground pepper

Broil chicken livers lightly on both sides. Set aside.

Slicer: Slice onions, using medium pressure. Empty bowl and place on paper towelling. Repeat with green peppers, then with mushrooms.

Heat oil in a large skillet or wok. Sauté onions for 1 or 2 minutes, stirring. Remove from pan. Repeat with peppers, then with mushrooms. Pour boiling water over pea pods to thaw. Pat dry. Add to skillet along with sautéed vegetables, soya sauce, garlic, brown sugar and ginger. Stir in chicken livers. Simmer for 2 or 3 minutes, stirring occasionally.

Make a well in the centre and stir in cornstarch/water mixture. Cook until sauce is clear and thickened, about 2 minutes longer, stirring constantly. Add pepper to taste. Serve on a bed of fluffy white rice.

Yield: 4 servings. Do not freeze, or vegetables will become soggy.

Variation: Stir in ½ cup toasted slivered almonds.

ITALIAN SEASONED CHICKEN WITH POTATOES

4 lb. chicken, cut in 8ths
salt & pepper, to taste
1 tsp. paprika
½ tsp. dry mustard
½ tsp. oregano
½ tsp. basil

¼ tsp. thyme
2 cloves garlic
1 large onion, quartered
½ c. chicken broth or water
4 medium potatoes, pared

Place chicken pieces in a large roasting pan and sprinkle with seasonings.

Steel Knife: Drop garlic through feed tube while machine is running. Process until minced. Scrape down sides of bowl. Add onion and process with 3 or 4 quick on/off turns, until coarsely chopped. Rub onion and garlic over chicken. If possible, let stand at least ½ hour to develop maximum flavor.

Add water or broth. Roast uncovered at 325°F for about 2 hours, or until tender and golden. About half an hour before chicken is done, insert **Slicer** in processor. Cut potatoes to fit feed tube. Slice, using very firm pressure. Add potatoes to chicken and sprinkle with additional seasonings. Baste occasionally, adding extra liquid if necessary.

Yield: 4 servings. Chicken freezes well, but omit potatoes if you plant to freeze this dish. Recipe may be doubled successfully and half may be frozen for a future meal.

MARINATED HERB CHICKEN √

3 lb. chicken, cut up	¼ tsp. pepper
1 clove garlic	¼ tsp. oregano
½ c. oil	1 c. flour
2 tsp. salt	1 tsp. paprika

Wash chicken pieces and dry well. Arrange in a 9'' x 13'' baking dish.

Steel Knife: Drop garlic through feed tube while machine is running. Process until minced. Add oil, salt, pepper and oregano. Process a few seconds to blend. Drizzle over chicken and marinate 3 to 4 hours, or overnight in refrigerator. Turn once.

Place flour in plastic bag and add chicken pieces, one or two at a time. Shake to coat. Dip again in marinade. Arrange in a single layer on an ungreased foil-lined cookie sheet. Sprinkle with paprika. Bake at 425°F for 1 hour.

Yield: 4 servings. May be frozen. Scrumptious!

MARINATED CASINO CHICKEN

2 broilers, cut in 8ths	1 pkg. dry onion soup mix
1 c. mushrooms	9 oz. jar red currant jam
1 c. bottled Casino salad dressing (8 oz. jar)	

Place chicken pieces in a large roasting pan.

Slicer: Slice mushrooms, using light pressure. Add to chicken.

Plastic or Steel Knife: Combine remaining ingredients and process for a few seconds to blend. Pour over chicken. Cover and marinate in refrigerator for 24 hours. Bake uncovered at 350°F for 2 hours, basting occasionally. Cover with foil if chicken becomes too brown. Serve over rice. Tastes even better the next day!

Yield: 8 servings. Freezes well.

HEAVENLY CHICKEN √
(You can use bottled or home-made salad dressings for
any of the variations of this recipe.)

2 broilers, cut in 8ths	9 oz. jar apricot jam
1 c. Italian Salad Dressing (p. 186)	1 pkg. dry onion soup mix

Place chicken pieces in a large roasting pan.

Steel Knife: Combine remaining ingredients and process for a few seconds, until blended. Pour over chicken. (May be marinated for several hours at room temperature or overnight in the refrigerator. Turn once.)

Bake uncovered at 350°F for about 2 hours, until nicely browned. Baste occasionally. Serve with rice.

Yield: 8 servings. Freezes well. (I like to freeze half for an emergency meal.)

VARIATIONS
Follow recipe above, using the following salad dressings and jams:-

Italian Salad Dressing (p. 186) and peach or pineapple jam.

Thousand Island Salad Dressing (p. 187) and apricot jam.

Sweet & Spicy French Dressing (p. 185) or bottled Catalina Dressing and peach or apricot jam.

Best Vinaigrette Dressing (p. 187) or bottled Herb Dressing and ½ c. orange marmalade plus ½ c. peach jam.

Any bottled low calorie dressing plus diet jam.

CRUNCHY SESAME CHICKEN (Fried)

24 soda or Ritz crackers
  (or ¾ c. bread crumbs)
½ tsp. salt
dash of pepper
dash of paprika

¼ c. sesame seeds
1 egg plus 2 tbsp. water
4 single chicken breasts,
  skinned and boned
oil for frying

Steel Knife: Process crackers with seasonings to make fine crumbs, about 30 seconds. Add sesame seeds and process 2 or 3 seconds longer to mix. Transfer to a flat plate or plastic bag. Process egg and water for 2 or 3 seconds. Transfer to a flat plate.

Dip chicken pieces in beaten egg, then in crumb mixture. Brown on medium heat in hot oil about 5 minutes on each side, until golden and crispy. Drain on paper towels. May be reheated uncovered at 400°F for 10 minutes.

Yield: 4 servings. May be frozen.

CRUNCHY SESAME CHICKEN (Baked)

Substitute 3 lb. chicken, cut in 8ths, or 4 chicken breasts (with skin and bone). Proceed as directed above for Crunchy Sesame Chicken. Do not fry, but bake uncovered at 400°F for 45 minutes to one hour, until done. May be frozen, but underbake slightly to avoid "reheated" flavor.

CRISPY RUSSIAN CHICKEN ✓

4 c. cornflakes (or 1 c.
  crumbs)
1 tsp. salt
¼ tsp. pepper

½ tsp. garlic powder
3½ lb. chicken, cut in 8ths
1 c. bottled Russian salad
  dressing (8 oz. jar)

Steel Knife: Process cornflakes with seasonings to make fine crumbs, about 20 seconds.

Wash chicken pieces and dry thoroughly. Coat generously on all sides with salad dressing. Roll in seasoned crumbs. Place on a cookie sheet lined with lightly greased foil. (May be prepared in advance up to this point and refrigerated.)

Bake uncovered at 350°F for one hour, until crisp and golden.

Yield: 4 servings. May be frozen.

TANGY ORANGE BARBECUE CHICKEN

2 chickens, cut in 8ths
6 oz. can frozen unsweetened
  orange juice (do not thaw)
¾ c. brown sugar, lightly
  packed
¾ c. bottled barbecue sauce

2 green peppers, halved &
  seeded
1 onion, halved
10 oz. can mandarin oranges,
  drained

Place washed and dried chicken pieces in roasting pan.

Steel Knife: Process orange juice, brown sugar and barbecue sauce until blended, about 10 to 15 seconds. Pour over chicken. Cover and bake at 350°F for 1½ hours. Uncover and bake ½ hour longer, basting occasionally.

Slicer: Slice peppers and onion, using light pressure. Add with drained mandarin oranges to chicken. Cook 10 to 15 minutes longer. Serve with fluffy white rice.

Yield: 8 servings. Tastes even better reheated. Freezes well.

MARINATED BARBECUED CHICKEN ✓

2 cloves garlic
½ c. oil
2 tbsp. white or wine vinegar
2 tsp. salt
dash pepper

2 tsp. paprika
1 tsp. dry mustard
½ tsp. chili powder
2 - 3 lb. chickens, cut in 8ths
(or 5 to 6 lb. chicken pieces)

Steel Knife: Drop garlic through feed tube while machine is running. Process until minced. Add oil, vinegar and seasonings. Process until blended, about 2 or 3 seconds longer.

Pour marinade over chicken pieces. Rub well to coat on all sides. Let marinate at room temperature for 1 hour, or overnight in the refrigerator. Pat chicken pieces very dry with paper towelling.

Place on the barbecue as far away from the hot coals as possible. (May also be baked on a lightly greased foil-lined cookie sheet at 400°F for 1 hour, or until browned and crispy.) Barbecue chicken for 35 to 45 minutes, turning very often to prevent scorching. It's a good idea to keep a water pistol or old Windex bottle filled with water on hand to extinguish any flare-ups. Delicious!

Yield: 8 servings. May be frozen.

PAPRIKA ROASTED CHICKEN ✓

2 large onions
3 lb. chicken, cut in 8ths
2 cloves garlic
¼ c. Worcestershire sauce

1½ tsp. salt
freshly ground pepper
1 tsp. dry mustard
2 tbsp. paprika

Slicer: Cut onions to fit feed tube. Slice, using firm pressure. Place in the bottom of an open roasting pan. Wash chicken pieces but do not dry. Place skin side down over onions.

Steel Knife: Drop garlic through feed tube while machine is running. Process until minced. Scrape down sides of bowl. Add remaining ingredients and process for a few seconds. Rub mixture over chicken pieces. Roast uncovered at 350°F for 1 hour. Turn pieces over and roast ½ hour longer, until golden. Baste occasionally. (Add a little water or wine if chicken begins to stick.) Par-boiled potatoes may be added during the last half hour of cooking.

Yield: 4 servings. Freezes well, but omit potatoes.

CHICKEN & VEGETABLES

3 large onions
2 medium zucchini (unpeeled)
3 or 4 carrots, scraped
5 or 6 potatoes, pared
salt, pepper & garlic
powder, to taste

1 tsp. oregano
2 chickens, cut in 8ths
½ c. white wine
⅔ c. bottled barbecue sauce
1 tbsp. lemon juice
1 tsp. onion flakes, if desired

Slicer: Cut vegetables to fit feed tube. Slice, using medium pressure. Arrange vegetables in layers in a large greased casserole. Sprinkle with seasonings. Arrange chicken in a single layer over vegetables. Season once again.

Steel Knife: Process wine, barbecue sauce, lemon juice and onion flakes for a few seconds to blend. Pour over chicken. Cover and bake at 375°F for 1 hour. Uncover and bake about ½ hour longer, until browned and tender. Baste occasionally.

Yield: 8 servings. May be frozen, but omit potatoes. Recipe may be halved, if desired.

POTATO CRUSTED CHICKEN ✓

(A delicious potato pancake flavour)

3½ lb. chicken, cut in 8ths
salt, pepper, paprika &
  garlic powder, to taste
2 or 3 medium onions, halved
2 tbsp. oil
1 egg

2 tbsp. water
1 c. instant mashed potato
  flakes
seasoning salt
¼ c. water

Wash chicken pieces and dry well. Sprinkle with salt, pepper, garlic and paprika. Refrigerate covered at least one hour or overnight for chicken to absorb flavoring.

Slicer: Slice onions, using medium pressure. Sauté in oil in a skillet until golden. Place in a large roasting pan.

Steel Knife: Blend egg with water for 2 or 3 seconds. Transfer to a flat dish. Dip chicken pieces first in egg, then in potato flakes. Sprinkle with seasoning salt and arrange in a single layer over onions. Add water. Bake covered at 350°F for one hour. Uncover and bake ½ hour longer. Baste occasionally.

Yield: 4 servings. May be frozen.

CHICKEN IN PINEAPPLE ORANGE SAUCE

2 chickens, cut in 8ths
salt and pepper, to taste
1 tbsp. paprika
2 cloves garlic
1 c. tomato sauce
6 oz. can frozen concentrated
  orange juice

¼ c. brown sugar, packed
½ tsp. dry mustard
½ tsp. cinnamon
½ tsp, ginger
14 oz. can pineapple chunks
1 medium orange

Sprinkle chicken with salt, pepper and paprika on all sides. Place in a roasting pan.

Steel Knife: Drop garlic through feed tube while machine is running. Process until minced. Scrape down sides of bowl. Add tomato sauce, orange juice, brown sugar, seasonings and ½ c. juice from pineapple. Process for 2 or 3 seconds to blend. Pour over chicken. Bake uncovered for about 2 hours at 350°F. Baste occasionally. If sauce cooks down too much, add a little pineapple juice. Add drained pineapple chunks 5 minutes before done.

Slicer: Cut orange in half lengthwise. Slice, using medium pressure. (You will have beautiful paper-thin slices of orange.) Serve chicken on a bed of fluffy white rice, spoon sauce over and garnish with orange slices.

Yield: 8 servings. Freezes well, but do not garnish until serving time.

STICKY CHICKY ✓

4 lb. chicken pieces	**Sauce:**
salt and pepper	2 cloves garlic
1 tsp. paprika	½ c. soya sauce
½ tsp. Accent, if desired	½ c. honey or corn syrup
½ tsp. garlic powder	2 tbsp. vinegar or lemon juice
1 tsp. dry mustard	½ tsp. ginger
	1 tbsp. cornstarch
	2 tbsp. cold water

Rub chicken pieces well with seasonings. Place in a casserole or open roaster, skin side down. Do not add any liquids. Roast at 400°F for 20 minutes, then turn skin side up and roast 15 minutes longer.

Steel Knife: Drop garlic through feed tube while machine is running. It is not necessary to peel garlic as the skin will dissolve during cooking. Process until minced. Add remaining ingredients except cornstarch and water; process 2 or 3 seconds, until blended. Pour sauce over chicken pieces. Reduce heat to 350°F. Cook ½ hour longer uncovered, basting occasionally.

Dissolve cornstarch in water. Stir into bubbling sauce. Return chicken to oven and cook 2 or 3 minutes longer. (If desired, sprinkle with 2 or 3 tbsp. sesame seeds to garnish.)

Yield: 6 servings. Freezes well.

BREADED CHICKEN FILLETS ✓

(Delicious and easy!)

6 single chicken breasts, skinned and boned	¼ tsp. garlic powder
15 Ritz crackers (or ½ c. crumbs)	½ tsp. paprika
1 tsp. salt	1 egg
¼ tsp. pepper	1 tbsp. water
	oil for frying

Wash and dry chicken breasts well.

Steel Knife: Process crackers with seasonings until fine crumbs are formed, about 20 to 30 seconds. Empty crumbs into a flat dish or a plastic bag.

Process egg with water for 2 seconds. Empty into a pie plate. Dip chicken pieces first into egg mixture, then into crumbs. Brown in hot oil over medium heat on both sides until golden brown. Total cooking time is about 6 to 8 minutes. Do not crowd frying pan. Drain well on paper towelling.

Yield: 4 to 6 servings. May be frozen. Allow for seconds!

Note: May be browned in advance and reheated uncovered at 400°F for about 10 minutes. Great with Best-Ever Scalloped Potatoes (p. 165) and Pineapple Carrots (p. 157).

HONEY GLAZED CHICKEN WINGS

2 dozen chicken wings   **1 c. Honey Garlic Sparerib Sauce (p. 122)**

Cut chicken wings in half at joint. Save wing tips to use in soup. Place chicken wings on a rack and bake at 400°F for 15 minutes. Turn and bake 15 minutes longer.

Prepare sauce as directed. Brush wings with sauce. Bake for 30 to 35 minutes longer, turning and brushing them with remaining sauce every 10 minutes or so.

Yield: 4 to 6 servings as a main course. To serve as an hors d'oeuvre, allow about 3 or 4 wings per person. Recipe makes 48 pieces. Freezes well.

HONEY GLAZED BABY DRUMS

Follow recipe for Honey Glazed Chicken Wings, but use 3 dozen chicken wings. Cut wings in two at joint, and only use "drumstick" portion for this recipe. The remaining portion of the wing may be used to make soup.

Bake as directed, brushing with sauce every few minutes.

Yield: 36 miniature drumsticks. Allow 6 to 8 drumsticks per person as a main dish, and 3 to 4 per person as an hors d'oeuvre. Freezes well.

CRANBERRY CHICKEN BALLS

2 lb. minced chicken (or 10 single chicken breasts, skinned and boned)
1 onion, halved
1 carrot, scraped and cut in 1" chunks
1 stalk celery
1 egg
½ tsp. garlic powder

1½ tsp. salt
¼ tsp. pepper
⅓ c. bread crumbs or matzo meal
2 - 14 oz. cans jellied cranberry sauce
½ tsp. cinnamon
2 - 8 oz. cans tomato sauce

Steel Knife: If chicken is not already minced, put about ⅓ of the chicken which you have cut into 1½" chunks into the processor bowl. Process until finely minced, about 10 seconds. Transfer to a mixing bowl. Repeat twice more with remaining chicken breasts, adding each in turn to the mixing bowl. Process onion, carrot and celery until minced. Add egg and seasonings and process a few seconds longer. Add with crumbs to chicken. Mix well.

Wet hands and form small meatballs as an appetizer or larger ones as a main course. Place on a foil-lined cookie sheet which has been lightly greased. Bake uncovered at 350°F about 25 to 30 minutes.

Steel Knife: Place cranberry sauce and cinnamon in processor bowl. Add tomato sauce through feed tube while machine is running. Process until blended. Transfer to an ovenproof casserole. Add meatballs and bake covered at 350°F for 1 hour, basting occasionally. Serve on a bed of fluffy white rice.

Yield: 6 to 8 servings as a main course, 10 to 12 servings as an appetizer. May be frozen.

CRANBERRY MEAT BALLS: Substitute 2 lb. ground beef or veal (or 2 lb. lean beef or veal, cut in 1½" chunks) for the chicken.

CHINESE CHICKEN WINGS

3 lb. chicken wings
salt & pepper, to taste
¼ tsp. garlic powder
paprika

Sauce:
2 cloves garlic
½ c. soya sauce
¼ c. ketchup or chili sauce
⅓ c. brown sugar, packed
2 tbsp. vinegar
¾ tsp. ginger
¼ tsp. chili powder

Cut chicken wings in two if serving as hors d'oeuvres. Discard wing tips, or save to use in soups. Sprinkle wings with seasonings. Bake in a single layer at 400°F for 35 to 40 minutes. Transfer to a casserole.

Steel Knife: Drop garlic through feed tube while machine is running. Process until minced. Add remaining ingredients for sauce and process for a few seconds to blend. Pour over wings. Cover and bake at 325°F for about one hour, basting occasionally. Serve with fluffy hot rice and chow mein as a main course.

Yield: 4 to 6 servings as main dish, 8 servings as an appetizer. Freezes well.

PINEAPPLE CHICKEN MEATBALLS

1½ lb. minced chicken (or 8
  single boneless and
  skinless chicken breasts)
1 small onion, halved
1 small potato, peeled and
  halved
2 eggs
1 tsp. salt
¼ tsp. pepper
⅓ c. bread crumbs
oil for frying

Sauce:
8 oz. jar Chinese cherry sauce
1½ c. Chinese Sweet & Sour
  sauce (p. 66)
8 oz. tin tomato sauce
14 oz. tin pineapple chunks,
  drained
1 green pepper, halved &
  seeded
1 onion, halved

Steel Knife: If chicken is not already minced, put about half of the chicken which you have cut into 1½'' chunks into the processor bowl. Process until finely minced, about 10 seconds. Transfer to a mixing bowl. Repeat with remaining chicken breasts. Process onion with potato until minced, about 8 to 10 seconds. Add eggs and seasonings and process a few seconds longer. Add with crumbs to chicken. Mix well.

Wet hands and form small meatballs as an appetizer or larger ones as a main course. Brown in hot oil on all sides. Drain well.

In a large saucepan, combine cherry sauce, sweet & sour sauce and tomato sauce. Heat to boiling. Add meatballs, cover and simmer for 1 hour. Add pineapple chunks.

Slicer: Slice pepper and onion, using firm pressure. Add to meatballs and simmer 5 to 10 minutes longer. Serve over hot fluffy white rice. Freezes well.

Yield: 4 to 6 servings as a main course, 8 servings as an appetizer.

Note: Veal may be substituted for the chicken, if desired.

MANDARIN CHICKEN BALLS ✓

½ small onion
1 lb. raw minced chicken or 2 c. cooked chicken, cut in chunks (discard skin and bones)
2 eggs
salt & pepper, to taste
¼ tsp. garlic powder
3 to 4 tbsp. crumbs
oil for frying

12 oz. jar Chinese cherry sauce or 1½ c. Chinese Sweet & Sour Sauce (p. 66)
¾ c. Chinese plum sauce
1 c. mushrooms
1 green pepper, halved & seeded
1 onion, halved
1 stalk celery, cut in thirds
10 oz. can drained mandarin oranges

Steel Knife: Process onion until minced, about 8 seconds. Add chicken, eggs, seasonings and crumbs. Process for 6 to 8 seconds, just until mixed. Make small meatballs. If using cooked chicken, brown in hot oil on all sides in a large skillet. Drain well. If using raw chicken, **either** brown in oil **or** bake at 400°F on a lightly greased baking sheet for 25 minutes.

Place chicken balls in a 2 quart ovenproof casserole. Combine sauces and pour over chicken. Simmer covered for about ½ hour, stirring occasionally. (May also be baked at 325°F for ½ hour.)

Slicer: Slice vegetables. Heat about 2 tbsp. oil in skillet and fry vegetables for 3 or 4 minutes over high heat. Stir into sauce along with drained oranges. May be prepared in advance and reheated. Delicious!

Yield: 4 servings. May be frozen, but it is best to add vegetables when reheating for maximum crunchiness.

Note: I often double this recipe and serve it as a company dish. Easy and economical. Leftover cooked turkey may be substituted for the chicken.

BREAD STUFFING

leftover bread or rolls to yield 2¼ c. soft bread crumbs
1 onion, halved
2 carrots, cut in 2" chunks
2 stalks celery, cut in 2" chunks

¼ c. fresh parsley
2 eggs
1 tsp. salt
freshly ground pepper
¼ tsp. thyme

Steel Knife: Make crumbs by dropping chunks of bread through feed tube while machine is running. Measure loosely packed and transfer to a large mixing bowl.

Steel Knife: Process vegetables until minced, about 8 seconds. Add eggs and process 2 or 3 seconds longer. Add with remaining ingredients to bread crumbs and mix well.

Yield: For a 5 lb. veal brisket, large capon, or 2 small roasting chickens. Stuff loosely.

MOSTLY VEGETABLES STUFFING

(Kind to the Calorie Conscious!)

2 onions	¾ tsp. salt
1 zucchini, unpeeled	freshly ground pepper
2 large carrots, peeled	⅛ tsp. oregano
2 eggs	⅛ tsp. basil
1 c. matzo meal	½ tsp. paprika

Grater: Cut vegetables to fit feed tube. Grate onions and zucchini, using medium pressure. Grate carrots, using firm pressure. Push vegetables to a side and insert **Plastic Knife** in processor bowl. Add remaining ingredients and process until well mixed, about 8 to 10 seconds.

Yield: for a 10 or 12 lb. turkey, or a large veal brisket, or 2 small chickens. Remove stuffing from poultry or meat if you plan to freeze it, and wrap them separately for freezing.

MINCED VEAL STUFFING

1 large clove garlic	2 tbsp. ketchup
1 lb. ground veal (or 1 lb. lean	1 egg
veal, cut into 1½" chunks)	¼ c. matzo meal
1 medium potato, peeled	½ tsp. Kitchen Bouquet or
1 large carrot, scraped	soya sauce, if desired
1 celery stalk	1 tbsp. instant onion soup mix
½ green pepper	dash of salt & pepper
1 small onion	

Steel Knife: Drop garlic through feed tube while machine is running. Process until minced. If meat is not already ground, put about half the meat into the processor bowl and process until finely chopped, about 8 seconds. Do not overprocess or meat will be tough. Transfer to a large mixing bowl. Repeat with remaining meat.

Grater: Cut vegetables to fit feed tube. Grate vegetables, using firm pressure. Add with remaining ingredients to meat and mix lightly with your hands to blend ingredients.

Use a a stuffing for veal brisket or shoulder (see recipe for Stuffed Veal Brisket, p. 120). Cook as directed. Scrumptious. May be frozen.

Note: Any cooked leftover vegetables may be puréed on the **Steel Knife** and added to the meat mixture.

BREAD & MUSHROOM STUFFING

Follow recipe for Stuffing Casserole (p. 178), but omit baking powder. Add ½ tsp. each of sage and thyme. Stuff turkey or veal brisket loosely. Cook according to recipe directions, but add about 10 minutes per pound to the cooking time. If desired, you may increase the mushrooms to 2 cups.

To freeze: Remove stuffing from veal brisket or turkey and freeze cooled stuffing separately.

Additional Recipes

Vegetables, Side Dishes & Salads

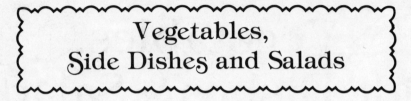

Vegetables, Side Dishes and Salads

- **Vegetables** should be peeled and sliced or chopped just before cooking in order to retain maximum flavor and vitamins. Cook only until tender.

- **Either** cook vegetables in about ½ cup boiling water (or enough water to just cover the vegetables). A vegetable steamer may also be used, and will retain all the vitamins and minerals in vegetables. Use a saucepan with a fairly tight fitting cover. Always open the cover away from you to prevent being burnt by the hot steam.

- **Steaming** vegetables takes about the same time as boiling, or perhaps a minute or two longer. Use about ½" boiling water in the bottom of the saucepan. Water should not touch vegetables.

- **Cooking time** of vegetables will vary depending on whether they are whole, sliced or chopped, and according to the type of vegetable being cooked. As an estimate, allow 3 to 4 minutes for grated vegetables, 5 to 6 minutes for sliced vegetables, and 10 to 15 minutes for whole vegetables. Taste and check.

- **Broccoli,** if the stalks are peeled, tastes delicious and tender when steamed. Stems should be peeled with a sharp knife. Discard the bottom half inch, which is usually quite tough. Steaming will take about 8 minutes. Broccoli tastes delicious with Hollandaise Sauce (p. 64).

- **Most vegetables** are delicious if seasoned with a little salt, freshly ground pepper and a little butter or margarine. Calorie counters may wish to use Low-Cal Butter or Margarine (p. 36) or a few drops of fresh lemon juice.

- **You can make gratinéed vegetables** easily by topping cooked vegetables with a White Sauce (p. 63) or Cheese Sauce (p. 64), then sprinkling with buttered seasoned bread crumbs. Bake about 15 to 20 minutes at 350°F, until bubbling and nicely browned.

- **Mushrooms** should be firm and white when you buy them. Caps should be tightly closed. Large mushrooms are excellent for stuffing. They are usually found at specialty fruit and vegetable stores, rather than pre-packaged. Mushroom stems may be reserved to use in sauces and soups. If you are able to buy a large quantity of mushrooms at a reasonable price (e.g. at open-air markets), why not try making Mushroom Duxelles (p. 161). It adds a gourmet touch to your cooking!

- **Leeks** are sometimes difficult to clean properly. Use white part only, plus about 2 or 3 inches of the green portion. Make 4 lengthwise cuts to within 1 inch from the roots so that the leek resembles a whisk broom. It will then be easy to wash and remove the sand and grit. Just swish in cold water. Dry well and slice or chop.

- **Potatoes** should not be stored in the refrigerator or they will develop a sweet taste.

- **Tomatoes** that you buy during the winter months are best bought on the green side. Let ripen at room temperature and use as ready, instead of purchasing them ripened and then refrigerating them. The flavor of room-temperature ripened tomatoes more closely resembles tomatoes picked from the vine.

- **Pasta** should be cooked in plenty of water. The general rule is 4 quarts or litres of water and 4 tsp. salt to each pound of pasta. Add gradually to rapidly boiling water. Do not cook pasta without salt or it will never taste right. A tablespoon of oil added to the cooking water will prevent boiling over and sticking.

- **Drain pasta** as soon as it is cooked. Do not let it remain in the pot of water. If you plan on using it later, it may be reheated quickly by placing in boiling water for a minute or so. Undercook slightly if you plan to reheat it later.

- **Spaghetti and macaroni** double when cooked. Noodles swell slightly. One pound of spaghetti yields 5 to 6 servings. One cup uncooked noodles (2½ oz. weight) yields 1¼ cups cooked and will yield 3 servings. Pasta freezes for 4 to 6 months.

- **Home-made pasta** is fun to make and very easy with a food processor. For the recipes called for in this book you may either use packaged pasta or home-made.

★★★★★★★★★★

ASPARAGUS CASSEROLE

1 can asparagus spears, well-drained	2 tbsp. flour
2 hard-cooked eggs	1 c. hot milk
3 oz. Swiss or Cheddar cheese (¾ c. grated)	salt & pepper, to taste
2 tbsp. butter or margarine	¼ c. cornflake crumbs or bread crumbs

Arrange asparagus in a greased 1 quart casserole.

Slicer: Slice eggs, using medium pressure. They will crumble somewhat. Place over asparagus.

Grater: Grate cheese, using medium pressure. Empty bowl and set aside. Wipe out bowl.

Steel Knife: Process butter with flour for 4 to 5 seconds. Pour in hot milk through the feed tube while the machine is running and process until blended. Add seasoning. Transfer to a saucepan and cook over medium heat, stirring, until bubbly and thickened. Pour over asparagus and eggs. Sprinkle with crumbs and top with grated cheese. Bake uncovered at 350°F for 20 to 25 minutes.

Yield: 4 servings.

Note: Recipe may be double successfully for a large crowd. If desired, add a 10 oz. can of drained sliced mushrooms. If you are in a hurry, a 10 oz. can of condensed cream of mushroom soup may be substituted for the butter, flour and milk.

FRENCH-STYLE GREEN BEANS

1 lb. fresh green beans	salt & pepper, to taste
boiling salted water, to cover	1 tsp. fresh lemon juice
2 tbsp. butter or margarine	

Slicer: Wash and trim beans. Cut in half to fit feed tube crosswise. Pack beans tightly so that they are lying on their sides in the feed tube. Slice, using very firm pressure. Repeat with remaining beans in as many batches as necessary.

Place in a saucepan with boiling salted water to cover. Cover and cook on medium heat for 8 to 10 minutes, until tender but still slightly crunchy. Drain well. Combine with remaining ingredients.

Yield: 4 servings. Best served fresh, but may be prepared in advance.

GREEN BEANS ALMONDINE

1 lb. fresh green beans	3 tbsp. butter or margarine
boiling salted water, to cover	¼ c. slivered almonds
1 onion, halved	salt & pepper, to taste

Slicer: Wash and trim beans. Cut in half to fit feed tube crosswise. Pack beans tightly so that they are lying on their sides in the feed tube. Slice, using very firm pressure. Repeat with remaining beans in as many batches as necessary.

Place in a saucepan with boiling salted water to cover. Cover and cook on medium heat for 7 to 8 minutes, until nearly tender. Drain well.

Steel Knife: Process onion with 2 or 3 quick on/off turns, until coarsely chopped. Melt margarine in a skillet. Add onion and sauté lightly. Stir in almonds and beans. Cook for 2 to 3 minutes, stirring to mix. Season to taste. May be prepared in advance, but best served fresh.

Yield: 4 servings.
Variation: Substitute garlic butter for regular butter.

ORIENTAL GREEN BEAN BAKE

2 -10 oz. pkgs. french style frozen green beans	1 or 2 cloves garlic
10 oz. pkg. frozen broccoli spears	2 - 10 oz. cans condensed cream of mushroom soup
8 oz. can water chestnuts, well-drained	2 tbsp. soya sauce
	dash pepper
10 oz. can sliced mushrooms, well-drained	3 oz. can french-fried onions

Cook beans and broccoli according to package directions, undercooking slightly. Drain well.

Slicer: Slice water chestnuts, using firm pressure. Combine with beans, broccoli and mushrooms in a lightly greased 9'' x 13'' oblong casserole. Mix well.

Steel Knife: Drop garlic through feed tube while machine is running. Process until minced. Add soup, soya sauce and pepper and blend with several on/off turns. Stir into vegetables. Top with french-fried onions. (May be prepared in advance up to this point and refrigerated.)

Bake at 350°F for 25 to 30 minutes, until bubbling and onion rings are nicely browned.

Yield: 8 servings.

CHEESY BROCCOLI CASSEROLE

10 oz. pkg. frozen broccoli, slightly thawed	2 c. creamed cottage cheese
	3 eggs
4 oz. Cheddar cheese (1 c. grated)	3 tbsp. butter, cut in pieces
	3 tbsp. flour

Cut broccoli into large pieces and place in a lightly buttered 2 quart casserole.

Grater: Grate cheese, using medium pressure. Remove **Grater** and insert **Steel Knife.** Add remaining ingredients to grated cheese except for broccoli. Process just until mixed, about 8 to 10 seconds. (Do not add salt.) Pour over broccoli and mix well. Bake at 325°F for about 1 hour.

Yield: 6 servings. May be frozen, but best prepared when needed. Reheats well.

Note: This casserole may be served as a side dish with dairy, or may be served as a main dish. It makes a different and interesting choice for a dairy buffet.

EASY BROCCOLI BAKE

2 - 10 oz. pkgs. frozen
broccoli spears (or
1 bunch fresh broccoli)
¼ lb. Cheddar cheese, cut in
chunks

10 oz. can cream of mushroom
or celery soup
½ c. cornflake or bread
crumbs (or 3 oz. can french
fried onions)
1 tbsp. butter or margarine

Cook broccoli until tender. (Follow package directions for frozen, or cook fresh broccoli for 10 to 12 minutes.) Drain well. Spread evenly in a buttered 1½ quart casserole.

Steel Knife: Process cheese until fine, about 15 to 20 seconds. Add soup and blend in with quick on/off turns. Spread over broccoli. Sprinkle with crumbs or onions. Dot with butter or margarine. Bake uncovered at 350°F for about 20 minutes.

Yield: 4 to 6 servings. May be prepared in advance and baked at mealtime.

BROCCOLI LATKES (Pancakes)

10 oz. pkg. frozen broccoli (or
½ bunch fresh broccoli, cut
in chunks)
1 small onion, halved
3 eggs

½ c. matzo meal or cracker
crumbs
¾ tsp. salt
dash pepper
oil for frying

Cook frozen broccoli according to package directions. (Cook fresh broccoli in boiling salted water until tender.) Drain thoroughly.

Steel Knife: Process onion until minced. Scrape down sides of bowl. Add eggs and broccoli and process until very finely chopped, about 20 seconds. Add matzo meal and seasonings and process a few seconds longer, until smooth.

Heat about 3 to 4 tbsp. oil in a large skillet. Drop in vegetable mixture from a tablespoon to make small pancakes. Flatten slightly with the back of the spoon. Brown on both sides. Drain on paper towelling. Add more oil if necessary.

Yield: about 1½ dozen small pancakes. May be frozen.

SPINACH LATKES (Pancakes)

Follow recipe for Broccoli Latkes (above), but substitute a 10 oz. pkg. of frozen or fresh spinach for the broccoli. Cook until tender and drain well. Squeeze out all moisture from spinach. Continue as directed.

BEAN LATKES (Pancakes)

Follow recipe for Broccoli Latkes (above), but substitute a 10 oz. pkg. frozen green beans or ½ lb. fresh green beans for the broccoli. Cook until tender and drain well. Continue as directed.

CAULIFLOWER LATKES (Pancakes)

Follow recipe for Broccoli Latkes (above), but substitute either 1 medium head of cauliflower or a 10 oz. pkg. frozen cauliflower for the broccoli. Cook until tender and drain well. Continue as directed.

APRICOT CANDIED CARROTS

2 lb. carrots, scraped and
  trimmed
½ c. boiling water

dash salt
½ c. apricot jam
8 marshmallows

Slicer: Cut carrots to fit feed tube. Slice, using firm pressure. Combine boiling water, salt and jam in a saucepan. Add carrots, cover and cook 35 minutes, or until tender. Remove cover and if necessary, let liquid boil down to a depth of ½''. Add marshmallows and stir until dissolved.

Yield: 6 to 8 servings. May be frozen.

Note: This dish reheats very well. You may heat it in the oven, if desired. If you prefer a sweeter taste, add ¼ cup honey along with the marshmallows.

CANDIED CARROTS

2 lb. carrots, scraped and
  trimmed
boiling salted water
½ c. brown sugar, packed

½ tsp. salt
dash pepper
12 marshmallows

Slicer: Cut carrots to fit feed tube. Slice, using firm pressure. Place in a heavy bottomed saucepan and cook in boiling salted water to cover until tender. Drain well. Add remaining ingredients and cook on low heat until marshmallows have melted, stirring often.

Yield: 6 to 8 servings. Freezes well. May be prepared in advance and reheated at 350°F for 20 minutes.

Note: For a quick version, substitute 2 - 14 oz. cans sliced carrots.

CARROT SOUFFLE

2 lb. carrots, scraped and
  trimmed
½ c. margarine, cut in chunks
3 eggs
¾ c. brown sugar, firmly
  packed

¼ c. flour
1½ tsp. baking powder
¾ tsp. baking soda

Slicer: Pack carrots tightly in feed tube. Slice, using firm pressure. Cook in boiling salted water until tender, about 10 to 15 minutes. Drain well.

Steel Knife: Process carrots with margarine until puréed, about 20 to 30 seconds, stopping machine to scrape down sides as necessary. Add remaining ingredients and process until blended, about 15 seconds.

Pour into a greased 1½ quart soufflé or baking dish. Place dish into a pan filled with 1'' of water. Bake uncovered at 350°F for about 1 hour. Serve immediately. Soufflé will sink slightly upon cooling. Do not freeze.

Yield: 6 servings.

Note: To avoid reheating the soufflé, you may prepare the batter earlier in the day, omitting baking powder and soda. Refrigerate until 1 hour before serving time. Stir in leavening and mix well. Bake as directed and serve immediately. This is a very moist and light dish, and is delicious with chicken or turkey.

PINEAPPLE CARROTS ✓

2 lbs. carrots, scraped &
trimmed
1 c. boiling water
1 tsp. salt
2 tbsp. cornstarch

1 c. unsweetened pineapple
juice
½ tsp. cinnamon, if desired
¼ c. sugar, or to taste

Slicer: Cut carrots to fit feed tube. Slice, using firm pressure. Cook in boiling salted water in a covered saucepan for 25 minutes, or until tender. Drain well.

Dissolve cornstarch in pineapple juice. Add with cinnamon and sugar to carrots and simmer until thickened, about 2 to 3 minutes.

Yield: 4 to 6 servings. Freezes well.

Calorie Trimmer's Version: Substitute artificial sweetener for the sugar.

CARROT MUFFINS

2 large carrots, scraped and
cut into 1" chunks
¾ c. margarine or shortening,
cut in chunks
½ c. brown sugar, packed
2 eggs
1 tbsp. lemon juice

3 tbsp. water
1¼ c. flour
1 tsp. baking soda
1 tsp. baking powder
¼ tsp. salt
¾ tsp. cinnamon

Steel Knife: Process carrots until finely minced, about 12 to 15 seconds. Add margarine, sugar and eggs. Process until well mixed, about 45 seconds. Add remaining ingredients and process with quick on/off turns, just until flour disappears.

Fill greased muffin tins ¾ full. Bake at 350°F about 30 minutes. Serve hot as a side dish with chicken or turkey. May be reheated.

Yield: about 1 dozen muffins. Freezes well.

CARROT RING

5 or 6 medium carrots, scraped &
cut into 1" chunks (about
1½ cups)
2 eggs
½ c. oil
½ c. brown sugar, packed

¼ c. orange juice or water
1½ c. flour
2 tsp. baking powder
1 tsp. baking soda
1 tsp. cinnamon

Steel Knife: Process carrots until finely minced, about 12 to 15 seconds. Add eggs, oil and brown sugar. Process until well mixed, about 45 seconds. Add remaining ingredients and process with 4 or 5 quick on/off turns, just until flour disappears.

Pour into a greased 6 cup ring mold or small Bundt pan. Bake at 350°F about 40 minutes, until done. Serve warm. Fill centre of ring with green peas or broccoli. Serve with roast chicken or turkey.

Yield: 8 servings. May be frozen.

CARROT LATKES (Pancakes) √
(Different and Delicious!)

6 medium carrots, peeled	dash pepper
1 onion	½ c. flour
3 eggs	½ tsp. baking powder
¾ tsp. salt	oil for frying

Grater: Cut carrots to fit feed tube and grate, using firm pressure. Measure 2 cups. Insert **Steel Knife** in processor bowl. Process onion until fine, about 6 to 8 seconds. Add remaining ingredients except oil. Process until blended, about 15 seconds.

Heat oil to ⅛'' depth in a large skillet. Drop carrot mixture from a large spoon into hot oil, and flatten patties with the back of the spoon. Brown on medium heat about 2 to 3 minutes on each side, until golden brown. Drain well on paper towelling.

Yield: 16 to 18 patties. Freezes well. (To reheat, place patties on a foil-lined cookie sheet and bake uncovered at 450°F for 8 to 10 minutes.)

Note: Miniatures make an excellent hors d'oeuvre for a cocktail party.

Yield: about 5 dozen.

ZUCCHINI LATKES (Pancakes) √
Follow recipe for Carrot Latkes (above), but substitute 3 medium zucchini for the carrots. After grating, salt lightly and let stand for 15 minutes. Press out excess moisture. Continue as directed.

MOCK KISHKA
(A yummy stuffing mixture baked in a roll, then sliced.)

½ c. margarine	2 medium onions
12 oz. pkg. Tam Tams or any crackers (about 3½ cups crumbs)	2 carrots, peeled 1 stalk celery salt and pepper, to taste

Melt margarine. Insert **Steel Knife** in processor. Process crackers until crushed, breaking them into the processor through the feed tube while the machine is running. Empty bowl. Process vegetables until minced, about 6 to 8 seconds. Add crumbs, seasonings and melted margarine to processor and process until blended.

Form into 3 rolls, about 1½'' in diameter, and wrap tightly in foil. (May be prepared in advance up to this point and refrigerated or frozen until needed. Thaw before baking.) Bake in foil on a cookie sheet at 350°F for 45 to 50 minutes. Slice in 2'' slices.

Yield: about 15 slices. (Allow for second and third helpings!) Freezes well.

CAULIFLOWER MUSHROOM BAKE

10 oz. pkg. frozen cauliflower	¼ lb. Cheddar cheese, cut in chunks
1 c. mushrooms	10 oz. can cream of mushroom soup
1 onion, halved	½ c. cornflake crumbs
2 tbsp. margarine or butter	

Cook cauliflower according to package directions. Drain well. Arrange evenly in a buttered 9'' pie plate.

Slicer: Slice mushrooms and onions, using light pressure. Sauté in 1 tbsp. margarine for 5 minutes. Add to cauliflower.

Steel Knife: Process cheese until fine, about 15 to 20 seconds. Add soup and blend in with quick on/off turns. Spread over cauliflower. Sprinkle with crumbs and dot with remaining margarine. Bake uncovered at 350°F for about 20 minutes.

Yield: 4 servings. May be prepared in advance and baked at mealtime.

CHINESE COMPANY CASSEROLE

2 leeks
2 onions
3 stalks celery
2 green peppers
¼ c. oil
1 pint mushrooms
8 oz. can water chestnuts, drained
½ lb. fresh bean sprouts

10 oz. pkg. frozen broccoli spears
6 oz. pkg. frozen pea pods
2 cloves garlic
10 oz. tin mushroom soup
1 c. water
¼ c. soya sauce
5 oz. can chow mein noodles

Cut leeks, onions, celery and green peppers to fit feed tube.

Slicer: Slice leeks and onions, using firm pressure. Slice celery and green peppers, using medium pressure. Heat oil in a large skillet or wok. Add sliced vegetables and brown over high heat, stirring constantly, for 3 to 4 minutes. Remove from heat and place in a large mixing bowl.

Slice mushrooms, using light pressure. Slice water chestnuts, using firm pressure. Add to skillet along with bean sprouts. Stir well. Cook for 2 to 3 minutes. Pour boiling water over broccoli and pea pods to separate.

Steel Knife: Drop garlic through feed tube while machine is running. Process until minced. Add soup, water and soya sauce and process a few seconds, until mixed. Combine all ingredients in mixing bowl **except** 1 cup chow mein noodles. Mix well. (May be prepared in advance up to this point.)

Bake in a lightly greased 9'' x 13'' pyrex baking dish at 375°F for 20 to 25 minutes, until piping hot. Top with reserved noodles during last 5 minutes of baking.

Yield: 8 to 10 servings. Best served fresh for maximum crunchiness. Excellent for the buffet table.

PEA PODS, PEPPERS & MUSHROOMS, CHINESE STYLE

2 onions
1 green pepper, halved & seeded
1 red pepper, halved & seeded
2 c. mushrooms
¼ lb. fresh pea pods (or 6 oz. pkg. frozen pea pods)
2 cloves garlic

1 tbsp. oil
2 tsp. instant chicken soup mix
1 tbsp. soya sauce
1½ tbsp. cornstarch dissolved in
¼ c. cold water
salt & pepper, to taste

Slicer: Cut onions and peppers to fit feed tube. Slice onions, using firm pressure. Transfer to a piece of paper towelling to absorb any excess moisture. Repeat with peppers, using light pressure. Pat dry on another piece of paper towelling. Repeat with mushrooms, using light pressure. Place on another piece of paper towelling. If pea pods are frozen, pour boiling water over to break them apart.

Steel Knife: Drop garlic through feed tube while machine is running. Process until minced, about 8 seconds.

Heat oil in a Wok or large skillet. Stir-fry garlic and onions over high heat for 30 seconds. Push to one side. Add peppers and stir-fry for 30 seconds longer. Push aside. Add mushrooms and stir-fry 30 seconds longer. Stir in pea pods, soup mix and soya sauce. Make a well in the centre of the Wok or skillet and blend the cornstarch/water mixture into the liquid. Cook until thickened, about 1 minute, stirring constantly. Add seasonings to taste and mix well.

Yield: 4 to 6 servings. Do not freeze.

CHINESE VEGETABLES ALMONDINE

(Easy and scrumptious. It takes more time to read the recipe than prepare it!)

10 oz. pkg. frozen peas
10 oz. pkg. frozen broccoli pieces
½ head cabbage (about 6 c. grated)
8 oz. can water chestnuts, drained
3 cloves garlic
2 onions, cut in chunks
1 c. slivered almonds
2 - 3 tbsp. oil
10 oz. tin whole mushrooms, drained
19 oz. can bean sprouts, drained & rinsed
8 oz. can bamboo shoots, drained

Sauce:
2 tbsp. oil or margarine
2 tbsp. flour
1 c. chicken broth
3 tbsp. soya sauce
freshly ground pepper

Cook frozen vegetables according to package directions, but undercook slightly.

Slicer: Cut cabbage to fit feed tube. Slice, using very light pressure. Set aside. Slice water chestnuts, using firm pressure. Set aside.

Steel Knife: Drop garlic through feed tube while machine is running. Process until minced. Scrape down sides of bowl. Add onions and process with 3 or 4 very quick on/off turns, until coarsely chopped.

Sauté almonds in hot oil in a wok or very large skillet. When golden, remove from pan and set aside. Add onions and garlic to wok and brown in hot oil for 2 minutes. Add mushrooms and brown lightly. Add cabbage and cook 2 minutes longer, stirring often. Add bean sprouts, water chestnuts, bamboo shoots, peas and broccoli. Mix well.

Sauce: Heat oil or margarine in a heavy saucepan. Add flour and cook for 1 minute over medium heat, stirring constantly. Add broth, soya sauce and pepper. Bring to a boil and simmer for 1 to 2 minutes. Combine with vegetables and mix well. Taste to adjust seasonings.

Transfer vegetables to a 9'' x 13'' greased casserole. (May be prepared in advance up to this point.) Bake uncovered at 350°F for 20 minutes. Sprinkle almonds over and bake 5 minutes longer.

Yield: 8 to 10 servings. May be frozen, but best served fresh.

PEA PODS & MUSHROOMS

6 oz. pkg. frozen pea pods
2 c. frozen peas
2 small onions
1 tbsp. margarine

10 oz. tin whole mushrooms, drained
salt and pepper, to taste
1 tsp. soya sauce

Cook pea pods and peas according to package directions, but undercook slightly.

Slicer: Slice onions, using heavy pressure. Sauté in margarine for 3 to 4 minutes. Add mushrooms and cook 1 minute longer. Add all remaining ingredients and toss to mix. Heat thoroughly.

Yield: 4 servings. Do not freeze.

SAUTEED GARLIC MUSHROOMS

2 cloves garlic
¼ c. margarine
1 lb. mushrooms (2 pints)

1 tsp. lemon juice
salt & pepper, to taste

Steel Knife: Drop garlic through feed tube while machine is running. Process until minced. Melt margarine in a heavy skillet. Stir in garlic and cook for 1 to 2 minutes.

Slicer: Stack mushrooms on their sides. Slice, using light pressure. Add to skillet and sauté on medium heat for 4 to 5 minutes, shaking pan to stir. Sprinkle with lemon juice, salt and pepper. Serve immediately.

Yield: 4 servings. Do not freeze.

MUSHROOM DUXELLES

1 onion or ½ c. shallots
¼ c. margarine (or butter)
1 pint mushrooms (about ½ lb.)

1 tbsp. lemon juice
¾ tsp. salt
¼ tsp. pepper

Steel Knife: Cut onion or shallots in chunks. Process until finely chopped, about 5 to 6 seconds. Melt margarine in a heavy skillet. Add onions and sauté on medium heat until transparent. Do not brown. Process mushrooms until finely chopped, about 8 to 10 seconds. Place in the corner of a tea towel and wring out mushrooms to remove excess moisture. Add mushrooms to skillet, sprinkle with lemon juice and cook, stirring, until dry, about 10 minutes. Add salt and pepper.

Duxelles will keep in refrigerator about 7 to 10 days if tightly covered. May be frozen. Many cooks freeze Duxelles in ice cube trays and transfer them to a tightly closed plastic bag. Frozen Duxelles Cubes may be added to stews and soups to add that ''gourmet'' touch.

Yield: about 1 cup.

ORIENTAL VEGETABLE DISH

2 pints (1 lb.) fresh
  mushrooms
8 oz. tin water chestnuts,
  drained
1 medium onion, halved
1 or 2 cloves garlic
½ c. butter or margarine

8 oz. tin bamboo shoots,
  drained
2 pkgs. frozen broccoli,
  cooked according to pkg.
  directions
salt and pepper, to taste

Slicer: Stack mushrooms sideways in feed tube. Slice, using light pressure. Slice water chestnuts and onion, using heavy pressure. Empty bowl.

Steel Knife: Drop garlic through feed tube while machine is running. Process until minced. Add butter and process until blended, scraping down sides of bowl as necessary. Place garlic butter in a large skillet. Melt over medium heat. Add onions, mushrooms and water chestnuts and sauté for 8 to 10 minutes, until golden. Add remaining ingredients and cook about 3 to 4 minutes longer over high heat, shaking pan often.

Yield: 8 servings. Do not freeze.

VEGETABLE CHOW MEIN

3 stalks celery
2 onions
1 green pepper
1 c. mushrooms
2 tbsp. corn or peanut oil
1 clove garlic, split
dash salt
¼ c. water or chicken broth

2 tbsp. soya sauce
¼ tsp. Accent, if desired
2 c. fresh or canned bean
   sprouts, washed and
   drained
2 tbsp. cornstarch
¼ c. cold water

Slicer: Cut vegetables to fit feed tube. Slice celery, using medium pressure. Transfer celery to paper towelling and pat dry. Repeat with remaining vegetables, using medium pressure for onions and light pressure for green pepper and mushrooms. Place each batch of vegetables in separate piles on paper towelling and pat dry.

Heat oil in a Wok until nearly smoking. Add garlic and salt; cook just until garlic has browned. Discard garlic. Add celery and cook over high heat, stirring constantly, about 30 seconds. Push up the sides of the Wok. Add onions and cook another 30 seconds. Push up the sides of the Wok. Repeat procedure with green pepper, then mushrooms. Add more oil if necessary. Add water, soya sauce and Accent. Reduce heat to medium, cover pan and cook 2 minutes longer. Uncover and stir in bean sprouts.

Push vegetables up the sides of the Wok and add cornstarch which has been dissolved in cold water. Stir into boiling liquid in the bottom of the Wok to make a thickened sauce. Stir all together and serve immediately on a bed of fluffy white rice. Garnish with chow mein noodles.

Yield: 4 to 6 servings. Do not freeze.

TUNA CHOW MEIN

Prepare basic recipe for Vegetable Chow Mein (above), but add two cans of well-drained flaked tuna along with the bean sprouts.

Yield: 4 to 6 servings. Do not freeze.

CHICKEN CHOW MEIN

Prepare basic recipe for Vegetable Chow Mein (above). Discard skin and bones from cooked leftover chicken and measure about 2 cups. (You will have enough to fill the feed tube twice.)

Slicer: Slice chicken, using very heavy pressure. Add to chow mein along with the bean sprouts. If desired, add 1 red pepper which has been sliced on the **Slicer,** using medium pressure. Season with salt & pepper.

Yield: 4 to 6 servings. Do not freeze.

BROCCOLI CHOW MEIN

Prepare basic recipe for Vegetable Chow Mein (above), but substitute 1 bunch of fresh broccoli for the mushrooms and bean sprouts. Cut broccoli flowers into individual flowerettes with a sharp knife. Using **Slicer,** slice broccoli stems, using medium pressure.

Begin with the celery, then the onions, then the green pepper, then the broccoli stems, then the broccoli flowerettes. Add liquid and seasoning, cover and cook for 2 minutes. Add corstarch-water mixture; cook until thickened, stirring to mix, and serve immediately. Delicious as a side-dish.

Yield: 4 to 6 servings. Do not freeze.

NO-FRY EGGPLANT PARMESAN

(Recipe may be halved for a small family, but I prepare
the full recipe and freeze the leftovers for another day.)

2 eggplants (about 1½ lb. each)
salt
3 oz. Parmesan cheese (¾ c.
  grated)
1 c. bread or cracker crumbs
dash salt & pepper
¼ tsp. garlic powder

½ lb. Mozzerella cheese (2 c.
grated)
2 eggs
2 tbsp. cold water
8 oz. can tomato or pizza
sauce
1 pkg. dry onion soup mix

Peel eggplant and slice lengthwise into ½'' slices. Sprinkle on both sides with salt. Let stand for 20 minutes. Pat dry on paper towelling to remove excess moisture.

Steel Knife: If Parmesan cheese is not already grated, break into small chunks with a chisel or blunt knife. Process until fine. Leave about ½ cup Parmesan cheese in processor bowl and set aside remaining ¼ cup. Add crumbs, salt, pepper and garlic powder to processor bowl. Process for 3 or 4 seconds to mix. Transfer to a sheet of waxed paper.

Grater: Grate Mozzerella cheese, using medium pressure. Set aside.

Steel Knife: Process eggs with cold water for 1 or 2 seconds. Transfer to a flat plate. Dip eggplant slices first in egg, then in crumb mixture. Arrange in a single layer on lightly greased cookie sheets.

Bake at 400°F for 20 minutes. Turn slices over and bake 15 minutes longer. Top each slice with 1 or 2 tbsp. sauce, some grated Mozzerella, about 1 tsp. reserved Parmesan cheese, and about 1 tsp. dry onion soup mix. Bake 12 to 15 minutes longer, until golden.

Yield: about 10 to 12 slices. Allow 1 or 2 slices per serving. Delicious with Caesar salad and garlic bread. May be frozen.

PROCESSOR MASHED POTATOES ✓

3 - 4 potatoes, peeled & cut in
  1½'' chunks (about 3 cups)
boiling salted water

¼ c. milk
3 tbsp. butter or margarine
salt & pepper, to taste

Cook potatoes in boiling salted water until tender. Drain well. Return saucepan to heat for about 1 minute to remove excess moisture from potatoes. Shake pan to prevent scorching.

Plastic Knife: (Do **not** use Steel Knife or potatoes will become a glue-like mess!) Add drained and dried potatoes. They should not come above the top of the blade, or they will not process properly.

Process potatoes with 4 to 5 quick on/off turns. Remove cover and cut through potatoes several times with a rubber spatula to push the larger chunks down towards the bottom of the bowl. Add milk and butter. Season to taste. Process about 15 to 20 seconds longer, scraping down sides of bowl once or twice. Mixture should be smooth and lump free. Do not overprocess.

Yield: 4 servings. Do not freeze for maximum flavor.

Note: Processing develops the starch in the potatoes, making them sticky rather than fluffy if you are not careful. If this happens, add 1 egg plus ½ tsp. baking powder and process on the **Steel Knife** about 20 to 30 seconds, until smooth and sticky. Spread in a greased 9'' pie plate, sprinkle with paprika and bake at 375°F about 30 minutes, or until brown and crusty.

EGGPLANT ITALIANO

(If you don't tell them it's eggplant, I won't.
It tastes like pizza without the crust.)

2 cloves garlic	1 eggplant (about 1¼ lbs.),
1 large onion, quartered	peeled
1 stalk celery	salt & pepper, to taste
1 green pepper	½ tsp. oregano
1 or 2 tbsp. oil, optional	19 oz. can tomatoes
1 c. mushrooms	¼ - ½ lb. Mozzerella cheese
	(1 - 2 cups grated)

Steel Knife: Drop garlic through feed tube while machine is running. Process until minced. Add onion and process with 3 to 4 quick on/off turns, until coarsely chopped.

Slicer: Cut remaining vegetables to fit feed tube. Slice celery and green pepper, using light pressure. Sauté with onion and garlic in hot oil in a large skillet about 5 minutes. (Oil may be omitted if you are using a teflon skillet.) Slice mushrooms, using light pressure. Add to skillet and sauté 1 minute longer.

French-Fry Blade or Slicer: Slice eggplant, using firm pressure. (If you do not have a French-Fry Blade, it is best to cut the eggplant so that it is half the width of the feed tube. In this way the slices will not be too large.) Add to skillet, stir well and cook about 5 minutes. Add seasonings and tomatoes. Cover and heat to simmering. (May be prepared in advance up to this point and refrigerated or frozen until needed.) Place in a greased shallow casserole. (Oven-to-table type is ideal.)

Grater: Grate cheese, using medium pressure. Sprinkle over eggplant. Bake at 375°F about 25 to 30 minutes, until bubbly and golden.

Yield: 4 to 6 servings.

Note: This is an excellent meal for calorie counters. Use maximum amount of Mozzerella cheese to give you your full protein for lunch, and eliminate oil. 4 servings of 294 calories each. If made as a side dish with minimum amount of cheese, recipe yields 4 servings of 194 calories each, or 6 servings of 129 calories.

BARBECUED LYONNAISE POTATOES √

4 large potatoes, pared	salt & pepper, to taste
2 small onions	paprika, to taste
2 tbsp. margarine	3 sprigs parsley

Cut a large sheet of heavy duty tinfoil or fold regular strength foil to double thickness. Insert **Slicer** in processor. Cut potatoes and onions to fit feed tube. Slice, using medium pressure. Arrange in ½'' thick layer in the centre of foil. Dot with margarine and sprinkle with seasonings.

Steel Knife: Chop parsley until minced, about 5 seconds. Sprinkle over potatoes. Wrap loosely, sealing all ends well.

Barbecue Method: Place on grill of barbecue about 4'' from hot coals. Cook about 20 minutes, turning package over after 10 minutes.

Oven Method: Bake at 450°F about 20 minutes. Do not turn.

Yield: 4 servings. Do not freeze.

OVEN-FRIED CHEESY POTATOES ✓

½ c. margarine or butter
6 medium potatoes, peeled
1 oz. Parmesan cheese (¼ c. grated)

salt and pepper, to taste
1 tsp. garlic powder
1 tsp. paprika

Preheat oven to 375°F. Melt margarine on a 15'' x 10'' x 1'' cookie sheet.

Slicer: Cut potatoes to fit feed tube. Slice, using firm pressure. Dip potatoes in melted margarine on both sides to coat. If cheese is not already grated, process on **Steel Knife** until fine. Sprinkle potatoes with cheese and seasonings. Bake at 375°F for 35 minutes, until crisp. Baste occasionally.

Yield: 4 to 6 servings. Do not freeze.

BEST-EVER SCALLOPED POTATOES ✓

4 to 6 medium potatoes, pared
salt & pepper, to taste
3 tbsp. margarine
3 tbsp. flour

2 tsp. instant chicken soup mix
1½ c. boiling water
paprika

Slicer: Cut potatoes to fit feed tube. Slice, using medium pressure. Arrange in layers in a well-greased 2 quart casserole. Sprinkle each layer with salt and pepper.

Steel Knife: Process margarine with flour and soup mix until blended, about 5 seconds. Pour boiling water through feed tube while machine is running and process until smooth. Transfer sauce to a heavy bottomed saucepan and cook over medium heat, stirring, until bubbly and thick. Add salt & pepper to taste. Pour hot sauce over potatoes. Sprinkle with paprika. Bake uncovered at 350°F for 1¼ hours, or until tender and golden brown.

Yield: 4 servings. Do not freeze.

SCALLOPED POTATOES & MUSHROOMS

2 medium onions, halved
1 pint mushrooms
2 tbsp. margarine

Best-Ever Scalloped Potatoes (above)

Slicer: Slice onions and mushrooms, using light pressure. Sauté in margarine for 8 to 10 minutes, until golden.

Follow directions for Best-Ever Scalloped Potatoes, but spread mushrooms and onions between layers of potatoes. Bake as directed.

Yield: 4 servings. Do not freeze.

EASY POTATO PANCAKES
(Single Processing Method — Fine Texture)

165

potatoes, pared	1 tsp. baking powder
	¾ tsp. salt
2 eggs	freshly ground pepper
⅓ c. flour	oil for frying

Steel Knife: Cut potatoes in chunks and onion in half. Place in processor with eggs and process until puréed, about 20 to 30 seconds. Add remaining ingredients except oil and process a few seconds longer to blend into a smooth mixture.

Pour oil to about ⅛'' depth into a large skillet. When hot, drop in potato mixture by large spoonfuls to form pancakes. Brown well on both sides. Drain well on paper towels.

Yield: about 2 dozen, or about 5 dozen miniatures for hors d'oeuvres. May be frozen.

To reheat: Place pancakes in a single layer on an ungreased foil-lined cookie sheet. Bake uncovered at 450°F for 7 or 8 minutes, until crisp and hot.

LACY POTATO PANCAKES
(Double Processing Method — Coarse Texture)

Use same ingredients as for Easy Potato Pancakes (above). Insert **Grater.** Cut potatoes to fit feed tube. Grate, using very light pressure. Empty bowl and place potatoes in a colander. Rinse under cold water to remove starch. (This will keep the pancakes from turning dark.) Grate onion, using medium pressure. Without emptying bowl, insert **Plastic Knife** in processor. Process all ingredients for a few seconds, just until mixed. (Some people prefer to use the **Steel Knife** and process the pancake mixture with 3 or 4 very quick on/off turns.)

Pour oil to about ⅛'' depth into a large skillet. When hot, drop in potato mixture by large spoonfuls to form pancakes. Flatten slightly with the back of the spoon. Brown well on both sides. Drain well on paper towels.

Yield: about 2 dozen, or about 5 dozen miniatures for hors d'oeuvres. May be frozen. Reheat as for Easy Potato Pancakes.

RICH MAN'S POTATO LATKES (Pancakes)
(Only poor people added flour or crumbs to stretch the number of latkes their recipe would yield. This recipe uses just potatoes and lots of eggs. They are delicious and very crisp.)

6 large potatoes, peeled	1 tsp. salt
1 onion, halved	¼ tsp. pepper
5 eggs	oil for frying

Cut potatoes into 1½'' chunks. Insert **Steel Knife.** Add 1 potato at a time. Process with 8 or 10 very quick on/off turns, until coarsely chopped. Empty bowl and transfer chopped potatoes to a colander or strainer. Repeat with remaining potatoes. Wash under cold running water to remove excess starch. Squeeze out excess moisture.

Process onion until minced, about 6 to 8 seconds. Add eggs and process 3 or 4 seconds longer. Place all ingredients in a large mixing bowl and mix well.

Pour oil to about ⅛'' depth into a large skillet. When hot, drop in potato mixture by small spoonfuls to form pancakes. Brown well on both sides. Drain well on paper towels.

Yield: about 40 bite-size latkes. Freezes well. To reheat, bake at 450°F for a few minutes, until crisp and hot. Do not cover.

POTATO KUGEL (Crispy Potato Pudding) √

(Your processor takes the hard work out of this family favorite!)

¼ c. oil	3 eggs
4 large potatoes, peeled & cut in chunks	1½ tsp. salt (or to taste)
	¼ tsp. pepper
1 large onion, quartered	¼ c. flour or potato starch

Place oil in an 8" square or 7" x 11" oblong Pyrex casserole. Preheat oven to 375°F. Place casserole in oven and heat until oil is piping hot, about 5 minutes.

Meanwhile, insert **Grater** in processor. Grate potatoes, using fairly light pressure. (The harder you press, the coarser the texture of the potatoes.) Transfer to a colander. (If you wish to wash out the starch and keep the potatoes white, rinse under cold running water.) Press out excess moisture and pat dry with paper towelling.

Steel Knife: Process onion until minced, about 6 to 8 seconds. Scrape down sides of bowl. Add eggs and seasonings. Process for 3 to 4 seconds. Combine with grated potatoes and flour in a large mixing bowl. Add about 3 tbsp. of the hot oil, leaving the remaining oil in the casserole. Mix well.

Pour in potato mixture. Sprinkle with a little additional oil on top. Bake uncovered at 375°F for about 1 hour, or until well-browned and crispy.

Yield: 6 to 8 servings. Do not freeze.

SWEET POTATO KUGEL

(An unusual pudding made from sweet potatoes. Great with poultry!)

4 medium sweet potatoes (about 2 lb.)	¼ tsp. nutmeg
	¼ tsp. cloves
1 onion, cut in chunks	¾ c. brown sugar, packed
6 eggs	½ c. flour
1 tsp. salt	½ tsp. baking powder
2 tsp. cinnamon (or to taste)	3 tbsp. oil

Grater: Pare sweet potatoes and cut to fit feed tube. Grate, using firm pressure. Empty into a large mixing bowl. You should have about 6 cups grated sweet potatoes.

Steel Knife: Process onion until minced, about 6 to 8 seconds. Add eggs, spices and brown sugar. Process until blended, about 8 to 10 seconds. Add to sweet potatoes. Add flour and baking powder and mix well.

Heat oil at 400°F in a 7" x 11" Pyrex baking dish. When hot, pour in sweet potato mixture and sprinkle a few drops of oil on top. Bake at 400°F about 1 hour, until nicely browned.

Yield: about 8 to 10 servings. Delicious with chicken or turkey. Freezes well. Recipe may be halved, if desired, and baked in a 1½ quart casserole.

RATATOUILLE

3 cloves garlic	1 eggplant (about 1¼ lb.),
1 large onion, quartered	peeled
1 green pepper, cut in 1"	½ tsp. basil
chunks	1 tsp. oregano
1 c. mushrooms	salt & pepper, to taste
2 tbsp. oil (optional)	19 oz. tin tomatoes
3 unpeeled zucchini (about 1 lb.)	5½ oz. tin tomato paste

Steel Knife: Drop garlic through feed tube while machine is running. Process until minced. Discard peel. Add onion and green pepper. Process with 3 or 4 quick on/off turns, until coarsely chopped.

Slicer: Slice mushrooms, using light pressure.

Sauté garlic, onion, green pepper and mushrooms in oil or on a teflon skillet on medium heat until golden, about 7 to 8 minutes.

Slicer or French Fry Blade: Cut zucchini and eggplant to fit feed tube. Slice, using heavy pressure. Add to skillet. Sauté 10 minutes longer, stirring occasionally. Add remaining ingredients, cover and simmer for 30 minutes, stirring occasionally. Serve hot or cold.

Yield: 6 to 8 servings. Freezes well.

SWISS RATATOUILLE CASSEROLE

1 c. slivered almonds	28 oz. can tomatoes
2 - 3 tbsp. oil	1½ tsp. salt
1½ lb. zucchini	1 tsp. pepper
1½ lb. eggplant	1½ tsp. basil
2 medium onions	1½ tsp. flour
2 tsp. instant chicken or beef	2 cloves garlic
soup mix (see Note)	½ lb. Swiss cheese slices

Sauté almonds in oil until golden. Remove from pan and set aside.

Slicer: Cut zucchini, eggplant and onions to fit feed tube. (You may peel the eggplant and zucchini if you wish.) Slice, using firm pressure. Empty bowl as necessary. Add vegetables to pan and sauté for 10 minutes. Add soup mix and cook 5 minutes longer. Add tomatoes, seasonings, flour and almonds.

Steel Knife: Drop garlic through feed tube while machine is running. Process until minced. Add to eggplant mixture. Transfer to a large casserole which has been lightly greased. Top with cheese slices. Bake at 400°F for 30 to 40 minutes.

Yield: 8 servings as a side dish, or 4 to 6 servings as a main dish. Serve with salad and garlic bread. Also delicious with fish.

To Freeze: Prepare eggplant mixture completely, omitting cheese. Place in a freezer-proof casserole and freeze until needed. Thaw and top with cheese slices. Bake as directed. If casserole is not completely thawed before baking, add a few minutes longer to the baking time.

Note: If you observe the Jewish dietary laws, use soup mix which is pareve (containing no actual chicken or beef).

CHINESE STYLE BOILED RICE

1 c. long grain rice   1 tsp. salt
1¾ c. cold water

Place rice in a fine strainer and rinse thoroughly under cold running water. Drain. Place in a 2 quart saucepan with 1¾ cups cold water and salt. Bring to a boil uncovered on high heat. Reduce heat to simmer, cover and cook 20 minutes, until dry. Turn off heat and let rice stand for 20 minutes, covered. Stir well while hot for separate fluffy grains.

Yield: 3 cups cooked rice (6 servings).

Note: Do not stir rice during cooking, or it will stick to bottom of pan. Keep leftover rice in refrigerator. Excellent for fried rice. Rice may become hard if frozen.

NO-FRY FRIED RICE ✓

(An easy company dish)

2 c. rice
¼ c. oil
1 pkg. dry onion soup mix
3 tbsp. soya sauce
1 green or red pepper, halved
  & seeded
8 oz. tin water chestnuts

10 oz. tin mushrooms, sliced
8 oz. tin bamboo shoots
3½ c. liquid (reserved juices
  from canned vegetables,
  plus cold water)
salt & pepper, to taste

Combine rice, oil, soup mix and soya sauce in a large casserole. Mix well.

Slicer: Slice pepper, using light pressure. Drain all canned vegetables and reserve liquid. Slice water chestnuts, using firm pressure. Add all ingredients except seasonings to casserole and mix. Cover and bake at 350°F for about 1 hour, or until all liquid is absorbed. Season to taste.

Yield: 8 to 10 servings. May be frozen or prepared in advance.

RICE PILAF

2 onions, quartered
1 stalk celery, cut in 2"
  chunks
½ green pepper, cut in 2"
  chunks
4 tbsp. margarine
1½ c. long grain rice
3 c. boiling water

2 tbsp. instant chicken soup
  mix
salt & pepper, to taste
½ tsp. dill weed
3 sprigs parsley
½ c. leftover chicken, if
  desired

Steel Knife: Process onions with 3 or 4 quick on/off turns, until coarsely chopped. Empty bowl. Process celery with green pepper, using 3 or 4 quick on/off turns, until chopped. Melt 3 tbsp. margarine in a heavy saucepan or skillet. Add vegetables and sauté on medium heat for 2 to 3 minutes. Add raw rice and cook 2 minutes longer, stirring. Add boiling water, soup mix and seasoning. Cover and simmer for 20 minutes.

Steel Knife: Process parsley until minced. Add chicken and process with quick on/off turns, until coarsely chopped. Add parsley, chicken and 1 tbsp. margarine to rice. Remove from heat and let stand covered for 10 minutes. Fluff with a fork.

Yield: 6 to 8 servings. May be frozen, but rice has a tendency to get hard after freezing.

CHINESE FRIED RICE ✓

3 c. cold boiled rice (see
　*Note)
3 green onions, cut in 3"
　lengths
1 stalk celery, cut in 2"
　lengths
½ c. cooked chicken, if desired

2 eggs
3 - 4 tbsp. oil
½ c. green peas (canned or
　frozen)
2 tbsp. soya sauce
pepper & Accent, to taste

*Note: Rice must be cold before you fry it to get the best results. Cook in advance, break up while still hot, and let stand until needed. Leftover boiled rice is ideal. It will keep for several days in the refrigerator. See recipe for Chinese Style Boiled Rice (p. 169).

Steel Knife: Process green onions and celery with 2 or 3 quick on/off turns, until coarsely chopped. Empty bowl onto a piece of wax paper and set aside. Discard skin and bones from chicken. Chop with 2 or 3 quick on/off turns. Set aside separately from vegetables. Process eggs for 2 or 3 seconds to mix.

Heat about 1 tbsp. oil in a large skillet or Wok. Add eggs and scramble them briefly. Remove from pan. Add remaining oil to pan. Add onions and celery and stir-fry for 30 seconds. Add rice and mix thoroughly, until heated through. Add remaining ingredients and stir well. (Frozen peas should be thawed first, but it is not necessary to pre-cook them.) Serve piping hot.

Yield: 4 to 6 servings.

To reheat: Place in a covered casserole in a 350°F oven for 15 minutes. Uncover and heat 5 to 10 minutes longer. May be frozen, but rice sometimes has a tendency to become a little hard. Flavor will not be affected.

BREADED ZUCCHINI ✓
(Zucchini remains crisp and crunchy)

3 medium unpeeled zucchini
　(about 1 lb.)
salt (about 1 tsp.)
1 egg, lightly beaten
1 c. toasted bread crumbs

½ tsp. salt
¼ tsp. pepper
¼ tsp. garlic powder
¼ tsp. oregano
oil for frying

Wash zucchini and pat dry. Trim off ends and cut zucchini to fit feed tube. Insert **Slicer.** Slice, using firm pressure. Sprinkle with salt and let stand 20 to 30 minutes to remove excess moisture. Pat dry. Dip into beaten egg, then into crumbs which have been combined with seasonings.

Heat about 3 tbsp. oil in a large skillet. Brown zucchini slices a few at a time on medium heat, about 2 or 3 minutes per side. Watch carefully to prevent burning. Drain on paper towels.

Yield: 3 to 4 servings. Do not freeze.

To reheat: Brown very lightly. Drain well on paper towels, then arrange in a single layer on cookie sheet. Refrigerate until needed. Bake at 425°F just until heated through and crispy.

Variation: Add 3 to 4 tbsp. grated Parmesan cheese to the bread crumb mixture.

CRISPY FRIED ZUCCHINI ✓
(As served at a favourite Montreal Italian restaurant)

Follow recipe for Breaded Zucchini (above), but eliminate beaten egg and substitute flour for bread crumbs. Coat zucchini slices with seasoned flour. Sauté them in hot oil. Delicious!

LEEK AND RICE CASSEROLE

4 leeks	boiling water
1 green pepper	1 c. tomato juice
2 stalks celery	1 c. cooked rice
2 tbsp. oil	salt and pepper, to taste

Soak leeks in cold water until clean. Dry well, and trim off most of tough green ends. Cut all vegetables to fit feed tube.

Slicer: Slice leeks, using firm pressure. Set aside separately. Slice green pepper and celery, using light pressure. Sauté celery and green pepper in oil on medium heat about 5 minutes, until golden. Stir in leeks. Add boiling water just to cover, and simmer for 5 minutes, covered. Add tomato juice, and bring to a boil. Add rice. Season to taste. Cover and simmer about 10 minutes, until leeks are tender. Freezes well.

Yield: 4 to 6 servings.

ZUCCHINI PUFFS

3 oz. Mozzerella cheese (¾ c. grated)	2 eggs
	½ tsp. salt
2 medium unpeeled zucchini (2 c. grated)	dash of pepper
	½ c. bread crumbs
½ small onion	

Grater: Grate cheese, using medium pressure. Empty bowl. Cut zucchini to fit feed tube. Grate zucchini, using firm pressure. Measure 2 cups, lightly packed.

Steel Knife: Process onion until minced, about 6 seconds. Add eggs and seasoning and process for 2 seconds. Add bread crumbs, zucchini and cheese to egg mixture. Process with 2 or 3 quick on/off turns, just until mixed. Do not overprocess.

Divide mixture evenly in 10 greased muffin cups. Bake at 375°F for 30 minutes. These will fall slightly upon standing but the taste and texture will not be affected. Serve hot.

Yield: 10 puffs of about 75 calories each. Freezes well.

SPINACH NOODLES

10 oz. fresh or frozen spinach	4 eggs
3 c. flour	2 tbsp. water
1 tsp. salt	

Discard stems from fresh spinach and wash the leaves well. Cook fresh spinach in the water clinging to the leaves in a covered saucepan for 3 to 4 minutes. (Cook frozen spinach according to package directions.) Drain and squeeze very dry.

Steel Knife: Process spinach until finely minced. Transfer to a small bowl. Wipe out processor bowl with paper towelling.

Steel Knife: Process flour and salt for 2 or 3 seconds. Add eggs, spinach and water and process until dough forms a ball around the blades and is well kneaded, about 25 to 30 seconds.

Divide dough into 8 equal pieces. Roll each piece on a floured board into an 8" square. Proceed as for Home-Made Pasta (p. 172).

Yield: 6 to 8 servings or 1½ lb. noodles.

Note: Uncooked noodles may be frozen up to 1 month or noodles may be stored for 2 or 3 days in the refrigerator in a large plastic bag. Flour noodles to prevent sticking.

HOME-MADE PASTA ✓

(The processor mixes up this delicious and easy pasta
in just 30 seconds! It is easily rolled and cut by hand,
or if it becomes a habit, invest in a pasta machine.)

1½ c. flour   1½ tbsp. water
½ tsp. salt   1 tbsp. oil, if desired
2 eggs

Steel Knife: Process flour with salt for 3 or 4 seconds. Add eggs and water and process until dough is well kneaded and forms a ball on the blades, about 25 to 30 seconds. Divide in four equal pieces. Roll each piece on a floured board into a 10" square. Dough should be as thin as possible. Let dry on towels about 20 minutes, turning each piece of dough over after 10 minutes for more even drying. (You may eliminate drying the pasta, if desired.)

Roll up each piece of dough jelly-roll style. Cut with a sharp knife into ½" wide strips (or whatever width you want noodles to be). Unroll and place on a lightly floured towel to dry for 1 to 2 hours. (The kids love to help unroll the dough and lay it out.) If noodles are used immediately, it is not necessary to dry them before cooking.

Bring 4 quarts of water to a boil. Add 4 tsp. salt. Cook noodles for about 3 or 4 minutes, or until "al dente" (slightly firm, but done). Cooking time will vary, depending on dryness of noodles. Drain immediately.

Yield: 3 to 4 servings, or about ¾ lb. noodles. This is the equivalent of a 12 oz. pkg.

Note: Uncooked noodles may be frozen up to 1 month, or may be stored for 2 to 3 days in the refrigerator in a plastic bag. Recipe may be doubled successfully and processed in one batch.

To Use Pasta Machine: Crank each piece of dough through the widest opening of machine rollers 4 or 5 times, flouring and folding it in half each time you run it through. Then reset the rollers and run the pasta through subsequent, ever-narrowing openings, until you have a long, thin length of pasta. (If it becomes too long and awkward to handle, just cut in half.) Flour the dough from time to time to prevent sticking. Spread on towels to dry for 20 minutes, turning each piece of dough over after 10 minutes. (You may eliminate drying the pasta, if desired.)

Change handle of the machine from roller to cutter position for thin or wide noodles. Roll pasta through desired cutters. Spread cut pasta to dry for 1 to 2 hours. Cook as directed.

FETTUCINE: Cut in ½" strips. Cook 3 to 5 minutes.

LASAGNA NOODLES: Cut in 2½" strips x 10". Cook 8 to 10 minutes.

CANNELLONI & MANICOTTI: Cut in 4" squares. Cook 7 to 8 minutes.

SPINACH LASAGNA NOODLES

Follow directions for Spinach Noodles (p. 171).

Divide dough in 3 equal pieces. Roll out each piece of dough on a well-floured board as thin as possible. Place on a towel and let dry for 20 minutes. Cut into strips 2½" wide by 10" long. Place on towels and let dry one to two hours. Cook in boiling salted water for 8 to 10 minutes, until "al dente", (slightly firm, but done). Drain well. Use in your favourite recipe.

Yield: 1½ lb. lasagna noodles.

NOODLE PANCAKES

½ - 12 oz. pkg. fine noodles
2 eggs
1 small onion

salt & pepper, to taste
oil for frying

Cook noodles according to package directions. Drain well and return to saucepan. Insert **Steel Knife** in processor. Process eggs with onion until blended, about 8 to 10 seconds. Add to noodles. Season to taste. Heat oil in skillet. Drop noodle mixture from a large spoon into hot oil. Brown on medium heat on both sides. Drain on paper towelling. Serve as a side dish with meat or chicken.

Yield: 16 to 18 latkes. Freezes well.

Note: These may be prepared in advance. To reheat, place in a single layer on a foil-lined baking sheet. Bake uncovered at 425°F 10 minutes, until hot and crispy.

SWISS STYLE NOODLES

½ -12 oz. pkg. broad noodles
   (about 3 cups cooked)
1 large onion, quartered
⅓ c. butter or margarine

¼ c. toasted bread crumbs
salt, pepper, paprika, to
   taste

Cook noodles according to package directions; drain well. Process onion on **Steel Knife** with 2 or 3 quick on/off turns, until coarsely chopped.

Sauté onion in margarine or butter in a large skillet until golden, about 8 to 10 minutes. Add bread crumbs and brown lightly, about 1 minute. Add noodles and seasonings and mix well.

Yield: 4 to 6 servings. Do not freeze.

Note: You may make your own noodles, if desired. Follow recipe for Home-Made Pasta (p. 172).

LOKSHIN KUGEL
(Noodle Pudding)

Home-Made Pasta (p. 172) or
   12 oz. pkg. medium or broad
   noodles
¼ c. oil

1 large onion, quartered
4 or 5 eggs
salt & pepper, to taste

Prepare noodles according to package or recipe directions. Drain well. Return to saucepan. Heat oil in a 7″ x 11″ pyrex baking dish at 425°F.

Steel Knife: Process onion with 2 or 3 quick on/off turns, until coarsely chopped. Stir into hot oil. Leave in oven about 5 minutes, until onions are lightly browned.

Steel Knife: Process eggs for 2 or 3 seconds. Combine with noodles and seasonings. Stir into oil/onion mixture. Bake uncovered at 400°F for 1 hour, until golden brown.

Yield: 8 to 10 servings. Freezes well.

NOODLE RAISIN KUGEL

Make Lokshin Kugel (above), but eliminate onion. Add ½ cup raisins, ¼ cup sugar and 1 tsp. cinnamon to noodle mixture. Bake as directed. Freezes well.

APPLE NOODLE KUGEL

Make Lokshin Kugel (above) but eliminate onion. Peel and core 3 apples. Insert **Grater** in processor. Grate apples, using medium pressure. Add grated apples, ⅓ c. white or brown sugar and ½ tbsp. cinnamon to noodle mixture. Bake as directed. May be frozen.

EASY MUSHROOM NOODLE KUGEL (Noodle Pudding)

Home-Made Pasta (p. 172) or   1 stalk celery, cut in 2"chunks
12 oz. pkg. broad noodles   2 tbsp. oil
1 clove garlic   10 oz. can condensed
1 large onion, quartered   mushroom soup
1 green pepper, cut in 2"   salt & pepper, to taste
chunks

Prepare noodles according to package or recipe directions. Drain well. Return to saucepan.

Steel Knife: Drop garlic through feed tube while machine is running. Process until minced. Process onion with 2 or 3 quick on/off turns, until coarsely chopped. Empty bowl. Process green pepper and celery with 3 or 4 quick on/off turns, until chopped. Sauté vegetables in hot oil for 5 minutes. Add vegetables, soup and seasoning to noodles and mix well. Place in a greased 7" x 11" pyrex baking dish. Bake uncovered at 350°F for 50 to 60 minutes.

Yield: 8 servings. Do not freeze.

TOMATO MUSHROOM KUGEL (Noodle Pudding)
(Tastes like Pizza!)

Follow recipe for Easy Mushroom Noodle Kugel (above), but substitute an 11 oz. can of tomato mushroom sauce for soup. Add ¼ tsp. oregano with the seasonings.

Yield: 8 servings. Do not freeze. Delicious!

WARM WATER KNISH DOUGH ✓
(A crisp dough which may be filled with cheese, potatoes, cooked ground meat or chicken.)

2 eggs   ½ tsp. salt
½ c. oil   2 tsp. baking powder
½ c. warm water   2½ c. flour

Steel Knife: Process eggs, oil and water until mixed, about 4 or 5 seconds. Add remaining ingredients and process **just** until blended, about 8 seconds. Do not overprocess or dough will become tough. Let dough stand about 10 minutes while you prepare your filling. (Suggested fillings:- Cheese, Potato, Corned Beef, Chicken, Chopped Liver, Meat.)

Divide dough in four. Take one piece, coat lightly on all sides with a little flour, and pat into a rectangle. Roll into a large rectangle, as thin as possible, on a floured board.

Place a row of filling along one side, about 1" from edge. Roll up. Using the edge of your hand, press down on roll, and with a sawing motion, cut through dough. Repeat every 2". Turn knishes on end and press cut edge in slightly. Repeat with remaining dough and filling. Bake on a lightly greased cookie sheet at 350°F for about 35 minutes, until golden brown.

Yield: 24 to 30 knishes. Freezes well, but underbake slightly.

To Freeze: Unbaked knishes may be successfully frozen. Freeze on a cookie sheet, then store in plastic bags in the freezer. Bake uncovered from frozen state at 350°F for 45 minutes, or until golden brown. This produces knishes having that "just-baked" flavour.

FLAKY POTATO KNISHES ✓
(A crisp baked dumpling filled with potatoes.)

Flaky Ginger Ale Pastry,　　　Potato Filling (p. 176)
double recipe (p. 305)

Prepare dough as directed and chill. (You will have 4 balls of dough.) Prepare filling and **cool completely.**

Roll out one portion of dough on a pastry cloth into a rectangle about 8'' x 12'', using a stocking cover on your rolling pin.

Place ¼ of the filling in a row along one edge, about 1'' from edges. Roll up. Using the edge of your hand, press down on roll, and with a sawing motion, cut through dough. Repeat about every 2''. Turn knishes on end, pressing ends in slightly. Repeat with remaining dough and filling.

Bake at 350°F on a lightly greased baking sheet for 35 to 40 minutes, until golden brown.

Yield: 2 dozen knishes. Delicious!

To Freeze: These knishes may be baked first, frozen up to 1 month, and reheated. Thaw, then reheat at 350°F about 12 to 15 minutes. Do not over-brown knishes on the first baking if you plan to freeze them.

Unbaked knishes may be successfully frozen. Freeze on a cookie sheet, then store in plastic bags in freezer. Bake uncovered from frozen state at 350°F for 45 minutes, or until golden brown.

KASHA KNISH
(A long roll of crispy dough filled with buckwheat groats.)

1 **large onion**　　　　　　　**salt and pepper, to taste**
3 **tbsp. oil or chicken fat**　　½ **recipe for Warm Water**
1 **c. kasha (buckwheat groats)**　　**Knish Dough (p. 174)**
2½ **c. boiling water (approximately)**

Steel Knife: Cut onion in chunks. Process with 3 or 4 quick on/off turns, until coarsely chopped. Sauté onion lightly in hot oil in a large skillet which has a cover. Add kasha and stir well. Brown over medium heat, stirring often. When nicely browned, add boiling water to cover. Add seasonings and stir well. Cover and simmer about 5 minutes, until water is absorbed. Let cool.

Prepare dough as directed. Place ½ the filling along one side, about 1'' from edge. Roll up, turning in ends. Do not cut. Repeat with remaining dough and filling. Bake at 350°F for 35 minutes, until golden brown. Slice to serve.

Yield: 2 rolls, each making 6 slices. Freezes well.

MEAT OR CHICKEN FILLING ✓

2 **lb. cooked leftover meat or**　　2 **eggs**
chicken (about 4 cups)　　**salt & pepper, to taste**
½ **c. leftover gravy (see Note)**

Steel Knife: Cut meat or chicken into 1½'' chunks. Process half the meat until minced, about 6 to 8 seconds. Add half the gravy, 1 egg and seasoning. Process 3 or 4 seconds longer, until mixed. Empty bowl and repeat with remaining ingredients.

Yield: about 4 cups filling. May be frozen.

Note: If you do not have any gravy, use chicken or beef broth. Fried onion may be added for additional flavor. Recipe may be halved, if desired.

POTATO FILLING √

m potatoes, peeled   ¼ c. oil or margarine
t in chunks   2 eggs
alted water   salt & pepper, to taste
3 or 4 onions, cut in chunks

Cook potatoes in boiling salted water until tender. Drain well. Return saucepan to heat for about 1 minute to remove excess moisture from potatoes. Shake pan to prevent scorching.

Steel Knife: Process half the onion, using 3 or 4 quick on/off turns, until coarsely chopped. Empty bowl and repeat with remaining onions. Sauté in oil until golden brown. Using **Steel Knife,** process eggs for 1 or 2 seconds.

Mash potatoes with potato masher. (To prepare on the processor, potatoes would have to be done in several batches, and there is always the problem of overprocessing.) Add onions, oil, eggs and seasonings and mix well.

Yield: about 4 cups filling. May be frozen.

Note: To make half the amount of potato filling, you might wish to use your processor. Use **Plastic Knife.** (The Steel Knife will produce a glue-like mess!) Add drained and dried potatoes. Chunks should be no larger than 1½''. Process potatoes with 4 or 5 quick on/off turns. Remove cover and cut through potatoes with a rubber spatula to push the larger chunks down towards the bottom of the bowl. Add eggs and seasonings. Process about 15 to 20 seconds longer, scraping down sides of bowl once or twice. Add onions and oil and process just a few seconds longer. Do not overprocess.

CORNED BEEF FILLING

1 lb. lean corned beef,   1 onion
smoked meat or pickled   3 eggs
brisket   ½ tsp. dry mustard

Cut meat into 1½'' chunks. Discard extra fat. Insert **Steel Knife** in processor. Process **half** the meat (about 1 cup) with the onion until ground, about 8 seconds. Empty bowl. Repeat with remaining meat. Add eggs, mustard and the first batch of ground meat back into the processor. Process with 3 or 4 quick on/off turns, **just** until mixed through.

Yield: about 2 cups filling. Use to fill knishes, kreplach, etc. Also ideal to fill turnovers made from your favorite pie dough. Freezes well.

CORNED BEEF AND POTATO FILLING

2 onions, quartered   2 medium potatoes, boiled &
3 tbsp. oil   mashed
1 lb. corned beef, smoked   2 eggs
meat or pickled brisket   salt & pepper, to taste

Steel Knife: Process onion with 3 or 4 quick on/off turns, until coarsely chopped. Sauté in hot oil until golden. Cut meat in 1½'' chunks. Trim away any fat. Process on **Steel Knife** until minced, about 8 seconds. Add meat to mashed potatoes along with onions, eggs and seasonings. Mix well.

Yield: about 3 cups filling. May be frozen.

CHINESE CREPES

Basic Crepe Batter (p. 102)   Egg Roll Filling (p. 42)

Prepare crêpes and filling as directed.

Place about 2 tbsp. filling on each crêpe, and roll up. Place in a greased 9'' x 13'' casserole. Bake at 400°F for 15 minutes, uncovered. You may top them with a little Spare Rib Sauce before baking, or serve them with Chinese Plum Sauce. Serves 4. Freezing is not recommended.

KREPLACH*

2 c. flour   2 large eggs
¼ tsp. salt   ¼ c. warm water

Steel Knife: Process all ingredients until dough forms a ball on the blades and is well-kneaded, about 25 to 30 seconds. Remove from bowl, wrap in plastic wrap or foil for about 15 minutes for easier handling. Meanwhile, prepare desired filling. (Cheese, leftover ground meat, chicken or liver.) You will need about 2 c. filling.

Divide dough in four. Cover portions of dough that you are not using. Shape dough with your hands into a square on a lightly floured board. Roll dough about ⅛'' thick into a 9'' square. Cut in 3'' squares.

Place 1 tbsp. filling in the centre of each square. Shape into a triangle by joining the 2 points diagonally opposite of each other. Seal completely by pinching edges together firmly. Press 2 points together to form a little ''purse'', if desired.

Boil uncovered in salted water for 15 to 20 minutes, until tender. Remove with a slotted spoon and drain well. Sprinkle with 1 tsp. oil (or butter) to prevent sticking. Repeat with remaining dough and filling.

Yield: 2½ to 3 dozen.

Freezing: Kreplach will freeze about 1 month. Uncooked kreplach may be frozen completely on a cookie sheet, then stored in a plastic bag until needed. Place on a cookie sheet, not touching each other, to thaw. Cook as directed above.

Cooked kreplach freeze well. Just make sure to sprinkle with oil before freezing. Thaw completely. May be served in soup, or browned in hot fat or butter until golden brown. You may also heat them at 350°F about 15 minutes in a covered casserole.

VARENIKAS*

Varenikas are prepared from the same dough as Kreplach (above), but the filling is different. Usual fillings are potato, kasha or fruit. (Try canned cherry or blueberry pie filling if you are in a hurry.) Varenikas are shaped like a half-moon, rather than triangular, and you do not join the 2 points to make a purse shape.

Potato varenikas are especially delicious when served with roasted chicken or meat and gravy. May be frozen.

The Jewish version of Wonton, Ravioli and Perogies.

STUFFING CASSEROLE

5 c. soft bread crumbs (see
  instructions below*)
3 tbsp. oil or margarine
2 medium onions, halved
1 green pepper, cut in 1"
  chunks
2 stalks celery, cut in 1" chunks

1 c. mushrooms
3 eggs
1 tsp. salt
dash of pepper
¼ tsp. garlic powder
1 c. chicken broth
1 tsp. baking powder

*Steel Knife: Use leftover crusts of bread, or any stale bread or rolls you have in your bread box. (I keep a plastic bag in the freezer and throw in any leftovers or stale ends.) Tear into 2" chunks and drop bread through the feed tube while the machine is running. Process until fine crumbs are formed. Measure 5 cups crumbs, loosely packed.

Heat oil in a large skillet. Meanwhile, process onions on **Steel Knife** with 3 or 4 quick on/off turns, until coarsely chopped. Add to skillet. Repeat with green pepper, then celery, then mushrooms, adding each in turn to the skillet. Brown vegetables quickly on medium-high heat. Remove from heat and cool slightly.

Process eggs for 2 or 3 seconds. Add with bread crumbs and remaining ingredients to skillet and mix well. Place in a greased 7" x 11" Pyrex baking dish and bake at 350°F for 40 to 45 minutes, until golden brown.

Yield: 6 to 8 servings. May be frozen.

Note: To use as a stuffing for turkey or veal brisket, omit baking powder. Add ½ tsp. each of sage and thyme, if desired. Stuff loosely. Add ten minutes per pound to the cooking time of poultry or roast.

SUPER COLESLAW

Coleslaw Mixture:

1 head cabbage (about 3 lb.)
3 medium carrots, peeled &
  trimmed
2 cloves garlic, peeled
3 green onions (shallots), cut
  in 2" pieces
1 green pepper, cut in long,
  narrow strips

Marinade:

1 c. white vinegar
½ c. sugar (see Note)
¾ c. oil
1 tsp. salt
¼ tsp. pepper

Slicer: Cut cabbage into wedges to fit feed tube. Discard core. Slice, using **very light** pressure. (If you prefer a finer texture, you may use the thin **Serrated Slicer** (use light pressure) or the **Grater** (use firm pressure).

Empty into a large bowl. I prefer using a young cabbage, if possible.

Grater: Cut carrots to fit feed tube crosswise. Grate, using firm pressure. Add to cabbage.

Steel Knife: Drop shallots and garlic through feed tube while machine is running. Process until minced.

Slicer: Stack green pepper vertically in feed tube. Process, using light pressure. Add to cabbage mixture.

Combine ingredients for marinade in a saucepan and bring to a boil. Pour hot marinade over coleslaw mixture and toss well. Transfer to a large jar, cover tightly and refrigerate.

Yield: about 12 to 16 servings. Do not freeze.

Note: This coleslaw will keep about 3 to 4 weeks in the refrigerator without becoming soggy. For calorie counters, eliminate all or part of the sugar. Add artificial sweetener to taste to the boiled marinade. If you boil the artificial sweetener, it may produce a bitter after-taste. Coleslaw will not keep as well if made with artificial sweetener.

CREAMY COLESLAW

Prepar Coleslaw Mixture for Super Coleslaw (p. 178), omitting garlic. Prepare the following dressing:-

1 c. Mayonnaise (p. 65)   2 tbsp. sugar (or to taste)
2 tbsp. lemon juice or vinegar   salt & pepper, to taste

Steel Knife: Prepare Mayonnaise as directed. Add lemon juice and sugar. Process a few seconds longer. Add to vegetables and mix well. Add additional salt and pepper to taste. Chill before serving.

Variation: Use ½ cup Mayonnaise and ½ cup sour cream.

COLESLAW MOLD

(Perfect for a summer buffet)

3 oz. pkg. lime jello   1 stalk celery
¾ c. boiling water   1 medium carrot, scraped &
¾ c. cold water   trimmed
1 tbsp. vinegar   ¼ small cabbage
½ c. mayonnaise   ¼ c. raisins, if desired

Dissolve jello in boiling water. Stir in cold water and vinegar. Blend in mayonnaise and chill until partially set.

Steel Knife: Cut vegetables in 2'' chunks. Process celery with carrot until minced, about 8 seconds. Empty bowl. Process cabbage with 4 or 5 quick on/off turns, until chopped. Fold vegetables and raisins into jello. Pour into a greased 1 quart mold and chill several hours until firm. Unmold.

Yield: 6 to 8 servings. Do not freeze.

TANGY MARINATED CARROT SALAD

2 to 3 lb. carrots, scraped &   ½ c. sugar
   trimmed   1 tsp. Worcestershire sauce
2 c. boiling salted water   1 tsp. pepper
1 green pepper, halved &   1 tsp. dry mustard
   seeded   1 tsp. dill weed
1 onion, halved   ¾ c. vinegar
10 oz. can tomato soup   ½ c. oil

Slicer: Cut carrots to fit feed tube. Pack tightly in an upright position. Slice, using firm pressure. Cook in boiling salted water for 1 minute. Drain well.

Slicer: Slice green pepper, using light pressure. Slice onion, using medium pressure. Add to carrots.

Steel Knife: Process soup with sugar, Worcestershire sauce and seasonings for 5 or 6 seconds. Add vinegar and oil through feed tube while machine is running. Process 8 to 10 seconds. Immediately pour soup mixture over carrots. Cover and marinate in the refrigerator for 10 to 12 hours before serving. Delicious hot or cold. 8 to 12 servings. Keeps about 1 week to 10 days in the refrigerator.

Note: Artificial sweetener may be substituted for the sugar, if desired.

MARINATED BEAN SALAD

1 large Spanish or Bermuda
onion
1 green pepper, halved &
seeded
1 red pepper, halved & seeded
14 oz. can cut green beans,
drained
14 oz. can cut wax (yellow)
beans, drained
10 oz. can baby lima beans,
drained

½ c. canned kidney beans,
drained
½ c. oil
¼ c. vinegar
salt & & pepper, to taste
1 tsp. dry mustard
2 - 3 tbsp. sugar
2 c. raw cauliflowerettes

Slicer: Cut onion to fit feed tube. Slice, using light pressure. Slice peppers, using light pressure. Combine all ingredients in a large bowl and toss to mix. Cover and refrigerate for at least 24 hours before serving.

Yield: about 12 servings. Will keep about 10 days in the refrigerator.

Note: You may substitute cooked fresh beans for canned, if desired.

MARINATED FRESH VEGETABLE SALAD

2 c. green beans
2 c. yellow beans
1 small head cauliflower,
broken into florets
1 green pepper, halved &
seeded
1 red pepper, halved & seeded
2 Spanish onions, quartered
1 stalk celery, cut to fit feed
tube
1 can artichoke hearts,
drained (if desired)
1 dozen black olives, if
desired

Marinade:
2 cloves garlic
1 c. vinegar
¼ c. oil
½ c. sugar
2 tsp. salt

Cut beans in half and boil for 2 or 3 minutes in boiling water to cover. Drain well.

Slicer: Slice cauliflower, using fairly firm pressure. Slice peppers, onions and celery, using medium pressure. Combine all vegetables in a large mixing bowl.

Steel Knife: Drop garlic through feed tube while machine is running. Process until minced. Add to saucepan along with vinegar, oil, sugar and salt. Bring mixture to a boil. Pour hot marinade over vegetables and mix well. Store in a glass gallon jar in the refrigerator. Will keep about 2 weeks.

Variation: Add 1 unpeeled zucchini and 1 bunch broccoli florets, sliced on the **Slicer.** Omit olives. If you wish, add 1 large carrot. Pack in feed tube crosswise. Slice with firm pressure. Carrot should be par-boiled with the beans before adding to salad.

SUPER SALADS

You will find your processor a great help in salad making. It is ideal to slice or chop vegetables, grate cheeses and make delicious salad dressings in moments. A salad dryer should be used to dry salad greens so that the dressing will cling to the greens rather than slide off the wet leaves and collect in a pool at the bottom of the salad bowl. The salad dryer is a good investment and is cheaper in the long run than using paper towelling; it is also easier than having to wash dishtowels with bits of lettuce clinging to them!

Lettuce should be torn into bite-sized pieces by hand rather than being sliced on the processor. After the lettuce has been dried, wrap in paper towels to absorb the last few drops of excess moisture and place in a plastic bag in your refrigerator. If adding dressing, add just at serving time; otherwise the salad will become limp and watery.

If dressing is not added to your salads, you may make a large salad bowl of mixed vegetables (except tomatoes) and store it in your refrigerator for a couple of days. If you have leftover salad which has had dressing added to it and has become limp, place it in a colander and rinse off the dressing. Process the leftover salad vegetables on the **Steel Knife** until finely chopped. Combine with equal parts of tomato juice and consommé, season to taste and you will have a quick Gazpacho!

The **Steel Knife** or **Plastic Knife** are used to make your salad dressings. Most vegetables will either be sliced on the **Slicer,** chopped with **quick on/off turns** using the **Steel Knife,** or ''diced'' by placing chunks of vegetables in the feed tube and processing on the **French-Fry Blade,** using very light pressure. It may be necessary to dry vegetables with a high water content (e.g. cucumbers, peppers) by placing between paper towels to absorb excess moisture.

You might wish to make layered salads rather than tossed salads. Use an attractive large glass serving bowl and as many different types of vegetables as you wish. Remember to vary the colors of the layers for maximum eye appeal.

Suggested Salad Ingredients:

Assorted salad greens:- Boston or iceberg lettuce; Romaine; fresh spinach; watercress; alfalfa sprouts; beans sprouts.

Carrots (use **Slicer** or **Grater.** Also nice with **French-Fry Blade.**)

Cherry tomatoes or tomato wedges. (Or use **French-Fry Blade**) to ''dice'' tomatoes. Drain before adding to salads.) Hand slicing is preferred for salads.

Onions:- scallions, Spanish onion or red onion. (Use **Slicer, French-Fry Blade** or **Steel Knife.**)

Cooked green or yellow beans. Broccoli or cauliflower florets (raw or par-boiled for a minute or two. Use **Slicer** if desired.)

Celery (Process on **Slicer** or **French-Fry Blade).**

Red or Green Peppers **(Slicer** or **French-Fry Blade.** Pat dry.)

Radishes (use **Slicer** or **Steel Knife).**

Cucumber, Mushrooms, Zucchini (use **Slicer**. Pat cucumbers and zucchini dry.)

Olives (green or black), marinated artichoke hearts, canned chick peas.

Grated cheese (use **Grater** or **French-Fry Blade):-** Cheddar, Swiss, Smoked Cheeses; Parmesan (process on **Steel Knife**).

Hard-cooked egg wedges (or use **Steel Knife**); cooked chicken, turkey, salami (use **Slicer**); cooked or canned fish such as salmon, tuna, halibut (use **Steel Knife**).

Croutons, artificial bacon bits (Bac-Os).

Potato cubes or slices (best done by hand as potatoes may crumble if sliced on the processor.)

FARMER'S SALAD

4 green onions (scallions), cut in 2" lengths
1 cucumber, peeled & cut to fit feed tube
6 radishes, trimmed

1 green pepper, halved & seeded
1 head lettuce, cut to fit feed tube
Yoghurt Cheese Dip (p. 38)
salt & pepper, to taste

Steel Knife: Drop scallions through feed tube while machine is running. Process until minced.

Slicer: Slice cucumber, radishes, pepper and lettuce, using light pressure. Empty bowl as necessary. Combine vegetables with remaining ingredients in a large mixing bowl and toss gently to mix.

Yield: 4 to 6 servings.

ORIENTAL LUNCHEON SALAD

Salad:
2 stalks celery, trimmed
4 scallions (green onions)
8 oz. can water chestnuts, drained
¼ Spanish onion
1 head lettuce, torn into bite-size pieces
2 - 7 oz. cans solid white tuna, drained
1 c. chow mein noodles, as garnish

Dressing:
½ c. mayonnaise
¼ c. red wine vinegar
¼ c. corn syrup
1 tbsp. soya sauce
½ tsp. ground ginger

Slicer: Cut celery and scallions to fit feed tube. Pack scallions in between the celery. Arrange in an upright position in the feed tube. Slice, using medium pressure. Slice water chestnuts, using heavy pressure. Slice onion, using very light pressure. Empty bowl as necessary.

Arrange lettuce on 6 chilled dinner plates. Arrange vegetables attractively over lettuce. Top with chunks of tuna. Chill until serving time. Top with dressing and garnish with chow mein noodles.

Yield: 6 servings.

Salad Dressing: Combine all ingredients and process on **Plastic or Steel Knife** for a few seconds, just until blended.

CAESAR SALAD ✓

3 heads Romaine lettuce (or 1
head Romaine and 1 head
iceberg lettuce)
1 egg, optional
1 can flat anchovies, optional
½ c. (approximately) corn or
olive oil
1 to 2 cloves garlic

¼ c. wine vinegar
1 tbsp. lemon juice
½ tsp. salt
freshly ground pepper
½ tsp. sugar
1 tsp. Worcestershire sauce
¼ - ⅓ c. Parmesan cheese
2 c. croutons (see below)

Wash lettuce and discard wilted leaves. Drain and dry thoroughly. (A lettuce spinner is ideal.) Tear lettuce into a large salad bowl. (May also be wrapped in paper towels and stored in a plastic bag in the refrigerator until needed.)

(Place egg in boiling water and simmer for 60 seconds. Cool under cold running water to stop cooking process. This is called a "coddled egg".)

Drain oil from anchovies into a measuring cup. Add corn or olive oil to measure ¾ cup. (If you don't like anchovies, increase corn or olive oil to ¾ cup.)

Steel Knife: Drop garlic through feed tube while machine is running. Process until minced, Discard peel. Add egg, oil, vinegar, lemon juice, seasonings, Worcestershire sauce and cheese. Process about 8 to 10 seconds to blend. (May be prepared in advance up to this point.)

Combine all ingredients in salad bowl and toss to mix thoroughly. Correct seasonings. Serve immediately.

Yield: 8 servings.

HOME-MADE CROUTONS ✓

2 c. stale French bread, crusts
removed

2 tbsp. butter or margarine (or
use garlic butter for a
delicious flavor)

Cut bread into ¼" cubes. Spread on a baking sheet and bake at 325°F for 10 to 15 minutes to dry out. Heat butter or margarine. Add bread cubes and sauté until golden, stirring constantly. Cool.

Note: May be prepared in advance and stored in the refrigerator in an airtight container for about a week. May be frozen. Thaw and crisp at 375°F for 4 or 5 minutes.

CUCUMBER SALAD

6 cucumbers, peeled (about 5
to 6 inches long)
1 tbsp. salt

1 onion, halved
Best Vinaigrette Dressing
(p. 187)
½ tsp. dill weed

Slicer: Cut cucumbers to fit feed tube. Slice, using medium pressure. (Long, thin, firm cucumbers are best.) Sprinkle with salt and place in the refrigerator with a plate on top of them to weigh them down. This releases the excess moisture. After 2 hours, place in a strainer and rinse off salt. Pat dry with paper towelling.

Slicer: Slice onion, using light pressure. Prepare dressing as directed, adding dill weed. Use about ¾ cup dressing. Combine all ingredients and mix well. Marinate at least 1 hour before serving.

Yield: 8 servings.

MUSHROOM AND ANCHOVY SALAD

1 head Romaine lettuce
1 oz. Parmesan cheese (¼ c. grated)
1 hard-cooked egg
¼ Spanish onion

1 pt. fresh mushrooms
1 tin anchovies, well-drained
½ c. toasted croutons (p. 183)
¾ c. Italian Salad Dressing (p. 186)

Trim any soft or rusty leaves from lettuce. Wash and dry thoroughly. If desired, wrap in a towel and place in a plastic bag in the refrigerator until needed.

If cheese is not already grated, process on **Steel Knife** until fine. Empty bowl. Process egg until minced, about 3 or 4 seconds. Empty bowl.

Slicer: Cut onion to fit feed tube. Slice, using very light pressure. Stack mushrooms on their sides. Slice, using light pressure. Combine lettuce, onion, mushrooms, anchovies and Parmesan cheese in a large attractive glass salad bowl. Reserve egg and croutons as garnish. Refrigerate salad.

About 10 minutes before serving, pour dressing over salad and toss well. Garnish with egg and croutons.

Yield: 8 servings.

CARROT & RAISIN SALAD

1 lb. carrots (about 5 or 6), scraped & trimmed
2 c. Sultana raisins

1 c. flaked coconut
honey to taste

Grater: Cut carrots to fit feed tube crosswise. Grate, using fairly firm pressure. Transfer to a mixing bowl and combine with remaining ingredients. Let stand several hours before serving to blend flavors.

Yield: 6 servings.

Note: Grated apple may be substituted for the coconut. Add 1 tbsp. lemon juice to the apples to prevent them from turning dark. If desired, moisten with a little mayonnaise.

SPINACH SALAD

2-10 oz. pkgs. fresh spinach
1 small red onion or ¼ Spanish onion
1 c. fresh mushrooms
1 c. raw cauliflowerettes, if desired

Best Vinaigrette Dressing (p. 187)
2 hard-cooked eggs
¼ c. artificial bacon bits (Bac-Os)
½ c. croutons

Wash spinach thoroughly and spin dry in a salad dryer. Tear into bite-size pieces and place in a large salad bowl.

Slicer: Slice onion, mushrooms and cauliflower, using medium pressure. Add to spinach. Refrigerate until serving time.

Steel Knife: Prepare dressing as directed. Refrigerate. Process eggs for 4 or 5 seconds, until coarsely chopped. At serving time, combine all ingredients except eggs. Toss to mix. Garnish with chopped eggs. Serve immediately.

Yield: 8 to 10 servings.

GREEK SALAD

2 large heads Romaine lettuce	½ lb. Feta cheese
1 red onion or ¼ Spanish onion	1 large clove garlic
	¾ c. olive oil
2 green peppers, halved & seeded	¼ c. lemon juice or wine vinegar
1 c. radishes	½ tsp. dry mustard
2 dozen black olives	½ tsp. oregano
1 pint cherry tomatoes or 2 large ripe tomatoes, cut into wedges	salt & pepper, to taste
	1 can flat anchovies, well-drained

Wash lettuce and spin dry in a salad dryer. Tear into bite-size pieces and place in a large salad bowl.

Slicer: Slice onion, peppers and radishes, using medium pressure. Add to salad bowl along with 16 olives (reserve remaining olives for garnish) and tomatoes.

Steel Knife: Process feta cheese with on/off turns, until crumbled. Add to salad. Wipe out bowl and blade.

Steel Knife: Drop garlic through feed tube while machine is running. Process until minced. Add oil, lemon juice, mustard and oregano. Process for a few seconds to blend. Pour over salad. Season lightly with salt and pepper (remember that the Feta cheese is salty). Toss well. Arrange anchovies like the spokes of a wheel over the top of the salad. Arrange reserved olives between the anchovies.

Yield: 8 servings.

SWEET & SPICY FRENCH DRESSING ✓

2 cloves garlic	½ c. vinegar
½ c. ketchup	½ c. sugar
½ tbsp. salt	½ tsp. paprika
½ tsp. dry mustard	½ tsp. Worcestershire sauce
1½ c. oil	

Steel Knife: Drop garlic through feed tube while machine is running. Process until minced. Discard garlic peel. Scrape down sides of bowl, add remaining ingredients and process until blended and creamy, about 25 to 30 seconds.

Yield: about 2¾ cups dressing. Do not freeze. Keeps about 2 months in the refrigerator in a tightly closed jar.

CREAMY GARLIC DRESSING ✓

2 cloves garlic, peeled	¼ c. buttermilk
2 tbsp. fresh parsley (or 1 tsp. dried)	salt and pepper, to taste
	dash tarragon
1 c. cottage cheese	2 tbsp. vinegar

Steel Knife: Drop garlic and parsely through feed tube. Process until minced. Add remaining ingredients and process until smooth and creamy, about 30 seconds, scraping down bowl once or twice. Chill before serving.

Yield: about 1¼ cups dressing. Contains about 15 calories per tablespoon.

CREAMY DILL SALAD DRESSING

½ c. mayonnaise
3 tbsp. vinegar
salt & pepper, to taste

½ tsp. dill weed
¼ tsp. garlic powder

Plastic Knife: Process all ingredients until blended, about 5 seconds.

Yield: about ⅔ cup. Refrigerate. Do not freeze. Recipe may be doubled.

GREEN GODDESS SALAD DRESSING

1 or 2 cloves garlic
4 green onions, cut in 2"
   pieces
¼ c. fresh parsley
½ can flat anchovies, drained

½ c. sour cream or yoghurt
1 c. Mayonnaise (p. 65)
2 tbsp. wine vinegar
1 tbsp. lemon juice
freshly ground pepper

Steel Knife: Drop garlic through feed tube while machine is running. Process until minced. Discard any peel. Add green onions, parsley and anchovies. Process until minced. Add remaining ingredients and process until blended, scraping down sides of bowl once or twice. Refrigerate.

Yield: about 1¾ cups. Will keep about 10 days in a tightly closed jar in the refrigerator.

ITALIAN SALAD DRESSING √

1 clove garlic
1 c. corn or olive oil
¼ c. wine vinegar
1 tbsp. lemon juice
1¼ tsp. salt
¼ tsp. pepper (fresh ground is
   best)

½ tsp. dry mustard
¼ tsp. oregano
¼ tsp. sugar
pinch of thyme
pinch of dill weed

Steel Knife: Drop garlic through feed tube while machine is running. Process until minced. Discard garlic peel. Scrape down sides of bowl, add remaining ingredients and process until blended, about 5 seconds.

Yield: about 1¼ cups dressing. Store in a tightly closed jar in the refrigerator. Keeps well. Do not freeze.

LO-CAL ITALIAN DRESSING √

(About 40 calories per tablespoon)

¼ onion (about 1 tbsp.
   minced)
½ clove garlic, peeled
¼ tsp. salt
dash pepper
¼ tsp. dry mustard

½ tsp. oregano
¼ tsp. basil
½ tsp. paprika
3 tbsp. oil
2 tbsp. water or chicken broth
¼ c. lemon juice

Steel Knife: Process all ingredients until blended, about 10 to 15 seconds.

Yield: ½ cup. Store in a covered bottle in refrigerator. Shake before serving. Do not freeze.

Note: Recipe may be doubled if desired.

BASIC VINAIGRETTE
(Oil & Vinegar Dressing)

¾ c. oil
¼ c. vinegar
1 tsp. salt

¼ tsp. freshly ground black
pepper

Plastic Knife: Process all ingredients for 3 or 4 seconds. Refrigerate.

Yield: 1 cup.

Note: you may use vegetable, peanut or olive oil. Vinegar may be wine, cider or tarragon vinegar. Lemon juice may be substituted for the vinegar. Add minced onion, garlic, ½ tsp. dry mustard and/or a pinch of sugar as a variation. Add 1 or 2 tbsp. caraway seeds for a delicious flavor.

BEST VINAIGRETTE DRESSING

1 small clove garlic
3 tbsp. parsley
¾ c. olive or corn oil
¼ c. wine vinegar

½ tsp. salt
¼ tsp. pepper
½ tsp. dried basil

Steel Knife: Drop garlic through feed tube while machine is running. Process until minced. Add parsley and process until minced. Add remaining ingredients and process for 1 or 2 seconds to blend. Refrigerate.

Yield: about 1 cup dressing.

RUSSIAN SALAD DRESSING

1 c. Mayonnaise (p. 65)
⅓ c. chili sauce or ketchup

few drops onion juice (or ¼ small
onion)
2 tbsp. chives, if desired

Steel Knife: Prepare mayonnaise as directed. Add remaining ingredients and process until mixed. (If using onion rather than onion juice, drop through feed tube while machine is running, rather than adding it directly to the processor bowl.)

Yield: about 1⅓ cups. Will keep about 2 weeks in a tightly covered jar or Tupperware container in the refrigerator. Do not freeze.

THOUSAND ISLAND DRESSING

Add 3 tbsp. relish or 2 small minced gherkins to Russian Salad Dressing (above).

YUMMY YOGHURT SALAD DRESSING

½ small onion
2 or 3 sprigs parsley
(about 2 tsp. dried)
1 c. plain yoghurt
3 tbsp. oil
1 tbsp. vinegar

½ tsp. salt
dash pepper
¼ tsp. oregano
¼ tsp. garlic powder
⅛ tsp. tarragon
⅛ tsp. basil

Steel Knife: Process onion with parsley for several seconds, until minced. Add remaining ingredients and process about 10 to 15 seconds longer. Transfer to a glass jar and refrigerate about 1 hour before serving to blend flavours.

Yield: 1¼ cups dressing. Contains about 22 calories per tablespoon. Will keep about 10 days in the refrigerator.

Variations: 1) Omit parsley, tarragon and basil. Add ½ tsp. dillweed.
               2) Add 2 tbsp. chili sauce or ketchup.

Yeast Doughs, Quick Breads & Muffins

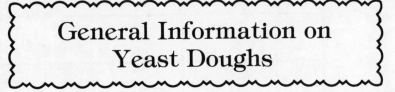

General Information on Yeast Doughs

Temperature: Ingredients should be warm. **Eggs** can be warmed by placing them in a bowl of warm water for a few minutes to remove the chill. **Milk** should be scalded (heated to just below boiling) and then cooled to lukewarm. Lukewarm water may be substituted for milk to make your recipe pareve. The crust will be more crisp, and the dough will have a less fine grain. Using the food processor, it is not necessary to melt the butter first, but you could let it stand at room temperature for a few minutes to soften slightly.

Quantity: Do not attempt to make more than 1 loaf at a time (about 3 cups flour).

Yeast: This is the ingredient which causes the dough to rise, and develops the flavor and texture of the dough. Yeast is available in two forms:

Active dry yeast: This comes in an envelope, and generally has an expiry date stamped on it. Store in the fridge or freezer, or in a cool dry place. Dissolve in warm, not hot water (105°F - 115°F) (about 43°C). It should feel like a baby's bath water. Too hot water will kill the yeast and too cold water will delay its action. Test water temperature by placing a few drops on the inside of the wrist. It should feel neither hot nor cold. One envelope yields about 2 tsp. yeast. Once you become addicted to making yeast doughs in your processor, you might wish to buy yeast at the health food store in bulk for a fraction of the cost.

Compressed cake yeast: Store tightly wrapped in the fridge. It will keep about 1 week. It may be stored in the freezer for several weeks if wrapped airtight. Yeast must be uniformly grey with no dark streaks. Dissolve in lukewarm water (85°F) (30°C).

1 envelope dry yeast (about 2 tsp.) = 1 cake compressed yeast (1 oz.)

Flour: Use all-purpose flour (bleached or unbleached), not self-rising or pastry flour. The flour is placed in the processor bowl along with the other dry ingredients and processed for 5 seconds to blend. If using solid shortening, cut into 1'' chunks and add to the machine along with the dry ingredients. Processing time will be about 20 seconds.

Always keep an extra ¼ to ⅓ cup flour in reserve ready to dump into the machine if you see that the motor is slowing down after you add the liquids. The adding of the flour will bring the speed of the machine back to normal, and the dough should gather itself into a mass or ball. The quantity of flour can vary according to the weather and the humidity. Hot, humid weather requires more flour.

N.B. The dough will not always form a **ball** around the blades (e.g. whole-wheat or rye breads). It is best to work with the dough as sticky as possible, using just **enough** flour to prevent the processor from slowing down or shutting off. This prevents doughs from being dry or heavy. Use just enough flour on your board to coat the outside of the dough so that it will not stick to your hands or the board.

Kneading: Empty the processor bowl onto a lightly floured board, wash the bowl and blade, and then lightly flour your hands. Knead dough for 1 to 2 minutes by hand, using just enough flour to keep dough from sticking. Dough will be smooth and elastic, and small air bubbles or ''blisters'' will form just below the surface. Poke your finger into the dough. If the dough springs up, it has been kneaded enough. Place dough in a bowl that has been greased with about 1 tsp. oil or soft butter, and turn it over so that all surfaces are greased. Make sure that bowl is large enough to allow the dough to double in bulk. Cover tightly with aluminum foil and allow to rise.

Rising at Room Temperature: Let rise until double in bulk in a warm place (75° - 85°F) (24° - 30°C). This will take about 1½ - 2 hours. Do **not** let dough get too warm in rising or it will develop a yeasty taste. Ideal places are:

1) Near, but not on, a warm stove.
2) In an unheated oven with a large pan of hot water beneath.
3) Turn on oven to 100°F for about 1 minute, turn off, and place dough in oven to rise. Keep the oven light on.

When double in bulk, punch dough down by plunging your fist into the centre of the dough, and fold outside edges into the centre. This releases the gases and redistributes the yeast cells. Allowing dough to rise a second time will improve the texture. Cover and let rise until double (about 45 minutes). Punch down again.

Rising Dough in Refrigerator: If desired, dough may be refrigerated after kneading. Round up in a greased bowl and cover with foil. Make sure that the bowl is large enough to allow for the dough to rise. Place in refrigerator until needed. Make sure that there is enough room between shelves for dough to rise.

Doughs made with water will keep 5 to 6 days in the fridge, and those made with milk will keep about 3 to 4 days. Cut off only as much dough as is needed, and return the remainder to the fridge. Let dough stand at room temperature for about ½ hour before shaping.

Note #1: Doughs made with butter will not rise as much in the fridge as doughs made with oil. This is because the butter will congeal in the fridge. If desired, you may let dough rise for 1 hour at room temperature, then place it in the fridge until needed.

Note #2: Dough may be placed in the fridge to slow down the rising process **at any time;** i.e. after the first kneading, after it has risen once and you have punched it down, or after it has been shaped. This is most convenient if you haven't time to complete the whole dough- making process in one day. Just make sure that dough is well covered to prevent drying out in the fridge, and always allow dough to rise double and the chill to come out before continuing with the recipe.

Shaping: It is necessary to punch the dough down before shaping it. Then let it rest for about 5 minutes for easier handling. You will find yeast dough very springy when you roll it out.

Final Rising: After dough has been shaped, it must rise once again. Place in baking pans, cover with a towel and let rise at room temperature **until double in bulk** (about 1 hour for room temperature doughs, about 2 to 3 hours for refrigerated doughs).

You can delay the final rise, if necessary, by placing shaped dough in the fridge immediately after shaping. Let stand at room temperature at least 30 minutes to remove chill. Make sure that dough is double in bulk. Then bake as directed.

Freezing: Dough may be frozen after the first or second rise (before shaping) **or** immediately after shaping. Cover airtight and freeze. Do not freeze twice before baking. The experts advise time limits ranging from 10 days to 1 month as a safe length of time.

To thaw: either place in fridge overnight, then complete the rising at room temperature, **or** thaw and complete the rising in a warm place. A frozen shaped loaf will thaw and rise double in about 6 to 7 hours at room temperature. Dough should be covered. Then bake as directed.

Freezing after Baking: Yeast products freeze very well. Wrap airtight when cool and freeze. Baked breads freeze for about 6 months; rolls and coffee cakes freeze about 4 to 6 months. **To thaw,** let stand at room temperature (covered to prevent drying) for about 1 hour, **or** wrap in foil and heat at 300°F for a few minutes (about 10 minutes for rolls and 20 to 25 minutes for coffee cakes.)

Glazing should be done when thawed, as glazes have a tendency to crack in the freezer.

Baking: Bake in a preheated oven as directed. There will be a final expansion known as "oven-spring" during the first few minutes of baking. At the end of the baking time, the yeast product will be evenly browned and sound hollow when crust is tapped lightly. Bake in middle or lower third of oven. If dough browns too quickly, cover loosely with foil.

Cooling: Breads should be removed from pans immediately after baking and cooled on a wire rack away from drafts. Glazing, if desired, is best done when coffee cakes and buns are still slightly warm.

SUMMARY

- Make recipes yielding 1 loaf or using no more than 3 cups of flour in the processor. The machine is so fast, you can make several recipes very quickly.

- Always begin with dry ingredients in the bowl; process to blend. Butter (or margarine) is processed with the dry ingredients. **Time:** about 20 seconds. (Melted shortening or oil is added with the liquids).

- Add yeast mixture next, then remaining liquid ingredients.

- Always keep a reserve of ¼ to ⅓ cup flour in case the motor slows down and the dough does not form a mass around the blades. Dump in the extra flour all at once through the feed tube. Dough should be kneaded for 30 to 40 seconds on the processor once it has massed together.

- Knead by hand for 1 to 2 minutes, or until dough is smooth and elastic.

- Rise the dough once, till double in bulk. Punch down. Some recipes call for a second rising. Dough may be risen at room temperature, or in the refrigerator.

- A good test to see if the dough has risen enough is to insert your finger to a depth of 1", and wait to see if the impression remains. If impression fills in, wait another 15 to 20 minutes before punching dough down.

- After dough has been shaped, it must rise once again, until double in bulk. Therefore, **there are 1 or 2 risings before shaping,** and **one rising after shaping.** Rising time will vary, depending on the temperature of the dough (i.e. whether it was risen in the refrigerator or at room temperature).

- Dough can be refrigerated at any point to slow down the rising process if you are busy and cannot complete the recipe at that time. Make sure to cover dough well.

- To give a nice shine to your coffee cakes and buns, brush with the juice from canned fruit (e.g. peaches, fruit cocktail, etc.) 10 minutes before the baking is completed. An alternate method is to brush shaped yeast doughs with an egg wash of 1 egg yolk plus 2 tsp. water just before you place them in the oven to bake.

- If yeast breads rise too long, the gluten strands will break and the bread will collapse. They should not rise more than double in bulk before baking.

- If the water to which the yeast is added is too hot, it will kill the yeast; if it is too cool, the yeast won't grow.

- Raisins which have dried out can be made plump and juicy once again by soaking them in boiling water for 3 or 4 minutes. Drain well before adding to your recipe.

- Brown sugar which has hardened can be salvaged easily. Just cut an apple in half and place it cut side up in the bag or container of brown sugar. A day or two later, discard the apple. Your sugar will be soft and moist once again!

- Add ¼ cup wheat germ to your favorite bread recipes to enrich them.

- If dough is too warm during the rising period, it will develop a yeasty taste. For processor recipes, use no more than 1 envelope dry yeast (or 2 tsp. dry yeast if you purchase it in bulk at the health food stores, which is much more economical).

CHALAH
(Braided Egg Bread)

1 tsp. sugar	⅓ c. oil
½ c. warm water (105° - 115°F)	2 eggs
1 pkg. yeast	¼ c. lukewarm water
3 c. flour (approximately)	1 egg yolk beaten with 1 tsp.
2 - 3 tbsp. sugar or honey	water
1 tsp. salt	poppy or sesame seeds

Dissolve sugar in ½ cup warm water in measuring cup. Sprinkle yeast over and let stand for 8 to 10 minutes. Stir to dissolve.

Steel Knife: Place flour, sugar and salt in processor. Pour dissolved yeast mixture over and process 12 to 15 seconds. While machine is running, add oil and eggs through feed tube and process until blended, about 10 seconds. Add water and process until dough gathers and forms a mass around the blades. (Have an additional ¼ - ⅓ cup flour ready in case the machine begins to slow down, and dump in through the feed tube if necessary.) Amount of flour will vary depending on whether large or extra-large eggs are used. Let machine knead dough about 30 seconds from the time the ball stage is reached. Dough should be sticky. Turn out onto a lightly floured board. Knead for 1 to 2 minutes, until smooth and elastic, adding just enough flour to prevent dough from sticking to your hands or to the board.

Round up in a large greased bowl, cover with foil and let rise in a warm place until double in bulk. (Dough may also be placed in refrigerator to rise. It can be kept up to 3 days before shaping and baking.) Punch down. If you have time, let the dough rise once again, or you may shape it at this point.

Divide dough into 3 equal portions. Roll with your hands into 3 long strands. Place on a greased baking sheet. Braid, then tuck ends under. Cover with a towel and let rise until double. Brush with beaten egg yolk and sprinkle with seeds. Bake at 400°F in the lower third of the oven for 30 minutes, until golden brown, and dough sounds hollow when tapped with your fingers. Cool away from drafts.

Yield: 1 large loaf. Freezes well.

Note: For a more festive loaf, divide dough into 4 equal portions. Form 3 strands into a large braid as directed. Divide the remaining portion into 3 smaller strands and form a smaller braid. Place the smaller braid on top of the large braid. Pinch in several places to join the two braids. Let rise and bake as directed.

HOLIDAY RAISIN CHALAH
(Round Egg Bread filled with raisins.)

Follow instructions for Chalah (above) using 3 tbsp. honey instead of sugar. Add ¾ c. Sultana raisins to dough about 20 seconds after it gathers into a mass around the blades. Process about 10 seconds longer to mix in raisins. Let dough rise as directed. Do not braid.

Roll dough between your palms into a long thick rope. Place on a greased baking sheet. Coil up like a snail starting from the centre and working outwards. Tuck end under. Cover with a towel and let rise until double in bulk. Brush with beaten egg yolk and sprinkle with poppy or sesame seeds. Bake at 400°F for 30 minutes, until golden brown.

Yield: 1 loaf. Freezes well.

CHALAH ROLLS (Bulkas)

Follow instructions for Chalah (p. 193) and let dough rise as directed. Do not braid.

Divide dough into 12 equal portions. Roll each portion between your palms into a rope about 8" long. Tie each piece in a knot. Place on a greased baking sheet, cover with a towel and let rise until double. Brush with beaten egg yolk and sprinkle with poppy or sesame seeds. Bake at 400°F for about 15 to 18 minutes, until golden brown.

Yield: 1 dozen rolls. Freezes well.

Note: To make miniature Bulkas, divide dough into 24 equal portions.

MINATURE CHALAH ROLLS

Follow instructions for Chalah (p. 193) and let dough rise as directed. Do not braid.

Divide dough into 12 equal portions. Shape each portion into 3 small thin strands. Braid, then tuck ends under. Place rolls on a greased baking sheet, cover and let rise until double. Brush with beaten egg yolk and sprinkle with poppy or sesame seeds. Bake at 400°F for 15 to 18 minutes, until golden brown.

Yield: 1 dozen rolls. Freezes well.

PITA √
(Sometimes called "pocket bread". Great for weight-watcher sandwiches. Just watch out for the filling!)

1 tsp. sugar	3¼ c. flour
¼ c. lukewarm water (105° - 115°F)	1 tsp. salt
1 pkg. yeast	1 c. lukewarm water

Dissolve sugar in lukewarm water. Sprinkle yeast over and let stand for 8 to 10 minutes, until foamy. Stir to dissolve.

Steel Knife: Place flour and salt in processor bowl. Add yeast and process 8 to 10 seconds to mix. Pour lukewarm water through the feed tube while the machine is running and process until dough is well kneaded and forms a ball on the blades. Once the dough has formed a ball, process 30 seconds longer.

Knead dough on a lightly floured board for 1 or 2 minutes, until smooth. Divide dough into 18 balls about 1½ to 2 inches in diameter. Roll each ball to ¼ inch thickness on a lightly floured board. Cover with a towel and let rise for ½ hour. Roll thinly once again and let rise ½ hour longer.

Preheat oven to 500°F. Place rolls on a greased baking sheet and bake about 8 minutes, or until puffed and golden. The centres of these rolls will be hollow. To fill, make a slit along one side and fill. Delicious stuffed with Felafel (p. 42), or use for your favorite sandwiches.

Yield: 18 rolls. May be frozen.

BEST-EVER ONION ROLLS

Chalah dough (p. 193)
2 onions, halved
¾ c. toasted bread crumbs
3 tbsp. oil
1 tsp. salt

dash pepper
1 tbsp. poppy seeds
1 tsp. caraway seeds, if desired

Follow instructions for Chalah dough and let rise as directed. Do not braid. Roll out on a floured surface into a large rectangle about ¼'' thick. Cut into 3'' squares.

Steel Knife: Chop onions with 3 or 4 quick on/off turns. Add remaining ingredients and process with 2 or 3 quick on/off turns to mix. Reserve about ½ cup filling to top rolls.

Place about 1 tbsp. of filling on each square and pinch tightly to seal. Place on a greased baking sheet. Brush with beaten egg yolk and sprinkle with about 1 tsp. reserved onion filling. Cover with a towel and let rise until double. Bake at 375°F for 18 to 20 minutes, until golden.

Yield: about 15 to 18 rolls. Freezes well.

HOME-MADE WHITE BREAD

1 pkg. yeast
½ c. lukewarm water (105° - 115°F)
3 c. flour
1½ tbsp. sugar

½ tbsp. salt
1 tbsp. margarine or oil
¾ c. scalded milk or lukewarm water

Sprinkle yeast over ½ c. lukewarm water. Let stand 8 to 10 minutes. Then stir to dissolve.

Steel Knife: Place flour, sugar, salt and shortening in food processor. Process 6 to 8 seconds. Add dissolved yeast and process about 10 seconds. Add milk or water through feed tube while machine is running. Process until dough forms a ball on the blades. Let machine knead dough about 30 to 40 seconds from the time the ball stage is reached. Turn out onto a lightly floured board. Knead for 1 to 2 minutes, until smooth and elastic. Round up in a large greased bowl, cover with foil, and let rise until double. Punch down. (If desired, you may rise dough a second time for a finer texture. First rising at room temperature will take about 1 to 1½ hours. Second rising will take about half the time.)

Roll dough on a lightly floured board into a 9'' x 12'' rectangle. Roll up, sausage-style, from the shorter side. Seal ends by pressing down with the edge of your hand. Place seam-side down in a greased 9'' x 5'' loaf pan. Cover with a towel, and let rise until double, about 1 hour.

Bake at 425°F for 25 to 30 minutes. Remove from pan and cool.

Yield: 1 loaf. Freezes well.

Note: May be baked free-form on a greased cookie sheet, if desired.

WHOLE WHEAT BREAD

Make White Bread (above), but use half Whole-Wheat flour.

DINNER ROLLS

Follow directions for Home-Made White Bread or Whole Wheat Bread (above) and let dough rise as directed. Punch down.

Divide dough into 12 equal portions. Shape each portion into a round ball. Place on a greased cookie sheet, cover and let rise until double in bulk. Bake at 375°F about 20 minutes, until golden.

Yield: 1 dozen rolls. Freezes well.

Note: Pareve White Bread (p. 197) may also be used to make dinner rolls. All these doughs are excellent to make hamburger and hot dog rolls.

BAGELS

Follow directions for Home-Made White Bread or Whole Wheat Bread. (p. 195) but increase flour to 3¼ cups. Let dough rise only 20 minutes.

Divide dough into 12 equal pieces. Roll each piece between the palms of your hands into an 8'' rope. Join ends to form a ring. Let rise for 20 to 30 minutes.

Bring about 4 cups of water to a rolling boil in a large pot. Add 1 tsp. salt and 1 tsp. honey. Drop 3 or 4 bagels at a time into boiling water. Cook for 30 seconds; flip over quickly and then remove from water. Repeat with remaining bagel.

Dip in poppy or sesame seeds. Place on a greased cookie sheet. Bake at 400°F about 25 minutes, until well-browned. It may be necessary to turn the bagel over for even browning.

Yield: 1 dozen. Freezes well.

Note: If baking bagels becomes a habit, you might want to invest in glazed ceramic floor tiles. These are available at your local tile dealer. Place tiles on the bottom rack of your oven. They should be touching. Preheat your oven as directed. Bake bagels directly on tiles. No baking pans are needed. This method may also be used for baking pizzas or any crusty types of bread. Baking directly on ceramic tiles produces a lovely, crisp crust.

VIENNA ROLLS

Follow directions for Home-Made White Bread (p. 195) or All-Purpose Pareve Dough (below). Let dough rise as directed.

Break off pieces of dough about the size of a large egg. Roll each piece with a rolling pin into a flat circle about ⅓'' thick. Place on a greased baking sheet, cover and let rise until double in bulk. Cut an "X" about ¼'' deep with a sharp knife. Brush with 1 egg yolk which has been blended with 1 tsp. water. Sprinkle with poppy seeds. Bake at 375°F about 20 minutes, until golden brown.

Yield: 10 rolls. Freezes well.

ALL-PURPOSE PAREVE* DOUGH

1 tsp. sugar	⅓ c. sugar
¼ c. warm water (105° - 115°F)	⅓ c. oil
1 pkg. yeast	2 eggs
3 c. flour	⅓ c. lukewarm water
½ tsp. salt	

Dissolve sugar in ¼ cup warm water in a measuring cup. Sprinkle yeast over and let stand for 8 to 10 minutes. Stir to dissolve.

Steel Knife: Place flour, salt and sugar in processor. Pour dissolved yeast mixture over and process for 12 to 15 seconds. While machine is running, add oil and eggs through feed tube and process until blended, about 10 seconds. Add water and process until dough forms a ball on the blades. Let machine knead dough about 30 to 40 seconds from the time the ball stage is reached. Turn out onto a lightly floured board, knead for 1 to 2 minutes, until smooth and elastic, adding only enough flour to keep dough from sticking. Round up in a large greased bowl and cover with foil.

Either let dough rise at room temperature until double in bulk (about 2 hours) **or** place in refrigerator and let rise overnight. Dough will keep in fridge for 4 to 5 days. Punch down and shape as desired.

This dough is excellent for cinnamon buns, dinner rolls, coffee cakes, etc. Refer to various recipes for exact instructions and baking times. Dough may be frozen before or after baking. Refer to Hints (p. 191).

Pareve means that no dairy or meat products are used in this recipe.

PAREVE* WHITE BREAD ✓

1 tsp. sugar	3 tbsp. sugar
½ c. warm water (105° - 115°F)	1 tsp. salt
1 pkg. yeast	½ c. warm water
2¾ c. flour	3 tbsp. vegetable oil

Dissolve sugar in ½ c. warm water. Sprinkle yeast over and let stand 8 to 10 minutes, until foamy. Stir to dissolve.

Steel Knife: Place flour, sugar and salt in processor and process 5 seconds. Add dissolved yeast through feed tube and process 10 seconds. Combine remaining water with oil and add through feed tube while machine is running. Process until dough forms a ball on the blades. Let machine knead dough about 30 to 40 seconds from the time the ball stage is reached.

Knead on a very lightly floured board 1 to 2 minutes, until smooth. Round up in a greased bowl, cover with foil, and let rise until double in bulk, about 1 to 2 hours. Punch down.

Roll dough on a lightly floured board into a 9'' x 12'' rectangle. Roll up, sausage-style, from the shorter side. Seal ends by pressing down with the edge of your hand. Place seam-side down in a greased 9'' x 5'' loaf pan. Cover with a towel, and let rise until double, about 1 hour.

Bake at 400°F for 20 minutes. Remove from pan immediately. Cool away from drafts.

Yield: 1 loaf. Keeps about 1 week. Freezes well.

Note: If desired, you may make individual dinner rolls, hamburger or hot dog rolls from this recipe. Just shape accordingly.

Pareve means that no dairy or meat products are used in this recipe.

PAREVE WHOLE WHEAT BREAD

Follow directions for Pareve White Bread (above), but use 1½ cups all-purpose flour and 1¼ cups whole wheat flour.

RAISIN BREAD ✓

Follow directions for Pareve White Bread (above) and let rise as directed. Punch down. Roll dough on a lightly floured board into a 9'' x 12'' rectangle. Sprinkle ½ to ¾ cup raisins evenly over dough. Roll up sausage-style from the shorter side. Seal ends. Let rise and bake as directed.

Yield: 1 loaf. Freezes well.

Note: If desired, sprinkle rectangle of dough with a mixture of ¼ cup brown sugar and ½ tsp. cinnamon as well as the raisins before rolling up.

100% WHOLE WHEAT BREAD ✓

1 pkg. yeast	2 tbsp. honey
½ c. lukewarm water (105° - 115°F)	½ c. milk, scalded & cooled to lukewarm (or ½ c. lukewarm water)
3¼ c. whole wheat flour (approximately)	2 tbsp. oil
1 tsp. salt	2 eggs

Sprinkle yeast over ½ cup lukewarm water. Let stand 8 to 10 minutes. Then stir to dissolve.

Steel Knife: Place 3 cups of flour, salt and honey in processor bowl. Process 5 or 6 seconds. Add dissolved yeast through feed tube while machine is running. Process about 10 seconds. Combine milk, oil and eggs in a measuring cup. Add through feed tube while machine is running. Batter will be very sticky. Dump in the reserved ¼ cup flour as the machine begins to slow down. Process until well mixed, about 30 seconds. Batter will **not** form a ball on the blades.

Empty onto a well floured board or counter. Flour surface of dough to make it manageable for kneading. Knead about 2 minutes, adding flour as necessary to prevent dough from sticking.

Place in a greased bowl and turn dough over so that all surfaces are greased. Cover and let rise until double in bulk. Punch down. Roll dough on a lightly floured board into a 9" x 12" rectangle. Roll up, jelly roll style, from the shorter side. Seal ends by pressing down with the edge of your hand. Place seam-side down in a greased 9" x 5" loaf pan. Cover and let rise until double. Bake at 375°F for 35 to 40 minutes. Remove from pan and cool.

Yield: 1 loaf. May be frozen.

Note: May also be shaped into rolls, if desired. Baking time will be about 20 minutes.

Yield: about 1 dozen rolls.

WHOLESOME OATMEAL BREAD

1 tsp. sugar	¼ c. molasses or honey
¼ c. warm water (105°F - 115°F)	1½ tsp. salt
1 pkg. yeast	½ c. oatmeal
2 tbsp. butter or margarine	1 c. boiling water
2 tbsp. brown sugar	2¾ c. flour (approximately)

Dissolve sugar in warm water. Sprinkle yeast over and let stand for 8 to 10 minutes. Stir to dissolve.

Steel Knife: While yeast is softening in warm water, place remaining ingredients except flour in processor bowl. Process with a few quick on/off turns to mix. Let stand until cool. Add yeast mixture plus 1 cup of flour. Process for 4 or 5 seconds. Add remaining flour and process until dough forms a ball on the blades. (If machine begins to slow down, dump in up to ¼ cup additional flour.) Once dough forms a ball, process for about 30 seconds, until well kneaded.

Turn out dough onto a lightly floured board and knead by hand for 1 or 2 minutes, until smooth and elastic. Place in a greased bowl and turn dough over to coat with oil on all sides. Cover with plastic wrap or aluminum foil and let stand until double in bulk, about 1½ to 2 hours. Punch down and let rise until double once again. Punch down.

Shape dough into a loaf and place in a greased 9" x 5" loaf pan or on a greased baking sheet. Cover with a towel and let rise until doubled, about 2 hours. Bake at 350°F for about 45 minutes, or until bread sounds hollow when tapped. Brush crust with a little butter when you take it out of the oven

Yield: 1 loaf. May be frozen.

BRIOCHE ✓

1 tsp. sugar	3 tbsp. sugar
¼ c. warm milk or water (105°F - 115°F)	¾ c. (1½ sticks) frozen butter, cut into 1" pieces
1 pkg. dry yeast	½ tsp. salt
2½ c. flour (approximately)	3 eggs

Dissolve 1 tsp. sugar in warm milk or water in measuring cup. Sprinkle yeast over and let stand 8 to 10 minutes. Stir to dissolve.

Steel Knife: Place flour, sugar, butter and salt in processor bowl. Process for about 20 seconds, until blended. Add dissolved yeast mixture and process another 5 seconds. Add eggs and process until dough forms a smooth ball. If machine begins to slow down, dump in another ¼ c. flour.

Turn out onto a lightly floured board and knead dough by hand for 1 to 2 minutes, until smooth. Place in a large greased bowl, turning to coat on all sides. Cover with plastic wrap or foil and let rise until double in bulk. Punch down. Cover once again and refrigerate overnight.

Shape ¾ of dough into a ball and place it in a greased round 1½ quart casserole or brioche mold. Cut a cross in the center of the dough and open it up. Shape remaining dough like a teardrop. Fit the point into the opening of the larger ball. Cover with a towel and let rise until double in bulk. If desired, brush with eggwash made from 1 egg yolk plus 1 tbsp. milk or water.

Bake at 350°F for 35 to 45 minutes, or until nicely browned and loaf sounds hollow when tapped. Turn out of pan to cool.

Yield: 1 loaf. May be frozen.

OLD-FASHIONED RYE BREAD

1 pkg. yeast	1 tbsp. caraway seeds
½ c. warm water (105°F - 115°F)	2 tbsp. honey or sugar
1½ c. all-purpose flour (approximately)	⅔ c. lukewarm water
1½ c. rye flour	1 tsp. instant coffee dissolved in 1 tbsp. boiling water
1½ tsp. salt	1 egg yolk lightly beaten with 2 tsp. water
1 tbsp. shortening or margarine	

Sprinkle yeast over warm water in measuring cup and let stand 8 to 10 minutes. Stir to dissolve.

Steel Knife: Place flours, salt, shortening and caraway seeds in processor. Pour dissolved yeast mixture over, and process 12 to 15 seconds. Add honey and lukewarm water; process dough about 15 to 20 seconds. Dump in an additional 3 to 4 tbsp. all-purpose flour through the feed tube if the dough seems too sticky, or if the machine slows down. Turn out onto a well-floured board or counter. (Dough will be somewhat sticky.) Flour surface of dough lightly. Knead about 2 minutes, until smooth and elastic, adding just enough all-purpose flour to prevent dough from sticking.

Round up in a greased bowl, cover and let rise in a warm place until double in bulk, about 2 hours. Punch down. Roll out into a 12" x 18" rectangle. Roll up sausage style from the 18" side. Seal ends by pressing down with the edge of your hand. Place bread on a well-greased cookie sheet, cover with a towel and let rise until double in bulk, about 2 hours. Brush with coffee mixture, then with beaten egg.

Bake at 375°F about 45 minutes, or until bread sounds hollow when tapped lightly. Cool thoroughly.

Yield: 1 large loaf. Freezes well.

ONION RYE BREAD

Prepare dough for Old-Fashioned Rye Bread as directed on p. 199. To shape, divide dough into 2 equal portions. Roll out each portion on a floured board into a 10'' x 15'' rectangle. Prepare the onion filling as directed in the recipe for Best-Ever Onion Rolls (p. 195). Spread the filling to within 1'' of edges of dough.

Roll up from the 15'' side jelly-roll style. Seal ends by pressing down with the edge of your hand. Place loaves on a well-greased cookie sheet (seam-side down), cover with a towel and let rise until double in bulk, about 2 hours. Brush with coffee mixture, then with beaten egg.

Bake at 375°F about 35 to 40 minutes, or until bread sounds hollow when lightly tapped. Cool thoroughly.

Yield: 2 loaves. Freezes well. Delicious!

RYE CRESCENTS

Prepare dough for Old-Fashioned Rye Bread as directed on p. 199. To shape, divide dough into 2 equal balls. Roll out each portion on a floured board into a 12'' circle. Cut each circle into 8 equal wedges. Beginning at outer edge, roll up. Place on a greased baking sheet with sealed point underneath. Curve into crescents. Cover with a towel and let rise until double in bulk, about 1 hour. Brush with coffee mixture, then with beaten egg.

Bake at 375°F for 20 to 25 minutes, until nicely browned.

Yield: 16 rolls. Freezes well.

LIGHT PUMPERNICKEL BREAD

1 pkg. yeast	1 tbsp. caraway seeds
½ c. warm water (105° - 115°F)	3 tbsp. molasses
1¾ c. all-purpose flour (approximately)	⅔ c. lukewarm water
	2 tbsp. corn meal
1½ c. rye flour	1 tsp. coffee dissolved in
1 tbsp. instant coffee	1 tbsp. boiling water
1½ tsp. salt	1 egg, lightly beaten
1 tbsp. shortening or margarine	

Sprinkle yeast over warm water in a measuring cup and let stand 8 to 10 minutes. Stir to dissolve.

Steel Knife: Place 1½ cups each of all-purpose and rye flours, coffee, salt, shortening and caraway seeds in processor. Add dissolved yeast mixture and process 12 to 15 seconds. Combine molasses and lukewarm water and add through the feed tube while the machine is running. As machine slows down, dump in approximately ¼ cup all-purpose flour through the feed tube and process 10 seconds longer. Dough will be sticky. Turn out onto a well-floured board or counter top. Flour dough surface lightly. Knead about 2 minutes, until smooth and elastic, adding just enough flour to keep dough from sticking.

Round up in a greased bowl, cover and let rise in a warm place until double in bulk, about 2 hours. Punch down. Shape into 1 large or 2 smaller round loaves. Line a baking sheet with tinfoil and grease it well. Sprinkle with corn meal. Place bread on pan; cover and let rise until double in bulk, about 2 to 3 hours. Brush with coffee mixture, then with beaten egg.

Bake at 375°F until done, about 45 minutes for a large loaf, and 35 to 40 minutes for smaller loaves. Cool thoroughly. Freezes well.

PARTY PUMPERNICKEL

Prepare Light Pumpernickel Bread as directed on p. 200. To shape, divide dough into 3 equal portions. Roll out each part into a 6'' x 15'' rectangle. Roll up sausage style from the 15'' side. Seal ends by pressing down with the edge of your hand. Taper ends slightly. Place on a greased baking sheet, cover and let rise until double in bulk. Brush with coffee mixture, then with beaten egg.

Bake at 375°F for about 30 minutes. When thoroughly cooled, slice very thin and serve with assorted spreads.

Yield: 3 loaves. Freezes well.

PUMPERNICKEL ROLLS

Prepare Light Pumpernickel Bread as directed on p. 200. To shape, divide dough into 12 pieces. Roll between the palms of your hands into slightly flattened balls. Place on a greased baking sheet, cover and let rise until double in bulk. Brush with coffee mixture, then with beaten egg. Bake at 375°F for about 20 to 25 minutes.

Yield: 1 dozen rolls. Freezes well.

CROISSANTS
(Light and flaky. Well worth the effort.)

1 pkg. yeast	½ tsp. salt
¼ c. warm water (105°F - 115°F)	1 c. milk, scalded & cooled to
2½ c. flour	lukewarm
2 tbsp. margarine or butter	½ c. chilled butter
1 tbsp. sugar	1 egg yolk plus 2 tsp. water

Sprinkle yeast over warm water and let stand for 8 to 10 minutes. Stir to dissolve.

Steel Knife: Process flour, margarine, sugar and salt for 10 seconds. Add dissolved yeast and process 5 or 6 seconds longer. Add milk through feed tube while machine is running and process until dough forms a ball on the blades. Let machine knead dough about 30 to 40 seconds from the time the ball stage is reached. Turn dough out onto a lightly floured board and knead for 1 to 2 minutes, until smooth and elastic.

Place in a large greased bowl and turn dough over so all surfaces are greased. Cover with foil and let rise at room temperature for 1½ hours, or until double in bulk. Punch down and refrigerate for ½ hour.

Steel Knife: Cut butter into chunks. Process until lump-free and smooth, about 45 seconds, scraping down sides of bowl. Refrigerate butter while you roll out the dough.

Roll dough into a rectangle about 8'' x 15'' on a floured board. Spread the lower ⅔ of the dough with the butter, leaving a ¼'' border around the edges. Fold the dough in three as if you were folding a business letter, folding from the top downwards. Turn dough in a quarter circle so that the dough resembles a book you are going to open. Roll into a rectangle, flouring dough as necessary. Fold into 3 as before. You have now completed 2 "turns". Repeat twice more, turning the dough a quarter turn each time. You will have completed 4 "turns" in all. Wrap in waxed paper and refrigerate for at least 2 hours.

Roll dough on a floured board into a 12'' square. Cut into nine 4''squares. Cut each square in half to form 18 triangles. Roll up from the wide side, stretching dough slightly, and shape into crescents. Place on a lightly greased foil-lined baking sheet with the point of the triangle underneath. Let rise about 1 hour at room temperature. Brush with egg/water mixture. Bake at 425°F for 12 to 15 minutes, until puffed and golden.

Yield: 18 croissants. Freezes well.

To thaw: Place frozen croissants on a greased baking sheet and heat at 400°F for about 5 minutes.

NORENE'S YUMMY YEAST DOUGH

1 tsp. sugar
¼ c. warm water (105° - 115°F)
1 pkg. yeast
⅓ c. lukewarm milk or water
3 c. flour

⅓ c. sugar
½ tsp. salt
½ c. butter or margarine (1 stick), cut in chunks
2 eggs

Dissolve sugar in ¼ cup water. Sprinkle yeast over and let stand for 8 to 10 minutes. Stir to dissolve. Meanwhile, heat milk until steaming but not boiling. Cool to lukewarm.

Steel Knife: Place flour, sugar, salt and butter in processor bowl. Process for about 20 seconds, until no large pieces of butter remain. Add dissolved yeast mixture and process another 5 seconds. Add eggs and milk through feed tube while machine is running. If machine begins to slow down, dump in up to an additional ¼ cup flour through the feed tube. Once dough has formed a mass or ball around the blades, process about 30 to 40 seconds longer.

Empty bowl onto a lightly floured board. Knead dough by hand for 1 to 2 minutes, until smooth and elastic. Small bubbles will begin to form under the surface of the dough, and it will not cling to your hands or to the board. Try to work with as little flour as possible in order to prevent dough from becoming too dry once it is baked.

Place dough into a large bowl which has been greased with about 2 tsp. oil, butter or margarine. Turn dough over so that all surfaces are lightly greased. Cover with tinfoil and let rise until double in bulk, about 2 hours at room temperature. Punch down and let rise until double once again, if desired.

Dough may be used to make Cinnamon Buns, Crescents, Chocolate Danish, etc. Refer to specific recipes for shaping and baking instructions. Dough may be frozen before or after baking. Refer to Hints (p. 191).

ALMOND TEA RING

Prepare Norene's Yummy Yeast Dough (above) or All-Purpose Pareve Dough (p. 196) as directed. When dough has doubled, punch down. Roll out on a floured board into one large (9'' x 18'') or two smaller (8'' x 12'') rectangles. Prepare the following filling:-

1½ c. almonds
¾ c. sugar
1 tbsp. lemon juice

1 egg yolk
⅓ - ½ c. strawberry or apricot jam

Steel Knife: Process almonds with sugar until finely ground, about 30 seconds. Add lemon juice and egg yolk and process about 5 seconds longer to mix.

Spread dough with jam to within 1'' of edges. Sprinkle with nut filling. Roll up like a jelly roll and join ends together to form a ring. Using a sharp knife, cut ring into 1'' slices about ⅔ of the way in towards the centre of the ring. (The inside of the ring will still be attached, but the outside edges will be cut right through as if you were making individual buns.) Turn cut sections on their sides, slightly overlapping.

When doubled in bulk, bake at 375°F for 25 to 30 minutes for a large ring, or about 20 to 25 minutes for smaller rings. Cool and glaze with White Glaze (p. 206) or Almond Glaze (p. 265). Garnish with toasted slivered almonds. Freezes well, but glaze after thawing.

SWEDISH TEA RING

Prepare Norene's Yummy Yeast Dough (p. 202) or All-Purpose Pareve Dough (p. 196) as directed. When dough has doubled, punch down. Roll out on a floured board into one large (9'' x 18'') or two smaller (8'' x 12'') rectangles.

Spread dough with about 2 to 3 tbsp. softened butter or margarine. Sprinkle with ½ cup Cinnamon-Sugar Mix (p. 206) and ½ cup sultana raisins. Chopped nuts may be added, if desired. Roll up like a jelly roll and join ends together to form a ring.

Using a sharp knife, cut ring into 1'' slices about ⅔ of the way in towards the centre of the ring. (The inside of the ring will still be attached, but the outside edges will be cut right through as if you were making individual buns.) Turn the cut sections on their sides, slightly overlapping.

When doubled in bulk, bake at 375°F for 25 to 30 minutes for a large ring, or 20 to 25 minutes for smaller rings. Cool and glaze with White Glaze (p. 206). Garnish with chopped nuts and maraschino cherries. Freezes well, but glaze after thawing.

DANISH ROLL

Prepare Norene's Yummy Yeast Dough (p. 202) or All-Purpose Pareve Dough (p. 196) and let rise as directed. Divide dough in two.

Roll out one portion of dough into an 8'' x 10'' rectangle. Brush with 1 to 2 tbsp. soft butter, sprinkle with ¼ c. Cinnamon-Sugar Mix (p. 206), and a handful of raisins (or ½ - 19 oz. can cherry or blueberry pie filling) to within ½'' of edges. Roll up like a jelly roll and seal edges well. Place across the width of a well-greased foil-lined cookie sheet. Repeat with remaining dough. Make sure to leave enough space between rolls on baking pan. Make several slashes across the top of each roll. When doubled in bulk, brush with egg wash (1 egg yolk blended with 2 tsp. water).

Bake at 375°F for about 25 to 30 minutes, until nicely browned.

Yield: 2 rolls. Freezes well.

CHEESE DANISH: Prepare Cheese Filling (p. 104). Spread ½ in a 2'' band along one edge of dough. Dough may also be sprinkled with a little cinnamon, sugar and raisins, if desired. Leave a 1'' border on all 3 sides. Roll up, sealing edges well. Repeat with remaining dough and filling. Let rise and bake as directed for Danish Roll.

HONEY PECAN ROLL

Norene's Yummy Yeast Dough (p. 202) or All-Purpose Pareve Dough (p. 196)	1½ c. pecans ½ c. honey 1 tsp. cinnamon

Follow directions for dough and let rise as directed. Punch down and divide into two equal pieces. Roll out each piece on a floured board into a 9'' x 12'' rectangle.

Steel Knife: Process nuts until coarsely chopped, about 8 to 10 seconds. Add honey and cinnamon; process with 2 or 3 quick on/off turns. Spread honey mixture evenly over each portion of dough to within 1'' of edges. Roll up like a jelly roll from the 12'' side. Seal ends. Place on a cookie sheet which has been lined with foil and well greased. Cover and let rise until double in bulk.

Bake at 350°F about 35 to 40 minutes, until golden brown. (You may brush the rolls with beaten egg yolk which has been mixed with 1 tsp. water. Brush before baking.)

Yield: 2 loaves. Freezes well.

Note: If desired, you may use honey to replace part or all of the sugar in the dough. However, dough will rise at a much slower rate.

CHOCOLATE DANISH

Follow directions for Norene's Yummy Yeast Dough (p. 202) or All-Purpose Pareve Dough (p. 196). Let rise as directed. Punch down and divide into two equal pieces. Roll out each piece on a floured board into a 9'' x 12'' rectangle. Prepare the following filling:-

⅓ c. walnuts (or any nuts you wish)
½ c. brown sugar, packed

2 tbsp. cocoa
1 tsp. cinnamon

Steel Knife: Process nuts until finely chopped, about 8 seconds. Empty bowl. Process remaining ingredients with several quick on/off turns to start, and then let machine run until mixed.

Spread each piece of dough with about 2 tbsp. softened margarine. Sprinkle with sugar mixture and nuts. Roll up like a jelly roll. If making a loaf, seal ends. Otherwise, cut in 1'' pieces. Place on a foil-lined cookie sheet which has been well-greased. Cover and let rise until double in bulk. Bake at 375°F for 25 to 30 minutes for a loaf shape, or about 18 to 20 minutes for individual danish. Freezes well. May be glazed with Chocolate Glaze (p. 265) or White Glaze (p. 206).

Yield: 2 loaves or about 16 danish.

Variation: Divide dough in half and roll into two circles. Sprinkle with filling ingredients. Cut each circle into 8 wedges. Beginning at outer edge, roll up. Place on a greased baking sheet with sealed point underneath. Curve into crescents. Cover; let rise until double and bake at 375°F for about 18 to 20 minutes.

Yield: 16 danish.

BUBBLE RING COFFEE CAKE √

Norene's Yummy Yeast Dough (p. 202) or All-Purpose Pareve Dough (p. 196)
½ c. walnuts
⅓ c. melted butter or margarine

¾ c. Cinnamon-Sugar Mix (p. 206)
¼ c. raisins
White Glaze (p. 206), if desired

Prepare desired dough and let rise as directed.

Steel Knife: Process nuts with 6 to 8 quick on/off turns, until coarsely chopped.

Form dough into forty 1'' balls. Roll first in melted butter, then in Cinnamon-Sugar Mix. Arrange in a greased 10'' tube pan or Bundt pan, sprinkling nuts and raisins in between layers.(Reserve about 2 to 3 tbsp. nuts to garnish baked cake.)

Cover and let rise until double in bulk. Bake at 375°F for about 30 to 35 minutes, until done. Loosen edges with a spatula and let stand for 15 minutes before inverting and removing from pan.

When cool, drizzle Glaze over. Sprinkle with reserved nuts. May be frozen, but glaze after thawing.

Yield: 10 to 12 servings.

CRESCENTS

Follow recipe for Norene's Yummy Yeast Dough (p. 202) or All-Purpose Pareve Dough (p. 196) and let rise as directed. Divide dough in half.

Roll one portion of dough into a circle about ¼'' thick. Spread with about 1 tbsp. softened butter or margarine, and sprinkle with about ¼ cup Cinnamon-Sugar Mix (p. 206). Roll lightly with rolling pin to press sugar mixture slightly into dough. Cut into 12 wedges for miniature buns, or 8 wedges for larger buns. Beginning at outer edge, roll up. Place on a greased baking sheet with sealed point underneath. Curve into crescents. Repeat with remaining dough.

Cover and let rise until double in bulk. Brush with egg wash (1 egg yolk blended with 2 tsp. water). Bake at 375°F for 15 minutes.

Yield: 24 small or 16 medium crescents. Freezes well.

Variation: Use filling for Chocolate Danish (p. 204) instead of cinnamon-sugar.

CINNAMON BUNS OR KUCHEN √

Norene's Yummy Yeast Dough (p. 202) or All-Purpose Pareve Dough (p. 196)
2 tbsp. soft butter or margarine

½ c. Cinnamon-Sugar Mix (p. 206)
⅓ c. raisins and / or chopped nuts, if desired

Prepare desired dough and let rise as directed. Roll into one large or two small rectangles. Spread with butter or margarine. Sprinkle with cinnamon-sugar, raisins and/or nuts. Roll lightly with rolling pin to press sugar mixture slightly into dough. Roll up like a jelly roll. Cut in 1'' slices. (Yields about 18 slices.)

Place in well-greased muffin tins or on well-greased foil-lined cookie sheets, leaving about 2'' between each bun. (For Kuchen, arrange in a well-greased 10'' springform pan or 2 greased 8'' round aluminum foil cake pans.) Cover and let rise until double in bulk. Brush with egg wash (1 egg yolk blended with 2 tsp. water).

Bake buns at 375°F for about 15 minutes, or Kuchen for about 25 to 30 minutes. May be glazed with White Glaze (p. 206). Freezes well, but glaze after thawing.

COFFEE RING: Roll dough into one large rectangle about 16'' x 20''. Fill and roll up as directed above. Cut into 8 thick slices. Place the slices in a single layer, cut-side up, in a greased 10'' tube pan. Cover; let rise until double in bulk. Bake at 375°F for about 30 to 35 minutes. May be frozen.

STICKY PECAN BUNS: Before placing buns in pans, prepare the following mixture:

¼ c. butter
½ c. brown sugar, packed
1 tbsp. water

9 glacé cherries, halved
1 c. pecans

Melt butter in a small saucepan. Add brown sugar and water; mix well. Place in muffin pans. Arrange cherries cut-side up evenly among pans.

Steel Knife: Chop pecans coarsely with several quick on/off turns. Sprinkle over sugar mixture. Arrange buns in pans. Cover, let rise and bake as directed. Immediately turn baking pans upside down on tray and let stand for about 1 minute so that sugar mixture will run over buns. May be frozen.

JAM BRAID

Follow recipe for Norene's Yummy Yeast Dough (p. 202) or All-Purpose Pareve Dough (p. 196) as directed. Divide dough in half. (Use half of dough for another recipe.) Roll one portion of dough into a rectangle about 6'' x 12'' and ½ inch thick. Use a sharp knife and cut dough lengthwise into 3 strips, leaving dough attached at one end. Braid strips and tuck ends under. Brush with a little melted butter. Cover and let rise until double in bulk. Bake at 375°F for 20 minutes. Ice with White Glaze (below) and fill crevices with about 3 to 4 tbsp. jam. Sprinkle with chopped nuts. May be frozen.

Yield: 1 loaf.

FAN TANS

Prepare Norene's Yummy Yeast Dough (p. 202) or All-Purpose Pareve Dough (p. 196) and let rise as directed. Divide in half. Roll one portion of dough into a 9'' x 10'' rectangle. Brush with soft butter. Sprinkle with ¼ c. Cinnamon-Sugar Mix (below). Cut into 6 strips of 1½'' wide x 10'' long. Stack evenly. Cut into ten 1'' strips. Place cut-side down in greased muffin cups. Repeat with remaining dough.

Cover and let rise until double in bulk. Bake at 375°F for 15 minutes.

Yield: about 20 buns. Freezes well.

WHITE GLAZE ✓

1 c. icing sugar	**2 tbsp. milk, water or juice**
½ tsp. vanilla	

Plastic Knife: Process all ingredients until blended, about 8 to 10 seconds, scraping down sides of bowl once or twice. Drizzle glaze over yeast breads or buns while still slightly warm. Decorate with chopped nuts, candied fruit or maraschino cherry halves. Glaze may crack slightly if frozen.

CINNAMON-SUGAR MIX ✓

Steel Knife: Combine 1 to 2 tbsp. cinnamon with 1 cup white sugar or 1 cup packed brown sugar in processor bowl. Process with quick on/off turns to start, then let machine run until well mixed.

Yield: 1 cup.

BANANA BREAD

(The large amount of soda as well as the long baking time at a low temperature gives the dark color to this banana bread. Delicious!)

3 medium very ripe bananas	**¼ c. oil**
(the blacker the better)	**1½ c. flour**
1 c. sugar	**½ c. buttermilk or sour milk**
3 tsp. baking soda	**(make sour milk with 1 tsp.**
dash salt	**lemon juice plus milk to**
2 eggs	**equal ½ cup)**

Steel Knife: Process bananas until puréed, about 15 to 20 seconds. You should have 1 cup banana purée. Add sugar, soda and salt and process for 30 seconds. Add eggs and oil and process until blended, about 10 seconds. Pour flour over, then add buttermilk or sour milk. Process 8 to 10 seconds longer, until smooth.

Line a 9'' x 5'' loaf pan with buttered parchment paper or aluminum foil. Pour in batter. Bake on middle rack of oven at 275°F for about 2½ hours, or until loaf tests done. (The long baking time at a low temperature is correct.)

Yield: 1 loaf. May be frozen.

ORANGE CORN BREAD

1 c. plus 3 tbsp. flour
½ tsp. salt
4 tsp. baking powder
¾ c. corn meal
1 medium seedless orange
   (do not peel)

3½ tbsp. sugar
½ c. margarine or butter,
   in chunks
1 egg
1¼ c. milk
¾ c. raisins

Steel Knife: Process dry ingredients until blended, about 5 seconds. Empty bowl.

Cut orange in quarters and discard seeds. Process on **Steel Knife** 20 seconds. Add sugar and margarine and process 1 minute. Pour egg and milk through feed tube while machine is running. Process 3 seconds. Add dry ingredients. Process, using on/off technique 3 or 4 times, **just** until blended. Add raisins and process 1 second longer.

Pour into a greased 9'' x 5'' loaf pan or 8'' square. Pan will be ⅔ full. Bake at 375°F for about 45 minutes, until cake tester comes out clean and dry. Serve warm or toasted with butter or preserves. Delicious!

Yield: 1 loaf. Freezes well.

NANA'S ZUCCHINI BREAD

3 c. flour
1½ c. sugar
1 tsp. cinnamon
1 tsp. salt
1 tsp. baking powder
¾ tsp. baking soda

1½ c. walnuts
1 c. raisins or currants
2 medium zucchini (2 c.
   grated)
3 eggs
1 c. oil

Steel Knife: Process flour with sugar, cinnamon, salt, baking powder and soda for 10 seconds, until blended. Transfer to a large bowl. Chop nuts coarsely with several quick on/off turns. Set aside ½ cup nuts. Combine remaining nuts with raisins in a small bowl and set aside.

Grater: Discard tips of zucchini. Peel if desired. (I don't, as there are vitamins in the skin. Just tell your children that the bits of green are pistachio nuts!) Grate, using medium pressure. Measure 2 cups. Add to flour mixture.

Steel Knife: Blend eggs with oil until light, about 45 seconds. Add to flour mixture. Stir until moistened. Add raisin/nut mixture. Pour into two greased and floured 9'' x 5'' loaf pans. Sprinkle with reserved nuts.

Bake at 350°F for about 45 to 50 minutes, until loaves test done. Cool for 15 minutes before removing from pans.

Yield: 2 loaves. Freezes well.

Variation: Eliminate raisins or currants. Add one 6 oz. package chocolate chips along with the nuts.

ZUCCHINI MUFFINS

Follow recipe for Nana's Zucchini Bread (above). Pour batter into greased or paper-lined muffin tins. Bake at 350°F about 25 minutes.

Yield: 24 to 30 muffins. Freezes well.

BANANA MUFFINS

½ c. butter or margarine, cut in
   chunks
2 eggs
1 tsp. vanilla
1¼ c. sugar

1 medium banana
1 tsp. baking soda
¾ c. buttermilk
1 tsp. baking powder
2 c. flour

Steel Knife: Process margarine, eggs, vanilla and sugar for 2 minutes, scraping down bowl once or twice. Do not insert pusher in feed tube. Break banana into 2'' pieces and add through feed tube while machine is running. Dissolve baking soda in buttermilk. Pour in through feed tube and process for 3 seconds. Add dry ingredients. Process with 4 quick on/off turns, **just** until flour disappears. Fill greased or paper-lined muffin tins ⅔ full. Bake at 400°F for 18 to 20 minutes.

Yield: about 18 muffins. Freezes well.

MOM'S BLUEBERRY MUFFINS ✓

½ c. butter or margarine, cut in
   chunks
¾ c. sugar
2 eggs
1 tbsp. vinegar plus milk to
   equal 1 cup

1 tsp. baking soda
2 tsp. baking powder
2 c. flour
1½ c. fresh or frozen
   blueberries

Steel Knife: Process butter, sugar and eggs for 2 minutes, scraping down bowl once or twice. Do not insert pusher in feed tube. Dissolve baking soda in vinegar-milk mixture. Pour in through feed tube and process for 3 seconds. Add dry ingredients. Process with 4 quick on/off turns, **just** until flour disappears. Carefully stir in blueberries by hand. Pour into greased or paper-lined muffin tins and bake at 375°F for 25 to 30 minutes.

Yield: about 2 dozen muffins. Freezes well.

HONEY BRAN MUFFINS ✓

(Grated carrots make these muffins moist and yummy!)

1½ c. whole wheat flour
1 tsp. salt
1½ tsp. soda
1 tsp. cinnamon
½ tsp. nutmeg
1½ c. bran
3 medium carrots (1 c. grated)

2 eggs
¼ c. oil
1½ c. milk or orange juice
2 tbsp. vinegar
½ c. honey
¼ c. molasses
½ c. raisins, if desired

Steel Knife: Process first 6 ingredients for 4 or 5 seconds. Transfer to a large mixing bowl. Cut carrots in 1'' chunks. Process until fine, scraping down bowl as necessary. Measure 1 cup and add to mixing bowl. Process eggs and oil for 2 or 3 seconds. Add with remaining ingredients to mixing bowl and stir with a wooden spoon just until blended. Do not overmix.

Spoon batter into paper lined muffin cups. Bake at 375°F for 20 to 25 minutes.

Yield: about 2 dozen. Freezes well.

DIET APPLE MUFFINS

2 slices bread, quartered	2 tsp. baking powder
2 apples, peeled, cored & quartered	2 tsp. vanilla
	1 or 2 tsp. cinnamon
2 eggs	artificial sweetener to equal
⅔ c. nonfat dry milk	2 tbsp. sugar

Steel Knife: Process bread with apple until coarsely chopped, about 6 seconds. Add remaining ingredients and process with 3 or 4 quick on/off turns, just until mixed. Pour into greased muffin tins. Bake at 375°F for 20 minutes, until puffed and browned. May be frozen.

Yield: 6 large muffins of 100 calories each or 12 small muffins of 50 calories each. Delicious for breakfast!

OATMEAL RAISIN MUFFINS √

1 c. flour	1 egg
½ tsp. salt	½ c. white sugar or brown
1 tsp. baking powder	sugar, firmly packed
½ tsp. baking soda	½ c. oil
1 c. quick-cooking rolled oats	¾ c. raisins
1 c. buttermilk or sour milk	

Steel Knife: Process flour, salt, baking powder and baking soda until blended, about 5 seconds. Transfer to a large mixing bowl. Place oats and buttermilk in processor bowl and let stand 2 or 3 minutes. Add egg, sugar and oil and process 10 seconds. Add to flour mixture along with raisins. Stir with a wooden spoon just enough to moisten. Spoon into muffin tins which have been lined with paper liners. Bake at 400°F for 18 to 20 minutes, until golden.

Yield: 12 to 15 muffins. Freezes well.

SUGAR-FREE BRAN MUFFINS √

(Moist, light & delicious)

1 c. flour (part whole-wheat, if desired)	1 c. All-bran
	1 egg
1 tsp. baking soda	2 tbsp. oil
1 tsp. baking powder	1 c. buttermilk (or 1 tbsp.
¼ tsp. salt	lemon juice plus skim milk
⅓ c. pitted dates (about 10)	to equal 1 c.)
artificial sweetener to equal ½ c. sugar	

Steel Knife: Place flour, soda, baking powder, salt, dates and sweetener in processor bowl. Process for 8 to 10 seconds, until dates are coarsely chopped. Add remaining ingredients and process with 2 or 3 quick on/off turns, **just** until mixed.

Divide batter evenly among 12 paper-lined muffin cups. Bake at 400°F for 20 to 25 minutes, until nicely browned.

Yield: 1 dozen muffins of about 95 calories each. Freezes well.

Note: Raisins may be substituted for the dates, but process only for about 5 seconds with the dry ingredients.

Desserts
& Tortes

ᵈDessert Hints

- **Marshmallows** went stale? Place a slice of fresh bread in the bag with the marshmallows and close tightly. A day or two later, discard the bread, and the marshmallows will be soft.

- **Whipping Cream** (35% cream) will turn to butter if it is warmer than 35°F when it is being whipped. Chill cream in the freezer for a few minutes before whipping to avoid this problem. Chilling the **Steel Knife** and the bowl will also help.

- **Fruit** may be ripened by storing it in a brown paper bag at room temperature for a few days. Refrigerate when ripe.

- **Fresh Fruit Salads:** Any fresh fruits in season (apples, pears, peaches, oranges, grapefruit, berries, melons). Bananas, watermelon and canteloupe should only be added to fruit salads which are to be eaten on the same day; otherwise the fruit will begin to ferment. To peel peaches, pour boiling water over; the skin will then peel off easily. Use watermelon in small amounts as it causes soggy fruit salad. Lemon juice will prevent discoloration of apples and bananas. An attractive glass bowl or brandy snifter will show off the fruits to advantage. A little liqueur may be added (e.g. Cointreau, Kirsch, Grand Marnier, or a little sherry or wine.)

- **Jell-O** which has set too firmly (especially in recipes which call for partially set Jell-O) can be melted or softened by placing the bowl of Jell-O into a bowl or sinkful of warm water. Then let it set again until desired consistency is reached.

- **Jell-O** may be thickened quickly either by substituting ice cubes for the cold water called for in the recipe, or by placing mixture in the freezer for about half an hour.

- **To unmold Jell-O molds:** It is important to allow air to get between Jell-O and the mold pan. Put pan into a sinkful of hot water for 5 seconds. Place serving plate over the pan and invert. Shake gently to loosen and allow air to enter. Mold will release.

- **To prevent** apple and banana slices from discoloring, sprinkle with a little lemon or pineapple juice.

- **Strawberries** taste fantastic when prepared in the following way:- Add 2 tbsp. brown sugar and 2 cups sour cream (or plain yoghurt) to 2 cups of sliced strawberries. Let stand 15 minutes for a melt-in-your-mouth flavor.

- **To prevent leakage** from springform pans when making mousses or Jell-O desserts, make sure Jell-O is partially set before placing mixture in pan. A crumb crust will also help.

- **To prevent** a skin from forming on cooked puddings, cover surface with waxed paper and remove when pudding is cool.

- **To make chocolate curls,** slightly warm a square of semi-sweet chocolate or a chocolate bar. Take long strokes on the flat side with a potato peeler. Chocolate may be grated on the **Grater** of the processor, using firm pressure, but it will not make curls. It is a good idea to grate several squares of chocolate at one time, and store it in a plastic bag in the refrigerator or freezer. Use as needed.

- **Women,** always being diet-conscious, may pass up cake, but will always go for light cold desserts (even though they may be loaded with calories)!

BASIC TORTE LAYERS

1 c. butter, cut in chunks	1 tsp. baking powder
½ c. sugar	2 c. flour
2 eggs	

Steel Knife: Process butter, sugar and eggs until well blended, about 1 minute. Add flour and baking powder. Process just until mixed, using on/off turns.

Divide dough into 5 or 6 equal portions. Roll out each piece of dough into an 8'' circle. Place on inverted 8'' layer pans. (It is not necessary to grease the pans.) Bake at 350°F until light brown, about 10 to 12 minutes. Remove from pans immediately and let cool. Fill and assemble as directed in any of the following recipes.

Yield: 5 to 6 layers. May be prepared in advance and frozen until needed.

CHOCOLATE LAYER TORTE

Basic Torte Layers (above)	1 c. chilled butter or
½ c. water	margarine, cut in chunks
¼ c. flour	1 c. icing sugar
¼ c. granulated sugar	2 tbsp. cocoa
1 square semi-sweet	½ c. sliced or slivered
chocolate, halved	almonds

Prepare Basic Torte Layers as directed. (May be prepared in advance and frozen.)

Steel Knife: Combine water, flour and sugar in processor bowl. Process until blended and no lumps remain, about 8 to 10 seconds. Transfer to a heavy-bottomed saucepan. Cook over medium heat, stirring constantly, until veiy thick, about 2 to 3 minutes. Add chocolate and stir until melted. Remove from heat and cool completely.

Steel Knife: Process butter with icing sugar until well-creamed, about 1 minute. Add cooled chocolate mixture and cocoa. Process until well blended, about 20 to 30 seconds, scraping down bowl as necessary.

Spread filling thinly between Torte Layers, ending with filling. Toast almonds on a baking sheet at 300°F for about 10 minutes. Cool completely. Garnish top of cake. Refrigerate at least 24 hours before serving. May be frozen.

Yield: 10 servings.

CINNAMON TORTE

Basic Torte Layers (above)	½ tsp. vanilla
3 c. chilled whipping cream	grated semi-sweet
⅓ c. icing sugar	chocolate, to garnish
1 tsp. cinnamon	

Prepare Basic Torte Layers as directed, adding 1½ tbsp. cinnamon to batter with dry ingredients. (May be prepared in advance and frozen.)

Cream may be whipped on an electric mixer or on processor using **Steel Knife.**(The electric mixer will yield a larger volume when whipped.) Place a heavy book under the back part of the base so that the processor is tipped forward. Pour cream through the feed tube while the machine is running and whip until it is the texture of sour cream, about 30 to 40 seconds. Do not insert pusher in feed tube. Add sugar, cinnamon and vanilla. Process about 10 seconds longer, or until cream is stiff and peaked. Do not overprocess.

Spread between Torte Layers, ending with whipped cream. Sprinkle with grated chocolate, and garnish with pecan halves, if desired.

Yield: 10 servings. Do not freeze.

NAPOLEON TORTE

Basic Torte Layers (p. 213)
4¾ oz. pkg. (6 serving size)
vanilla pudding (not instant)
2⅓ c. milk

1 c. chilled whipping cream
(or 1 envelope dessert
topping plus ½ c. milk)
Icing sugar to garnish

Prepare Basic Torte Layers as directed.

Cook pudding according to package directions, using 2⅓ cups milk. Cover top of cooked pudding with a piece of waxed paper and refrigerate until completely cold.

Steel Knife: Tip processor forward by placing a thick book underneath base. Do not insert pusher in feed tube. Process whipping cream or dessert topping until stiff, (about 45 seconds for whipping cream, and 2 minutes for dessert topping.) Add chilled pudding and blend until smooth, about 15 to 20 seconds.

Spread cream filling between Torte Layers, ending with crust. Sprinkle heavily with icing sugar. Refrigerate 24 hours. Cut with a very sharp knife.

Yield: 8 to 10 servings. Do not freeze.

Variation: Arrange sliced bananas (sprinkled with lemon juice to prevent darkening) between layers along with custard mixture. Other fruits may be substituted, if desired (e.g. peaches, mandarin oranges).

SOUR CREAM TORTE

Basic Torte Layers (p. 213)
1½ c. walnuts
1½ c. sour cream

1 tsp. vanilla
½ c. icing sugar (or to taste)

Prepare Basic Torte Layers as directed. (May be prepared in advance and frozen.)

Steel Knife: Process nuts until finely chopped, about 15 seconds. Add sour cream, vanilla and icing sugar. Process a few seconds longer to mix. Spread filling between Torte Layers, ending with crust. Refrigerate at least 24 hours before serving. Before serving, sprinkle generously with sifted icing sugar. Do not freeze.

Yield: 10 servings.

HAZELNUT (FILBERT) TORTE

¾ c. filberts
2 squares semi-sweet
chocolate, halved
¾ c. margarine or butter, cut in chunks

¾ c. sugar
2 eggs
¾ c. flour
¾ tsp. baking powder

Steel Knife: Process nuts with chocolate until ground, about 45 seconds. Empty bowl. Process margarine with sugar for 30 seconds. Add eggs and process 1 minute longer. Add flour and baking powder. Process with 3 or 4 quick on/off turns. Add chocolate and nuts. Process for 4 or 5 seconds, just until mixed into batter.

Spread batter evenly into two 9'' round layer pans which have been well-greased. Bake at 350°F for 30 to 35 minutes, until layers test done. Cool 10 minutes before removing from pans. Fill and frost with Mocha Butter Cream (p. 269) or Chocolate Buttercream Icing (p. 268). Freezes well.

Yield: 8 to 10 servings.

Note: Recipe may be doubled and Torte can be made in four layers if desired. If doubling recipe, process in 2 batches.

BLACK FOREST TORTE

(Authentic Swiss Recipe. Fantastic! As this is a torte rather than a cake the layers will be very thin.)

Chocolate Torte:
1 c. unblanched almonds
12 rusks, broken into pieces
   (See Note)
4 squares semi-sweet
   chocolate
¼ c. water or coffee
1 c. butter, cut into chunks
1 c. sugar
6 egg yolks
6 egg whites

Filling and Garnish:
2 cans Bing cherries, drained
   & pitted (reserve ¼ c. juice)
¼ c. Kirsch
2 c. whipping cream, chilled
3 tbsp. sugar
1 square semi-sweet
   chocolate
whole unblanched almonds
maraschino cherries

Steel Knife: Chop almonds coarsely, about 15 seconds. Transfer to a large mixing bowl. Process rusks to make fine crumbs. Add to nuts. Melt chocolate with water or coffee in the top of a double boiler or in a saucepan over low heat. Cool. Process butter with sugar and egg yolks until well beaten, about 1 minute. Scrape down sides of bowl once or twice, as necessary. Add cooled chocolate mixture and process about 8 to 10 seconds to blend, scraping down sides of bowl as necessary. Add nuts and rusks. Blend in with quick on/off turns. Transfer mixture to large mixing bowl.

Using electric mixer, beat egg whites until stiff but not dry. Stir a little into the chocolate mixture to lighten it, then fold in remaining whites carefully with a rubber spatula.

Pour into a greased and floured 10'' springform pan. Bake at 350°F for 50 to 60 minutes. Cool completely. Remove from pan and split into 3 layers. (May be frozen at this time and thawed when needed.)

Combine ¼ c. cherry juice with the kirsch. Whip cream until nearly stiff. Beat in sugar. (An electric mixer is preferred in order to achieve maximum volume and a very light texture.)

Grater: Grate chocolate, using firm pressure.

To Assemble Torte:

Sprinkle bottom layer of torte with about ¼ cup of the cherry liquid. Spread with a layer of whipped cream. Top with second torte layer. Moisten with remaining cherry liquid. Spread with a layer of whipped cream, then with drained cherries, then with whipped cream once again. Top with a third layer of cake. Ice completely with remaining whipped cream.

Garnish with grated chocolate on the top and sides of the torte. Decorate the outer edge of the top of the torte with almonds and cherries. Refrigerate for several hours before serving. Freezes well.

Yield: 12 to 16 servings.

To Thaw: Remove from freezer and place in refrigerator overnight.

Note: Rusks are toasted, dried bread slices and are found in the cracker or gourmet section of your supermarket. You may substitute 12 slices of French bread sliced ¾'' thick. Place slices on a cookie sheet and bake uncovered at 250°F for 1 hour, until dry and golden brown.

LINZER TORTE
(A lattice-topped jam & nut delight)

¾ c. almonds
1½ c. flour
½ c. butter or margarine, cut in chunks
½ c. icing sugar
1 tsp. grated lemon rind, if desired

1 egg
1¼ c. strawberry jam (raspberry, peach or apricot jam may be used)

Steel Knife: Process nuts with ¼ cup of flour until very finely chopped, about 30 seconds. Empty bowl. Process remaining flour with butter and icing sugar about 10 seconds, until crumbly. Add nut-flour mixture, rind and egg. Process until blended, about 10 or 15 seconds. Press ¾ of the dough into the bottom and about ¼'' up the sides of a lightly greased 9'' spring form pan to form a shallow shell about ¼'' in thickness. Fill evenly with jam. Roll out remaining dough on a floured board or pastry cloth and cut in ½'' wide strips. Make lattice-work over the top of the torte.

Bake at 350°F for 45 minutes. When cooled, fill any spaces between lattice-work with more jam. Dust with additional icing sugar.

Yield: 10 servings. May be frozen.

CHOCOLATE FANTASY TORTE

1 c. pecans
1 square semi-sweet chocolate
8 oz. pkg. chocolate wafers
⅓ c. melted butter
2 tbsp. sugar
½ c. chilled butter, cut in chunks

1½ c. icing sugar
3 eggs
3 squares unsweetened chocolate, melted & cooled
1½ c. chilled whipping cream
½ c. maple syrup
4 c. colored miniature marshmallows

Steel Knife: Chop pecans coarsely with several quick on/off turns. Empty bowl.

Grater: Grate chocolate, using firm pressure. Reserve for garnish. Wipe out bowl with paper towelling.

Steel Knife: Break chocolate wafers into chunks and process until fine crumbs are formed, about 20 to 30 seconds. Measure 1½ cups crumbs. Process with melted butter and 2 tbsp. sugar until blended, about 6 to 8 seconds. Press into the bottom of a 10'' springform pan. Bake at 375°F for 7 to 8 minutes. Cool. Wash bowl and blade.

Steel Knife: Process ½ cup butter with icing sugar and eggs for 45 seconds. Do not insert pusher in feed tube. Add cooled chocolate and process until blended, about 20 seconds, scraping down bowl as necessary. Pour over crust. Place in freezer while preparing topping.

Cream may be whipped on electric mixer, or on processor using the **Steel Knife.** Tip processor forward by placing a thick book underneath base. Do not insert pusher in feed tube. Whip cream with maple syrup until thick, about 45 seconds. Fold in marshmallows and pecans with a rubber spatula. Spread over chocolate layer. Garnish with reserved grated chocolate. Refrigerate overnight. (May be frozen. Remove from freezer one hour before serving.)

Yield: 12 servings.

Note: Vanilla wafers may be substituted for chocolate wafers, if desired.

GRASSHOPPER TORTE

8 oz. pkg. chocolate wafers
½ c. butter or margarine, melted
9 oz. jar marshmallow cream (or 1 pkg. marshmallows melted with ¼ c. milk)
¼ c. milk (or green creme de menthe liqueur)

1 tsp. peppermint extract (omit if using liqueur)
few drops green food coloring (omit if using liqueur)
2 c. whipping cream (or 2 envelopes dessert topping mix plus 1 c. milk)

Steel Knife: Break cookies into chunks and process to make fine crumbs, about 30 seconds. Add melted butter and process a few seconds longer, until mixed. Reserve ½ cup crumbs for topping. Press remaining crumbs into the bottom of an ungreased 9" springform pan or into the bottom and up the sides of a 10" pie plate. Chill while preparing filling.

Combine marshmallow cream with liqueur, (or with milk, peppermint extract and food coloring.) (If using packaged marshmallows, melt with ¼ c. milk over low heat, stirring constantly. Cool, stirring every 5 minutes. Stir in liqueur.)

Whip cream or dessert topping until stiff. It is preferable to use an electric mixer in order to achieve maximum volume, but if you wish, you may use the **Steel Knife** and whip the cream or topping on the processor. Fold in marshmallow mixture. Pour over crust. Top with reserved crumbs, cover with aluminum foil and freeze several hours or overnight. (May be prepared in advance and frozen until needed.)

Yield: 8 to 10 servings. Delicious!

Variation: Instead of garnishing with chocolate wafer crumbs, garnish with whipped cream and grated semi-sweet chocolate at serving time.

TIA MARIA TORTE

2 c. chilled whipping cream
¼ c. icing sugar
Chocolate Chip Cookies (2 lb. package or 4 to 5 dozen home-made)
⅔ c. milk

⅔ c. Tia Maria liqueur
1 square semi-sweet chocolate
12 maraschino cherries, well-drained

Whip cream with sugar on electric mixer until stiff. Set aside. (Processor may be used, but will not yield enough volume.) Dip cookies quickly into milk, then into liqueur. Arrange in a single layer in the bottom of an ungreased 10" springform pan. Fill in spaces with pieces of cookies which have also been dipped. Spread a layer of whipped cream over cookies. Repeat twice more with remaining cookies and whipped cream, ending with whipped cream. Reserve about ½ cup whipped cream and place in a pastry bag fitted with a star tube. Pipe rosettes around the edge of the Torte.

Grater: Grate chocolate, using firm pressure. Sprinkle over top of Torte. Garnish rosettes of whipped cream with cherries. Refrigerate overnight.

Yield: 12 servings.

MALAKOV CREAM CAKE

(To blow your mind — and your diet!)

3 squares unsweetened chocolate	2 tbsp. rum, cognac or brandy
1 c. unsalted butter, cut into chunks	1 - 16 oz. sponge cake
1¾ c. icing sugar	1½ c. whipping cream, chilled
3 egg yolks	2 tbsp. sugar or icing sugar
¼ c. milk	whole almonds
	maraschino cherries
	grated semi-sweet chocolate

Melt chocolate over low heat. (Chopping chocolate first on the **Steel Knife** until fine will make it melt very quickly.) Cool completely.

Steel Knife: Process butter and sugar until well creamed and light, about 1 minute. Add egg yolks and process another 20 seconds, until well blended. Scrape down sides of bowl as necessary. Blend in milk and liqueur for a few seconds, then add cooled chocolate. Process about 10 seconds longer, scraping down sides of bowl once or twice.

Cut cake into 1'' squares with a sharp knife. Arrange a layer of cake squares in a lightly buttered 9'' pie plate or 8'' spring form pan, leaving spaces between the cake so that the cream can go in between. Pour half of chocolate cream over. Repeat with remaining cake and chocolate cream. Cover with waxed paper and weigh down with a heavy plate. (I usually put several jars of odds and ends from the refrigerator on top of the plate to help force the buttercream between the cake squares.) Refrigerate for several hours or overnight. (May be frozen until needed and then thawed in the refrigerator overnight.) Remove waxed paper.

Steel Knife: Place a heavy book under the back part of the base of the processor so that the machine is tipped forward. Do not insert pusher in feed tube. Process whipping cream until the texture of sour cream. Add sugar and process until stiff, about 10 seconds longer. Spread over chocolate layer. (You may use a pastry decorating set to pipe rosettes of whipped cream around the border.) Arrange almonds and cherries decoratively around the edges, and sprinkle with grated chocolate. Chill until serving time.

Yield: 8 to 10 servings. (As this dessert is sinfully rich, I usually serve small slices. However, they always come back for seconds!) May be frozen.

Variation: Omit chocolate. Process ¼ lb. roasted almonds on the **Steel Knife** until fine. Empty bowl. Prepare buttercream as directed, adding ground almonds with on/off turns. You may also substitute ⅓ cup strong coffee to replace the milk and liqueur, if desired.

EASY CHEESE CAKE (8" or 9")

Crust:
18 single graham wafers (about 1½ c. crumbs)
6 tbsp. soft butter or margarine, cut in small chunks
2 tbsp. sugar
½ tsp. cinnamon

Filling:
1½ lb. cream cheese (half cottage cheese may be used), cut in chunks
3 eggs
1 c. plus 2 tbsp. sugar
2 tsp. vanilla

Crust: Insert **Steel Knife** in processor. Break wafers into chunks. Process until coarse crumbs are formed. Add remaining ingredients and process until blended, about 5 or 6 seconds. Pat into the bottom of a lightly greased 8'' or 9'' spring form pan. Wash and dry bowl and blade.

Filling: Process ingredients for filling on **Steel Knife** until blended and creamy, about 30 seconds. Pour over crust. Bake at 375°F for 35 minutes. Edges should be brown and set. Turn off heat and leave cake in oven with door partly open until cool, about 1 hour. Top will crack slightly and cake may fall.

You may top this cheese cake with any of the toppings listed below. Refrigerate.

Yield: 9 - 10 servings. Cheese cake may be frozen, but crust may not be as crisp. Topping is best added when cheese cake is thawed.

EASY CHEESE CAKE (10")

Use a 10'' spring form pan. Increase the filling ingredients to 2 lb. cream cheese, 4 eggs, 1½ cups sugar and 1 tbsp. vanilla. It is not necessary to increase the ingredients for the crust. Baking time should be increased by 5 minutes.

Yield: 12 servings.

CHEESE CAKE TOPPINGS

1) **Canned Pie Fillings:** Use a 19 oz. can of cherry, blueberry or pineapple pie filling. Spoon over cheese cake. Chill 3 to 4 hours.

2) **Mandarin Orange Topping:** Drain three 10 oz. cans mandarin oranges. Pat dry. Arrange in an attractive design over cooled cheese cake. Melt 1 cup red currant or apple jelly with 2 tsp. water over low heat. Brush over fruit to glaze. Chill 3 to 4 hours. Chocolate wafers may be substituted for graham wafers to make the crust.

3) **Peach Topping:** Drain a 28 oz. tin of peach slices, reserving 1 cup juice. Pat fruit dry. Arrange in an attractive design over cooled cheese cake. Place reserved peach syrup in a saucepan with 1 tbsp. corn starch and 2 tsp. lemon juice. Blend well. Cook over medium heat until syrup thickens, stirring constantly. Cool. Spoon over peaches. Chill 3 to 4 hours.

4) **Fresh Strawberry Topping:** Hull and slice 2 pints of strawberries in half lengthwise. Arrange cut-side down in an attractive design over cooled cheese cake. Melt 1 cup red currant jelly or strawberry jelly with 2 tsp. water over low heat. Brush over fruit to glaze. Chill 3 to 4 hours.

5) **Fresh Strawberry Glaze:** Hull 2 pints of strawberries. Slice about 3 cups in half lengthwise and arrange cut-side down in an attractive design over cooled cheese cake. Process remaining cup of berries on the **Steel Knife** until crushed, about 3 or 4 seconds.

Combine crushed berries with ¾ c. sugar, ¼ c. cold water and 1½ tbsp. potato starch or corn starch in a saucepan. Simmer gently for about 2 minutes, stirring constantly. Stir in 1 tsp. butter or margarine. Cool slightly. Spoon over cheese cake. Chill 3 to 4 hours.

MINI CHEESE CAKES

Follow recipe for Easy Cheese Cake (p. 219). Divide crumb mixture evenly among muffin tins which have been lined with paper cupcake liners. Top with cheese mixture. Bake at 375°F for about 10 minutes. Top with assorted toppings (e.g. cherry, blueberry, pineapple, strawberry). Refrigerate.

Yield: about 18 to 24 miniature cheese cakes. (The 10'' cheese cake recipe will make about 24 minis; the 8'' or 9'' will make about 18.)

Note: An easy topping for these miniatures is a spoonful of thick jam.

CHOCOLATE CHEESECAKE (Baked)

Very rich — but very delicious!

8 oz. pkg. chocolate wafers (about 1¾ c. crumbs)	1 lb. cream cheese, cut in chunks
½ c. butter or margarine, melted	¾ c. sugar
½ tsp. cinnamon	4 eggs
2 tbsp. white or brown sugar	½ c. sour cream
2 - 6 oz. pkgs. chocolate chips	½ c. whipping cream
	1 tbsp. icing sugar

Steel Knife: Break wafers in pieces and drop through feed tube while machine is running. Process until fine crumbs are formed. Add butter, cinnamon and sugar; process a few seconds longer to blend. Press into the bottom of a lightly greased 9'' springform pan, reserving ⅓ cup crumbs for topping. Wash and dry bowl and blade.

Melt chocolate chips on low heat; cool. Using **Steel Knife,** process cheese with sugar for about 1 minute. Do not insert pusher in feed tube. Add eggs one at a time through the feed tube, processing to blend thoroughly. Scrape down sides of bowl as necessary. Add chocolate and sour cream; process about 20 seconds longer, scraping down bowl to blend batter.

Pour chocolate mixture over crust and sprinkle with reserved crumbs. Bake at 350°F for 50 to 55 minutes. Edges of cake will be set, but the centre will be somewhat soft and runny. Turn off oven and let cake cool in oven for ½ hour with the door partly open. Surface of cake will crack slightly.

When completely cooled, place on a serving plate, removing sides of pan. Insert **Steel Knife** in processor. Place a heavy book under the back part of the base so that the machine is tipped forward. Whip cream until thick, about 35 to 40 seconds. Do not insert pusher in feed tube. Add icing sugar and process a few seconds longer, until stiff. Transfer to a pastry bag fitted with a star tube. Garnish cake with rosettes of whipped cream. Top each rosette with a chocolate chip, or sprinkle with grated chocolate. Refrigerate.

Yield: 12 to 15 servings. May be frozen, but thaw in refrigerator. As this cheesecake is extremely rich, serve very small portions.

DREAMY CREAMY CHOCOLATE CHEESECAKE (Unbaked)

1 **square semi-sweet chocolate**
8 **oz. pkg. chocolate wafers**
½ **c. melted butter or margarine**
2 **envelopes dessert topping (e.g. Dream Whip)**
1 **c. milk**
1 **lb. cream cheese, cut in chunks**

2 **tbsp. Kahlua or Tia Maria, if desired**
⅔ **c. sugar**
2 **- 6 oz. pkgs. chocolate chips, melted & cooled**
1 **c. whipping cream (or 1 envelope dessert topping plus ½ cup milk)**

Grater: Grate chocolate, using firm pressure. Set aside to use as a garnish.

Steel Knife: Break wafers in half and drop through feed tube while machine is running. Process until fine crumbs are formed. Add butter and process a few seconds longer to blend. Press into the bottom of an ungreased 10'' springform pan. Bake at 350°F for 7 to 8 minutes. Cool. Wash bowl, cover and blade.

Tip processor forward by placing a thick book underneath the base. Using **Steel Knife,** process dessert topping with milk for 2 minutes, until stiff. Do not insert pusher in feed tube. Remove book from under base. Add cream cheese chunks through feed tube while machine is running. Process until smooth. Add liqueur, sugar and chocolate. Process until smooth and light, about 2 minutes, scraping down sides of bowl as necessary. Pour over crust. Wash bowl and blade.

Steel Knife: Tip processor forward once again, using a thick book underneath the base. Process until stiff, about 35 to 40 seconds for cream and 2 minutes for dessert topping. Decorate cheesecake using a pastry decorator to pipe whipped cream in an attractive design. Sprinkle with reserved grated chocolate. Refrigerate 6 to 8 hours, or overnight.

Yield: 12 servings. May be frozen. Thaw overnight in refrigerator.

Note: Recipe may be halved, if desired, using a 9'' pie plate. Decrease crumbs to 1¼ cups and butter to ⅓ cup. Do not decrease whipping cream for topping.

LIGHT'N'LEMONY CHEESE DESSERT

3 **oz. pkg. (4 serving size) lemon Jell-O**
1 **c. boiling water**
1⅓ **c. cottage cheese**

1 **envelope dessert topping mix (Dream Whip, etc.)**
½ **c. milk**

Dissolve Jell-O in boiling water. Chill until partially set (the consistency of unbeaten egg whites).

Steel Knife: Process cottage cheese until smooth and creamy (creamed cottage cheese is ideal). Add Jell-O and process until well mixed, about 30 seconds. Scrape down sides of bowl as necessary.

Combine dessert topping with milk and prepare according to package directions, using electric mixer for maximum volume. Add to lemon/cheese mixture and process until blended and smooth, about 20 seconds longer.

Pour into a baked 9'' graham wafer crust, or into 8 individual glass serving dishes. If desired, garnish with whole strawberries. Refrigerate 3 to 4 hours.

Yield: 8 servings. Do not freeze. Contains about 114 calories per serving, excluding graham wafer crust and strawberries.

Note: Substitute low-calorie gelatin dessert (D-Zerta) to reduce calories to about 77 per serving.

CREAMY PINEAPPLE CHEESECAKE
(Unbaked)

20 single graham wafers (about
    1¾ c. crumbs)
½ c. soft butter or margarine,
    cut in chunks
3 tbsp. brown sugar
3 oz. pkg. lemon Jell-O
1 cup boiling water

2 c. marshmallows
2 lb. dry cottage cheese or
    cream cheese
3 tbsp. sugar
14 oz. can crushed pineapple,
    drained

Steel Knife: Break wafers into pieces. Process wafers to make coarse crumbs, about 20 seconds. Add butter and brown sugar and process until blended, about 5 or 6 seconds longer. Press into the bottom of a 10″ springform pan, reserving about 3 tbsp. crumbs for topping. Bake at 375°F for 7 to 8 minutes, until golden. Cool.

Dissolve Jell-O in boiling water in a saucepan. Add marshmallows and stir over low heat until melted. Refrigerate for 1 hour, or place in freezer for ½ hour, until thickened.

Steel Knife: Process cheese about 45 seconds, until smooth and well creamed. Add thickened Jell-O mixture and sugar. Process until blended, about 15 seconds, scraping down bowl as necessary. Add pineapple and process with 3 or 4 quick on/off turns. Pour over crust. Sprinkle with reserved crumbs. Chill overnight.

Yield: 12 servings. Do not freeze.

STRAWBERRY DREAM CHEESECAKE

Follow recipe for Creamy Pineapple Cheesecake (above). Instead of lemon Jell-O and crushed pineapple, substitute strawberry Jell-O and 1 pint fresh strawberries.

Slicer: Slice berries, using gentle pressure. Fold berries into cheese mixture by hand.

Yield: 12 servings. Do not freeze.

Note: If desired, garnish with whipped cream or dessert topping instead of sprinkling with graham wafer crumbs. Pipe in an attractive design using a pastry bag and star tube. Decorate with whole strawberries.

LEMON TRIFLE
(A delightful and refreshing dessert)

1 pkg. lemon pie filling
2¼ c. whipping cream (500 mL)
¼ c. sugar
1 sponge or angel cake, cut in
    1″ squares

14 oz. can pineapple chunks,
    well-drained
10 oz. can mandarin oranges
    well-drained

Prepare pie filling according to package directions. Cool completely.

Steel Knife: Tip processor forward by placing a thick book underneath. Do not insert pusher in feed tube. Whip cream until texture of sour cream. Add sugar and process a few seconds longer, until stiff. Set aside half the whipped cream for the garnish. Add cooked lemon mixture to whipped cream and process with several quick on/off turns to blend, scraping down bowl as necessary.

Arrange half the cake in a 2½ to 3 quart glass bowl. Add half the pineapple, then top with half the lemon cream. Repeat with remaining cake, pineapple and lemon cream. Garnish with reserved whipped cream and arrange orange segments in an attractive design. Refrigerate 4 to 6 hours.

Yield: 12 servings. Do not freeze.

TERRIFIC TRIFLE

(Easy to Make and Delicious to Eat!)

6 serving size pkg. vanilla instant pudding	¼ c. rum, Cointreau, Grand Marnier, sherry or your favorite liqueur
1½ c. sour cream or plain yoghurt	2 bananas
1½ c. milk	1 tbsp. lemon juice
1 pint strawberries, hulled	1 pint (500 mL) chilled whipping cream
1 sponge cake, broken into 1" chunks	¼ c. sugar or icing sugar
	grated semi-sweet chocolate

Steel Knife: Process pudding with sour cream for a few seconds. Gradually add milk through feed tube while machine is running, stopping machine once or twice to scrape down sides of bowl. Process for about 20 seconds. Empty mixture into another bowl. Wash and dry bowl and blade.

Slicer: Reserve several strawberries for garnish. Slice remaining berries, using gentle pressure.

Place ⅓ of cake on the bottom of a 3 qt. glass serving bowl. Sprinkle with 2 tbsp. liqueur. Arrange strawberries over cake and cover with half of pudding. Place another ⅓ of cake over pudding and sprinkle with remaining liqueur.

Slicer: Cut bananas to fit feed tube. Slice, using light pressure. Sprinkle with lemon juice. Arrange bananas over cake and cover with remaining pudding. Top with balance of cake. Wash and dry bowl.

Steel Knife: Tip processor forward by placing a thick book underneath base. Do not insert pusher in feed tube. Whip cream until the texture of sour cream, about 35 to 40 seconds. Add sugar and process a few seconds longer, until stiff. Do not overprocess. Garnish trifle with whipped cream, grated chocolate and reserved strawberries. (I sometimes dip the tops of the berries in icing sugar.) Chill several hours or overnight.

Yield: 16 to 20 servings. Do not freeze, and do not make more than a day in advance. Leftovers will keep about 2 or 3 days at the most.

Note: In an emergency, I have assembled this trifle in 15 minutes and served it almost immediately to unexpected company. I always keep sponge cake layers in my freezer as they thaw quickly. Use any desired combination of fresh, frozen or well-drained canned fruits (e.g. peaches, oranges, pineapple chunks, blueberries, raspberries, etc.). Dessert topping may be substituted for whipping cream and sugar.

For a Large Crowd

Use 2 packages (4 serving size) vanilla instant pudding, 2 cups sour cream, 2 cups milk, extra cake and 3 different kinds of fruit.

Yield: 25 to 30 servings.

For a Small Crowd

Use 1 package (4 serving size) vanilla instant pudding. 1 cup sour cream, 1 cup milk. The amount of cake and fruit should be decreased slightly.

Yield: about 12 servings. May also be made in individual glass serving dishes.

BLACK FOREST TRIFLE

1 pkg. chocolate pudding (6 serving size)
3 c. milk
1 angel or sponge cake
19 oz. can cherry pie filling
2 c. whipping cream, chilled

2 tbsp. icing sugar
1 square semi-sweet chocolate
¼ c. slivered toasted almonds
maraschino cherries to garnish

Cook pudding with milk according to package directions. Do not use instant pudding. Cover surface of pudding with waxed paper to prevent a skin from forming. Let cool.

Break up cake in 1'' pieces and place half in a 3 quart glass bowl. Add half of pudding, then half of pie filling. Repeat with remaining cake, pudding, and filling.

Tip processor forward by placing a thick book underneath base. Do not insert pusher in feed tube. This will increase the volume of whipped cream. Whip cream using **Steel Knife** until the texture of sour cream. Add sugar and process a few seconds longer, until stiff. Garnish trifle. Wash and dry bowl and cover.

Grater: Grate chocolate, using firm pressure. Sprinkle over whipped cream. Decorate with almonds and cherries. Chill overnight.

Yield: 12 servings. Do not freeze.

HEAVENLY CHOCOLATE TRIFLE

(Watch out for the Chocolate Monsters!)

1 square semi-sweet chocolate
12 oz. pkg. chocolate chips
4 eggs
¼ c. sugar
2 envelopes dessert topping mix

1 c. cold milk
1 large angel food cake
1½ c. whipping cream, chilled
3 tbsp. icing sugar
3 oz. pkg. slivered almonds (if desired, toast at 300°F for a few minutes)

Grater: Grate semi-sweet chocolate, using firm pressure. Set aside. Melt chocolate chips over very low heat until melted. Cool.

Steel Knife: Process eggs with sugar until well beaten, about 30 seconds. Add melted chocolate chips and process until well blended, stopping machine to scrape down sides of bowl as necessary. Using electric mixer, whip dessert topping with milk until stiff. Add to processor and process until blended, scraping down sides of bowl two or three times. This should take about 10 to 15 seconds.

Tear cake into bite-size pieces. Place half of cake pieces in the bottom of a 3 quart glass serving bowl. Pour over half the chocolate mixture. Repeat with remaining cake and filling. (May be frozen at this point , if desired. Thaw overnight in refrigerator.)

Use electric mixer or processer (**Steel Knife**) to whip the cream. When nearly stiff, add icing sugar and whip until stiff. (If using processor, place a heavy book under the back part of the base so that the machine is tipped forward. Do not insert pusher in feed tube. Cream will be heavier in texture if made on the processor and will not yield as much volume.)

Top trifle with whipped cream. Garnish with reserved grated chocolate and toasted almonds. Chill several hours or overnight before serving.

Yield: 12 to 16 servings. A real company dessert.

JELL-O WHIP TRIFLE

(Less Fattening than Most Trifles)

Easy Jell-O Whip (below)
1 envelope dessert topping mix
½ c. milk
3 c. miniature colored marshmallows

4 c. sponge cake, cut in 1" squares
maraschino cherries, pineapple chunks, etc.

Prepare Easy Jell-O Whip as directed, but leave mixture in processor bowl and place in refrigerator to thicken while you prepare the dessert topping. Whip dessert topping with milk on electric mixer until light and fluffy. (The processor will not provide enough volume.) Fold in Jell-O and marshmallows.

Place ⅓ of mixture in an attractive large glass serving bowl. Arrange half of cake in a single layer over Jell-O. Repeat until all ingredients are used, ending with Jell-O mixture. Garnish with cherries (or the same fruit you have used in the Jell-O mixture) in an attractive design. Refrigerate 3 to 4 hours or overnight.

Yield: 10 servings. Do not freeze.

Note: If desired, you may prepare an additional envelope of dessert topping mix to top the trifle, rather than ending with the Jell-O mixture. Garnish as desired.

P.S. Miniature marshmallows only contain about 2 calories each.

EASY JELL-O WHIP

3 oz. pkg. Jell-O, any flavor
1 c. boiling water
8 ice cubes

14 oz. can fruit cocktail, pineapple chunks, peaches or any desired fruit, well-drained

Steel Knife: Process Jell-O with boiling water for 30 seconds. Drop in ice cubes at 5 second intervals through feed tube while machine is running. Be sure to cover the opening at the top of the feed tube with the palm of your hand to prevent mixture from splashing. Whip until mixture triples in volume and ice is completely blended, about 2 to 4 minutes. Do not insert pusher in feed tube. Mixture will become light and foamy and will nearly fill processor bowl. Fold in fruit by hand. Pour into individual serving dishes. Refrigerate. Mixture will be firm and ready to serve in about 20 to 30 minutes.

Yield: 8 servings. Do not freeze.

Note: To remove the syrup from the canned fruit, wash well in a strainer under cold running water. (This hint is for the calorie-conscious.)

STRAWBERRY YOGHURT DELIGHT

2 c. (1 pint) strawberries, hulled
2 c. plain yoghurt

1 tsp. lemon juice
artificial sweetener to equal
¼ c. sugar (or to taste)

Steel Knife: Process strawberries until puréed, about 10 seconds, scraping down sides of bowl if necessary. Add remaining ingredients and process a few seconds longer to blend.

Pour into 8 glass dessert dishes. Chill.

Yield: 8 half-cup servings of about 47 calories each. If desired, top each serving with a strawberry.

MILLES FEUILLES DESSERT

(A Favorite Family or Company Dessert)

18 double graham wafers (approximately)
2 pkgs. (4 serving size) vanilla instant pudding
2 c. sour cream or plain yoghurt
2 c. milk
2 c. whipping cream plus 2 tbsp. icing sugar (or 2 envelopes dessert topping mix plus 1 c. milk)

2½ c. icing sugar
6 tbsp. milk
½ tsp. vanilla
2 squares semi-sweet chocolate, melted (or approximately ¼ c. canned chocolate syrup)

Arrange half the wafers closely together in the bottom of an ungreased 9" x 13" Pyrex oblong pan. Fill any spaces with pieces of broken wafers.

Steel Knife: Process pudding with sour cream for a few seconds. Gradually add milk through feed tube while machine is running, stopping machine once or twice to scrape down sides of bowl. Process for about 20 seconds, until smooth. Immediately pour over graham wafer base. Refrigerate for about 15 minutes, until thickened. Wash and dry the bowl, blade and cover.

Steel Knife: Place a heavy book under the base of the processor so that the machine is tipped forward. Process whipping cream with icing sugar (or dessert topping with milk) until stiff. Spread carefully over pudding. Top with remaining wafers.

Plastic Knife: Process icing sugar with milk and vanilla until blended, about 6 to 8 seconds. Spread carefully over wafers.

Drizzle parallel lines of chocolate over icing about 1" apart, down the **length** of the dessert. Draw the dull side of a knife across the **width** of the dessert, cutting through the chocolate lines about every 2" to make a decorative pattern. Chill for several hours before serving. Do not freeze. May be prepared in advance. Will keep about 3 days in the refrigerator. Cut in oblongs about 2" x 3".

Yield: about 18 servings.

Note: Recipe may be halved, if desired, and prepared in an 8" square pan.

Yield: about 8 servings. (Cut in oblongs about 2" x 4".)

PINEAPPLE SHERBET

Open a 14 oz. or 19 oz. can of pineapple chunks (in its own juice) and place can in freezer until nearly frozen, about 2 to 3 hours.

Steel Knife: Process pineapple until the texture of sherbet, stopping processor several times to scrape down sides of bowl. Place in glass serving dishes. Serve immediately.

Yield: 3 to 4 servings.

Note: In order to make sherbet at a moment's notice, freeze pineapple chunks and juice in ice cube trays. Store in freezer until needed. Process no more than one cup "pineapple ice cubes" at a time until sherbet consistency. Any fruit in its own juice can be substituted for pineapple chunks (e.g. pears, peaches, etc.).

PALM SPRINGS DESSERT

(A Dieter's Delight!)

16 single graham wafers
3 oz. pkg. any flavor Jell-O (or 2
   envelopes D-Zerta gelatin)
2 c. plain yoghurt (see Note
   below)

1 c. fruit cocktail, rinsed
   under cold water and well
   drained
1 envelope dessert topping
   mix
½ c. cold milk

Line a 7'' x 11'' utility Pyrex dish with graham wafers. Trim to fit, reserving leftover pieces of wafers.

Plastic or Steel Knife: Process leftover wafers to make fine crumbs. Reserve as a garnish. Process Jell-O powder with yoghurt for 5 to 6 seconds. Spread in a layer over graham wafers. Arrange fruit cocktail over yoghurt mixture.

Whip dessert topping mix with cold milk on electric mixer until stiff. (If you wish, you may use the processor, but you will not have enough volume so you would have to use 2 envelopes dessert topping plus 1 cup cold milk.) Spread whipped topping over fruit. Garnish with reserved crumbs. May be garnished with additional fruit, if desired. Refrigerate for 6 to 8 hours. May be frozen. Thaw overnight in refrigerator.

Yield: 8 to 12 servings, depending on how large the servings are! Your guests will never believe that this is a low calorie dessert.

Note: You can change this dessert easily by using different flavors of Jell-O and yoghurt; the fruit used can also be changed. Some suggestions are:-

• Lime or lemon Jell-O, drained crushed pineapple, plain yoghurt.
• Peach Jell-O, drained sliced peaches or fruit cocktail, plain or peach yoghurt.
• Strawberry Jell-O, sliced fresh strawberries, plain or strawberry yoghurt.
• Raspberry Jell-O, raspberries, plain or raspberry yoghurt.
• Cherry Jell-O, drained pitted cherries or blueberries, plain or cherry yoghurt.
• Orange Jell-O, drained mandarin oranges, plain or orange yoghurt.

SOUR CREAM FRUIT DELIGHT

(People who hate sour cream will never know if you don't tell!)

36 single graham wafers (3 c.
   crumbs)
¼ c. sugar
⅔ c. butter, melted
1 pint sour cream (2 c.)
½ c. sugar

1 tbsp. vanilla
28 oz. tin fruit cocktail, well
   drained
19 oz. tin crushed pineapple,
   well drained

Steel Knife: Break up half the graham wafers and place in processor bowl. Drop remaining wafers through feed tube while machine is running. Process until fine crumbs are formed, about 25 to 30 seconds. Add ¼ cup sugar and the butter. Process about 5 seconds longer, until mixed. Reserve 1 cup crumbs for topping. Press remaining crumbs into the bottom and up the sides of an ungreased 10'' spring form pan.

Combine sour cream, ½ c. sugar, vanilla and drained fruit in a large mixing bowl. Stir carefully to mix. Pour into crust. Top with reserved crumbs.

Bake at 350°F for 30 minutes. Cool thoroughly. Refrigerate overnight.

Yield: 10 to 12 delicious servings. Do not freeze.

ORANGE SHERBET BAVARIAN

3 oz. pkg. orange Jell-O
1 c. boiling water
1 pint orange sherbet
(about 2 cups)
10 oz. tin mandarin oranges,
drained

½ c. frozen blueberries,
thawed & drained
sweetened whipped cream,
to garnish

Dissolve Jell-O in boiling water in a 2 cup Pyrex measure.

Steel Knife: Break sherbet up into large chunks and place in processor bowl. While machine is running, add dissolved Jell-O through feed tube in a slow and steady stream. Process until blended, about 20 to 30 seconds. Chill until thickened, about 20 minutes. Fold in oranges and blueberries very carefully, reserving a few berries and oranges for garnish. Spoon into 8 individual serving dishes. Garnish with whipped cream and reserved fruit.

Yield: 8 servings. Do not freeze.

Note: Recipe may be doubled or tripled and made in a large mold or an attractive glass serving bowl. **Either** process ingredients in 2 or 3 batches using the processor, (otherwise you will have leakage from the bottom of the processor bowl) **or** dissolve Jell-O in boiling water in a large mixing bowl, and add sherbet by spoonfuls, stirring to blend. When partially set, fold in fruit and spoon into mold. Chunks of sponge or angel cake may be folded in, if desired. Will serve a large crowd.

PARTY RAINBOW MOUSSE

Prepare two or three flavors of any of the following Jell-O mousses:-

Strawberry Mousse (p. 229)
Raspberry Mousse (p. 229)
Orange Mousse (p. 229)
Lemon Mousse (p. 229)
Lemon Marshmallow Mousse (p. 230)
Peach Mousse (p. 230)
Frosty Lime Mousse (p. 230)

Chill each flavor in separate mixing bowls until partially set, about 20 minutes. Spread first flavor in a glass serving bowl. Chill 5 minutes. Then add the next flavor. Make sure that each layer is set just enough so that the different colors will not run into each other, but are not completely set, or the layers will separate. You can make as many layers as your serving bowl will hold. (Three layers will fill a 3 quart bowl and will serve 18 to 20 people.)

Steel Knife: Place 2 cups chilled whipping cream plus 2 tbsp. sugar in processor bowl. (You may substitute 2 envelopes dessert topping mix plus 1 cup milk, if desired.) Place a thick book underneath the base of the processor so that the machine is tipped forward. Process until stiff, about 45 seconds for whipped cream and 2 minutes for dessert topping. Do not insert pusher in feed tube to incorporate more air. Garnish Mousse. Decorate with maraschino cherries, or repeat any of the fruits which are included in the Mousse layers. Do not freeze.

STRAWBERRY MOUSSE

1 pint strawberries, hulled
3 oz. pkg. strawberry Jell-O
1 c. boiling water

2 c. vanilla or strawberry
ice cream (1 pint or ½ litre)

Reserve 8 strawberries as garnish. Insert **Slicer** in processor. Slice remaining strawberries, using light pressure. Empty bowl. Dissolve Jell-O in boiling water in a 2 cup Pyrex measure.

Steel Knife: Break ice cream up into large chunks and place in processor bowl. While machine is running, add dissolved Jell-O through feed tube in a slow and steady stream. Process until blended, about 20 to 30 seconds. Chill until thickened, about 20 minutes. Fold in fruit with a rubber spatula. Pour into 8 parfait glasses or a baked 9'' graham wafer crust. Garnish with reserved berries.

Yield: 8 servings. Do not freeze.

RASPBERRY MOUSSE

15 oz. pkg. frozen raspberries,
thawed
3 oz. pkg. raspberry Jell-O

2 c. vanilla ice cream (1 pint
or ½ litre)

Drain juice from raspberries and measure 1 cup. (Add additional water if necessary.) Bring juice to a boil. Add Jell-O and stir to dissolve thoroughly.

Steel Knife: Combine ingredients as described in recipe for Strawberry Mousse (above).

Yield: 8 servings.

ORANGE MOUSSE

3 oz. pkg. orange Jell-O
1 c. boiling water
2 c. vanilla ice cream (1 pint or
½ litre)

10 oz. can mandarin oranges,
well drained

Dissolve Jell-O in boiling water in a 2 cup Pyrex measure.

Steel Knife: Combine ingredients as described in recipe for Strawberry Mousse (above).

Yield: 8 servings.

Variation: Omit canned mandarin oranges and substitute 2 oranges, peeled and halved. Slice on **Slicer,** using light pressure.

LEMON MOUSSE

3 oz. pkg. lemon Jell-O
1 c. boiling water
2 c. vanilla ice cream (1 pint or
½ litre)

14 oz. can fruit cocktail, well
drained

Dissolve Jell-O in boiling water in a 2 cup Pyrex measure.

Steel Knife: Combine ingredients as described in recipe for Strawberry Mousse (above). **Yield:** 8 servings.

LEMON MARSHMALLOW MOUSSE

3 oz. pkg. lemon Jell-O
1 c. boiling water
2 c. vanilla ice cream (1 pint or ½ litre)

14 oz. can pineapple chunks, well drained
1 c. miniature marshmallows

Dissolve Jell-O in boiling water in a 2 cup Pyrex measure.

Steel Knife: Combine ingredients as described in recipe for Strawberry Mousse (p. 229), adding marshmallows with fruit.

Yield: 8 servings.

PEACH MOUSSE

3 oz. pkg. peach Jell-O
1 c. boiling water
2 c. vanilla ice cream (1 pint or ½ litre)

14 oz. can peach slices, well drained

Dissolve Jell-O in boiling water in a 2 cup Pyrex measure.

Steel Knife: Combine ingredients as described in recipe for Strawberry Mousse (p. 229). **Yield:** 8 servings.

FROSTY LIME MOUSSE

14 oz. can crushed pineapple
3 oz. pkg. lime Jell-O

2 c. vanilla ice cream (1 pint or ½ litre)

Drain juice from pineapple and measure 1 cup, adding additional water if necessary. Bring juice to a boil. Add Jell-O and stir to dissolve thoroughly.

Steel Knife: Combine ingredients as described in recipe for Strawberry Mousse (p. 229).

Yield: 8 servings.

CHOCOLATE POTS OF CREAM (Chocolate Mousse)

6 oz. pkg. chocolate chips
2 squares semi-sweet chocolate
dash salt
7 oz. table cream or whipping cream

¼ c. milk
4 egg yolks
1 tbsp. Kahlua, cognac or coffee, if desired

Steel Knife: Place chocolate chips, cut-up chocolate and salt in processor. Heat cream and milk almost to boiling and pour over chocolate. Process until noise has stopped and mixture is smooth and creamy. Add egg yolks and liqueur and process 30 seconds longer. Pour into parfait glasses or individual white ceramic serving pots. Refrigerate 4 hours. Let stand 10 minutes at room temperature before serving.

Yield: 6 servings.

Note: May be garnished with whipped cream and grated chocolate, if desired. May be frozen.

VICTORIAN CHOCOLATE MOUSSE

(Pale chocolate color. Very light and creamy.)

2 c. chilled whipping cream (or 2 envelopes dessert topping plus 1 c. milk)	**²⁄₃ c. chocolate chips** **4 egg yolks** **3 tbsp. sugar**

Tip processor forward by placing a thick book underneath base. Do not insert pusher in feed tube. Whip cream or dessert topping using **Steel Knife.** Process until stiff peaks form, about 45 seconds for cream or 2 minutes for dessert topping. Empty bowl. Melt chocolate over low heat, but do not cool.

Steel Knife: Process egg yolks with sugar and chocolate about 45 seconds. Add most of whipped cream, reserving about ¼ cup for garnish. Blend into chocolate with several quick on/off turns, scraping down bowl as necessary.

Pour into 8 parfait glasses and refrigerate until set, about 1 hour. Garnish each with a little of the reserved whipped cream. Sprinkle with a few chocolate chips, if desired.

Yield: 8 servings. May be frozen. Thaw overnight in refrigerator.

MARSHMALLOW AMBROSIA

2 - 10 oz. cans mandarin oranges, drained	**2 pts. sour cream (use ½ yoghurt to reduce calories, if desired)**
2 - 19 oz. cans fruit cocktail, drained	**10 oz. pkg. colored miniature marshmallows**
10 oz. can pineapple chunks, drained	**8 chocolate wafers (or 4 macaroons)**
½ c. coconut, if desired	

Place fruit in a colander and rinse under cold running water. Dry well. Combine with remaining ingredients except chocolate wafers in a large mixing bowl and mix gently. Transfer to a large attractive glass serving bowl.

Insert **Steel Knife** in processor. Break cookies in half and drop through feed tube while machine is running. Process until fine crumbs are formed. Sprinkle over sour cream/fruit mixture. Cover and chill overnight. (Recipe may be halved, if desired.)

Yield: 16 to 20 servings.

APPLE CRUMBLE

½ c. butter or margarine, cut in chunks	**6 to 8 apples, cored & halved (peel if desired)**
1 c. flour	**1 tsp. cinnamon**
¾ c. brown sugar, packed	

Steel Knife: Process butter, flour and brown sugar about 8 seconds, until crumbly. Empty bowl.

Slicer: Slice apples, using medium pressure. Empty into a lightly greased 9'' square baking pan. Sprinkle with cinnamon. Sprinkle reserved crumb mixture over apples. Bake at 375°F for 35 to 45 minutes. Serve hot or cold.

Yield: 8 servings. May be frozen.

Note: Prepare batches of crumb mixture and freeze in plastic bags. When needed, sprinkle over desired fruit (no need to thaw crumbs). Bake until tender. Some suggested fillings:- sliced peaches, pears, canned pie filling. An easy and delicious dessert.

LEMONADE SOUFFLE

(Light and Refreshing)

2 - 3 oz. pkgs. lemon Jell-O
2¾ c. boiling water
6 oz. frozen lemonade
   concentrate
2 envelopes dessert topping
   mix

1 c. milk
⅓ c. peach or apricot jam
1 c. graham wafer crumbs or
   granola (approximately)
8 glacé cherries

Dissolve Jell-O in boiling water in a mixing bowl. Add lemonade and stir until melted. Chill until partially set, about 2 hours.

Steel Knife: Place a thick book underneath the base of the processor so that the machine is tipped forward. Do not insert pusher in feed tube. Process dessert topping with milk until stiff, about 2 minutes. Remove book from under base. Remove about ½ cup whipped topping from processor bowl and set aside.

Add Jell-O and jam to remaining whipped topping. Process together for about 10 or 15 seconds, scraping down sides of bowl as necessary. Pour mixture into a 6 cup soufflé dish. Chill several hours or overnight. Place reserved whipped topping into a pastry bag outfitted with a star tube. When soufflé is somewhat set, pipe rosettes decoratively around border and sprinkle with crumbs. Garnish with glacé cherries, if desired.

Yield: 6 to 8 servings. Do not freeze. If desired, may also be placed in individual glass serving dishes (about 10 smaller servings).

PUDDING PARFAIT

1½ c. fresh strawberries
1 envelope dessert topping
   mix
2 c. milk

1 pkg. (4 serving size) instant
   vanilla pudding
1 c. graham wafer crumbs or
   granola (approximately)

Hull strawberries, reserving 8 whole berries for garnish. Insert **Slicer** in processor. Slice berries, using very light pressure. Empty bowl. Wash and dry the cover and bowl.

Steel Knife: Process dessert topping with ½ cup milk until stiff. (Place a heavy book under the back part of the base of the processor so that the machine is tipped forward in order to increase the volume produced.) Remove cover and sprinkle instant pudding over topping. Add remaining 1½ cups milk through the feed tube while the machine is running. Scrape down as necessary. Process until smooth and well blended, about 20 to 30 seconds in all.

Spoon half of pudding mixture into 8 parfait glasses. Sprinkle with crumbs or granola. Top with sliced strawberries. Add remaining pudding, sprinkle with remaining crumbs and garnish each parfait with a whole strawberry. Chill about 1 hour before serving.

Yield: 8 servings. Do not freeze.

Note: You may substitute chocolate pudding and chocolate wafer crumbs for vanilla pudding and graham wafer crumbs. Eliminate strawberries. Garnish with rosettes of whipped cream, if desired.

BISCUIT TORTONI
(An Elegant but Easy Dessert)

½ c. almonds
¾ c. dried macaroon crumbs
  (about 5 or 6 macaroons)
2 tbsp. rum, sherry or vanilla

2 c. whipping cream
¼ c. icing sugar
4 maraschino cherries, halved

Steel Knife: Process almonds until fine, about 20 seconds. Empty into a bowl. Process macaroons for 6 to 8 seconds to make crumbs. Measure and add to almonds. Set aside about ⅓ cup almond/macaroon mixture as a garnish. Add rum and about ¾ cup unwhipped whipping cream to remaining almonds and macaroons. Stir to moisten.

Steel Knife: Tip processor forward by placing a heavy book underneath the base of the machine. Do not insert pusher in feed tube. Process remaining whipping cream until the texture of sour cream, about 35 seconds. Add sugar and process a few seconds longer, until stiff.

Pour almond/macaroon/cream mixture over whipped cream. Blend in with 3 or 4 quick on/off turns. Spoon into paper cups (or paper cupcake liners). Sprinkle reserved crumb mixture over, and garnish each one with a cherry half. Freeze until firm, about 4 hours.

Yield: about 8 servings.

TANGY HOT FRUIT COMPOTE

Follow recipe for Deep Dish Tutti-Fruiti Cake (p. 258), making the filling only. Combine filling ingredients in a lightly greased 7'' x 11'' Pyrex utility dish, mixing gently. Cover with tinfoil and bake at 350°F for 45 to 50 minutes. Serve hot. Delicious!

Yield: 10 to 12 servings. May be prepared in advance and reheated.

FROZEN PEACH DESSERT

(Quick, easy and refreshing. Almost
like ice cream.)

19 oz. tin peaches (See Note)
⅓ c. sugar
⅓ - ½ c. peach brandy

⅛ tsp. almond extract
1 c. whipping cream

Drain peaches in a strainer, reserving ½ cup peach juice. Measure 2 cups drained peaches. (Del Monte brand is best.)

Steel Knife: Process peaches with the reserved peach juice, sugar, brandy and extract. Purée until smooth. Meanwhile, whip cream on electric mixer until stiff. Add whipped cream to peach purée. Blend in with 3 or 4 on/off turns.

Pour mixture into a 1 quart mold. (A 6 cup Tupperware mold is also ideal, and very easy to unmold.) Freeze until firm. Unmold by placing mold in hot water for about 10 seconds, then shake to loosen. Repeat if necessary. (Tupperware mold will release easily.) Freeze until about 15 minutes before serving time. Let stand to soften slightly. May be garnished with mint leaves.

Yield: 8 servings.

Note: Canned apricots and apricot brandy may be substituted, if desired. Cointreau is also delicious.

CRUNCHY APPLE CRISP

¾ c. brown sugar, packed
½ c. flour
½ c. butter or margarine, cut in
  chunks
⅓ c. oatmeal, granola, or
  graham wafer crumbs

1 tsp. cinnamon
6 apples, peeled, cored &
  halved
½ c. raisins, if desired

Steel Knife: Combine all ingredients except apples and raisins and process until crumbly, about 8 seconds. Empty bowl.

Slicer: Slice apples, using medium pressure. Place in a greased 9'' square or 10'' round pie plate. Stir in raisins. Sprinkle with reserved crumb mixture. Bake at 375°F for 35 to 40 minutes. Serve warm with ice cream.

Yield: 6 to 8 servings. Freezes well.

PISTACHIO PINEAPPLE DELIGHT

(Watergate Dessert)

Refreshing, delicious and quick.
A delightful ending to any meal!

½ c. pecans or walnuts
2 envelopes dessert topping
  mix (Dream Whip)
1 c. cold milk
1 pkg. (4 serving size) instant
  pistachio pudding

14 oz. can crushed pineapple
  or pineapple chunks, with
  juice
1½ c. miniature marshmallows

Steel Knife: Process nuts until coarsely chopped, about 6 to 8 seconds. Empty bowl.

Steel Knife: Process dessert topping with milk until stiff, about 2 minutes. Remove cover and sprinkle pudding mix over topping. Replace cover and start machine. Add pineapple and juice through feed tube while machine is running. Scrape down sides of bowl. Sprinkle marshmallows and nuts over mixture. Mix in with 2 or 3 very quick on/off turns. Do not overprocess.

Pour into a 6 cup soufflé dish or attractive glass serving dishes. Refrigerate for several hours, until well chilled. (Using pineapple which has been refrigerated before adding to the dessert will speed up the process.) Soufflé may be garnished with rosettes of whipped cream and additional chopped nuts.

Yield: about 8 servings as a dessert soufflé, or 10 to 12 servings in individual dishes. Do not freeze.

CHERRY CREPES JUBILEE

Basic Crêpe Batter (p. 102)
19 oz. tin cherry pie filling

6 tbsp. Kirsch (cherry liqueur
  or cognac)

Prepare crêpes as directed. Combine half the pie filling with 2 tbsp. Kirsch. Place about 2 tbsp. filling on the lower ⅓ of crêpe and roll up. Repeat with remaining crêpes.

Place crêpes in a chafing dish. Spoon remaining cherries around crêpes. Heat remaining Kirsch. Pour carefully over crêpes and ignite with a match. When flames have burned out, serve immediately. Makes 6 to 8 servings. Delicious served with vanilla ice cream.

ICE CREAM CREPES

Basic Crêpe Batter (p. 102)   **Vanilla Ice Cream**
Quicky Chocolate Sauce
(p. 67)

Prepare crêpes and sauce as directed. Keep warm.

Slice ice cream into rectangles slightly larger than the size of a bread stick. Place ice cream on the lower ⅓ of crêpe, roll up, and top with chocolate sauce. Serve 2 to each person.

Variations: Use any flavor ice cream or sherbet, and top with Sundae sauce or jam, or whipped cream and chopped nuts for those who are not diet-conscious! Sugared strawberries are also great over ice cream crêpes.

Note: This is an easy dessert to whip up if you keep a batch of frozen crêpes in the freezer for unexpected company.

Additional Recipes

Cakes & Icings

How to Adapt Cake Recipes to your Food Processor

- **Use the Steel Knife** rather than the Plastic Knife to mix cake batters. You will have much less chance of leakage from the bottom of the processor bowl.

- **If your recipe calls for sifting** dry ingredients together, process them for 5 to 10 seconds, until blended. Leave the pusher in the feed tube. Empty mixture into another bowl.

- **Nuts, chocolate,** etc., should be chopped first, while the processor bowl is dry, to prevent extra washing of the bowl and blades.

- **Fillings for coffee cakes** should also be processed first, before preparing the cake batter.

- **Paper towelling** is very handy to wipe out the processor bowl for easy clean-ups between steps.

- **Arrange all ingredients** on countertop before beginning your recipe. The processor is so quick that it will take about ⅓ the time to mix up your cake batters.

- **Always cut butter** or margarine into chunks before processing. Use directly from the refrigerator (unless otherwise indicated) for best results. The speed of the blades will cause soft butter to melt, producing a heavy texture in the finished cake.

- **Creaming Method (Steel Knife)**
  1) Process butter, sugar, eggs and flavoring for about 2 minutes, until well mixed.
  2) Do not insert pusher in feed tube for maximum volume.
  3) Stop the machine once or twice to scrape down batter from the sides of the bowl with a rubber spatula.
  4) Add liquids and process quickly, about 3 seconds. They may be added either through the feed tube or directly into the processor bowl.
  5) Add combined dry ingredients over the top of the batter and turn the machine on and off very quickly, about 3 or 4 times. It may be necessary to scrape down the sides of the bowl once again.
  6) Process **just** until flour mixture disappears. Do not overprocess, or your cakes will be tough and heavy.

- **Alternate Creaming Method (Steel Knife)**
  1) Process butter and sugar for 35 to 45 seconds, until well mixed.
  2) Do not insert pusher in feed tube for maximum volume.
  3) Stop the machine once or twice to scrape down batter from the sides of the bowl with a rubber spatula.
  4) Add eggs one at a time and process for 15 seconds after each addition.
  5) Add flavorings and liquids; process for 3 seconds.
  6) Add combined dry ingredients as directed in Steps 5) and 6) of Creaming Method (above).

- **The light and fluffy texture** achieved when creaming butter, sugar and eggs on an electric mixer cannot be achieved with the processor; however, it still produces delicious, light cakes.

- **Capacity of the food processor:** A general guideline is to make cakes not exceeding 2 cups of flour. To check if a recipe will fit in the processor, total the volume of all the ingredients. It should not exceed more than 6½ cups. (Capacity of some processors may vary. Check your manual.) Calculate each egg as ¼ cup liquid.

- **If the amount of batter is too large** for your processor, process all the ingredients with the exception of the flour and leavening. Then transfer all ingredients to a large mixing bowl and stir with a wooden spoon for about 30 seconds, just until batter is blended.

- **The processor** may produce cakes which are slightly smaller in volume than those made in an electric mixer. Just add an extra ½ tsp. baking powder to your old favorites when using the processor.

- **Cakes mixes** may be made in the processor. Begin with the dry ingredients and add liquids through the feed tube while the machine is running. Process for about 1½ minutes.

- **Pusher** should be in the feed tube when combining dry ingredients.

- **Pusher** should **not** be in feed tube when creaming ingredients, in order to incorporate more air into the batter.

- **Sugar** sometimes gathers along the rim of the processor bowl, making it difficult to turn the machine on and off. If this happens, just wipe the rim of the bowl and the cover with a damp cloth.

- **An easy way to clean cake batter off the Steel Knife:** Empty most of the cake batter from processor bowl. Replace bowl and knife back onto the base of your machine; cover, then start the motor once again. Centrifugal force will spin your blade clean in seconds!

- **Sponge or Chiffon cakes** should **not** be made in the processor.

- **Egg whites in the processor:** The food processor is **not** recommended for whipping egg whites. Use an electric or hand mixer, or a wire whisk to achieve best results. Egg whites should increase seven times in volume. With the processor, the whites will only increase about 4 times in volume and will not be very stiff.

- **Most icings** are easily made in the processor. Use the **Steel or Plastic Knife** and process all ingredients until smooth and blended, usually about 10 or 15 seconds. Scrape down sides of bowl with a rubber spatula as necessary.

CAKE HINTS

- **Unfrosted cakes will freeze** for 4 to 6 months. It is easier if you freeze frosted cakes first, then wrap. Frosted cakes will keep 2 to 3 months. Thaw wrapped, at room temperature. It will take from 1 to 3 hours to defrost, depending on the size of the cake.

- **Keep** cakes and squares covered while defrosting to prevent drying out.

- **Cakes** will become stale more quickly once they have been frozen.

- **If necessary,** cakes can be frozen a second time; however, they will be drier.

- **Whipped cream** cakes freeze very well. Defrost overnight in the refrigerator, **not** at room temperature. Keep chilled.

- **Assemble** all ingredients and read the recipe through completely before starting.

- **Grease cake pans** thoroughly with shortening. Add flour and shake to coat bottom and sides of pan. Dump out excess flour.

- **Do not** use butter or margarine to grease cake pans, or cake may stick to pan. Low calorie sprays such as Pam may be used to grease your baking pans instead of shortening and flour.

- **When baking cupcakes** or muffins, fill any empty muffin cups ⅓ full with water to prevent discoloring or burning of pan.

- **For easy clean up,** line muffin tins with paper cupcake liners.

- **When baking layer cakes** or several cakes at once, refrigerate extra batter until the oven is free.

- **Bang** cake pans firmly against the counter top in order to settle any large air bubbles which might have formed in the batter.

- **Baking pans** should not touch each other or the sides of the oven in order to have proper circulation of heat.

- **Always preheat oven** to required temperature before placing cake batters, cookies or yeast doughs in oven. Do not open oven door for first fifteen minutes of baking.

- **Place** cake pans on the centre rack or in the lower third of the oven. Bundt or tube pans should be placed on the lowest rack.

- **To remove cakes from pan,** always let cake stand a few minutes. Allow 5 minutes for layers, 10 minutes for square or rectangular cakes and 15 to 20 minutes for Bundt cakes.

- **Loosen** edges with a knife and invert. If cake is left in pan too long, it may stick and be difficult to remove. If cake is removed too soon, especially large cakes, they may break when you invert them.

- **When cake is baked,** it will shrink slightly from the sides of the pan and will feel firm to the touch. Cakes should spring back and will not retain the imprint of your fingertips. A toothpick or skewer inserted in the centre of the cake will come out dry.

- **Incorrect** oven temperatures often cause poor results. If the oven temperature is too low to start, the cake may rise too much before it sets. If the temperature is too high, the top crust will set before the cake has completed its rising, and then your cake will crack.

- **An oven thermometer** is a good investment. If your oven is incorrect, you can adjust the temperature dial according to the thermometer.

- **Lower** temperature by 25°F (10°C) if using dark or glass baking pans.

- **Do not** frost cakes until they are completely cool. Wrap well to prevent drying out.

- **It is easier** to assemble layer cakes if you place the bottoms of the cakes together. Dip knife in hot water several times to help spread icing easily.

- **Cakes** are more enthusiastically received when served to a small group of seated guests rather than on a buffet table.

- **To make sour milk,** measure 1 tbsp. vinegar or lemon juice into a measuring cup and add milk to equal 1 cup. Sour milk is interchangeable with buttermilk.

- **Skim milk** may be substituted for whole or 2% milk in your cakes.

- **Sour cream and yoghurt** may be interchanged in baking. If adding baking soda to yoghurt, combine in a large enough bowl, as the yoghurt will nearly double in volume.

- **Butter and margarine** are generally interchangeable in most recipes. Do not melt unless recipe indicates otherwise. Do **not** substitute oil for butter or margarine in baking.

- **Margarine** is not less fattening than butter. A tablespoon of margarine or butter contains 100 calories. However, most margarines are much healthier for you as they contain poly-unsaturated fats.

- **Do not** use diet margarine or whipped margarine in your baking.

- **Use** leftover juice from canned fruit as part of liquid in baking. You may also substitute water, juice, or non-dairy creamers which have been diluted with water for the milk in cake recipes.

- **Measure liquids** in a glass measuring cup. The 1 cup mark (or 2 cup mark) should be about ½'' below the rim of the cup to avoid spillage. There should be a pouring spout.

- **To measure liquids** in a measuring spoon, the spoon should be filled until it cannot hold another drop.

- **To measure shortening** or butter, use the displacement method. Fill a 2 cup glass measuring cup with cold water to the 1 cup mark. Drop fat into the water, making certain it is completely immersed. If you require ½ cup butter for your recipe, add enough butter to raise the water level to 1½ cups. You will then have 1 cup of water and ½ cup butter. (For ¾ cup butter, the water level will rise to 1¾ cups, for ⅓ cup butter, the water level will rise to 1⅓ cups, etc.) Spill out water.

- **An alternate method** is to press butter or margarine into a dry measure. Press firmly to make certain there are no hollows underneath.

- **Baking powder,** cocoa and baking soda sometimes have a tendency to pack down in their containers. Stir to loosen before measuring.

- **Baking powder** may lose its strength if kept on the pantry shelf for more than a year.

- **Many** homemakers keep an open box of baking soda in their refrigerator to absorb food odors. Do not use this soda in your baking!

- **An easy substitute** for one square (1 oz.) of unsweetened chocolate is 3 tbsp. cocoa plus 1 tbsp. butter or margarine in baking.

- **A 6 oz. package (170 grams) of chocolate chips** contains 1 cup, not ¾ cup.

- **Chocolate** may be melted easily by placing it in a saucepan or double boiler while still in its paper wrapper, open side up. A microwave oven is also excellent; allow about 3 minutes at high power. Another method is to place the chocolate in a pyrex measuring cup and melt it in the oven while it is preheating.

- **Honey** which has become sugary should be heated in its jar in a pot of hot water.

- **To measure brown sugar,** pack firmly into a measuring cup. Level with a straight edge knife.

- **Brown sugar** which has hardened can be salvaged easily. Just cut an apple in half and place it cut-side up in the bag or container of brown sugar. A day or two later, discard the apple. Your sugar will be soft once again. Storing brown sugar in a tightly closed container in the refrigerator will keep it soft.

- **Raisins** which have dried out can be made plump and juicy once again by soaking them in boiling water. Let stand for 3 to 4 minutes and drain well. An alternate method is to steam them in a vegetable steamer.

- **If raisins, dates or currants** sink to the bottom of your cake, toss them with a little flour to coat them lightly before adding them to the batter.

- **Store nuts and coconut** in the freezer. They will keep for at least a year without spoiling. It is not necessary to defrost before using them.

- **All recipes in this book call for all-purpose flour,** unless otherwise indicated. It may be bleached or unbleached, depending on your preference.

- **Instant Blending Flour** may be used if desired. (Robin Hood Mills produces it in Canada, and Wondra Flour is available in the U.S.A.). It is excellent for crepes, blending into sauces and gravies, etc. because it does not lump. It is also used for general baking purposes.

- **To substitute** cake flour for all-purpose flour, **add** 2 tbsp. more per cup. To substitute all-purpose flour for cake flour, **subtract** 2 tbsp. per cup.

- **When measuring flour,** do **not** use a glass measuring cup. It is difficult to get an accurate measure without banging the cup to level off the flour. This causes the flour to pack down, and results in using as much as an extra 2 tbsp. flour per cup. **Always** use a set of dry measuring cups (1 cup, ½ cup. ⅓ cup and ¼ cup).

- **Aerate** flour by mixing it through with a spoon to loosen it, since flour has a tendency to settle during standing. Dip the cup into the flour, filling it to overflowing. Level off with the straight edge of a knife. **Never** bang the cup on the counter or your recipe will end up with too much flour. This can cause heavy or dry cakes, or cracks in the top.

- **Eggs** should be at room temperature for baking. They may be warmed quickly by placing them in a bowl of warm water for a few minutes.

- **Eggs** separate easiest directly from the refrigerator.

- **To remove** bits of yolk from whites when separating eggs, touch with a damp cloth, or remove with a piece of egg shell.

- **Egg whites** give the most volume when they are allowed to stand until they reach room temperature before beating. They can be warmed quickly by placing the bowl they are in into a bowl of warm water. Stir to warm evenly.

- **Egg whites** will not whip perfectly if they contain any particles of egg yolk, or if the bowl they are beaten in or the beaters are moist, or if they are greasy.

- **A copper bowl** is excellent for beating egg whites. Otherwise, add ¼ tsp. cream of tartar for every 4 egg whites to prevent them from deflating and becoming weepy.

- **Cream of tartar** and flavoring should be added to the whites when they become frothy (large bubbles appear on the surface, and the mixture begins to turn white.)

- **Soft peaks stage** is when the mixture stands in peaks which recede as soon as they are formed.

- **Stiff but not dry** is when the peaks are stiff and sharply pointed, but their surfaces shine and the color is uniformly white. If the bowl is turned upside down, the whites will not fall out.

- **Stiff and dry** is when the peaks resemble soap suds, take on a dull shine, and break apart in chunks when lifted with a fork.

- **When making meringues,** begin adding sugar when the whites form soft peaks. Add 1 tbsp. at a time, and beat the mixture until you cannot feel the sugar granules when you rub the meringue between your fingertips. It should look like marshmallow creme.

- **Always** fold whites into your batter very gently so that they will retain as much of their volume as possible. A rubber spatula is ideal. Add about ¼ of the stiffly beaten whites to the batter and stir to blend. Empty the remaining egg whites onto the top of the batter, then cut down from the top centre of the mixture to the bottom of the bowl. Draw the spatula across the bottom of the bowl towards you until you reach the edge of the bowl, then up and out. Rotate the bowl ¼ turn after each cut and fold movement. Use the edge of the spatula like a knife when cutting through the batter. This should not take more than a minute, and don't be too thorough in order not to deflate the whites.

- **Reserve** left-over yolks to use in baking. Two yolks may be substituted for 1 whole egg.

BAKING FAULTS

Cracked or Peaked Surface:	Oven too hot; too much flour; batter overmixed; not enough liquid; cake batter not spread right into corners.
Sunken:	Too much sugar, shortening or baking powder; underbaking; opening oven door too soon; not enough eggs or flour.
Poor Volume:	Not enough baking powder; overmixing; uneven oven temperature (too hot at top); too much shortening or liquid. Ingredients too cold or too warm.
Too pale:	Too little sugar; underbaked.
Too brown:	Overbaked; oven temperature too high; too much sugar.
Tunnels and holes inside:	Overmixing after flour is added; too much flour; too much baking powder; undercreaming the fat and sugar.
Heavy, Rubbery Layer on Bottom:	Too much liquid; batter undermixed.
Dry:	Insufficient shortening or sugar; overbaked; too much flour or not enough liquid; cake not covered when completely cooled.
Tough:	Overmixed; overbaked; insufficient shortening.
Compact & Heavy:	Too much sugar, liquid, shortening or flour.
Cake sticks to Pan:	Undergreasing of pan; butter used to grease pan; cake left in pan too long.
Cake Breaks When Removed from Pan:	Removed from pan without allowing time to cool before loosening and inverting. A good guide is 10 minutes for small cakes, and 15 to 20 mins. for large cakes. Sponge and chiffon cakes should cool inverted for at least 1 hour. (Do not grease.) Regular cakes: undergreasing of pans.
Uneven Height:	Oven temperature not even. Batter not spread evenly in pan.

- **Refer** to page 23 for **Metric Measures for Baking Pans & Casseroles** and **Metric Baking Temperatures.**

CAKE PANS, BAKING TEMPERATURES & TIMES

If you don't have the pan size called for in a particular recipe, use the following guide to interchange baking pans. Baking times are approximate.

Use:	Instead of:
Two 8" or 9" round layer pans (1¾" deep) (350°F for 25 to 35 minutes)	7" x 11" oblong or 9" square pan (350°F for 40 to 50 minutes)
Three 8" or 9" round layer pans (1¾" deep) (350°F for 25 to 35 minutes)	Two 8" square pans (350°F for 35 to 40 minutes)
Two 8" or 9" round layer pans (1¾" deep) (350°F for 25 to 35 minutes)	9" x 13" oblong pan (350°F for 40 to 50 minutes)
9" x 5" x 3" loaf pan (350°F for 40 to 50 minutes)	8" square pan (350°F for 35 to 40 minutes)
Two 8" x 4" x 3" **or** 9" x 5" x 3" loaf pans (350°F for 40 to 50 minutes)	9" x 13" oblong pan (350°F for 40 to 50 minutes) **or** 12 cup Bundt pan (10") (325°F for 50 to 60 minutes)
9" square pan (350°F for 40 to 45 minutes)	7" x 11" oblong pan (350°F for 40 to 50 minutes)
9" or 10" tube pan (325°F for 50 to 60 minutes)	12 cup Bundt pan (10") See **Note*** (325°F for 50 to 60 minutes)
9" x 13" oblong pan (350°F for 40 to 50 minutes)	12 cup Bundt pan or 9" or 10" tube pan (325°F for 50 to 60 minutes)

*Note: A 10" tube pan holds about 18 cups of batter, whereas a 10" Bundt pan will only hold about 12 cups batter. Therefore, you can switch from a 12 cup (10") Bundt pan to a 10" tube pan, but you cannot always switch the opposite way around.

Cupcakes: Any cake batter may be baked in muffin tins. Fill ⅔ full. Bake at 400°F for about 18 to 20 minutes. To avoid greasing pans, line with paper liners.

APPROXIMATE CAPACITIES OF CAKE PANS (Filled to the brim)

8" square pan	holds 8 cups
9" square pan	holds 9 cups
8" x 4" loaf pan	holds 6 cups
9" x 5" loaf pan	holds 8 cups
9" tube pan or 10" Bundt	holds 12 cups
10" tube pan	holds 18 cups
8" round x 1¾" deep	holds 5 cups
9" round x 1¾" deep	holds 6 cups
7" x 11" oblong pan	holds 10 cups
9" x 13" oblong pan	holds 12 cups

If you have pans other than those listed above, measure the amount of liquid they will hold when filled to the brim. Interchange them accordingly for your favorite recipes.

FAMILY APPLE CAKE ✓

(Sure to become a favorite of your family!)

Filling:
8 or 9 apples, peeled, cored
   & halved (6 cups sliced)
½ c. brown sugar, packed
1 tbsp. cinnamon
¼ tsp. allspice, if desired
½ c. raisins, if desired
2 tbsp. flour

Batter:
1 c. shortening or margarine,
   cut in chunks
4 eggs
1¾ c. sugar
1 tsp. vanilla
½ c. apple juice or whiskey
2¾ c. flour
4 tsp. baking powder

Slicer: Slice apples, using firm pressure. Transfer to a large bowl and mix with remaining ingredients for filling. Wipe the bowl and the cover with paper towelling.

Steel Knife: Process shortening with eggs, sugar and vanilla for 2 minutes, scraping down bowl once or twice. Do not insert pusher in feed tube. Add juice and process for 3 seconds. Add flour and baking powder. Process with about 6 quick on/off turns, **just** until flour mixture disappears. Scrape down sides of bowl as necessary.

Spread ⅓ of batter in a greased and floured 12 cup Bundt pan or 10'' tube pan. Arrange half of apple filling over batter. Do not allow filling to touch sides of pan. Repeat until all ingredients are used, ending with batter.

Bake at 350°F for about 70 to 75 minutes, or until cake tests done. Cool for 20 minutes before removing from pan. Dust with icing sugar when cool.

Yield: 12 servings. May be frozen.

APPLE COFFEE CAKE ✓

Topping:
½ c. brown sugar, packed

½ c. walnuts
1 tsp. cinnamon

Steel Knife: Process ingredients for topping with 4 quick on/off turns, until nuts are coarsely chopped. Transfer to a small bowl.

Batter:
2 large apples, peeled, cored
   & quartered
½ c. butter or margarine, cut in
   chunks
½ c. sugar
½ c. brown sugar, packed
1 egg

½ tsp. baking soda
½ c. buttermilk or sour milk
1 tsp. baking powder
½ tsp. cinnamon
¼ tsp. nutmeg
⅛ tsp. cloves
1½ c. flour

Steel Knife: Process apples with several quick on/off turns, until coarsely chopped. Remove from bowl. Process butter, sugars and egg for 2 minutes, until well mixed. Do not insert pusher in feed tube. Stop machine once or twice to scrape down sides of bowl. Dissolve baking soda in milk. Add to creamed mixture and process for 3 seconds. Add baking powder, spices and flour. Blend in with 3 or 4 quick on/off turns, just until flour almost disappears. Add apples and process with 2 or 3 quick on/off turns to mix. Do not overprocess.

Pour batter into a greased and floured 8'' square baking pan. Sprinkle with topping. Bake at 350°F for 40 to 45 minutes. Delicious served warm with ice cream.

Yield: 9 servings. Freezes well.

APPLE STREUSEL CAKE

Topping:
½ c. margarine, cut in chunks
1¼ c. flour
½ c. sugar
¾ tsp. cinnamon

Filling:
8 apples, peeled, cored &
halved
⅓ c. sugar
1 tsp. cinnamon
2 tbsp. flour

Batter for Basic Pareve Cake (p. 255)

Steel Knife: Process ingredients for topping until crumbly, about 8 to 10 seconds. Empty into a small bowl.

Slicer: Slice apples, using firm pressure. Transfer apples to a large bowl and mix with remaining ingredients for filling. Wipe out processor bowl with paper towelling.

Steel Knife: Prepare batter for Basic Pareve Cake as directed. Pour the batter into a greased and floured 9'' x 13'' baking pan. Spread apples evenly over batter. Sprinkle with topping. Bake at 350°F for 50 to 60 minutes, until cake tests done.

Yield: 15 servings. May be frozen, but topping will become moist from the apples.

DEEP DISH APPLE CAKE ✓

Follow recipe for Deep Dish Tutti-Fruiti Cake (p. 258), but substitute the following filling:

10 to 12 large apples, peeled,
cored & halved
1 c. sugar

1 tbsp. cinnamon
1 tbsp. lemon juice

Slicer: Slice apples, using firm pressure. Transfer to a mixing bowl and toss with remaining filling ingredients. Baked cake freezes well.

Yield: 15 servings.

LATTICE APPLE CAKE

Dough:
1 medium seedless orange
1 c. sugar
3 eggs
1 tsp. vanilla
¾ c. oil
3 c. flour
2 tsp. baking powder

Filling:
7 or 8 apples, peeled, cored &
halved
¾ c. white or brown sugar,
packed
1 tbsp. cinnamon
½ c. sultana raisins, if desired

Cut orange in four, but do not peel. Insert **Steel Knife** in processor. Process orange until fine, about 20 to 25 seconds. Add remaining ingredients for dough and process until mixed, about 12 to 15 seconds, scraping down sides of bowl if necessary. Press ⅔ of the dough into the bottom and 1'' up the sides of a greased 10'' springform pan. Reserve remaining dough for topping, flouring it lightly.

Slicer: Slice apples, using firm pressure. Transfer to a bowl and mix with remaining ingredients for filling. Spread evenly over dough in pan.

Flour your hands to facilitate handling of dough for lattice topping. Roll pieces of dough between your palms into thin ropes and arrange in a criss-cross design to form lattice-work over filling. Bake at 350°F for about 1 hour, until golden brown. Cool completely. Sprinkle with icing sugar, if desired. Freezes well.

Yield: 12 servings.

Note: Cake may also be baked in a greased 9'' x 13'' baking pan.

LATTICE APPLE BLUEBERRY CAKE ✓

Follow directions for Lattice Apple Cake (p. 246), but substitute the following filling:-

4 apples, peeled, cored & halved	**2 c. fresh or frozen blueberries, well drained**
¾ c. white or brown sugar, packed	**1 tbsp. cinnamon**
	¼ c. flour

Slicer: Slice apples, using firm pressure. Transfer to a mixing bowl and toss lightly to mix with remaining filling ingredients. Baked cake freezes well.

Yield: 12 servings.

APPLESAUCE DATE & NUT CAKE

1 c. walnuts	**¼ tsp. cloves**
1 c. pitted dates	**½ c. butter or margarine, cut in chunks**
2 c. + 2 tbsp. flour	
1 tsp. baking soda	**1½ c. brown sugar, packed**
1 tsp. baking powder	**4 eggs**
2 tsp. cinnamon	**2 tsp. vanilla**
¼ tsp. nutmeg	**1 c. applesauce**

Steel Knife: Process nuts until coarsely chopped, about 6 to 8 seconds. Empty into a small bowl. Place dates and 2 tbsp. flour in processor bowl. Process until coarsely chopped, about 8 seconds. Add to nuts. Place remaining dry ingredients in processor bowl. Process until blended, about 6 to 8 seconds. Transfer to a large bowl.

Process butter, brown sugar, eggs and vanilla for 2 minutes. Do not insert pusher in feed tube. Add applesauce and process for 3 seconds. Add reserved dry ingredients and process with 3 or 4 quick on/off turns, **just** until blended. Add nuts and dates. Mix in with 2 or 3 additional quick on/off turns. Scrape down bowl as necessary.

Pour batter into a greased and floured 10'' tube pan or 12 cup Bundt pan. Bake at 350°F for 55 to 60 minutes, until cake tests done. Freezes well.

Yield: 12 servings.

Note: If desired, batter may be baked in two 9'' x 5'' loaf pans at 350°F for 45 to 50 minutes, until done.

APPLESAUCE SPICE CAKE
(Kids love this version.)

Follow recipe for Applesauce Date & Nut Cake (above), but eliminate walnuts, dates and 2 tbsp. flour.

If desired, add ¾ cup raisins with 2 or 3 quick on/off turns after you have blended in the flour mixture.

Variation

Before making batter, combine the following ingredients in the processor to make a Streusel Topping:-

¼ c. margarine or butter, cut in chunks	**½ c. sugar**
¾ c. flour	**½ tsp. cinnamon**

Steel Knife: Process mixture until crumbly, about 8 to 10 seconds. Empty bowl. Prepare batter as directed. Pour into a greased and floured 9'' x 13'' baking pan. Sprinkle with Streusel Topping. Bake at 350°F for 45 to 50 minutes.

Yield: 12 to 15 servings. Freezes well.

SPICY PUMPKIN LOAF

Follow recipe for Applesauce Date & Nut Cake (p. 247) but substitute 1 cup canned pumpkin for the applesauce, and 1 cup raisins for the chopped dates. Bake in two greased 9'' x 5'' loaf pans at 350°F for 45 to 50 minutes, until done. Freezes well.

Yield: 2 loaves.

YOGHURT BANANA CAKE

(My son Doug loves any cake, as long as it's banana!)

½ c. butter or margarine, cut in chunks	2 large bananas (very ripe)
	1 tsp. baking soda
1½ c. sugar	¾ c. plain yoghurt
2 eggs	1 tsp. baking powder
1 tsp. vanilla	2 c. flour

Steel Knife: Process butter, sugar, eggs and vanilla for 2 minutes, scraping down bowl once or twice. Do not insert pusher in feed tube. While machine is running, drop chunks of banana through feed tube. Process until blended.

Meanwhile, dissolve baking soda in yoghurt. Let stand for 1 to 2 minutes. Yoghurt will nearly double in volume, so use a 2 cup measuring cup. Add to batter and process for 3 seconds. Add flour and baking powder. Process with 4 quick on/off turns, just until flour mixture disappears. Bake in a greased and floured 9'' square baking pan at 350°F for 50 minutes, until cake tests done. Cool 10 minutes. Remove from pan. Freezes well.

Yield: 9 servings.

If desired, frost with Banana Frosting (p. 266). Garnish with walnut halves.

Note: Sour cream may be substituted for yoghurt, if desired. Sugar may be reduced to 1¼ cups, but will produce a lighter colored cake.

BANANA ORANGE CAKE: Substitute orange juice for yoghurt. Do **not** dissolve baking soda in juice. Decrease baking soda to ½ tsp., increase baking powder to 2 tsp. and add to batter along with flour.

CHOCOLATE CHIP BANANA CAKE

Follow recipe for Yoghurt Banana Cake (above), but add 1 or 2 squares of semi-sweet or unsweetened chocolate, halved.

Using **Steel Knife,** process chocolate until finely chopped, about 25 to 30 seconds. Remove from bowl. Continue with recipe for Yoghurt Banana Cake, and add chocolate with dry ingredients. Bake as directed. Freezes well.

Yield: 9 servings. Frost with Chocolate Cocoa Frosting (p. 267) or Banana Frosting (p. 266).

BANANA NUT CAKE

Follow recipe for Yoghurt Banana Cake (above), but add ¾ cup walnuts, pecans or brazil nuts.

Using **Steel Knife,** process nuts with several quick on/off turns, until coarsely chopped. Remove from bowl. Continue with recipe for Yoghurt Banana Cake, and add chopped nuts with one or two quick on/off turns after the flour has been blended into the batter. Bake as directed. Freezes well.

Yield: 9 servings. May be frosted with Chocolate Frosting, (p. 267), Chocolate Cocoa Frosting (p. 267) or Banana Frosting (p. 266). Garnish with appropriate nuts.

BLUEBERRY BUNDT CAKE ✓

¾ c. butter or margarine, cut in
    chunks
1½ c. sugar
3 eggs
1 tsp. vanilla
4 tsp. vinegar plus milk to
    equal 1½ cups

1½ tsp. baking soda
3 tsp. baking powder
3 c. flour
2 c. fresh or frozen
    blueberries (do not thaw)

Steel Knife: Process butter, sugar, eggs and vanilla for 2 minutes, scraping down bowl once or twice. Do not insert pusher in feed tube. Dissolve soda in vinegar-milk mixture. Pour in through feed tube and process for 3 seconds. Add dry ingredients. Process with 4 quick on/off turns, **just** until flour disappears. Carefully stir in blueberries by hand. Pour into a greased and floured 12 cup Bundt pan. Bake at 325°F for 1 hour, until cake tests done. Let cool 15 minutes. Invert and remove from pan. Dust with icing sugar, if desired.

Yield: 12 servings. Freezes well.

BLUEBERRY CRUMBLE CAKE ✓

2¼ c. flour
1¼ c. sugar
¾ c. butter or margarine, cut in
    chunks
1 tsp. baking soda

1 c. sour cream or plain
    yoghurt
1 tsp. baking powder
2 eggs
1½ c. fresh blueberries

Steel Knife: Process flour, sugar and butter until fine crumbs are formed, about 12 to 15 seconds. Remove 1 cup of crumb mixture from processor bowl and set aside. Dissolve baking soda in sour cream or yoghurt. Add to processor bowl along with baking powder and eggs. Process for 6 to 8 seconds, just until blended, scraping down sides of bowl with a rubber spatula as necessary. Stir in blueberries by hand.

Spread batter evenly in a greased and floured 9'' square baking pan. Sprinkle with reserved crumb mixture. Bake at 375°F for 40 to 45 minutes, until done.

Yield: 9 servings. Delicious served warm or at room temperature. May be frozen.

CARAMEL PECAN CAKE

(Quick, easy and delicious - and from a mix!)

½ c. pecans
19 oz. pkg. white or yellow
    cake mix
1 pkg. (4 serving size) caramel
    instant pudding

1 c. sour cream
4 eggs
½ c. oil

Steel Knife: Chop pecans with 4 or 5 quick on/off turns, until coarsely chopped. Empty bowl. Place cake mix, pudding and sour cream in processor. Add eggs and oil through feed tube while machine is running and process for 2 minutes, stopping machine once or twice to scrape down. Add pecans and process with 3 or 4 quick on/off turns, just until mixed.

Bake in a greased and floured 12 cup Bundt pan or 10'' tube pan at 325°F for 50 to 60 minutes, until cake tests done. Cool 15 minutes; invert and remove from pan. Dust with icing sugar when cool. Freezes well.

Yield: 12 servings.

BURNT SUGAR CAKE

½ c. sugar	3 eggs
½ c. boiling water	1 c. milk
½ c. margarine or butter, cut in	2⅓ c. flour
chunks	2½ tsp. baking powder
1⅓ c. sugar	½ tsp. salt
1 tsp. vanilla	

Melt ½ cup sugar in a heavy skillet on medium heat until clear and dark brown, stirring constantly to prevent sugar from burning. Remove from heat and carefully stir in boiling water. Return mixture to heat and simmer until lumps melt and mixture is syrupy. Let cool.

Steel Knife: Process margarine, sugar, vanilla and eggs for 2 minutes, scraping down bowl once or twice. Do not insert pusher in feed tube. Add milk and ¼ cup burnt sugar syrup. Process for 3 seconds. Add dry ingredients. Process with 4 quick on/off turns, **just** until flour disappears. Scrape down bowl as necessary. Pour batter into a greased and floured 9 cup Bundt pan or two 9'' layer pans. Bake layers at 350°F for 30 to 35 minutes, or Bundt cake at 325°F for 45 to 55 minutes. Cool and frost with Fluffy Burnt Sugar Icing (see recipe below). If freezing cake, do not frost.

Yield: 8 to 10 servings.

Fluffy Burnt Sugar Icing

½ c. brown sugar, packed	¼ c. corn syrup
2 tbsp. reserved burnt sugar	2 egg whites
syrup	1 tsp. vanilla
1 tbsp. water	

Blend brown sugar, reserved syrup, water and corn syrup in a saucepan. Cover and bring to a boil. Uncover and cook until 242°F on a candy thermometer, or until mixture spins a 6'' to 8'' thread when dropped from a fork. Beat egg whites on an electric mixer until stiff peaks form. Pour syrup slowly in a thin stream into egg whites. Beat until mixture holds stiff peaks. Add vanilla. Frost cake.

NUTRITIOUS CARROT CAKE

3 carrots scraped & trimmed	2 c. flour
1 apple, peeled & cored	2 tsp. baking soda
3 eggs	1 tsp. baking powder
1¼ c. sugar	2 tsp. cinnamon
1 c. oil	1 c. raisins

Grater: Cut carrots to fit feed tube. Grate, using firm pressure. Cut apple to fit feed tube. Grate, using medium pressure. Measure carrots and apple to equal 2 cups lightly packed.

Steel Knife: Process eggs with sugar for 1 minute. Do not insert pusher in feed tube. While machine is running, add oil through feed tube. Process 45 seconds longer. Add carrots and apple and process about 8 to 10 seconds, until blended. Add dry ingredients. Process with 3 or 4 quick on/off turns, **just** until flour disappears. Sprinkle raisins over batter. Give one or two more quick on/off turns. Scrape down bowl as necessary.

Pour batter into a well-greased 12 cup Bundt pan or 9'' x 13'' baking pan. Bake at 350°F for about 40 to 50 minutes, until cake tests done. When cool, ice with Cream Cheese Icing (p. 268). Freezes well.

Yield: 12 to 15 servings.

CARROT SPICE CAKE

Prepare Zucchini Spice Cake as directed on p. 264, but instead of zucchini, substitute 4 medium carrots which have been scraped, trimmed and cut to fit feed tube. Grate, using firm pressure. Cake freezes well.

Yield: 12 to 15 servings.

CARROT PINEAPPLE CAKE

Prepare Zucchini Spice Cake as directed on p. 264, but instead of zucchini, substitute 4 medium carrots which have been scraped, trimmed and cut to fit feed tube. Grate, using firm pressure

Drain a 10 oz. can crushed pineapple very thoroughly. Add to batter along with nuts and raisins. Glaze baked cake with Orange Glaze (p. 265), if desired. Freezes well, but glaze cake after thawing.

Yield: 12 to 15 servings.

EASY AND GOOD CARROT LOAF

8 oz. jar junior baby food	**1½ c. flour**
carrots	**1 tsp. baking powder**
(or 1 c. carrot purée)	**1 tsp. baking soda**
1 c. sugar	**½ tsp. cinnamon**
2 eggs	**½ c. raisins, if desired**
¾ c. oil	

If you wish to prepare you own carrot purée, peel and trim three large carrots. Cut in 1'' pieces. Process on **Steel Knife** with 4 or 5 quick on/off turns, until coarsely chopped. You should have approximately 1½ cups chopped carrots. Place in a saucepan with 1 cup boiling water and a dash of salt. Cover and simmer about 15 minutes, or until tender. Process on **Steel Knife** until puréed, about 25 to 30 seconds. Measure 1 cup purée.

Add sugar and eggs to carrot purée. Process for 15 to 20 seconds. While machine is running, add oil through feed tube. Process for 35 to 40 seconds. Add flour, baking powder, soda and cinnamon. Process with 3 or 4 quick on/off turns, **just** until flour disappears. Add raisins with 1 or 2 on/off turns.

Pour into a greased 9'' x 5'' loaf pan. Bake at 350°F for 55 to 60 minutes, until loaf tests done. Cool 15 minutes and remove from pan. When completely cooled, frost completely with Cream Cheese Icing (p. 268). If desired, sprinkle with coconut. Freezes well.

Yield: 1 loaf.

COCKEYED CAKE
(Fudgy and Fast.
There are no eggs in this cake.)

1½ c. flour	**5 tbsp. corn oil**
1 c. sugar	**1 tbsp. vinegar**
⅓ c. cocoa	**1 tsp. vanilla or peppermint**
1 tsp. baking soda	**extract**
½ tsp. salt	**1 c. cold water**

Steel Knife: Process dry ingredients for 10 seconds, until blended. Add remaining ingredients and process 6 to 8 seconds longer, just until blended.

Pour into a greased 8'' square baking pan. Bake at 350°F for 30 minutes.

Yield: 9 servings. Freezes well.

PAREVE* CHOCOLATE CAKE ✓

(Big, Moist, Dark and Delicious. Sure to be a favorite in your house.)

⅔ c. cocoa
2¼ c. flour
2 c. sugar
1½ tsp. baking powder
1½ tsp. baking soda

¾ tsp. salt
1½ tsp. instant coffee
1½ c. orange juice or water
3 eggs
1¼ c. oil

Steel Knife: Combine all dry ingredients in processor bowl. Process until blended, about 10 seconds. Add orange juice and eggs. Start processor and add oil through feed tube while machine is running. Process batter for 45 seconds. Do not insert pusher in feed tube and do not overprocess.

Pour batter into a well-greased 10'' tube pan or 12 cup Bundt pan. Bake at 350°F for 55 to 60 minutes, until cake tests done. Cool for 20 minutes before removing cake from pan. Freezes well.

Yield: 12 servings.

Note: This amount of cake batter may be too large for some processors. If this is the case, then make Easy Chocolate Cake, which is quite similar, but is a slightly smaller cake. See recipe below.

Pareve means that no dairy or meat products are used in this recipe.

EASY CHOCOLATE CAKE ✓

1½ c. sugar
2 c. flour
½ c. cocoa
dash of salt
1 tsp. instant coffee
1 tsp. baking powder

1 tsp. baking soda
1¼ c. milk, orange juice or water
3 eggs
¾ c. oil

Steel Knife: Combine all dry ingredients in processor bowl. Process until blended, about 10 seconds. Add milk and eggs. Start processor and add oil through feed tube while machine is running. Process batter for 45 seconds. Do not insert pusher in feed tube and do not overprocess.

Pour batter into a well-greased and floured 9 or 12 cup Bundt pan or 9'' tube pan. Bake at 325°F for about 55 to 60 minutes, until cake tests done. Cool for 20 minutes before removing from pan. Ice with your favorite chocolate frosting. Freezes well.

Yield: 10 servings.

CRUNCHY CHOCOLATE CAKE

¾ c. walnuts
¾ c. sugar
3 tbsp. flour
½ tbsp. cocoa

3 tbsp. melted butter or margarine
Batter for Chocolate Yoghurt Cake (p. 253)

Steel Knife: Process nuts until coarsely chopped, about 6 to 8 seconds. Add sugar, flour, cocoa and butter. Process just until mixed, about 3 to 4 seconds. Empty bowl. Prepare batter for Chocolate Yoghurt Cake as directed. Pour into a greased and floured 9'' x 13'' baking pan. Sprinkle with nut topping. Bake at 350°F about 45 minutes, or until cake tests done. Freezes well.

Yield: 12 to 15 servings.

CHOCOLATE YOGHURT CAKE

½ c. butter or margarine, cut in chunks
1 c. white sugar
1 c. brown sugar, lightly packed
4 eggs

1 tsp. vanilla
4 squares unsweetened chocolate, melted & cooled
1 tsp. baking soda
1 c. plain yoghurt
2 c. flour

Steel Knife: Process butter, sugars, eggs and vanilla for 2 minutes, scraping down bowl once or twice. Do not insert pusher in feed tube. Add melted chocolate and process until blended, about 10 seconds, scraping down sides of bowl as necessary. Dissolve baking soda in yoghurt in a mixing bowl (yoghurt will nearly double in volume, so make sure that bowl is large enough). Add yoghurt and flour to processor. Process with 3 or 4 quick on/off turns, **just** until blended, scraping down bowl if necessary.

Pour batter into a greased and floured 12 cup Bundt pan or 10'' tube pan. Bake at 325°F for about 50 minutes, or until cake tests done. Let cool for 15 to 20 minutes before removing from pan. When cool, ice with Chocolate Glaze (p. 265). Cake freezes well. Do not freeze if glazed.

Yield: 12 servings.

Variation: To add nuts to cake, process 1 cup walnuts or peanuts on **Steel Knife** until coarsely chopped, about 6 seconds. Empty bowl and prepare cake batter as directed. Add nuts to batter once flour is blended in. Process with 1 or 2 quick on/off turns, just until mixed. Bake as directed.

Note: You may prepare half the recipe if desired, and bake in a greased and floured 8'' square baking pan at 350°F for 35 to 40 minutes, until cake tests done.

CHOCK FULL OF CHIPS CUPCAKES

Prepare batter for Chocolate Yoghurt Cake (above). After flour and yoghurt are blended in, sprinkle 1 cup chocolate chips over the top of the batter. Mix in with one or two very quick on/off turns. Pour batter into muffin tins which have been lined with paper liners. Bake at 400°F for about 18 to 20 minutes, until done.

Yield: about 24 to 30 cupcakes. Freezes well. Frost with your favorite chocolate frosting.

Variation: Add ¾ tsp. cinnamon to batter along with flour.

CHOCOLATE SWISS CAKE ✓

Follow recipe for Chocolate Mocha Cake (p. 254) or Chocolate Yoghurt Cake (above), and pour batter into three greased and floured 9'' layer pans. Bake at 350°F about 25 minutes, until layers test done. Cool completely. Freeze layers until firm. Split each layer in half crosswise, using a very sharp knife.

Steel or Plastic Knife: Place 2½ cups chilled whipping cream in processor bowl. Do not insert pusher in feed tube. Place a heavy book under the back part of the base so that the machine is tipped forward. Whip cream until the texture of sour cream, about 35 seconds. Add 3 to 4 tbsp. sugar and process a few seconds longer, until stiff. Spread between layers and assemble cake. Top with whipped cream. Do not frost sides. Garnish with grated chocolate and maraschino cherries. Refrigerate.

Yield: 12 servings. May be frozen. Thaw in refrigerator.

Note: For a lighter textured whipped cream, it may be whipped on an electric mixer.

CHOCOLATE MOCHA CAKE ✓

¾ c. soft butter or margarine, cut in chunks	2 tsp. instant coffee
	2 tbsp. boiling water
1½ c. sugar	1 c. milk
4 eggs	2 c. + 2 tbsp. flour
2 tsp. vanilla	2 tsp. baking powder
3 squares unsweetened or semi-sweet chocolate, melted & cooled	½ tsp. baking soda
	½ tsp. salt

Steel Knife: Process butter, sugar, eggs and vanilla for 2 minutes, scraping down bowl once or twice. Do not insert pusher in feed tube. Add melted chocolate and process until blended, about 10 seconds. Dissolve instant coffee in boiling water. Add to milk. Add half of flour to processor and process with 2 or 3 on/off turns, until nearly blended. Add remaining ingredients. Process with 3 or 4 quick on/off turns, **just** until blended.

Pour batter into a greased and floured 12 cup Bundt pan or three 9'' layer pans. Bake Bundt cake at 325°F for 45 to 50 minutes, until cake tests done. Bake layers at 350°F about 25 minutes. When cool, frost with Koko-Moko Buttercream Icing (p. 268) or double recipe of Mocha Butter Cream (p. 269). If baked in a Bundt pan, glaze with Chocolate Glaze (p. 265). Freezes well.

Yield: 12 servings.

CHOCOLATE MINT CAKE ✓

Follow recipe for Chocolate Yoghurt Cake (p. 253), but substitue 1 tsp. peppermint extract for vanilla. Pour batter into 3 greased and floured nine inch layer pans. Bake at 350°F about 25 minutes, until layers test done. When cool, frost with Chocolate Mint Frosting (p. 267) or Peppermint Butter Icing (p. 270). Freezes well.

Yield: 12 servings.

SOUR CREAM FUDGE CAKE
(Guaranteed to Please!)

¼ c. butter	¾ tsp. baking soda
1 c. sugar	¾ c. sour cream
2 eggs	1 c. less 2 tbsp. flour
1 tsp. vanilla	
2 squares unsweetened chocolate, melted and cooled	

Steel Knife: Process butter, sugar, eggs and vanilla for 2 minutes. Do not insert pusher in feed tube. Add melted chocolate and process until blended, about 10 seconds. Scrape down sides of bowl with rubber spatula as necessary. Dissolve baking soda in sour cream; add to batter and process 3 seconds. Add flour and process with 3 or 4 quick on/off turns, **just** until blended.

Pour batter into a greased and floured 8'' square baking pan. Bake at 350°F for about 45 minutes, until cake tests done. Frost with your favourite frosting. Freezes well.

Yield: 9 servings.

Note: This recipe may be doubled and baked in a 10'' tube pan at 325°F for 1 hour and 10 minutes or until done. For layers, bake in three 9'' round pans at 375°F for 25 to 30 minutes, until done. Delicious with Pecan Coconut Frosting (p. 269).

CHOCOLATE CHIP BUNDT CAKE
(From a Mix)

19 oz. pkg. chocolate or white cake mix	1 c. sour cream
	4 eggs
1 pkg. (4 serving size) instant chocolate pudding	½ c. vegetable or corn oil
	6 oz. pkg. chocolate chips

Steel Knife: Place cake mix, pudding and sour cream in processor. Add eggs and oil through feed tube while machine is running. Process for 2 minutes. Do not insert pusher in feed tube. Stop machine once or twice to scrape down batter. Sprinkle chocolate chips over batter. Process with 2 or 3 quick on/off turns, just to mix chocolate chips through batter without processing them.

Pour batter into a greased and floured 12 cup Bundt pan or 10'' tube pan. Bake at 325°F for 50 to 60 minutes, until cake tests done. Cool 15 to 20 minutes. Loosen edges with a long narrow spatula and invert onto a serving plate. Cool. Glaze if desired, or dust with icing sugar. Yummy! One of the best chocolate cakes you will ever taste.

Yield: 12 servings. Freezes well.

Note: If chocolate chips sink to the bottom of the cake (this happens with some cake mixes), try shaking chips with a little cocoa in a plastic bag before adding them to the cake batter.

FAVORITE CHOCOLATE CHIP CAKE
(Just one of the many recipes shared by my friend Marilyn!)

1⅓ c. flour	1 c. sugar
1½ tsp. baking powder	2 eggs
1 tsp. baking soda	1 c. sour cream or yoghurt
1 tsp. cinnamon	½ - ¾ c. chocolate chips
6 tbsp. soft butter or margarine	

Steel Knife: Process flour, baking powder, baking soda and cinnamon for 5 seconds. Empty into another bowl. Process butter, sugar and eggs for 2 minutes, scraping down bowl once or twice. Do not insert pusher in feed tube. Add sour cream or yoghurt and process for 3 seconds. Add dry ingredients. Process with 4 quick on/off turns, **just** until flour mixture disappears. Pour into a greased and floured 9'' square or 7'' x 11'' baking pan. Sprinkle chocolate chips evenly over batter. Bake at 350°F about 35 to 40 minutes, until cake test done. Yummy! Freezes well.

Yield: 9 to 10 servings.

BASIC PAREVE* CAKE
(Even though there is no butter or milk in this recipe,
the oil and juice make a moist and yummy cake.)

2 eggs	¾ c. orange or apple juice
1 c. sugar	2 c. flour
1 tsp. vanilla	3 tsp. baking powder
½ c. oil	½ tsp. salt

Steel Knife: Process eggs with sugar and vanilla for 1 minute. Do not insert pusher in feed tube. Add oil and process 1 minute longer. While machine is running, add juice through feed tube and process for 3 seconds. Add dry ingredients. Process with 4 quick on/off turns, **just** until flour disappears. Pour into a greased and floured 9'' square or 7'' x 11'' oblong baking pan. Bake at 350°F for about 40 to 50 minutes, until cake tests done. Freezes well. Ice with your favorite frosting. Delicious with Chocolate Cocoa Frosting (p. 267) or Peanut Butter Frosting (p. 268).

Yield: 9 to 12 servings.

*Pareve means that no dairy or meat products are used in this recipe.

BEST COFFEE CAKE ✓

Topping:
¾ c. almonds or pecans
½ c. brown sugar, packed
2 tsp. cinnamon

1 tbsp. cocoa
6 oz. pkg. chocolate chips

Steel Knife: Process nuts with brown sugar, cinnamon and cocoa until nuts are finely chopped, about 6 or 8 quick on/off turns. Transfer to a small bowl and mix in chocolate chips. Wipe processor bowl clean with paper towelling.

Batter:
6 tbsp. butter or margarine
1 c. sugar
2 eggs
1 tsp. vanilla

1 tsp. baking soda
1 c. sour cream or yoghurt
1⅓ c. flour
1½ tsp. baking powder

Steel Knife: Process butter, sugar, eggs and vanilla for 2 minutes, scraping down bowl once or twice. Do not insert pusher in feed tube. Dissolve baking soda in sour cream or yoghurt. Add to batter and process for 3 seconds. Add flour and baking powder. Process with 4 quick on/off turns, **just** until flour disappears. Scrape down bowl if necessary.

Pour half the batter into a greased and floured 9'' square baking pan. Sprinkle with half the topping. Repeat with remaining batter and topping. Bake at 350°F for 40 to 45 minutes, until cake tests done. Freezes well.

Yield: 9 servings.

CHOCOLATE FLAKE COFFEE CAKE

Steel Knife: Process 1 or 2 squares semi-sweet chocolate, halved, until finely chopped, about 20 to 25 seconds. Empty into a small bowl.

Continue with recipe for Best Coffee Cake (above), adding chocolate to the batter with the flour and baking powder.

CRUNCHY COFFEE CAKE

Follow recipe for Best Coffee Cake (above) but use the following topping:-

3 tbsp. butter or margarine
⅔ c. graham wafer crumbs
⅓ c. brown sugar, packed

2 tsp. cinnamon
½ c. filberts or walnuts

Steel Knife: Process all ingredients for topping until nuts are finely chopped, about 10 to 12 seconds.

COCONUT CRUMBLY CAKE

Follow recipe for Best Coffee Cake (above), but use the following topping:-

¼ c. flour
⅓ c. brown sugar, packed

¼ c. butter or margarine
½ c. coconut

Steel Knife: Combine all ingredients except coconut in processor; process for 6 to 8 seconds. Add coconut and process with two or three quick on/off turns.

Prepare batter as directed. Pour entire batter (rather than half the batter) into baking pan. Top with coconut mixture. Bake as directed.

PAREVE* COFFEE CAKE

½ c. walnuts
½ c. brown sugar, packed
2 tsp. cinnamon
⅛ tsp. cloves, if desired
⅛ tsp. allspice, if desired

¼ c. flour
3 tbsp. melted margarine
Basic Pareve Cake Batter
(p. 255)

Steel Knife: Place nuts, sugar, spices, flour and margarine in processor. Process with 4 quick on/off turns, until nuts are finely chopped. Empty bowl and wipe out with paper towelling. Prepare Basic Pareve Cake as directed. Pour half the batter into a greased and floured 9'' square or 7'' x 11'' oblong baking pan. Sprinkle with half the topping. Repeat with remaining batter and topping. Bake at 350°F for 45 to 55 minutes, until cake tests done. Freezes well.

Yield: 9 to 10 servings.

Variations: Use Topping for Best Coffee Cake (p. 256) or Crunchy Coffee Cake (p. 256).

*Pareve means that no dairy or meat products are used in this recipe.

MARBLED STREUSEL COFFEE CAKE
(They'll come back for seconds!)

Filling:
1 c. walnuts or pecans
½ c. coconut
½ c. brown sugar, packed
2 tsp. cinnamon
2 tbsp. cocoa

Batter:
¾ c. soft butter or margarine
1½ c. sugar
3 eggs
2 tsp. vanilla
3 c. flour
1½ c. sour milk (See Note)
1½ tsp. baking soda
1½ tsp. baking powder
¼ tsp. salt
½ c. coconut
1 square semi-sweet chocolate, melted and cooled

Steel Knife: Chop nuts coarsely with several quick on/off turns. Remove half the nuts from the processor and set aside to add to cake batter. Add remaining ingredients for filling to processor and process for just a few seconds. Empty bowl.

Batter: Process butter, sugar, eggs and vanilla for 2 minutes. Do not insert pusher in feed tube. Add half of flour and process with 2 or 3 on/off turns, until nearly blended. Add sour milk, baking soda, baking powder, salt and remaining flour. Process with several quick on/off turns, **just** until blended. Add reserved ½ cup nuts and coconut. Process with 1 or 2 more quick on/off turns.

Pour ½ of batter into a greased and floured 10'' Bundt or tube pan. Drizzle half of melted chocolate over batter. Cut through with a knife. Sprinkle with ¾ of filling. Add remaining batter and drizzle once again with melted chocolate. Cut through second layer of batter with a knife. Top with remaining filling.

Bake at 350°F for 55 to 60 minutes. Let cool 15 minutes before inverting cake to remove from pan. Re-invert cake so that nut filling is on top. When cool, glaze with White Glaze (p. 266). Freezes well, but do not glaze if freezing.

Yield: 12 to 15 servings.

Note*: To make sour milk, measure 4 tsp. vinegar or lemon juice into a measuring cup. Add milk to equal 1½ cups. Yoghurt or sour cream may be substituted for sour milk. Batter will be thicker and will require slightly more processing time to blend.

SOUR CREAM COFFEE CAKE

Prepare filling for either Marbled Streusel Coffee Cake (p. 257) or Best Coffee Cake (p. 256). Set aside.

Prepare Marbled Streusel Coffee Cake batter, but substitute 1½ cups sour cream for the sour milk. Batter will be somewhat thicker and you will need 5 or 6 on/off turns to blend in the dry ingredients.

Pour half the batter into a greased and floured 10'' tube pan or Bundt pan. Sprinkle with half of filling. Top with remaining batter and filling. (Melted chocolate may either be omitted or cut into batter as in recipe for Marbled Streusel Coffee Cake.)

Bake at 350°F for 55 to 60 minutes. Cool 15 minutes before removing from pan. Freezes well.

Yield: 12 to 15 servings.

CUPCAKES

Make your favorite cake recipe, but pour batter into muffin tins which have been lined with paper liners. Fill ⅔ full. Bake at 400°F for about 18 to 20 minutes, or until done.

Batter for 8'' square or 9'' x 5'' loaf pan yields 12 to 14 cupcakes.

Batter for 9'' square pan or 7'' x 11'' oblong pan yields 18 to 20 cupcakes.

Batter for 9'' x 13'' oblong pan or 12 c. Bundt pan yields 24 to 30 cupcakes.

BUTTERFLY CUPCAKES

Make your favorite cupcakes. When cool, cut a slice from the top of each cupcake and pipe with your favorite icing or sweetened whipped cream. Cut the removed tops in half. Press into icing to look like wings. Sprinkle with icing sugar.

DEEP DISH TUTTI-FRUITI CAKE

Filling:

28 oz. tin sliced peaches, drained
19 oz. tin pineapple chunks, drained
10 oz. tin mandarin oranges, drained
1 c. pitted prunes
¼ c. orange Tang crystals
19 oz. tin cherry pie filling

Batter:

1 c. sugar
¾ c. oil
3 eggs
¼ c. orange or apple juice
2 c. flour
2 tsp. baking powder
1 tsp. vanilla or orange extract

Combine ingredients for filling in a lightly greased 9'' x 13'' pyrex baking dish. Mix well.

Steel Knife: Process sugar with oil and eggs for 5 seconds. Add remaining ingredients for batter and process just until blended, about 8 to 10 seconds. Spread over fruits. Bake at 350°F for 55 to 60 minutes. If desired, sprinkle batter with a mixture of 2 tbsp. sugar and ½ tsp. cinnamon before baking, or sprinkle cooled, baked cake with sifted icing sugar.

Yield: 15 servings. May be frozen.

Note: A combination of 7 to 8 cups assorted fresh fruits in season may be used instead of canned fruits and prunes. Slice fruits on **Slicer,** adjusting pressure of pusher according to texture of fruit being sliced. Soft fruits require light pressure, firmer fruits require firmer pressure. (e.g. peaches, plums, nectarines, berries). Stir Tang crystals and pie filling into fruits. Then prepare batter and bake as directed.

DARK RICH FRUIT CAKE

(This is a variation of the delicious cake that my mother made for my wedding.)

1 lb. sultana raisins	2 tsp. cinnamon
1 lb. dark seedless raisins	1 tsp. nutmeg
1 lb. candied mixed fruits	1 tsp. cloves
1 lb. nuts (almonds, pecans, walnuts, etc. or a combination)	1 seedless orange, quartered (do not peel)
1 lb. candied (glacé) cherries	1 c. margarine or butter, cut in chunks
3½ c. flour	1½ c. sugar
1 tsp. baking powder	6 eggs
½ tsp. baking soda	½ c. grape or apple jelly
2 tbsp. cocoa	¼ c. brandy

Pour boiling water over raisins to cover completely. Let stand for 2 to 3 minutes. Drain well and pat dry. Place in a very large mixing bowl. Add candied mixed fruits.

Steel Knife: Chop nuts in batches of about 1 cup at a time. Process for 6 to 8 seconds, or until coarsely chopped. Time will depend on type of nuts being processed. (e.g. Almonds will take longer than walnuts.) Add to mixing bowl. Process cherries in 2 batches with ¼ cup flour until coarsely chopped, using about 4 quick on/off turns. Add to mixing bowl with an additional 1 cup flour. Mix very well.

Combine remaining flour with leavening, cocoa and spices in processor bowl. Process for about 10 seconds. Add to mixing bowl. Process orange until fine, about 20 seconds. Add to mixing bowl.

Process margarine, sugar and eggs for 2 minutes, until well blended. Do not insert pusher in feed tube. Add jelly and process 8 to 10 seconds to blend. Add brandy and process 2 or 3 seconds longer. Add to mixing bowl.

Stir with a wooden spoon until thoroughly mixed. Batter will be very heavy. Line desired baking pans with well greased brown paper or parchment, or aluminum foil. Fill pans to within 1'' from the top. Bake at 275°F.

Yield: about 8 lb. fruitcake.

TIME: *Bake loaf cakes about 3 hours. **Yield:** 3 loaves (9'' x 5'' x 3'')
      *Bake in tube pan about 3½ to 4 hours. **Yield:** 1 cake (10'' tube pan).
      *Bake in 9'' x 13'' pan about 3 hours. **Yield:** 1 cake and 1 loaf.
      *Bake small cakes about 1¾ to 2 hours. Small tinfoil pans are ideal.

Cool completely. Wrap in aluminum foil. If desired, wrap cakes in brandy-dampened cloth and store in an airtight container in a very cool place in order to ripen. Freezes well.

Shiny Glaze: Combine ½ cup golden corn syrup and ¼ cup water in a saucepan. Bring to a boil and remove from heat. Cool to lukewarm. Pour over cooled cake.

GENIE'S BIRTHDAY CAKE

(An old-time Winnipeg favorite.)

Base:
⅓ c. soft shortening or
   margarine
¼ c. icing sugar
1 c. flour
½ tsp. baking powder
1 tsp. vanilla

Cake:
½ c. soft shortening or
   margarine
¾ c. sugar
2 eggs
1 tsp. vanilla
½ c. milk
2 tsp. baking powder
½ tsp. salt
1⅓ c. flour

Base: Insert **Steel Knife.** Process all ingredients until blended, about 10 seconds. Grease an 8'' square baking pan, then line with wax paper, leaving about 1'' of paper extending beyond the top of the pan on either side. Press dough firmly into the bottom of the pan. Bake at 350°F for 12 to 15 minutes. Cool and remove from pan. Place on a serving plate and peel off wax paper.

Cake: Using **Steel Knife,** process shortening, sugar, eggs and vanilla for 2 minutes. Do not insert pusher in feed tube. Add milk and process 3 seconds. Add dry ingredients and process with 3 or 4 quick on/off turns, **just** until flour disappears. Scrape down bowl as necessary.

Pour batter into a greased and floured 8'' square pan. Bake at 350°F for 35 to 40 minutes. Cool 10 minutes and remove from pan.

Prepare Genie's Icing (p. 268). Spread baked base with a thin layer of icing. Cover with baked, cooled cake. Frost completely, reserving about ½ c. icing. Add a few drops of food coloring to icing and pipe leaves and flowers with a cake decorating set. Coat sides of cake with chocolate shot or grated sweet chocolate.

Yield: 8 to 10 servings. Freezes well.

CINNAMON MARBLE CAKE

½ c. butter or margarine, cut in
   chunks
1¼ c. sugar
3 eggs
¾ c. plain yoghurt

2 c. flour
1 tsp. baking soda
¼ c. brandy or rum
1 tbsp. cinnamon
2 tbsp. sugar

Steel Knife: Process butter with sugar and eggs for 2 minutes. Do not insert pusher in feed tube. Add yoghurt and process 3 seconds. Add flour, baking soda and brandy. Process with 4 quick on/off turns, just until blended. Scrape down bowl if necessary.

Pour into a well-greased 9'' square baking pan. Combine cinnamon and sugar. Sprinkle over cake. Cut through with a knife to give a marbled effect. Smooth out surface of cake with a rubber spatula. Bake at 350°F for 45 minutes, until cake tests done. Freezes well. If desired, frost with Cinnamon Icing (p. 266).

Yield: 9 servings.

HARVEY WALLBANGER CAKE

19 oz. pkg. orange cake mix
1 pkg. (4 serving size) vanilla
   instant pudding
4 eggs

½ c. oil
¾ c. orange juice
⅓ c. Galliano liqueur
3 tbsp. vodka

Steel Knife: Place dry ingredients in processor bowl. Add liquid ingredients through feed tube while machine is running. Process for 2 minutes, stopping machine once or twice to scrape down sides of bowl. Pour into a greased and floured 12 cup Bundt pan or 10'' tube pan. Bake at 325°F for 50 to 60 minutes, until cake tests done. Cool 15 minutes; then invert pan and remove cake. When completely cool, glaze with Galliano Glaze (p. 265). Cake freezes well. (If glazing cake, glaze after defrosting.)

Yield: 12 servings.

MARBLE MARVEL CAKE
(Chocolate syrup added to the batter makes this
Marble Cake fudgy and delicious!)

¾ c. margarine or butter, cut in
   chunks
1½ c. sugar
3 eggs
1½ tsp. vanilla
¾ c. milk, orange juice or
   water

2½ c. flour
2 tsp. baking powder
¼ tsp. salt
½ c. canned chocolate syrup
¼ tsp. baking soda

Steel Knife: Process margarine, sugar, eggs and vanilla for 2 minutes, scraping down bowl once or twice. Do not insert pusher in feed tube. Add milk through feed tube while machine is running. Process for 3 or 4 seconds. Add flour, baking powder and salt. Process with 4 or 5 quick on/off turns, scraping down bowl once or twice, **just** until mixed. Pour ⅔ of batter into a well-greased 12 cup Bundt pan or 10'' tube pan. Add chocolate syrup and baking soda to remaining batter in processor. Process for a few seconds, just until blended. Scrape down bowl as necessary. Pour chocolate batter over white batter. Cut through batters in a swirl design with a spatula or a fork.

Bake at 325°F for 60 to 70 minutes, until cake tests done. Cool 20 minutes before removing from pan. Ice with your favorite chocolate icing, or glaze with Chocolate Glaze (p. 265). Freezes well.

Yield: 12 servings.

PISTACHIO MARBLE CAKE
(From a Mix)

19 oz. pkg. white or yellow
   cake mix
4 serving size pistachio
   instant pudding
½ c. orange juice

½ c. water
4 eggs
½ c. oil
¾ c. canned chocolate syrup

Steel Knife: Place dry ingredients in processor bowl. Add remaining ingredients except chocolate syrup through feed tube while machine is running. Process for 2 minutes. Do not insert pusher in feed tube. Pour ¾ of batter into a greased and floured 10'' Bundt pan. Add chocolate syrup to remaining batter and process a few seconds longer, just until mixed. Pour over batter in pan.

Bake at 350°F for 50 to 60 minutes, until cake tests done. Cool 15 minutes before removing from pan. Freezes well.

HONEY COLA CAKE

2¼ c. flour
2 tsp. baking powder
1 tsp. baking soda
2 tsp. cinnamon
¾ c. brown sugar, packed

3 eggs
1 c. liquid honey
¾ c. oil
½ c. cola beverage (regular or low-cal)

Steel Knife: Process flour, baking powder, baking soda and cinnamon until blended, about 10 seconds. Empty into another bowl. Process brown sugar with eggs for 30 seconds. Do not insert pusher in feed tube. Add honey and oil; process 1½ minutes longer. Remove cover and add dry ingredients. Pour cola over. Process with 4 or 5 quick on/off turns, **just** until batter is blended. Immediately remove processor bowl from base and pour batter into a well-greased 12 cup Bundt pan or 10'' tube pan. Bake at 325°F for approximately 1 hour, until cake tests done. Let cool for 20 minutes before removing from pan. This cake keeps very well, and is sure to please. Freezes well.

Yield: 12 servings.

Note: If desired, substitute strong tea, coffee, orange juice or club soda for the cola. You may add 1 or 2 tbsp. cocoa with the dry ingredients to give a darker color.

If you wish to add raisins and/or nuts, they should be processed before the other ingredients. Using the **Steel Knife,** chop about ½ cup walnuts, pecans or almonds with several quick on/off turns, until coarsely chopped. Empty bowl. Place ½ to ¾ cup Sultana raisins in the processor bowl along with ¼ cup of the flour called for in the recipe. Process with several on/off turns to chop coarsely. Empty bowl. (Chopping the raisins and coating them with flour will help prevent them from sinking to the bottom of the cake during baking.) Proceed with recipe as directed. After flour has been added to batter, add raisins and/or nuts with 2 or 3 very quick on/off turns to mix into batter. Bake as directed.

POPPY SEED BUNDT CAKE

½ c. poppy seeds
1 c. buttermilk or sour milk
1 c. butter or margarine, cut in chunks
1½ c. sugar

4 eggs
2 tsp. vanilla or orange extract
2½ c. flour
2 tsp. baking powder
1 tsp. baking soda

Soak poppy seeds in milk for at least ½ hour.

Steel Knife: Process butter, sugar, eggs and vanilla for 2 minutes. Do not insert pusher in feed tube. Remove cover and add poppy seed/milk mixture to batter. Process for 3 or 4 seconds to blend. Add dry ingredients and process with 5 or 6 on/off turns. Mix through with a rubber spatula if batter is not completely blended.

Pour batter into a greased and floured 12 cup Bundt pan. Bake at 325°F for 50 to 60 minutes, until cake tests done. Cool 15 minutes before removing from pan. Freezes well.

Yield: 12 servings.

Variation

Before preparing batter, combine 2 tsp. cocoa, 1 tsp. cinnamon and ⅓ cup white or brown sugar in processor bowl. Process with the **Steel Knife** for a few seconds to blend. Empty bowl and set aside.

Prepare batter. Pour half the batter into pan, sprinkle with cocoa mixture, and scatter about ½ cup chocolate chips on top. Add remaining batter. Bake as directed.

FRESH ORANGE CAKE

2 medium seedless oranges
¾ c. margarine or butter, cut in
    chunks
1½ c. sugar

3 eggs
2 c. flour
2 tsp. baking powder
¼ tsp. salt

Steel Knife: Cut oranges in quarters, but do not peel. Process until fine, about 20 seconds. Add margarine, sugar and eggs. Process until well mixed, about 2 minutes. Do not insert pusher in feed tube. Scrape down sides of bowl once or twice. Add remaining ingredients and process with 3 or 4 quick on/off turns, **just** until flour disappears.

Pour batter into a 9'' square baking pan which has been greased and floured, or two 8'' or 9'' layer pans. Bake square cake at 350°F for about 40 to 45 minutes, or layers for 25 to 35 minutes, until cake tests done. Cool 10 minutes before removing from pans. When completely cool, frost with Orange Icing (p. 269).

Yield: about 9 servings. Freezes well. Garnish with drained mandarin oranges and chopped nuts, if desired.

RAISIN SPICE CAKE

2 c. flour
1 tsp. baking powder
2 tsp. cinnamon
¼ tsp. cloves
¼ tsp. Allspice
½ c. butter or margarine, cut in
    chunks

1 c. sugar
2 eggs
1 tsp. vanilla
1 c. sour cream
1 tsp. baking soda
½ c. raisins

Steel Knife: Process flour, baking powder, cinnamon, cloves and Allspice about 5 seconds, until blended. Empty bowl. Process butter, sugar, eggs and vanilla for 2 minutes, scraping down bowl once or twice. Do not insert pusher in feed tube. Meanwhile dissolve soda in sour cream. Add to creamed mixture and process 3 seconds. Add dry ingredients. Process with 3 quick on/off turns, just until flour mixture **almost** disappears. Add raisins and repeat 2 more quick on/off turns to mix raisins through batter without processing them. Pour into a greased and floured 9'' square baking pan. Bake at 350°F for 45-55 minutes, until cake tests done. When cool, frost with Cinnamon Icing (p. 266). Freezes well.

Yield: 9 servings.

Hint: To prevent raisins from sinking, toss lightly with 2 tbsp. flour called for in recipe.

LATTICE PEACH CAKE

Follow directions for Lattice Apple Cake (p. 246), but substitute the following filling:-

8 large, fresh, firm peaches	**1 tbsp. lemon juice**
(see Note)	**½ c. flour**
1 c. sugar	**1 tsp. cinnamon**

Pour boiling water over peaches. Drain well. The skin will peel off very easily. Cut in half and remove pits.

Slicer: Slice peaches, using medium pressure. Drain well and pat dry with paper towelling. Mix together with remaining filling ingredients. Baked cake freezes well.

Yield: 12 servings.

Note: Two 28 oz. cans peach slices (well-drained and dried with paper towelling) may be substituted for fresh peaches, if desired.

ZUCCHINI SPICE CAKE

(Delicious and nutritious. If you don't tell them, they won't know!)

2 c. flour	**2 medium zucchini (2 c.**
2 tsp. baking soda	**grated)**
1 tsp. baking powder	**3 eggs**
½ tsp. salt	**2 c. sugar (or 1½ c. brown**
1 tbsp. cinnamon	**sugar, packed)**
¼ tsp. Allspice, if desired	**1 c. oil**
1 c. walnuts	**2 tsp. vanilla**
	1 c. raisins

Steel Knife: Process dry ingredients about 10 seconds to blend. Empty into a large mixing bowl. Process nuts until chopped, about 6 seconds. Empty into a small bowl.

Grater: Grate unpeeled zucchini, using medium pressure. Empty into a measuring cup and measure loosely packed.

Steel Knife: Process eggs with sugar for 1 minute. Do not insert pusher in feed tube. While machine is running, add oil and vanilla through feed tube. Process about 45 seconds. Add zucchini and process about 8 to 10 seconds. Remove cover and add dry ingredients. (See **Note.**) Process with 3 or 4 quick on/off turns, **just** until flour disappears. Sprinkle nuts and raisins over batter. Give 1 or 2 more quick on/off turns.

Pour batter into a greased and floured 9'' x 13'' baking pan or 12 cup Bundt pan. Bake at 350°F for 55 to 60 minutes, or until cake tests done. Cool 15 minutes before removing from pan. When completely cooled, ice oblong cake with Cream Cheese Icing (p. 268) or drizzle White Glaze (p. 266) over Bundt cake. Also delicious without icing. This cake keeps very well. Freezes well.

Yield: 12 to 15 servings.

Note: This amount of batter will nearly completely fill the bowl of the standard-size food processor, but it will not overflow. If the amount of batter is too great for your brand of food processor, reverse the procedure and add the zucchini mixture to the dry ingredients in the mixing bowl. Mix with a wooden spoon until blended, about 45 seconds. Stir in nuts and raisins.

Variation: Substitute 1 cup chocolate chips for the raisins, if desired.

ALMOND GLAZE

½ c. sliced or slivered   2 tbsp. milk or water
  almonds, if desired   ½ tsp. almond extract
1 c. icing sugar

Place almonds on a cookie sheet and toast at 300°F for about 10 minutes, stirring once or twice. Let cool.

Plastic Knife: Process all ingredients except almonds until smooth, about 6 to 8 seconds. Scrape down sides of bowl as necessary. Drizzle over your favorite cake or sweet yeast breads. (e.g. Almond Tea Ring). Decorate with toasted almonds. Do not freeze glaze.

Yield: about ½ cup glaze.

CHOCOLATE GLAZE

1½ c. icing sugar   1 square unsweetened
2 tbsp. milk or water   chocolate, melted and
                                    cooled

Plastic Knife: Combine all ingredients and process for 6 to 8 seconds to blend, scraping down sides of bowl once or twice. Drizzle over your favorite cake. Excellent on Swedish Tea Ring (p. 203) or your favorite Bundt cake. It is preferable to glaze cakes that are not being frozen, as glazing has a tendency to crack in the freezer. Otherwise, glaze cakes after thawing.

Yield: about ¾ cup glaze.

GALLIANO GLAZE

1 c. icing sugar   1 tbsp. Galliano
1 tbsp. vodka

Plastic Knife: Process all ingredients until blended, about 8 to 10 seconds, scraping down sides of bowl once or twice. Drizzle over cooled cake. Do not freeze glaze.

Yield: about ½ cup.

ORANGE GLAZE

1 tsp. orange peel (zest)   3 tbsp. orange juice
2 c. icing sugar   1 tsp. vanilla

Using a potato peeler, peel rind from an orange, making sure not to use any of the bitter white part. Using **Steel Knife** process all ingredients together until blended, about 15 seconds. Scrape down if necessary. Drizzle over a large Bundt cake. If desired, garnish with mandarin oranges. Do not freeze. Delicious on Zucchini Spice Cake (p. 264) or Carrot Pineapple Cake (p. 251).

Yield: about 1 cup.

LEMON GLAZE

Follow recipe for Orange Glaze (above), but substitute lemon juice and zest for orange.

Yield: about 1 cup. Do not freeze.

WHITE GLAZE

1 c. icing sugar   ½ tsp. vanilla
2 tbsp. milk or water

Plastic Knife: Process all ingredients until smooth, about 6 to 8 seconds. Scrape down sides of bowl as necessary. Drizzle over your favorite cake or sweet yeast breads (e.g. Swedish Tea Ring p. 203).

Yield: about ½ cup.

BANANA FROSTING

2 tbsp. butter or margarine   ½ tsp. lemon juice
2" piece of banana (about 2   1¼ c. icing sugar
   tbsp.)   (approximately)
pinch of salt

Steel Knife: Process butter with banana for several seconds, until blended. Add remaining ingredients and process until smooth. Add a little extra icing sugar if frosting is too loose.

Yield: for a 9" square cake. Freezes well.

BUTTER ICING

¼ c. butter or margarine   2 - 3 tbsp. hot milk or cream
dash of salt   1 tsp. vanilla (or desired
2 c. icing sugar   flavoring)

Steel Knife: Combine all ingredients and process until smooth and blended, about 10 to 15 seconds. Scrape down sides of bowl as necessary.

Yield: for two 9" layers or a 9" x 13" oblong cake.

Variations: Substitute various flavorings for vanilla (e.g. maple, almond, butterscotch, etc.)

CINNAMON ICING

1 c. icing sugar   ½ tsp. vanilla
2 tbsp. soft butter or   2 tbsp. sour cream
   margarine   ½ tsp. cinnamon

Steel Knife: Process all ingredients until smooth, about 10 seconds. Scrape down sides of bowl as necessary.

Yield: for a 9" square cake. Recipe may be increased by 1½ times to frost a 9" x 13" cake. Freezes well.

PAREVE* CHOCOLATE ICING

2 squares unsweetened   2½ c. icing sugar
   chocolate, melted & cooled   1 egg
3 tbsp. soft margarine

Steel Knife: Process all ingredients until smooth and blended, about 10 seconds, scraping down bowl if necessary.

Yield: For a large cake. Freezes well.

*Pareve means that no dairy or meat products are used in this recipe.

ROCKY ROAD FROSTING

Stir ½ cup chopped nuts and 1 cup miniature marshmallows into your favorite chocolate icing. May be frozen.

CHOCOLATE FROSTING

1 square unsweetened
chocolate, melted & cooled
¼ c. soft butter or margarine
1½ c. icing sugar

2 - 3 tbsp. cream, milk, sour
cream or boiling water
½ tsp. vanilla

Steel Knife: Process all ingredients until smooth and blended, about 10 seconds. Scrape down sides of bowl as necessary.

Yield: for a 9'' square cake. Freezes well.

Variation: Substitute ½ tsp. peppermint extract for vanilla.

CHOCOLATE COCOA FROSTING

1 c. icing sugar
2 tbsp. soft butter or
margarine
2 tbsp. cocoa

2 tbsp. milk or hot water
½ tsp. vanilla
pinch of salt

Steel Knife: Process all ingredients until smooth and blended, about 10 seconds. Scrape down sides of bowl as necessary.

Yield: for a 9'' square cake. Freezes well.

Note: Recipe may be doubled for a large cake.

CHOCOLATE MINT FROSTING

3 c. icing sugar
⅓ c. soft butter or margarine
⅓ c. cocoa

5 - 6 tbsp. milk
¾ tsp. peppermint extract

Steel Knife: Process all ingredients until smooth and blended, about 10 seconds. Scrape down bowl once or twice.

Yield: for a large cake. Freezes well.

ONE-TWO-THREE MINT FROSTING

Place chocolate mint patties directly on top of an 8'' or 9'' square chocolate cake immediately upon removing it from the oven. As the patties melt, spread them evenly with a knife or spatula over the cake. May be frozen. Easy and delicious!

CHOCOLATE FUDGE FROSTING

6 oz. pkg. chocolate chips
3 tbsp. butter or margarine
dash of salt

3 c. icing sugar
½ c. milk
1 tsp. vanilla

Melt chocolate chips with butter or margarine on low heat. Cool completely.

Steel Knife: Combine all ingredients in processor, using slightly less than ½ cup milk. Process until smooth and blended, about 15 seconds. If icing seems too thick, add a few more drops of milk. If icing is too loose, add a tbsp. or two more of icing sugar.

Yield: For two 9'' layers, or a 9'' x 13'' cake. May be frozen. **Note:** Icing will thicken somewhat upon standing.

CHOCOLATE BUTTERCREAM ICING
(Smooth, rich and creamy!)

1 c. soft butter	2 c. icing sugar
½ c. cocoa	4 tbsp. milk or cream
¼ tsp. vanilla	

Steel Knife: Cut butter into 1'' chunks. Process with remaining ingredients until smooth and blended, about 15 to 20 seconds. Scrape down sides of bowl once or twice.

Yield: to fill and frost two or three 9'' layer cakes, or a large cake. Freezes well.

KOKO-MOKO BUTTERCREAM ICING

1 tsp. instant coffee	¼ tsp. vanilla
1 tbsp. boiling water	⅓ c. cocoa
1 c. soft butter, cut in chunks	2 - 3 tbsp. milk or cream
2 c. icing sugar	

Dissolve coffee in boiling water. Insert **Steel Knife** in processor. Combine all ingredients and process until smooth and blended, about 15 to 20 seconds. Scrape down sides of bowl once or twice.

Yield: to fill and frost two or three 9'' layer cakes or a large cake. Freezes well.

CREAM CHEESE ICING

¼ c. soft butter or margarine	2 c. icing sugar
¼ lb. softened cream cheese	¼ tsp. salt

Steel Knife: Process all ingredients until smooth, about 10 seconds.

Yield: for a 9'' x 13'' cake or two 9'' layers. Freezes well.

GENIE'S ICING
(A whipped Butter Icing)

1 c. sugar	1 c. unsalted butter,
2 tbsp. cornstarch	margarine or shortening,
1 c. milk	softened

Steel Knife: Place sugar and cornstarch in processor bowl. Add milk through feed tube while machine is running. Blend until smooth. Transfer to a saucepan and cook on medium heat, stirring often, until mixture comes to a boil. Cook 1 minute longer. Remove from heat and cover surface of mixture with waxpaper. Cool thoroughly.

Using an electric mixer, cream butter or shortening until light and fluffy. Add cooled mixture and beat at high speed at least 5 minutes. Tint if desired.

Yield: for two 9'' layers. May be frozen.

Note: The icing may be made on the processor using the **Steel Knife,** but will not have the same light fluffy texture as when beaten with electric mixer. The taste will not be affected. Processing time is about 2 minutes.

PEANUT BUTTER FROSTING

1½ c. icing sugar	4 - 5 tbsp. milk or hot water
6 tbsp. peanut butter	

Steel Knife: Process all ingredients until smooth and blended, about 10 seconds. Scrape down sides of bowl as necessary.

Yield: For a 9'' square cake. Freezes well.

MOCHA BUTTER CREAM

½ c. soft butter or margarine   2 tsp. instant coffee dissolved
1½ c. icing sugar   in 4 tsp. boiling water

Steel Knife: Process all ingredients until blended, about 10 to 15 seconds. Scrape down bowl if necessary.

Yield: for two 9'' layers or a 9'' square. Freezes well.

MOCHA FROSTING

¼ c. soft butter or margarine   1 tsp. instant coffee dissolved
dash of salt   in 2½ tbsp. boiling water
2 c. icing sugar
1 tsp. vanilla

Steel Knife: Combine all ingredients and process until smooth and blended, about 15 to 20 seconds. Scrape down sides of bowl as necessary.

Yield: for two 9'' layers or a large cake. Freezes well.

ORANGE ICING

¼ c. butter or margarine   ½ tsp. vanilla
dash sait   1 tsp. grated orange rind, if
2 c. icing sugar   desired
2 - 3 tbsp. orange juice

Steel Knife: Combine all ingredients and process until smooth and blended, about 15 seconds. Scrape down sides of bowl as necessary. For a deeper orange color, add a few drops each of red and yellow food coloring.

Yield: For two 9'' layers or a 9'' x 13'' cake.

LEMON ICING: Substitute lemon juice for orange juice, and lemon rind for orange rind.

PINEAPPLE ICING

Follow recipe for Orange Icing (above), but substitute ¼ c. crushed pineapple (with juice) for the orange juice and rind.

Yield: for two 9'' layers or a 9'' x 13'' oblong cake. Freezes well.

PECAN COCONUT FROSTING

1 c. evaporated milk   1 tsp. vanilla
1 c. sugar   1 c. pecans
½ c. butter or margarine   1¼ c. flaked coconut
3 egg yolks

Combine all ingredients except nuts and coconut in a heavy saucepan. Cook over medium heat, stirring, until thickened, about 12 minutes.

Steel Knife: Process pecans with 6 or 8 quick on/off turns, until chopped. Add with coconut to saucepan and beat until thick enough to spread.

Yield: To fill and top three 9'' layers. (Do not ice sides of cake.) Delicious on Sour Cream Fudge Cake (p. 254). May be frozen.

PEPPERMINT BUTTER ICING

1 peppermint candy cane   ½ tsp. peppermint extract
  (about ⅓ c. crushed)   few drops red food coloring
6 tbsp. soft butter   4 - 5 tbsp. hot milk or cream
3 c. icing sugar

Steel Knife: Break peppermint candy into 1" pieces. Start machine and drop candy through feed tube while machine is running. Process for a few seconds, until coarsely crushed. Empty bowl and set aside.

Combine remaining ingredients and process until smooth and blended, about 10 to 12 seconds, scraping down sides of bowl if necessary. Delicious with chocolate cake layers. Use crushed candy as a garnish for top of cake.

Yield: to fill and frost 2 - 9" layers or a large cake. Icing may be frozen.

WHIPPED CREAM

2 c. chilled whipping cream   ¼ c. granulated or icing sugar
  (35%)

Steel Knife: (Plastic Knife may be used if desired, but there is more splashing.) Place a heavy book under the back part of the base of the processor so that the machine is tipped forward. Whip cream until the texture of sour cream, about 35 seconds. Do not insert pusher in feed tube. Add sugar and process about 10 seconds longer, or until stiff. Do not overprocess.

Yield: To fill and frost two 9" layers (about 3 cups whipped cream). Refrigerate. May be frozen.

CHOCOLATE WHIPPED CREAM

Follow recipe for Whipped Cream (above), but increase sugar to ½ cup, and add ¼ cup cocoa when adding the sugar.

Yield: about 3½ cups.

COFFEE WHIPPED CREAM

Dissolve 2 tsp. instant coffee in 2 tbsp. boiling water. Cool completely. Follow recipe for Whipped Cream (above), adding the coffee along with the sugar.

Yield: about 3 cups.

MOCHA WHIPPED CREAM

Follow recipe for Whipped Cream (above), but increase sugar to ½ cup, and add 2 tsp. instant coffee and 2 tbsp. cocoa when adding the sugar.

Yield: about 3¼ cups.

WHIPPED DESSERT TOPPING

1 envelope dessert topping   ½ c. cold milk
  mix (such as Dream Whip)   1 tsp. vanilla

Steel Knife: Place a heavy book under the back part of the base of the processor so that the machine is tipped forward. Do not insert pusher in feed tube. Process all ingredients until stiff, stopping machine once or twice to scrape down sides of bowl.

Yield: about 1½ cups whipped topping.

(Note: You will have a smaller yield when you use the processor rather than an electric mixer.)

Variations: Add ¼ cup cocoa and ¼ c. icing sugar to the whipped topping. Process just until blended. (Or try 2 tsp. instant coffee and 2 tbsp. cocoa plus ¼ cup icing sugar.)

Any of the above variations may be doubled, if desired.

Cookies &
Squares

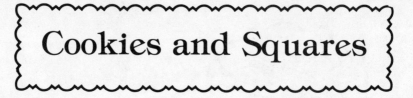

Cookies and Squares

- **Use the Steel Knife** to make cookies and squares. Most cookie recipes can be adapted easily to the processor. Process butter or margarine with sugar until well-creamed, about 1 or 2 minutes. Eggs can either be processed with the butter and sugar, or added through the feed tube one at a time. Flour and other dry ingredients should be blended in with quick on/off turns, just until blended. Some recipes call for allowing the cookie dough to come to a ball on the blades.

- **As a good guide,** don't make cookie recipes calling for more than 2 or 2½ cups of flour in your processor. Although some recipes will work well, it depends on the amount of dough the recipe makes, and sometimes it may not become properly mixed.

- **If recipe calls for chopped nuts,** dates, etc., process first before you make the batter. Empty nuts or dates from bowl, make batter, then add nuts, dates, chocolate chips, etc. with quick on/off turns. Some recipes may require you to mix these into the dough with a spatula or wooden spoon in order to prevent overprocessing and to keep some texture.

- **If chopping dates, cherries** or other sticky fruit, add 2 to 4 tbsp. of the flour called for in the recipe to prevent fruit from sticking to the blade. Use on/off turns.

- **It is not necessary** to soften butter or margarine before creaming them on the **Steel Knife.** Cut into chunks and use directly from the refrigerator. Some scraping down from the sides of the bowl with a rubber spatula may be necessary from time to time.

- **Remember that ½ cup butter** or margarine is the equivalent of ¼ lb. or one stick.

- **Butter and margarine** are interchangeable in most recipes. Shortening may also be substituted, but there will be a slight difference in flavor. Use part butter and part shortening instead of all shortening.

- **Try adding** chopped Brazils, peanuts, filberts or pistachios to your cookie recipes as an interesting change.

- **Icing sugar** is another name for confectioner's sugar or powdered sugar. Sprinkle on cookies once they are completely cooled, or the sugar will melt and not look as attractive.

- **Evaporated milk and sweetened condensed milk** are **not** interchangeable. Read labels carefully when you are shopping so that you don't buy the wrong product.

- **Substitute granola** for half the graham wafer crumbs in cookies and squares for an interesting taste and texture.

- **Broken leftover cookies** may be processed on the **Steel Knife** and used to make crumb crusts instead of always using graham wafers. This is also a good idea on how to use up that batch of cookies that the kids just don't like. (It does happen sometimes!)

- **If you are short** on cookie sheets, cut a piece of aluminum foil to fit your cookie sheet. While the first pan of cookies is baking, place the next batch of cookies on foil. Place foil on your cookie sheet as soon as you have emptied it from the first batch of cookies. Baking on aluminum foil also saves clean-ups.

- **Always cool cookies** before transfering them to your cookie jar in order to prevent them from sticking to each other.

- **Bake cookies** on the middle rack of your oven. If baking 2 pans at once, place racks so they divide the oven evenly into thirds. Switch pans for the last few minutes for even browning.

- **Cookies and squares** freeze well. Keep a supply of assorted cookies in your freezer. They will usually defrost in about 15 minutes or so, depending on size. Serve squares in pretty colored cupcake liners for eye appeal. Most cookie doughs can be frozen unbaked for several months.

✶✶✶✶✶✶✶✶✶

CHOCOLATE TURTLE COOKIES

½ c. butter or margarine, cut in chunks	¼ tsp. baking soda
½ c. brown sugar, lightly packed	¼ tsp. salt
2 eggs (reserve 1 egg white)	pecan halves or pieces
1 tsp. vanilla	Chocolate Fudge Frosting, half recipe (p. 267)
1½ c. flour	

Steel Knife: Process butter, sugar, 1 egg plus 1 yolk and vanilla for 2 minutes. Add flour, soda and salt and process **just** until dough is mixed and begins to gather in a ball around the blades. On/off turns will help you to avoid overprocessing dough.

Shape dough into 1 inch balls. Flatten each ball slightly. Arrange pecans in groups of three on lightly greased cookie sheets so that they resemble the head and feet of a turtle. Dip flattened balls of dough in unbeaten egg white and press gently onto nuts, allowing the tips of the nuts to show.

Bake at 375°F for 10 to 12 minutes. Cool completely. Ice tops with chocolate icing.

Yield: about 3 dozen cookies. Freezes well. Yummy!

CHOCOLATE CHIP COOKIES √

½ to 1 c. pecans or walnuts, if desired	1 tsp. vanilla
1 c. margarine or butter, cut in chunks	2¼ c. flour
¾ c. sugar	1 tsp. baking soda
¾ c. brown sugar, packed	½ tsp. salt
2 eggs	12 oz. pkg. chocolate chips (2 cups)

Steel Knife: Process nuts until coarsely chopped, about 8 to 10 seconds. Empty bowl. Process butter, sugars, eggs and vanilla for 1 minute. Add dry ingredients and process with several quick on/off turns, just until blended. Stir in chocolate chips and nuts by hand.

Drop by small spoonfuls onto a foil-lined cookie sheet which has been lightly greased. Bake at 375°F for 10 to 12 minutes, until lightly browned.

Yield: about 7 to 8 dozen. Freezes well.

BANANA CHOCOLATE CHIP DROPS
(A soft cake-like cookie. Kids will love them!)

²⁄₃ c. shortening or margarine,   2½ c. flour
    cut in chunks   2 tsp. baking powder
½ c. white sugar   ¼ tsp. soda
½ c. brown sugar, packed   pinch salt
2 eggs   6 oz. pkg. chocolate chips
½ tsp. vanilla
2 large ripe bananas (about 1
    cup)

Steel Knife: Process shortening, sugars, eggs and vanilla for 2 minutes, scraping down sides of bowl as necessary. While machine is running, drop in chunks of banana and process until blended. Add dry ingredients and process just until flour disappears, using quick on/off turns. Dough will be very soft, like a thick cake batter. Sprinkle chocolate chips over batter and mix in with 3 or 4 quick on/off turns.

Drop from a teaspoon onto greased cookie sheets. Bake at 400°F 10 to 12 minutes, until golden.

Yield: about 6 dozen. Freezes well.

CHOCOLATE CHIP OATMEAL COOKIES
(Watch out for the Cookie Monster!)

½ c. margarine, cut in chunks   1¾ c. flour
½ c. oil   ½ tsp. salt
1 c. brown sugar, lightly   1 tsp. baking soda
    packed   2 c. oatmeal
1 tsp. vanilla   ½ c. flaked coconut
¼ c. boiling water   ²⁄₃ c. chocolate chips

Steel Knife: Process margarine, oil, sugar and vanilla for 2 minutes, scraping down sides of bowl occasionally. Add boiling water and blend for a few seconds. Add flour, salt, soda and oatmeal. Process with several on/off turns, **just** until mixed. Stir in coconut and chocolate chips with a wooden spoon or spatula.

Form into 1'' balls. Place on lightly greased cookie sheets. Flatten completely with a fork in a criss- cross pattern. Bake at 325°F for 18 to 20 minutes, until golden brown.

Yield: about 6 dozen. Freezes well.

CHOCO-CRUNCHOS

½ c. chocolate chips   3 tbsp. milk
1 tbsp. butter or margarine   dash of salt
1 c. walnuts or peanuts   1 tsp. vanilla
1½ c. icing sugar   2½ c. coconut (approximately)

Melt chocolate chips with butter over low heat. Cool.

Steel Knife: Process nuts with several quick on/off turns, until coarsely chopped. Empty bowl. Process icing sugar with milk, salt, vanilla and melted chocolate about 15 seconds, until blended. Add reserved nuts and 1 cup of the coconut. Process with on/off turns, just until mixed. Form into 1'' balls. Roll in remaining coconut. Place on a lightly greased cookie sheet and refrigerate. May be frozen. Kids will love these.

Variation: Decrease coconut to 1 cup and add to chocolate mixture as directed. Roll balls in crushed peanuts instead of coconut.

COCONUT OATMEAL BAR COOKIES
(Easy and delicious!)

½ c. walnuts
⅔ c. rolled oats
½ c. fine coconut
1⅓ c. flour

1 c. margarine or butter, cut in chunks
⅔ c. brown sugar, packed

Steel Knife: Process nuts until coarsely chopped, about 6 to 8 seconds. Empty into a large mixing bowl. Add rolled oats and coconut.

Process flour, butter and sugar until mixed, about 20 seconds. Add to mixing bowl. Mix to a crumbly mass with your fingertips. Pat onto a greased cookie sheet (15'' x 10'' x 1''). Bake at 300°F for 40 to 45 minutes. Cool and cut into squares with a sharp knife.

Yield: about 5 dozen cookies. Freezes well.

COCONUT CHEESE BALLS

(This recipe was given to me by Sandra Bercovitch, who spent many hours helping me type recipes for my book.)

12 maraschino cherries, drained & dried
½ lb. cream cheese, in chunks
2 tbsp. crushed pineapple, well-drained

1 tbsp. sugar
¼ tsp. vanilla
½ tsp. grated lemon rind
1 c. toasted coconut

Steel Knife: Process cherries with 2 or 3 quick on/off turns. Add remaining ingredients except coconut. Process with 3 or 4 quick on/off turns, just until blended. Place mixture in freezer about 20 minutes for easier handling.

Meanwhile, toast coconut on a tinfoil-lined baking sheet at 250°F for 10 minutes, stirring occasionally. Let cool. Shape cheese mixture into 1'' balls, using a teaspoon. Roll in coconut. Freeze until needed. Thaw 15 minutes before serving.

Yield: 2 dozen.

Note: Smooth type dry cottage cheese (pot cheese) may be substituted for cream cheese.

MELTING MOMENTS

¾ c. butter or margarine, cut in chunks
⅓ c. brown sugar, packed
1 tsp. vanilla

1½ c. flour
1 c. pecans or walnuts
icing sugar

Steel Knife: Process butter and brown sugar with vanilla for 1 minute, or until well creamed. Sprinkle flour and nuts over. Process with several on/off turns, just until mixed.

Form into 1'' balls. Place on an ungreased cookie sheet and bake at 350°F for about 20 minutes. When cool, sprinkle heavily with icing sugar. These definitely live up to their name!

Yield: about 3½ dozen. May be frozen.

CINNAMON TWISTS ("S" COOKIES) ✓

(A variation of the recipe in "Second Helpings Please" — a favorite of kids from 1 to 100 years old! My grandmother always made these for me.)

½ c. sugar
1 tbsp. cinnamon
3 eggs (extra-large)

1 c. brown sugar, lightly packed
¾ c. oil
2 tsp. baking powder
3 c. flour

Steel Knife: Place ½ cup sugar and the cinnamon in processor bowl. Process with several quick on/off turns to start, and then let machine run until well mixed. Empty mixture onto a flat plate.

Place eggs, brown sugar and oil in processor. Process on **Steel Knife** until blended, about 4 or 5 seconds. Add baking powder and flour. Process with several on/off turns, **just** until flour disappears. Do not overprocess.

Using about 1 tbsp. dough for each cookie, roll between your palms to form a pencil-shaped roll. Shape into twists, crescents, rings, the letter "S", or any initial you wish. (Kids love to make all sorts of designs!) Roll in cinnamon-sugar mixture.

Place on greased cookie sheets and bake at 375°F for 12 to 15 minutes, or until nicely browned. (Baking time will depend on the size of the cookies, especially if the children are "assisting" you.)

Yield: about 5 dozen. Freezes well, if you can put them away quickly enough!)

MERINGUE HORNS

Dough:

2 tsp. sugar
¼ c. warm water (105° - 115°F)
1 pkg. yeast
1 c. butter or margarine, cut in chunks
2 c. flour
2 egg yolks

Filling:

2 squares semi-sweet chocolate
2 egg whites
½ c. sugar
¾ - 1 c. coconut or sesame seeds
icing sugar to garnish

Dough: Dissolve sugar in warm water. Sprinkle yeast over and let stand 8 to 10 minutes. Stir to dissolve.

Steel Knife: Process butter with flour until crumbly, about 10 seconds. Add egg yolks and yeast mixture. Process until a soft dough is formed, about 15 seconds. Wrap dough in plastic wrap and refrigerate overnight.

Filling: Insert **Grater** in processor. Grate chocolate, using firm pressure.

Using electric mixer, beat egg whites at high speed until soft peaks form. Gradually add sugar and beat until stiff.

Divide dough into 6 balls. Roll each ball of dough on a floured board or pastry cloth into a circle about ⅛'' thick. Cut into 8 wedges. Spread with meringue and sprinkle with grated chocolate. Beginning at outer edge, roll up. Roll in coconut or sesame seeds. Place on a greased cookie sheet, point-side down.

Bake at 350°F for 18 to 20 minutes. Cool. Sprinkle with icing sugar.

Yield: 4 dozen. May be frozen.

OH HENRY'S
(Really quick to make and quick to disappear!)

1 c. salted peanuts, walnuts or Brazil nuts	6 oz. pkg. butterscotch chips
6 oz. pkg. chocolate chips	3 oz. can chow mein noodles

Steel Knife: Chop walnuts or Brazil nuts with several quick on/off turns, until coarsely chopped. Peanuts do not need chopping.

Melt chocolate and butterscotch chips in large saucepan over very low heat or in the top of a double boiler. Stir in noodles and nuts. Drop from a teaspoon onto a lightly greased baking sheet. Refrigerate or freeze.

Yield: about 3½ dozen. My kids eat these right from the freezer!

ORANGE NUT COOKIES

¾ c. walnuts	1 egg
rind of an orange	⅓ c. orange juice
1 c. sugar	1½ tsp. baking powder
½ c. butter or margarine, cut in chunks	¼ tsp. salt
	3 c. flour

Steel Knife: Process nuts with 6 quick on/off turns, until coarsely chopped. Empty bowl.

Using a potato peeler, remove the orange rind (zest), making sure not to include any of the bitter white pith. Place in processor along with the sugar. Use 4 or 5 on/off turns to start; then let machine run until finely minced, about 30 seconds. Add butter and egg. Process until creamed, about 1 minute. Add juice and process for 5 seconds.

Add dry ingredients. Process with several on/off turns, **just** until blended. Nuts should be added for the last few on/off turns in order not to overprocess. Roll dough into 1'' balls. Place on a lightly greased cookie sheet and flatten with a fork which has been dipped into flour. Bake at 375°F for 12 to 15 minutes, until golden brown.

Yield: about 6 to 7 dozen. May be frozen.

Variation: Roll balls of dough in a mixture of cinnamon and sugar before flattening them with a fork. Delicious!

OLD FASHIONED PEANUT BUTTER COOKIES ✓
(Brings back memories of childhood years)

½ c. soft butter or margarine	1¼ c. flour
½ c. peanut butter	½ tsp. baking powder
½ c. sugar	½ tsp. baking soda
½ c. brown sugar, packed	½ c. chocolate chips, if desired
1 egg	

Steel Knife: process butter, peanut butter, sugars and egg until well-creamed, about 1 minute. Add flour, baking powder and soda and process with on/off turns, just until blended. Roll into 1'' balls and place about 3'' apart on an ungreased foil-lined cookie sheet. Flatten in a criss-cross fashion with a fork which has been dipped in flour. If desired, press 3 or 4 chocolate chips into each cookie.

Bake at 375°F for 10 to 12 minutes, until golden. Cool slightly before removing from pan.

Yield: about 3½ dozen cookies. Freezes well.

Note: These cookies will spread during baking.

PEANUT BUTTER KRISPIES

(No-Bake)

2 c. peanuts	1 c. icing sugar
1 c. peanut butter	2 tbsp. milk (approximately)
(home-made or commercial)	3 c. Rice Krispies cereal
2 tbsp. soft butter or	
margarine	

Steel Knife: Process 1 cup of peanuts at a time. Chop with 6 or 8 quick on/off turns, until coarsely chopped. Empty bowl and repeat with remaining nuts. Set aside.

Steel Knife: Process peanut butter, butter, icing sugar and milk together until smooth and blended, stopping machine once or twice to scrape down sides of bowl.

Place cereal in a large mixing bowl. Stir in peanut butter mixture. Shape into 1'' balls and roll in chopped peanuts. Store in refrigerator.

Yield: about 3 dozen. May be frozen.

CINNAMON NUT ROGELACH
(Crunchy Crescents)

Cream Cheese Pastry (p. 303)	$\frac{1}{3}$ c. sugar
or Flaky Ginger Ale Pastry (p. 305)	1 tsp. cinnamon
$\frac{2}{3}$ c. walnuts	1 egg white, lightly beaten

Prepare dough as directed. Divide into 2 balls. (Ginger Ale Pastry should be chilled first.) Flour dough lightly. Roll out one portion of dough on a pastry cloth or floured board into a circle about $\frac{1}{16}$'' thick.

Steel Knife: Process walnuts, sugar and cinnamon until nuts are fairly fine, about 12 to 15 seconds.

Sprinkle dough with about ¼ c. of cinnamon/nut mixture. Cut with a sharp knife into 12 triangles. Roll up from the outside edge towards the center. Repeat with remaining dough and filling.

Dip first in egg white, then in cinnamon/nut mixture. Place on a greased, foil-lined cookie sheet. Bake at 375°F for 18 to 20 minutes, until lightly browned.

Yield: 2 dozen. Freezes well. Scrumptious!

Note: Ingredients for filling may be doubled successfully in one batch. Extra filling may be stored in a plastic bag in the freezer.

POPPY SEED BUTTER BALLS

1 c. butter or margarine, cut in	¼ c. orange or apple juice
chunks	2¼ c. flour
1 c. icing sugar	$\frac{1}{3}$ c. poppy seeds
½ tsp. vanilla	

Steel Knife: Process butter, sugar and vanilla for 2 minutes, scraping down sides of bowl as necessary. Add remaining ingredients and process just until dough forms a ball, about 10 to 15 seconds. Shape into 1'' balls and arrange on ungreased cookie sheets. Bake at 350°F about 18 to 20 minutes, until bottoms are brown. Cool and sprinkle with icing sugar.

Yield: about 5 dozen. Freezes well.

CHOCOLATE CHIP ROGELACH
(Chocolate chip and nut-filled crescents.
Quick to make and sure to please!)

Cream Cheese Pastry (p. 303)
  or Flaky Ginger Ale Pastry (p. 305)
½ c. brown sugar, lightly
  packed

¼ c. walnuts
1 tsp. cinnamon
2 tbsp. cocoa
4 tbsp. chocolate chips

Prepare dough as directed. Divide into 2 balls. (Ginger Ale Pastry should be chilled first.) Flour dough lightly. Roll out one portion of dough on a pastry cloth or floured board into a circle about ⅟₁₆" thick.

Steel Knife: Process brown sugar, nuts, cinnamon and cocoa until nuts are finely chopped, about 12 to 15 seconds.

Sprinkle dough with ¼ c. the chocolate/nut mixture. Cut with a sharp knife into 12 triangles. Sprinkle about 2 tbsp. chocolate chips around the outer edge of the triangles, making sure that there are 3 or 4 chips on each triangle. Roll up carefully from the outside edge towards the centre. Place on an ungreased foil-lined cookie sheet. Repeat with remaining dough and filling. Bake at 375°F for 18 to 20 minutes, until lightly browned. May be sprinkled with icing sugar when cool, if desired.

Yield: 2 dozen. Freezes well.

Note: Ingredients for filling may be doubled successfully in one batch. Extra filling may be stored in a plastic bag in the freezer.

CHOCOLATE ROGELACH
(Ground chocolate and nut-filled crescents.)

Cream Cheese Pastry (p. 303)
  or Flaky Ginger Ale Pastry (p. 305)
¼ c. sugar (white or brown)

½ tsp. cinnamon
⅓ c. chocolate chips
⅓ c. walnuts or almonds

Prepare dough as directed. Divide into 2 balls. (Ginger Ale Pastry should be chilled first.) Flour dough lightly. Roll out one portion of dough on a pastry cloth or floured board into a circle about ⅟₁₆" thick.

Steel Knife: Process sugar, cinnamon, chocolate chips and nuts until finely chopped, about 25 to 30 seconds.

Sprinkle dough with ¼ c. of chocolate/nut mixture. Cut with a sharp knife into 12 triangles. Roll up from the outside edge towards the center. Place on an ungreased foil-lined cookie sheet. Repeat with remaining dough and filling. Bake at 375°F for 18 to 20 minutes, until lightly browned. May be sprinkled with icing sugar when cool, if desired.

Yield: 2 dozen. Freezes well.

Note: Ingredients for filling may be doubled successfully in one batch. Extra filling may be stored in a plastic bag in the freezer.

MARSHMALLOW RUM BALLS

¾ pkg. chocolate wafers (8 oz. size)

2 c. whipping cream (or 2 envelopes dessert topping mix plus 1 c. milk)

2 tsp. rum extract or 2 tbsp. rum

1 package marshmallows (about 40)

Steel Knife: Break cookies into pieces. Process until fine crumbs are formed, about 20 to 30 seconds. Transfer to another bowl and reserve.

To whip cream or dessert topping, you may use an electric mixer, or the **Steel Knife** of the processor. Place a heavy book under the back part of the base of the processor so that the machine is tipped forward. Do not insert pusher in feed tube for maximum volume. Whip cream until stiff, about 45 seconds. If desired, add about 3 tbsp. sugar during the last few seconds of processing. (Dessert topping will take about 2 minutes of processing time.) Add rum and blend a few seconds longer. Transfer to a large mixing bowl. Add marshmallows and mix well. Refrigerate overnight. Marshmallows will soften and absorb whipped cream.

Roll each marshmallow in chocolate wafer crumbs. Place in cupcake papers and freeze until needed. Remove from freezer about 5 or 10 minutes before serving.

Yield: about 40. Freezes well. So easy, and yet so good!

YUMMY RUM BALLS

(No-Bake)

1 c. pecans or walnuts

½ c. Sultana raisins

¼ c. rum

8 oz. pkg. vanilla wafers

2 tbsp. cocoa

½ c. corn syrup

½ c. butter or margarine

½ c. chocolate chips

chocolate trimettes, coconut and / or chopped nuts

Steel Knife: Chop nuts with 6 or 8 quick on/off turns. Set aside. Process raisins until ground, about 8 to 10 seconds. Combine in a small bowl with rum and let soak half an hour.

Break cookies in chunks. Drop through feed tube while machine is running and process to make fine crumbs. Add cocoa, corn syrup, nuts and raisins. Process with on/off turns to blend thoroughly. Wet your hands and roll crumb mixture into 1'' balls. Place on a foil-lined cookie sheet and refrigerate for 20 minutes, or until firm.

Melt butter with chocolate chips on low heat. Dip balls in cooled chocolate mixture, then in trimettes, coconut, and/or chopped nuts. Refrigerate or freeze. Let stand about 5 minutes (if you can wait that long!) before serving. Serve in tiny petit four papers.

Yield: 3½ to 4 dozen balls.

SESAME NOTHINGS
(These expand from almost nothing into large crunchy puffs.)

This recipe is ideal for the processor. It used to take my mother 20 minutes of mixing on the electric mixer, and I remember watching the batter climb up the beaters. The processor mixes up the batter in about 2 minutes. Although the instructions are long, these are really easy to make and are sure to become a family favorite. Buy sesame seeds at the bakery or health food store in bulk for maximum economy.

3 eggs
2 tbsp. sugar (or artificial
  sweetener to equal 2 tbsp.
  sugar)
dash salt

½ c. oil
1 c. flour
¾ c. sesame seeds
2 additional tbsp. sugar

Preheat oven to 500°F.

Steel Knife: Process eggs with sugar and salt for about 30 seconds, or until light. Pour oil through the feed tube in a steady stream while the machine is running. Process 1 minute longer. Add flour by heaping spoonfuls through the feed tube while the machine is running. Process 30 to 40 seconds longer. (The Cuisinart will automatically shut off after about 40 seconds because the batter is very sticky. If you have an inexpensive processor, take care not to let the machine shut itself off or you may require a service call.)

Combine sesame seeds with remaining sugar on a flat plate. Take a scant teaspoon of dough and use another spoon to push it off into the sesame seeds. Coat dough with sesame seeds. Stretch dough about 3 inches long and twist to make an elongated twisted finger. Roll again in sesame seeds. Place cookies on 2 greased foil-lined cookie sheets, making sure to leave room between each cookie.

Reduce heat to 400°F and place cookies on middle rack of oven. Bake for 7 to 8 minutes. Reduce heat to 300°F and bake 10 to 12 minutes longer. Shut off oven and let cookies remain in oven for 10 minutes longer to dry.

Yield: about 36 to 40 cookies. They puff up and are light, crunchy and fantastic. May be frozen.

Variation: Roll in poppy seeds and sugar instead of sesame seeds and sugar.

EYER KICHEL
(Crisp egg cookies which are as light as a feather. Low in calories.)

Prepare batter for Sesame Nothings as directed above. Instead of shaping into elongated twisted fingers, drop batter from a teaspoon onto a greased cookie sheet, leaving about 3'' between cookies. If desired, sprinkle with a little sugar. Bake as directed above. Excellent for the diabetic as these can be made sugar-free.

Yield: 40 cookies containing about 40 calories each if made with artificial sweetener, 43 calories if made with sugar.

SESAME CRESCENTS

½ c. butter or margarine, cut in
chunks
½ c. brown sugar, packed
1 egg plus 1 egg yolk
1 tsp. vanilla

1½ c. flour
¼ tsp. soda
½ c. sesame seeds (about)
3 tbsp. sugar

Steel Knife: Process butter, brown sugar, egg, egg yolk and vanilla for 2 minutes. Add flour and soda and process **just** until dough is mixed and begins to gather in a ball around the blades.

Using about 1 teaspoon of dough for each cookie, shape into crescents. Roll in a mixture of sesame seeds and sugar. Place on a greased cookie sheet and bake at 375°F for about 10 minutes, until golden.

Yield: about 3 ½ dozen cookies. Freezes well.

GRANOLA CRESCENTS

Follow directions for Sesame Crescents (above), but omit sesame seeds and 3 tbsp. sugar. Process ½ to ¾ c. Harvest Crunch or granola on **Steel Knife** until fine. Shape cookies into crescents and roll in granola. Bake as directed.

Yield: about 3 ½ dozen cookies. Freezes well.

NUTTY CRESCENTS

Follow directions for Sesame Crescents (above), but substitute ½ to ¾ cup nuts for the sesame seeds. Process on **Steel Knife** with the 3 tbsp. sugar until finely chopped, about 15 seconds. Shape cookies into crescents and roll in nut/sugar mixture. Dip in unbeaten egg white. Bake as directed.

Yield: about 3½ dozen. Freezes well.

SPRITZ COOKIES

(Make in a cookie press, or roll out and cut into fancy shapes.)

2¼ c. flour
¾ c. sugar
½ tsp. salt
¼ tsp. baking powder
1 c. margarine or shortening,
cut in chunks

1 egg plus cold water to
equal ¼ cup
1 tsp. vanilla

Steel Knife: Place dry ingredients and margarine in processor bowl. Process about 10 seconds, until crumbly. Add remaining ingredients and process until a soft dough is formed. This will take about 1 minute. Dough will be very crumbly when you first add the egg and vanilla. Stop machine several times to cut through dough with a rubber spatula.

Force dough through a cookie press into various shapes onto an ungreased cookie sheet. (Dough may also be rolled out and cut into various shapes with cookie cutters, or shaped into walnut-sized balls and flattened with the bottom of a glass which has been dipped into flour to prevent sticking.) Garnish with candy sprinkles, if desired.

Bake at 400°F about 10 minutes, until edges are delicately browned.

Yield: about 6 dozen. Freezes well.

SHORTBREAD COOKIES

1 c. butter (2 sticks), cut in chunks
½ c. icing sugar

½ c. cornstarch or potato starch
1½ c. flour
½ tsp. vanilla

Steel Knife: Process butter with icing sugar until well creamed, about 1 minute. Add cornstarch, flour and vanilla. Process with several on/off turns, just until dough is well mixed and begins to gather together in a ball around the blades.

Shape rounded teaspoonfuls of dough into small balls. Place on an ungreased cookie sheet and flatten in a criss-cross pattern with the floured tines of a fork. Bake at 350°F for about 12 to 15 minutes, or until edges are slightly browned.

Yield: about 4 dozen. These melt in your mouth!

Variation: Chop 1 cup walnuts, pecans or almonds on the **Steel Knife,** using on/off turns. Empty bowl. Make cookie dough as directed above. Add chopped nuts once the flour has been blended into the dough. Process with 2 or 3 on/off turns to mix.

SUGAR COOKIES

2 eggs
¾ c. sugar
½ c. oil

¼ c. orange juice or water
2 tsp. baking powder
3 c. flour

Steel Knife: Process eggs with sugar, oil and juice until blended, about 5 or 6 seconds. Add baking powder and flour. Process just until mixed, using on/off turns.

Divide dough into 4 pieces Roll each piece on a floured board or pastry cloth into a rectangle. Dough should be about ⅛" thick. Using assorted cookie cutters, cut in different shapes. Dip each cookie lightly in granulated sugar. Place sugar-side up on a greased cookie sheet. Bake at 375°F for 8 to 10 minutes, until golden brown.

Yield: about 5 dozen. May be frozen.

POPPY SEED COOKIES (MOON COOKIES)

Follow directions for Sugar Cookies as directed (above), but add ¼ cup poppy seeds with the dry ingredients. Cut and bake as directed.

Yield: about 5 dozen. May be frozen.

TOM THUMB COOKIES

¾ c. almonds or walnuts
1½ c. flour
½ c. butter or margarine, cut in chunks
½ c. icing sugar

½ tsp. almond extract
1 egg
your favorite jam (about ½ c. strawberry, raspberry, peach etc.)

Steel Knife: Process nuts with ¼ c. flour until very finely chopped. Empty bowl. Process remaining flour with butter and icing sugar about 10 seconds, until crumbly. Add nut/flour mixture, flavoring and egg. Process until blended, about 15 seconds.

Shape dough into 1" balls. Place on a lightly greased cookie sheet and press your thumb into the centre of each cookie to make an indentation. Fill with a bit of jam. Bake at 350°F for 15 to 18 minutes, until golden.

Yield: about 4 dozen. Freezes well.

WALNUT BRANDY COOKIES

1 c. walnuts
1 c. soft butter (do not use
   margarine)
1 c. icing sugar
1 tsp. vanilla

4 tbsp. brandy (or milk or
   juice)
2 c. flour
¼ tsp. salt

Steel Knife: Process nuts until chopped, about 6 to 8 seconds. Empty bowl. Process butter, icing sugar and vanilla about 2 minutes. Add brandy and process 3 seconds. Add flour, salt and nuts. Process **just** until mixture gathers in a ball around the blades. Chill dough in freezer for 20 minutes for easier handling. Form into 1'' balls and place 2'' apart on an ungreased cookie sheet. Bake at 325°F for 20 minutes, or until golden.

Yield: 5 dozen. Freezes well.

BASIC OIL DOUGH

1 medium seedless orange
2 eggs
¾ c. sugar

½ c. oil
2 tsp. baking powder
2¾ c. flour

Steel Knife: Quarter orange, but do not peel. Process until fine, about 25 seconds. Add eggs, sugar and oil. Process for 10 seconds. Add baking powder and flour. Process with several on/off turns, **just** until flour is blended into dough. Do not overprocess. Dough will be fairly sticky. Remove from bowl with a rubber spatula onto a lightly floured board. Use as directed in any of your favorite recipes. This dough is excellent for Hamentaschen (p. 287), Mandel Bread (below) and Roly Poly (p. 288).
Best frozen after baking.

MANDEL BREAD
(Almond cookies first baked in a long roll, then sliced and toasted.)

1 c. almonds   Basic Oil Dough (above)

Steel Knife: Chop almonds coarsely, about 12 to 15 seconds. Empty bowl. Prepare dough as directed, adding nuts to the dough along with the flour and baking powder. Shape into 3 rolls, flouring your hands for easier handling. Place on a greased cookie sheet. Bake at 350°F for 25 minutes. Dough will be cake-like, and not quite baked. Slice into ½'' slices with a sharp knife. Place cut-side down on the cookie sheet and return Mandel Bread to oven at 250°F for 1 hour, or until dry and crisp. (The low temperature prevents over-browning.) Keeps very well in a tightly closed cookie tin.

Yield: about 4 to 5 dozen. May be frozen.

Variation: After slicing rolls, dip each slice into a mixture of cinnamon and sugar. Then dry in oven as directed.

HAMENTASCHEN
(A filled triangular-shaped cookie. You'll love them!)

Cream Cheese Pastry,
double recipe (p. 303)
or Basic Oil Dough (p. 286)

Prune Filling, Apricot Raisin
Filling or Date Filling (below)

Prepare desired dough as directed. If using Cream Cheese Pastry, prepare in two batches. Prepare desired filling. Divide dough into 4 pieces. Flour each piece of dough lightly. Roll out on a floured board or pastry cloth to ¼'' thickness. Cut in 3'' circles. Place a spoonful of filling on each circle. Bring sides upwards to meet. Pinch to form a triangle. Place on a greased cookie sheet. If desired, brush with 1 egg yolk which has been blended with 1 tsp. water.

Bake Cream Cheese Pastry Hamentaschen at 400°F for about 15 minutes, and Oil Dough Hamentaschen at 350°F for 25 to 30 minutes. Freezes well.

Yield: about 4 dozen.

PRUNE FILLING

1 **medium seedless orange**	1½ **c. raisins**
12 **oz. pkg. pitted prunes**	2 **tbsp. sugar, if desired**

Steel Knife: Cut orange in quarters, but do not peel. Process half the orange until fine, about 20 seconds. Add **half** the remaining ingredients. Process until fine, about 15 to 20 seconds. Empty processor bowl. Repeat with remaining ingredients.

Yield: about 2½ cups filling. May be prepared in advance and refrigerated or frozen.

Note: It is a good idea to feel the prunes with your fingertips to make sure that no pits have been overlooked before packaging. Otherwise, you could damage the Steel Knife.

If you wish to add nuts, process about ¼ cup walnuts for 4 to 5 seconds. Empty bowl and process remaining ingredients. Add nuts and process a few seconds longer.

APRICOT RAISIN FILLING

1 **medium seedless orange**	1½ **c. sultana raisins**
8 **oz. pkg. dried apricots**	3 **to 4 tbsp. sugar**

Steel Knife: Cut orange in quarters, but do not peel. Process **half** the orange until fine, about 20 seconds. Add **half** the remaining ingredients. Process until fine, about 15 seconds. Empty processor bowl. Repeat with remaining ingredients.

Yield: about 2 cups filling. May be prepared in advance and refrigerated or frozen.

DATE FILLING

¼ **c. walnuts**	1 **tsp. grated lemon rind, if**
2 **c. pitted dates**	**desired**
½ **c. sultana raisins**	½ **tsp. cinnamon**

Steel Knife: Chop walnuts coarsely, about 4 or 5 seconds. Empty bowl. Process dates with raisins, rind and cinnamon until minced, about 15 to 20 seconds. Add nuts with 1 or 2 quick on/off turns.

Yield: about 2 cups filling. May be prepared in advance and refrigerated or frozen.

ROLY POLY

Prepare Basic Oil Dough (p. 286) as directed. Divide into 3 balls. (If desired, you may use Cream Cheese Pastry (p. 303) or Flaky Ginger Ale Pastry (p. 305), but divide dough into 2 balls.) Flour each ball lightly. Roll out into a rectangle.

Spread about 3 to 4 tbsp. jam to within 1'' of edges of rectangle. Sprinkle with about 3 tbsp. each of chopped nuts, raisins, coconut and grated chocolate. Arrange strips of Turkish Delight or maraschino cherries along one edge. Roll up like a jelly roll, turning in ends. Place on greased, foil-lined cookie sheet. Brush with a little beaten egg yolk which has been blended with 2 tsp. water.

Bake at 350°F for 35 to 45 minutes. Slice with a sharp knife. Keeps well. May be frozen.

Note: If desired, eliminate jam and sprinkle each piece of dough with 2 tbsp. each Graham wafer crumbs and brown sugar. Also delicious with candied mixed fruit.

ALMOND CRISP BARS

(Warning — These may become habit-forming!)

½ c. butter or margarine, cut in chunks	1 egg yolk
¼ c. granulated sugar	½ c. flour
¼ c. brown sugar, lightly packed	½ c. rolled oats or granola
½ tsp. vanilla or almond extract	¾ c. chocolate chips
	1 tbsp. butter
	¼ c. almonds

Steel Knife: Process ½ cup butter with sugars, flavoring and egg yolk for 45 seconds. Add flour and process for 4 or 5 seconds to mix. Add oats or granola and process with several quick on/off turns to mix.

Spread mixture with a rubber spatula in a greased 8'' square baking pan. Bake at 350°F for 25 minutes, until golden. Meanwhile, melt chocolate chips with 1 tbsp. butter, mixing to blend well. Spread over base.

Steel Knife: Process almonds until fine, about 15 or 20 seconds. Sprinkle over chocolate. Cut into squares while still warm.

Yield: about 25 squares. Freezes well.

Note: Recipe may be doubled and baked in a greased 10'' x 15'' jelly roll pan, increasing baking time slightly. Sprinkle half the squares with chopped nuts and half the squares with ½ c. shredded coconut.

YUMMY PEANUT BUTTER SQUARES

1 c. butter or margarine (2 sticks), cut in chunks	¼ c. brown sugar
2 c. flour	¾ c. peanut butter
	6 oz. pkg. chocolate chips

Steel Knife: Process butter with flour and brown sugar until well blended, about 15 to 20 seconds. Press evenly into a lightly greased 9'' x 13'' baking pan. Bake at 375°F for about 15 to 20 minutes, until browned. Cool.

Melt peanut butter with chocolate chips, stirring to blend. Spread over cooled base. Cover and refrigerate. Cut into squares.

Yield: about 45 squares. Can be frozen.

BASIC BROWNIES

(Moist and Fudgy)

⅓ c. butter or margarine
⅔ c. sugar
2 tbsp. water
6 oz. pkg. chocolate chips
2 eggs

¾ c. flour
½ tsp. baking powder
1 tsp. vanilla or peppermint
  extract
¾ c. walnut pieces

Combine butter, sugar and water in a saucepan and bring to a boil, stirring constantly.

Steel Knife: Process hot butter mixture with chocolate chips until smooth and blended and chocolate pieces have melted, about 15 to 20 seconds. Add eggs through feed tube while machine is running, and process a few seconds longer. Add remaining ingredients and process with 3 or 4 quick on/off turns, just until nuts are chopped. Scrape down sides of bowl as necessary.

Spread batter evenly in a greased 8" square baking pan. Bake at 350°F for about 30 minutes.

Yield: 25 brownies. Freezes well. If desired, ice with your favorite chocolate frosting, and sprinkle with additional chopped nuts.

PEPPERMINT PATTY BROWNIES

Prepare Basic Brownies (above) as directed. As soon as you remove Brownies from oven place chocolate mint patties directly on top. The heat of the Brownies will cause the patties to melt. Spread them evenly with a knife or a spatula. The white cream filling will blend in with the chocolate. Cool slightly before cutting into squares.

Yield: 25 brownies. Freezes well.

TWO-TONE MINT BROWNIES

Prepare Basic Brownies (above) as directed. Cool completely. Prepare the following topping:-

2 c. icing sugar
¼ c. butter or margarine,
  cut in chunks

few drops green food coloring, if
  desired
1 - 2 tbsp. milk
1 tsp. peppermint extract

Steel Knife: Process all ingredients until smooth, about 10 to 15 seconds, scraping down sides of bowl as necessary. Icing should be very thick. Spread over cooled Brownies. Let stand for 10 minutes.

Chocolate Glaze:

½ c. chocolate chips

1 tbsp. butter

Melt chocolate chips with butter, stirring to blend well. Spread over mint topping. When firm, cut into squares.

Yield: 25 brownies. Freezes well, if you can hide them fast enough!

CHOCOLATE MARSHMALLOW BROWNIES

Prepare Basic Brownies (p. 289) as directed. As soon as Brownies are baked, top with a single layer of miniature marshmallows (white or colored), or regular-sized marshmallows which you have cut in half. Return pan to oven for 5 minutes, until marshmallows are melted and puffy. Cool completely. Frost with the following icing:-

1½ c. icing sugar	3 tbsp. cocoa
3 tbsp. soft butter or	3 tbsp. milk
margarine	½ tsp. vanilla

Steel Knife: Process all ingredients until smooth and blended, about 10 to 15 seconds.

BUTTERSCOTCH BROWNIES

½ c. walnuts	¼ c. melted butter or
1 c. brown sugar, packed	margarine
1 egg	¾ c. flour
1 tsp. vanilla or butterscotch	1 tsp. baking powder
extract	dash salt

Steel Knife: Process nuts until coarsely chopped, about 5 to 6 seconds. Empty bowl. Process brown sugar with egg, flavoring and butter for 30 seconds, or until blended. Add dry ingredients and process a few seconds to blend. Sprinkle nuts over and mix in with 2 or 3 quick on/off turns.

Spread mixture evenly in a well-greased 8'' square baking pan. Bake at 350°F for 25 minutes. Edges will pull away from sides of pan. Do not overbake. Cut in squares while warm.

Yield: 25 squares. Freezes well.

BUTTER TART SLICE

Base:

Base:	Topping:
½ c. butter or margarine, cut in chunks	1½ c. brown sugar, lightly packed
1½ c. flour	¼ c. melted butter
2 tbsp. icing sugar or brown sugar	2 eggs
	1 tbsp. vinegar
	1 tsp. vanilla
	1 c. raisins

Steel Knife: Combine butter, flour and icing sugar. Process until well blended, about 20 seconds. Press into the bottom of a lightly greased 9'' square baking pan. Bake at 350°F for 10 minutes.

Steel Knife: Process all ingredients for topping except raisins until well mixed. Add raisins and blend in with 1 or 2 quick on/off turns. Pour over base. Bake about 30 to 35 minutes longer, until nicely browned. Cool and cut into squares.

Yield: 25 squares. May be frozen.

Variation: Omit raisins. Sprinkle ¾ cup pecan halves or pieces over baked base before adding topping. Bake as directed.

BY CRACKY BARS

½ c. walnuts
1 c. sugar
¾ c. butter or margarine, cut in chunks
2 eggs
1 tsp. vanilla
⅓ c. milk

1½ c. flour
¼ tsp. baking soda
1 square unsweetened chocolate, melted
15 single graham wafers (approximately)
1 c. chocolate chips

Steel Knife: Process nuts until chopped, about 6 to 8 seconds. Empty bowl. Process sugar, butter, eggs and vanilla one minute. Add milk through feed tube while machine is running. Process 3 seconds. Add flour and baking soda. Process just until blended with 3 or 4 quick on/off turns. Remove half of batter, and set aside. Add melted chocolate and nuts to batter in processor, and process with quick on/off turns just until blended, stopping machine to scrape down once or twice.

Spread chocolate batter evenly in a greased 9" x 13" baking pan. Arrange wafers over batter to cover. Mix chocolate chips into remaining batter and spread over wafers. Bake at 350°F about 35 minutes, until cake tester comes out dry. Cut into squares.

Yield: about 3 dozen. Freezes well.

EASY CHEESE DREAMS

Base:

½ c. walnuts
¼ c. brown sugar, lightly packed
¾ c. flour
6 tbsp. butter or margarine, cut in chunks

Topping:

½ lb. cream cheese, cut in chunks
1 egg
¼ c. sugar
1 tsp. almond extract
1 tbsp. lemon juice
2 tbsp. milk

Steel Knife: Combine all ingredients for base in processor bowl. Process with several on/off turns, until crumbly. Pat mixture into a lightly greased 8" square baking pan. Bake at 350°F for 15 minutes. Remove from oven.

Steel Knife: Process all ingredients for topping until well blended, about 30 seconds. Scrape down sides of bowl as necessary. Spread over base. Return to oven and bake 25 minutes longer. When cool, cut in squares. Refrigerate.

Yield: about 2 dozen. May be frozen.

Variation: Reserve about ½ cup crumbly mixture from base. Sprinkle over cheese topping and bake as directed.

CHOCOLATE CHIP NUT CHEWS

Base:	Topping:
½ c. butter or margarine, cut in chunks	1 c. walnuts or peanuts
½ c. sugar	1 c. brown sugar, packed
1 c. flour	2 eggs
6 oz. pkg. chocolate chips	½ tsp. vanilla
	2 tbsp. flour
	½ tsp. baking powder
	½ c. coconut

Steel Knife: Process butter, sugar and flour about 20 seconds, until blended. Press into a lightly greased 8'' square pan. Bake at 350°F about 15 minutes. Remove from oven and top with chocolate chips.

Steel Knife: Process nuts until coarsely chopped, about 6 to 8 seconds. Empty bowl. Process brown sugar, eggs and vanilla for 30 seconds. Add remaining ingredients and mix in with 2 or 3 quick on/off turns. Spread over chocolate chips. Bake about 25 minutes longer. Cool and cut in squares.

Yield: 25 squares. Freezes well.

CHOCOLATE CHIP COCONUT CHEWS

Follow recipe for Chocolate Chip Nut Chews (above), but increase coconut to 1½ cups and reduce nuts to ½ cup.

Yield: 25 squares. Freezes well.

DREAM SQUARES

Follow recipe for Chocolate Chip Nut Chews (above), but increase coconut to 1 cup, and omit chocolate chips. When completely cooled, frost with the following icing:-

1 c. icing sugar	½ tsp. vanilla or almond extract
2 tbsp. soft butter or margarine	1 - 2 tbsp. milk

Steel Knife: Process all ingredients until smooth and blended, about 10 to 15 seconds, scraping down bowl as necessary. Frost squares. Cut with a sharp knife.

Yield: 25 squares. May be frozen.

CRUMBLY JAM SQUARES

¼ lb. Cheddar cheese (1 c. grated)	3 tbsp. sugar
½ c. butter or margarine, cut in chunks	1 tsp. baking powder
1½ c. flour	1 c. apricot jam, orange marmelade or apple jelly

Steel Knife: Cut cheese into 1'' chunks. Process until finely chopped, about 15 seconds. Add butter and process 30 seconds longer, scraping down bowl once or twice. Add flour, baking powder and sugar. Process 10 to 15 seconds longer, until crumbly.

Press half the mixture into an ungreased 8'' square pan. Spread with jam. Sprinkle remaining crumbs over top. Bake at 350°F about 30 minutes. Cool. Cut into squares. Freezes well.

Yield: 25 squares.

FRENCH UNBAKED CAKE

½ c. walnuts	2 tbsp. cocoa
¼ c. butter or margarine	½ tsp. vanilla
1 egg	16 double graham wafers
¼ c. lightly packed brown sugar	Frosting (see below)

Steel Knife: Chop nuts with several quick on/off turns. Empty bowl. Melt butter in a saucepan or the top of a double boiler. Still using the **Steel Knife,** process egg, brown sugar and cocoa for a few seconds, until mixed. Add to saucepan and cook just until thickened, like custard. Do not boil or mixture will curdle. Add vanilla.

Break up wafers into chunks about the size of cornflakes. Place in a large mixing bowl along with **half** the nuts. Pour chocolate mixture over wafers and mix with a wooder spoon until wafers are quite well coated with chocolate. Spread evenly in a greased 8'' square baking pan. Prepare frosting.

2 c. icing sugar	3 to 4 tbsp. milk
¼ c. soft butter or margarine	1 tsp. vanilla
2 tbsp. cocoa	pinch of salt

Steel Knife: Process all ingredients for frosting until smooth and blended, about 10 to 15 seconds. Scrape down sides of bowl as necessary. Spread over squares in a fairly thick layer. Swirl icing with a knife. Sprinkle with reserved nuts. Refrigerate. Cut into squares.

Yield: about 25 squares. May be frozen.

HALFWAY SQUARES

(They're half gone before you look around!)

⅓ c. butter, cut in chunks	½ tsp. vanilla
1 egg, separated	4 tbsp. water
¼ c. granulated sugar	4 squares semi-sweet
¼ c. brown sugar, packed	chocolate
1 c. flour	½ c. brown sugar, packed
¾ tsp. baking powder	

Steel Knife: Process butter with egg yolk, granulated sugar and ¼ cup brown sugar for about 45 seconds, until blended. Add flour, baking powder and vanilla and process with several on/off turns, until mixed. Pat down into the bottom of a greased 8'' square baking pan. Set aside.

Melt water and chocolate together over low heat, stirring. Spread evenly over base.

Using an electric mixer, beat reserved egg white until stiff. Gradually beat in remaining ½ cup brown sugar. Spread carefully over chocolate layer, trying not to marble the egg white mixture with the melted chocolate. Bake at 375°F for about 25 minutes. When cool, cut into squares. Do not freeze.

Yield: 25 squares.

Variation: Substitute ½ cup chocolate chips for the water and semi-sweet chocolate. Sprinkle chocolate chips over base (do not melt). Top with egg white & sugar mixture & bake as directed.

HEAVENLY SQUARES

Base:

½ c. walnuts
¼ c. brown sugar, lightly
   packed
¾ c. flour
6 tbsp. butter or margarine,
   cut in chunks

Topping:

1 c. pitted dates
5 tbsp. flour
¼ c. maraschino cherries,
   well-drained
2 eggs
1 c. brown sugar, lightly
   packed
½ tsp. baking powder
1¼ c. coconut
½ c. chocolate chips

Steel Knife: Combine all ingredients for base in processor bowl. Process with 6 on/off turns, until crumbly. Pat mixture into a lightly greased 8'' square pan. Bake at 350°F for 15 minutes. Remove from oven.

Steel Knife: Process dates with 2 tbsp. flour until coarsely chopped, about 6 to 8 seconds. Empty bowl. Pat cherries dry on paper towelling. Process with 1 tbsp. flour, giving 2 very quick on/off turns. Add to dates. Process eggs, brown sugar, baking powder and remaining 2 tbsp. flour until well blended, about 30 seconds. Add dates, cherries, coconut and chocolate chips. Mix in with several quick on/off turns.

Spread mixture over base. Return to oven and bake 25 to 30 minutes longer, until set and golden brown. Cut in squares while warm.

Yield: about 25 squares. Freezes well.

HELLO DOLLY SQUARES

(My daughter Jodi adores these!)

½ c. walnuts, almonds or
   pecans
1¼ c. graham wafer crumbs (or
   15 single graham wafers)
½ c. butter or margarine

1½ c. chocolate chips
½ c. raisins, if desired
1½ c. coconut
14 oz. can sweetened
   condensed milk

Steel Knife: Process nuts until coarsely chopped, about 6 to 8 seconds. Empty bowl. If using graham wafers, break in chunks. Process to make fine crumbs, about 25 to 35 seconds.

Place margarine in a 9'' x 13'' baking pan and melt in 350°F oven. Mix in crumbs and spread evenly in pan. Sprinkle with chocolate chips, raisins, coconut and nuts. Drizzle condensed milk over evenly. Bake at 350°F for 25 to 30 minutes. Cool and cut into squares.

Yield: about 4 dozen. Freezes well.

Variation: Substitute 1½ cups granola for graham wafer crumbs. Delicious! Any leftover cookies may be made into crumbs and used.

HUNGARIAN PASTRY SQUARES

¾ c. walnuts
½ c. butter, cut in chunks
¼ c. white sugar
¼ c. brown sugar, packed
2 eggs, separated
1 tsp. vanilla
1½ c. flour

½ tsp. baking soda
½ tsp. baking powder
dash salt
⅔ c. strawberry jam (approximately)
2 tbsp. icing sugar

Steel Knife: Process nuts until finely chopped, about 8 to 10 seconds. Empty bowl. Process butter, sugars, egg yolks and vanilla about 30 seconds. Add dry ingredients and process with several on/off turns just until mixed. Place in a greased 8'' square pan and press down firmly. Spread a thin layer of jam over base. Sprinkle with half of nuts.

Beat egg whites on electric mixer at high speed until stiff, adding icing sugar gradually. Spread over jam and nuts. Sprinkle with remaining nuts. Bake at 375°F for approximately 30 minutes, until well browned. Cool. Cut in small squares.

Yield: about 25 squares. Freezes well.

LEMON SLICE

1 c. flour
½ c. butter or margarine, cut into chunks
2 tbsp. icing sugar

1 pkg. lemon pie filling
1 envelope dessert topping
½ c. cold milk
½ tsp. lemon extract or vanilla

Steel Knife: Process flour with butter and icing sugar until blended, about 15 to 20 seconds. Press mixture into an ungreased 8'' square baking pan. Bake at 375°F for 15 minutes. Cool.

Cook lemon pie filling according to package directions, substituting 1 whole egg for the egg yolks called for in the directions. Cool. Spread over crust.

Steel Knife: Combine dessert topping with milk and lemon extract in processor bowl. Tip machine forward by placing a heavy book under the back part of the base. Process dessert topping until stiff, about 2 minutes. Do not insert pusher in feed tube. Spread over lemon pudding. Chill and cut into squares.

Yield: 25 squares. Do not freeze.

LEMON SQUARES

Base:
1 c. butter or margarine, cut in chunks
2 c. flour
½ c. sugar

Topping:
4 eggs
¼ c. lemon juice
2 c. sugar
¼ c. flour
1 tsp. baking powder

Base: Insert **Steel Knife** . Process butter, sugar, and flour until crumbly, about 20 seconds. Press into a lightly greased 9'' x 13'' baking pan. Bake at 350°F for 20 minutes.

Topping: Combine all ingredients and process on **Steel Knife** until blended, about 10 seconds. Pour over base. Bake 25 minutes longer. Cut in small squares when cool. Melts in your mouth!

Yield: about 48 squares. Freezes well.

MARSHMALLOW COCONUT SQUARES

1 c. walnuts or pecans
1½ c. graham wafer crumbs (or
   18 single graham wafers)
½ c. butter or margarine
2 c. coconut
1½ c. miniature marshmallows

14 oz. tin sweetened
   condensed milk
4 squares semi-sweet
   chocolate, melted (or ¾ c.
   chocolate chips, melted)

Steel Knife: Process nuts until coarsely chopped, about 6 to 8 seconds. Empty bowl. If using graham wafers, break in chunks. Process to make fine crumbs, about 25 to 35 seconds.

Melt butter or margarine in a 9'' x 13'' baking pan. Stir in crumbs to make a crust. Sprinkle with coconut, nuts and marshmallows. Drizzle condensed milk (do **not** use evaporated milk) over top. Bake at 350°F for 25 to 30 minutes. Remove from oven and drizzle with melted chocolate. Cool and cut into squares.

Yield: about 4 dozen. Freezes well.

NANAIMO CRUNCH BARS

(Sure to be a favorite in your family!
No baking required for this delicious square.)

Base:
½ c. butter or margarine
¼ c. sugar
⅓ c. cocoa
1 egg
1 tsp. vanilla
½ c. walnuts
1½ c. granola cereal or graham
   wafer crumbs (or any cookie
   crumbs)
1 c. coconut

Filling:
¼ c. soft butter or margarine
2 tbsp. vanilla pudding
   powder or custard powder
3 tbsp. milk
2 c. icing sugar

Glaze:
4 squares semi-
   sweet chocolate
1 tsp. butter or margarine

Base: Combine butter, sugar, cocoa, egg and vanilla in the top of a double boiler. Cook over boiling water, stirring, until smooth and thickened and mixture resembles custard. Chop nuts using **Steel Knife,** using 6 or 8 quick on/off turns. Add with granola or crumbs and coconut to saucepan. Mix well. (If necessary, you can make your own crumbs by processing graham wafers or plain cookies on the **Steel Knife** until fine crumbs are formed.) Press mixture into a buttered 9'' square pan.

Filling: Using **Steel Knife,** process all ingredients for filling until well mixed, about 15 to 20 seconds. Stop machine and scrape down sides of bowl once or twice. Spread over base.

Glaze: Melt chocolate over hot water. Add butter and mix well. Spread over the filling. Refrigerate. Cut in squares.

Yield: about 2 dozen. Freezes well.

PECAN JAM SQUARES
(A Prize-Winner)

Base:

½ c. butter or margarine, cut in chunks
½ c. brown sugar, packed
1 c. flour
½ c. strawberry jam

Topping:

1 c. pecans
2 eggs
1 c. brown sugar, packed
1 tsp. vanilla
1 tbsp. flour
¼ tsp. baking powder
3 tbsp. icing sugar (to garnish)

Steel Knife: Process all ingredients for base except jam about 20 seconds. Press into a lightly greased 8'' square pan. Bake at 350°F for 15 minutes. Spread with jam.

Steel Knife: Chop nuts coarsely, about 8 to 10 seconds. Empty bowl. Process remaining ingredients for topping except icing sugar until mixed, about 10 to 15 seconds. Add pecans and mix in with 2 or 3 quick on/off turns. Spread over base. Bake about 25 minutes longer. Cool completely and sprinkle with icing sugar. Cut into squares.

Yield: about 25 squares. Freezes well.

PINEAPPLE CHEESE CAKE SQUARES

36 single graham wafers (3 c. crushed)
½ c. melted butter or margarine
14 oz. tin crushed pineapple, well-drained
18 maraschino cherries

2 tbsp. flour
1 lb. cream cheese or cottage cheese
½ c. sugar
1 tsp. vanilla
4 eggs

Steel Knife: Break up half the graham wafers and place in processor bowl. Drop remaining wafers through feed tube while machine is running. Process until fine crumbs are formed, about 25 to 30 seconds. Add melted butter and blend about 5 seconds longer, until mixed. Place half the crumbs into a lightly greased 8'' square Pyrex baking dish. Reserve remaining crumb mixture. Wash and dry bowl and blade.

Empty pineapple into a sieve and set aside to drain thoroughly. Press out excess juice with the back of a spoon. (Calorie counters may wish to wash out the syrup under cold running water.)

Steel Knife: Pat cherries dry with a paper towel. Place in processor bowl with flour. Process with 1 or 2 **very quick** on/off turns. Set cherries aside. Wipe out bowl with paper towelling.

Steel Knife: Cut cheese in chunks. Place in processor with sugar, vanilla and **one** egg. Start machine and add remaining eggs one at a time through feed tube. Process until smooth and blended, about 30 seconds. Add cherries and pineapple; mix in with 1 or 2 quick on/off turns. Pour over graham wafer base. Top with reserved crumbs. Bake at 350°F for about 30 minutes. Chill before serving.

Yield: about 25 squares. If frozen, crust may become soggy.

Note: For a lighter texture, separate the eggs. Process the yolks with the cheese mixture as directed. Beat the whites stiff on an electric mixer. Fold into cheese mixture.

Calorie Counter's Version

Omit cherries and flour. Use cottage cheese instead of cream cheese, and substitute artificial sweetener for the sugar. One square contains about 100 calories.

Pies & Pastries

Hints to be Successful at Pastry Making

- Have ingredients as cold as possible. Butter &/or shortening should be frozen.
- Cut shortening &/or butter into 1'' pieces and arrange around the bottom of the processor bowl. Then add flour and salt. Processing with an on/off motion 4 or 5 times will help you control the texture of the flour-fat mixture.
- Mixture should look like coarse oatmeal.
- Add cold water (or liquid) through the feed tube in a thin stream while the machine is running. In about 15 seconds, the dough will begin to gather around the blades.
- It is not necessary to process until the ball stage (the dough forms a ball around the blades). If you are inexperienced, you can overprocess the dough, and end up with a cardboard texture.
- If the dough does not seem to gather together and is too dry, add a little extra liquid, **a little at a time,** and whirl until it begins to hold together.
- If the dough is sticky to the touch after you remove it from the bowl, knead in a little extra flour with your fingers until it feels right. Do not overhandle.
- Always **chill dough in the refrigerator for at least** ½ **hour** (or 15 minutes in the freezer) before using for easier handling.
- **N.B. An alternate procedure** to produce perfect pastry for the beginner:
  1) Process the dry ingredients for 5 seconds.
  2) Turn off machine, press frozen or very cold shortening down against the blades, and turn the machine rapidly on and off until the mixture looks like coarse oatmeal.
  3) Remove cover, and sprinkle water over mixture 1 or 2 tbsp. at a time, using a fork to stir in just enough liquid to make the dough come clean from the sides of the container and hold together. (You may remove the blade, if desired.)
  This method takes a few seconds longer, but you're less likely to overwork the dough and produce more professional results if you are inexperienced.

HOW TO ROLL DOUGH

- TAKE YOUR TIME!
- A pastry cloth and stocking cover on your rolling pin makes for easy rolling and eliminates excessive flour, which can make your crust tough. A linen towel which has flour rubbed in can be used instead of a pastry cloth. Anchor it under the edges of your pastry board.
- Rolling dough on wax paper which is floured is an alternate method. Wet counter so that wax paper will adhere.
- Flour your rolling pin or rolling pin cover to prevent sticking.
- Roll dough equally in all directions, making sure to keep pastry round.
- Check often to make sure that dough is not sticking. If it does, lift up carefully with a floured spatula, and add a **little** more flour.

• Always roll from the center of the dough to the outside edge, using light strokes and a lifting motion.

• If using wax paper, place a sheet on top of dough when it is party rolled out and then continue rolling.

• To measure correct size of circle, turn pie plate upside down over pastry. Pastry should be 1½'' - 2'' larger than pie plate.

• If cracks form along the outside edge of the circle, press them together as they form, in order to prevent them from enlarging.

HOW TO PLACE DOUGH IN PAN

• Fold dough in half carefully, then in half again. Place point at centre of pie plate, and unfold carefully.

• Do not stretch pastry. It will shrink during baking.

• To minimize shrinking during baking, refrigerate pie shell before baking for 20 to 30 minutes, if you have time.

• Ease pastry into pan by using your thumbs to press sides in a downward direction.

• For a **One Crust Pie,** the bottom edge should have a ½'' overhang, which is then folded under. For a **Two Crust Pie,** the top crust should have the overhang, which is then folded under the bottom crust (not under the rim of the pie plate!).

• For a lattice-top pie, the bottom crust has an overhang, which is folded over the lattice. Flute as desired.

PIE PANS

• Pyrex, aluminum or dull metal pans are best. Aluminium foil reflects the heat, and therefore, if you are baking in foil pans, place them on an aluminum or teflon cookie sheet before placing in oven.

• A 9'' pie plate holds about 4 cups filling and serves 8; an 8'' pie plate holds about 3 cups filling and serves 6.

• If using a quiche pan which has a lift-out bottom and a fluted or rippled sharp edge, just roll your rolling pin over the edge and the excess pastry will automatically cut itself away. An 11'' quiche pan may be used instead of a 9'' pie plate.

• Pastry which has a high proportion of shortening to flour does not require greased baking pans. (Cookie crusts do.)

FREEZING

• Pies may be baked first, and then frozen. Thaw at room temperature for 5 to 6 hours, then heat at 350°F for 15 mins. for that just-baked taste.

• If you don't have time to wait for the pie to defrost before serving, then preheat oven to 425°F and heat pie until warm throughout, about 20 mins. To prevent overbrowning, cover loosely with tinfoil.

• Unbaked pastry may be frozen for 1 to 2 months; baked pie shells may be frozen 2 to 4 months. Bakes pies can be frozen for about 3 months.

• Freeze pies immediately, whether they are baked or unbaked.

- Unbaked pies freeze successfully. Freeze, then wrap well. To bake, preheat oven to 450°F. Bake for 15 to 20 mins. (After first 15 minutes, cut slits in top of pie.) Reduce heat to 375° and bake 45 mins. longer.

- Unbaked pies should not have slits cut in them before freezing.

- Wrap well with foil, then store in a plastic bag which is tightly closed.

- Do not use a Pyrex pie plate if you plan to freeze pie and then bake it from the frozen state. The pan could crack from extreme temperature changes.

TOPPINGS

- For a shiny top, brush the top crust with milk before baking.

- For a glazed top, brush top crust lightly with beaten egg before baking.

- For a sugary top, moisten top crust with water, and sprinkle with sugar before baking.

EDGINGS

Fluted Edge: Place left thumb and forefinger (barely touching about ½" below the tip) on the outside edge of the pie plate, with your fingertips pointing inwards. With the forefinger of your other hand, **push** along the inside rim **outwards** between your thumb and forefinger, as if you are pinching your right forefinger. Repeat every inch or so. This forms a V-shape fluting. Reverse hands if you are left-handed.

Ruffle Edge: Place left thumb and forefinger about ½" apart on the outside edge of the pie plate, with your fingertips pointing inwards. With the forefinger of your other hand, **pull** pastry gently in towards the centre of the plate. Repeat every inch or so. This forms a rounded, ruffled edge. Reverse hands if you are left-handed.

Pinched Stand-up Edge: Use thumbs and forefingers of both hands. Place them along the edge of the pie, with your thumbs along the outer edge and your forefingers pointing inwards. Your hands should be about ½" apart. Pinch dough, pushing fingers together so that they "kiss", making a stand-up edge. Repeat every ½" or so.

LATTICE-TOP PIES

Prepare pastry for any 2-crust pie. Roll out dough for bottom crust and line pie plate. Trim to ½" beyond edge of pie plate. Roll out second ball of dough. Using a sharp knife or pastry wheel, cut dough into ½" strips. Use a ruler to keep strips straight. You will need approximately 12 strips.

Fill pie shell with desired filling. Carefully lay 6 of the strips over the filling, about 1" apart, and parallel to each other. Carefully fold every other strip halfway back.

Place the 7th strip across the centre of the pie at right angles to those already in place. Unfold the folded pastry strips, and fold back the strips that were straight. Repeat with 8th strip, placing it 1" away from the 7th strip. Repeat this weaving process until all strips have been used.

Trim pastry strips even with the bottom crust. Fold under, and flute edges as desired.

Alternate (Easy) Method: Cut 12 strips as directed above. Lay half the strips 1" apart across pie, twisting them. Arrange remaining strips at right angles, also twisting them. Press ends of strips into rim of crust. Fold bottom pastry over the lattice-work. Seal and flute.

Pastry Problems:

Dough dry and hard to work with:	Insufficient liquid; dough is too cold; dough was not shaped into a round and flattened before chilling and rolling.
Pastry is hard when baked:	Too much water; overmixing; excess flour on pastry board; dough overhandled.
Baked pastry is tough:	Insufficient shortening; overmixing shortening and flour; overhandling; oven temperature is too low.
Too pale:	Oven temperature is too low; underbaked.
Too dark:	Oven temperature is too high; overbaked.
Soggy lower crust:	Pastry is overhandled; too much filling; filling too moist; pastry soaked before baking started; pie baked too high in oven; oven temperature is too low. (Brush shell with unbeaten egg white before adding filling.)
Apple pie has large air space under top crust of pie:	Apples not packed tightly into shell; apples sliced too thick; pastry not rich enough; apples not mounded higher in the centre of the shell.
Crust thick and doughy:	Insufficient fat; too much water; water not cold enough; pastry rolled too thick; oven temperature is too low.
Crust shrinks while baking:	Pastry rolled too thin; pastry overhandled or stretched when fitted into pan; too much water; oven temperature too low; pastry not chilled for ½ hour before baking.
One crust pie shell has bumps and does not lie flat enough:	Pastry not pricked enough; oven temperature too low.

★★★★★★★★★

CREAM CHEESE PASTRY

(An excellent all-purpose dough. A favourite of my students because it is so quick and easy.)

¼ lb. butter (or margarine), cut in chunks
¼ lb. cream cheese (or cottage cheese)

1 c. flour
2 tbsp. sugar, optional

Steel Knife: Combine all ingredients in processor bowl. Process until dough forms a ball on the blades, about 18 to 20 seconds. Chilling is not necessary.

This dough freezes well. It may be used to make Roly Poly (p. 288), Hamentaschen (p. 287), any of the Rogelach recipes (p. 280-281), Cheese Roll (p. 95) or Turnovers (p. 95). It is also great to make miniature quiches. Press about 1 tbsp. dough into medium size ungreased muffin cups. Fill with any quiche filling. (It is not necessary to prebake the dough before adding the quiche filling.) Bake at 400°F about 20 minutes, until golden.

STANDARD BUTTER PASTRY

¼ lb. frozen butter (1 stick)   ½ tsp. salt
¼ c. frozen shortening   ½ c. ice water
2 c. flour

Steel Knife: Cut butter and shortening into about 6 or 8 pieces. Arrange around the bottom of the processor bowl. Add flour and salt. Turn machine on and off quickly (about 2 to 3 seconds at a time) for 4 or 5 times, until the mixture begins to look like coarse oatmeal.

Add water in a slow stream through the feed tube while the machine is running. Process **just** until the dough begins to gather around the blades, about 10 to 12 seconds after all the liquid is added. Remove dough from machine, press into a ball, divide into 2 equal pieces and wrap each piece in plastic wrap or foil. Chill in refrigerator for at least ½ hour (or in freezer for 15 minutes) while you prepare the filling. Each piece of dough should look like a large, thick hamburger patty.

Roll out on a lightly floured board (or preferably use a pastry cloth and rolling pin stockinette cover). Use a light, lifting motion. Roll equally in all directions, making sure to keep dough circular and mending cracks as they form. Roll about 2'' larger than pie plate, about ⅛'' thick.

Yield: Two 9'' crusts or 12 medium tart shells. Freezes well.

Note: Dough may be stored in the refrigerator for 3 to 4 days. Allow dough to stand for a few minutes to soften slightly so that it will be easier to roll.

PAREVE* PIE CRUST (BASIC PASTRY)

⅔ c. frozen shortening   1 tsp. vinegar
2 c. flour   scant ½ c. ice water (about 3½
½ tsp. salt   ounces)

Steel Knife: Place chunks of shortening around the bottom of the processor bowl. Add flour and salt. Process with about 5 or 6 quick on/off turns, stopping to check texture, until mixture begins to look like coarse oatmeal. Do not overprocess. Add vinegar.

With machine running, add liquid in a steady stream through the feed tube **just** until the dough begins to gather around the blades, about 10 to 12 seconds after the liquid is added. Immediately remove dough from machine, press into a ball, divide in two and wrap each piece in foil or plastic wrap. Each piece of dough should look like a large, thick hamburger patty. Refrigerate for at least 1 hour before rolling out. (May be made 2 or 3 days in advance.)

Roll out dough on a lightly floured board (or preferably use a pastry cloth and a rolling pin stockinette cover). Roll equally in all directions, making sure to keep dough circular and mending cracks as they form. Roll about 2'' larger than pie plate, about ⅛'' thick.

Yield: Two 9'' pie crusts. Freezes well.
*Pareve means that no dairy or meat products are used in this recipe.

EGG PASTRY

Follow directions for Pareve Pie Crust (above), but instead of using all water, use 1 egg plus enough ice water to equal a scant half cup. This pastry is ideal to make turnovers as it is crisp and golden in color. May also be used to make your favorite pies.

Yield: Two 9'' pie crusts. Freezes well.

FLAKY GINGER ALE PASTRY

1 c. + 1 tbsp. flour
½ c. frozen margarine, cut in 6
   or 8 pieces

¼ c. gingerale, 7-Up, Fresca or
   soda water
½ tbsp. vinegar

Steel Knife: Process flour and margarine with on/off turns (about 2 to 3 seconds at a time) for 4 or 5 times, until the mixture begins to look like coarse oatmeal. Combine gingerale with vinegar and add through feed tube while machine is running. Process **just** until the dough begins to gather in a mass around the blades, about 8 to 10 seconds. Do not overprocess.

Remove dough from machine, divide into two balls, wrap in waxed paper and chill in the refrigerator at least 1 hour, or overnight. The colder the dough, the easier it is to roll. Dough may be frozen baked or unbaked.

Excellent for Tuna Strudel (p. 86), Mushroom Pinwheels (p. 45), Roly Poly (p. 288), Cheese Roll (p. 95), Cinnamon Nut Rogelach (p. 280), Chocolate Rogelach (p. 281) and Chocolate Chip Rogelach (p. 281).

Note: Recipe may be doubled in one batch successfully.

SOUR CREAM PASTRY
(Very rich and flaky. Almost like a mock puff pastry.)

1 c. chilled butter, cut in 1"
   chunks

1½ c. flour
½ c. cold sour cream

Steel Knife: Process butter with flour until the consistency of coarse oatmeal, using about 8 on/off turns. Add sour cream and process **just** until the pastry begins to cling together around the blades and form a ball. You will have to scrape down the sides of the bowl once or twice. Do not overprocess Divide dough in two, wrap in plastic wrap and refrigerate at least 4 hours or overnight.

Let dough stand for about 5 minutes to remove the chill and ease the rolling. Roll out on a lightly floured board or on a pastry cloth, using a rolling pin stockinette cover for easier rolling.

Excellent for tarts, turnovers, pies and strudels.

Yield: two 9'' pie crusts or 2 dozen medium tarts. Freezes well. Dough will keep in refrigerator for 4 or 5 days.

Note: Suggested recipes with this pastry are Butter Tarts (p. 309), Pizza Tarts (p. 46), Cherry or Apple Strudel (p. 318).

9'' PIE SHELL

Prepare your favourite pastry recipe as directed. Carefully transfer to a pie plate. Trim off overhanging edges, **leaving about ½'' excess.** Turn under, flute edges or press with tines of fork. Prick bottom of pastry all over with fork. (This prevents dough from puffing up.) Chill for half hour before baking to prevent crust from shrinking. Bake at 425°F about 10 minutes, until golden.

Note: If your recipe calls for a **partially baked shell,** (e.g. for quiche), line pastry with aluminum foil and weigh it down with uncooked rice or dried beans. Bake at 400°F for 10 minutes, remove paper and beans or rice, and bake 5 minutes longer. Cool slightly and fill.

TWO CRUST PIE

Prepare your favourite pastry recipe as directed. Divide in two. Roll out one portion. Transfer to your pie plate, and trim off all overhanging edges. Sprinkle with 2 tbsp. bread crumbs, or brush with a little unbeaten egg white. Fill as desired. Roll out top crust, fold in half and make several slits. Carefully unfold over filling and trim off excess dough, **leaving ½" excess.** Turn this under the bottom crust. Flute. Bake fruit pies at 425°F about 50 minutes.

ALMOND PAT-A- CRUST

(Easy for beginners.)

¼ c. almonds   ¼ c. softened butter, cut in
1 c. flour   chunks
3 tbsp. sugar

Steel Knife: Process almonds until coarsely chopped, about 10 seconds. Add flour and sugar and process 2 or 3 seconds longer. Add butter and process until well mixed, about 15 seconds.

Pat firmly and evenly into the bottom and up the sides of an ungreased 9" pie plate. Bake at 400°F for 16 to 18 minutes, until golden. Cool and fill as desired. Excellent for cream pies, fruit flans, etc.

Yield: one 9" pie crust. May be frozen.

Note: Any type of nuts may be substituted for the almonds. Just adjust processing time according to hardness of nuts.

GRAHAM WAFER CRUST

(Melting of the butter is not necessary!)

18 single graham wafers   6 tbsp. butter or margarine,
   (about 1½ c. crumbs)   cut in chunks
                                  3 tbsp. white or brown sugar

Steel or Plastic Knife: Break wafers into chunks. Process until coarse crumbs are formed. Add butter and sugar and process a few seconds longer, until blended. Pat into the bottom and up the sides of a lightly greased 9" pie plate. Either bake at 375°F for 7 to 8 minutes, or refrigerate 2 to 3 hours. If frozen, the crust will not be as crisp.

Variation: Substitute ½ c. almonds or walnuts for 6 of the graham wafers.

CHOCOLATE, VANILLA WAFER OR GINGER SNAP CRUST

Prepare as for Graham Wafer Crust, but substitute 28-30 chocolate wafers **or** 24 ginger snaps **or** 36 vanilla wafers for graham wafers.

Note: Any leftover cookie crumbs may be used. Use 1½ c. crumbs.

OATMEAL COOKIE PIE CRUST

10 large oatmeal cookies (or   ¼ c. butter or margarine,
   enough to make 1½ c. crumbs)   melted

Steel Knife: Break cookies into chunks and process until fine crumbs are formed, about 25 to 30 seconds. Add melted butter and process a few seconds longer, just until mixed.

Press into the bottom and up the sides of a 9" pie plate. Bake at 375°F for 7 to 8 minutes. **Yield:** One 9" pie crust. If frozen, the crust will not be as crisp.

BUTTER CRUNCH TOPPING

(Excellent on apple or peach pie)

1½ c. Granola	1 tsp. cinnamon
½ c. brown sugar, lightly packed	unbaked 9" apple or peach pie (omit top crust)
¼ c. cold butter or margarine, cut in 1" pieces	

Steel Knife: Place granola, brown sugar, butter and cinnamon in processor. Process until crumbly, about 6 seconds. Sprinkle over unbaked pie. Bake at 400°F for 45 minutes.

Yield: To top a 9" pie.

Note: Cover loosely with foil to prevent overbrowning during last 20 minutes of baking. Freezes well.

FAMILY APPLE PIE

Standard Butter Pastry (p. 304)	½ to 1 cup sugar (to taste)
2 tbsp. bread crumbs	1 tsp. cinnamon
8 large apples, cored and peeled	4 tbsp. flour

Prepare pastry as directed. Roll out one portion into a large circle and place in a 9" pie plate. Trim off overhanging edges. Sprinkle with crumbs.

Slicer: Cut apples to fit feed tube. Slice, using medium pressure. You should have 6 to 7 cups. The processor bowl should be nearly full. Combine in a mixing bowl with sugar, cinnamon and flour.

Fill shell, mounding apples higher in the centre. Roll out remaining dough and cut several slits. Place over apple filling. Trim away edges, leaving ½" border all around. Tuck under bottom crust. Flute edges.

Bake at 425°F about 45 to 50 minutes. May be frozen baked or unbaked.

To freeze unbaked pie: Do not cut slits in top crust. Wrap well and freeze. To bake, preheat oven to 450°F. Bake for 15 minutes. Cut slits in top. Reduce heat to 375°F and bake 45 minutes longer.

FAMILY PEACH PIE

Prepare as for Family Apple Pie (above), but substitute 8 large peaches for apples. Peel by pouring boiling water over peaches, then place in cold water. Peel, cut in half and remove pits. Slice. Increase flour to ⅓ cup.

CRUMBLY APPLE PIE

Follow directions for Family Apple Pie (above), but do not make a top crust and use only ½ cup sugar to sweeten. Prepare following topping:

1 c. flour	½ c. brown sugar, packed
¼ lb. cold butter, cut in 1" pieces	½ tsp. cinnamon

Steel Knife: Wipe bowl dry with paper towelling. Process all ingredients for topping about 8 to 10 seconds, until well blended. Sprinkle over apples. Bake at 400°F for 45 to 50 minutes. Delicious! May be frozen. Serve warm or cold.

Note: Any fruit may be substituted for the apple filling (e.g. peaches, pears, blueberries, etc.).

APPLE FLAN

½ recipe Standard Butter   ¼ c. sugar
   Pastry (p. 304)   2 tbsp. margarine or butter
3 tbsp. bread crumbs   ¾ c. apple jelly
6 to 8 large apples

Prepare pastry as directed. Roll out chilled dough on a floured pastry cloth into a large circle. Transfer to an 11'' quiche pan with a removeable bottom. Trim away excess edges. Sprinkle with crumbs. Chill while you prepare filling.

Peel and core apples. Cut to fit feed tube.

Slicer: Slice apples, using medium pressure. Arrange attractively in pie shell. Sprinkle with sugar and dot with bits of butter.

Bake at 400°F for 65 to 70 minutes, until well-browned. Melt apple jelly in a small saucepan. Brush over apples. May be frozen.

Note: Glaze may be omitted. Instead, prepare topping as for Crumbly Apple Pie (p. 307). Sprinkle over apple filling and bake.

APPLE MERINGUE PIE

5 apples, peeled & cored   1 tbsp. flour
½ c. sugar   2 tbsp. cold water
½ c. white wine or apple juice 9'' baked pie shell
1 tbsp. butter   2 egg whites
½ tsp. cinnamon   ¼ c. sugar
dash salt   ¼ c. apricot jam
1 tsp. vanilla   1 tsp. Kirsch

Slicer: Cut apples to fit feed tube. Slice, using firm pressure. Transfer to a saucepan. Add ½ cup sugar, wine, butter, cinnamon and salt. Simmer uncovered until tender, about 5 minutes. Add vanilla. Dissolve flour in cold water and add to apples. Cook 1 minute longer. Mixture should be thick. Spoon into cooled pie shell.

Using electric mixer, beat egg whites until foamy. Add sugar one tablespoon at a time and beat until stiff peaks form. Place meringue in a pastry bag and pipe in a lattice design over the pie. Bake at 375°F for 7 to 8 minutes, until meringue is golden. Fill spaces between lattice work with apricot jam which has been thinned with Kirsch.

Yield: 6 to 8 servings.

To Freeze: Pie shell may be frozen unbaked. Pop in the oven while still frozen and bake at 475°F for 8 to 10 minutes. Filling may be prepared and frozen separately in a pie plate which has been lined with foil. Thaw almost completely before adding to pie shell. Do not freeze meringue.

BLUEBERRY APPLE PIE

Follow recipe for Family Apple Pie (p. 307), but substitute the following filling:

3 to 4 apples, cored and   ¾ to 1 c. sugar
   peeled   ⅓ c. flour
1½ c. fresh or frozen   1 tsp. cinnamon
   blueberries (drained)

Slicer: Cut apples to fit feed tube. Slice, using medium pressure. Combine with remaining filling ingredients and mix well. Assemble and bake as directed. May be frozen.

BLACK BOTTOM PIE

(Well worth the effort. Sure to make a hit.)

Ginger Snap Crust (p. 306)	¼ c. cold water
½ c. sugar	2 tsp. rum extract
2 tbsp. flour	3 egg whites
dash of salt	½ c. sugar
2 c. milk	1 c. whipping cream (chilled)
3 egg yolks	2 tbsp. icing sugar
6 oz. pkg. chocolate chips	grated chocolate to garnish
1 envelope (1 tbsp.) unflavored gelatin	

Prepare crust as directed and bake at 375°F for 7 to 8 minutes. Cool completely.

Combine ½ c. sugar with flour and salt in a saucepan. Gradually stir in milk. Bring to a boil, stirring. Boil for 1 minute. Remove from heat.

Steel Knife: Process egg yolks for 2 or 3 seconds. Add half of the hot mixture to the egg yolks and process for 8 to 10 seconds, until blended. Return mixture to saucepan and boil 1 minute longer. Remove from heat.

Steel Knife: Process chocolate chips until finely chopped. Add 1 cup of the hot mixture to the chocolate and process until chocolate is melted. Scrape down sides of bowl as necessary so that mixture is well blended. Pour into baked crust.

Soften gelatin in cold water for 5 minutes. Add to remaining hot custard mixture and stir until gelatin is dissolved. Chill until mixture is partially set and mounds slightly when dropped from a spoon. Stir in rum extract.

Beat egg whites on electric mixer until foamy. Gradually add sugar, beating until stiff peaks are formed. Fold into partially set custard. Spread over chocolate layer. Chill several hours, until firm.

Steel Knife: Place a thick book under the back part of the processor base so that the machine is tipped forward. Do not insert pusher in feed tube. Whip cream until the texture of sour cream. Add icing sugar and process until stiff, about 10 seconds longer. Garnish pie. Sprinkle with chocolate.

Yield: 6 to 8 servings. Do not freeze.

BUTTER TARTS

½ c. butter, cut in chunks	½ tsp. vanilla
1½ c. brown sugar, lightly packed	½ c. raisins
2 eggs	2 dozen medium tart shells, unbaked (see recipe for
1 tbsp. lemon juice	Sour Cream Pastry (p. 305))

Steel Knife: Process butter with brown sugar and eggs for about 1 minute, scraping down sides of bowl once or twice. Mixture should be well creamed. Add lemon juice and vanilla and process a second or two longer. Divide raisins evenly among tart shells. Fill about ⅔ full with creamed mixture.

Bake at 375°F until golden brown, about 18 to 20 minutes. Cool completely.

Yield: 2 dozen tarts. May be frozen.

CHOCOLATE FLECKED MARSHMALLOW CREAM PIE

8 oz. pkg. chocolate or vanilla
  wafers (about 1½ c. crumbs)
⅓ c. melted butter or
  margarine
1 square unsweetened
  chocolate

32 marshmallows
¾ c. milk
dash salt
2½ c. whipping cream (500 mL)
2 tbsp. icing sugar
maraschino cherries, halved

Steel Knife: Process wafers until coarse crumbs are formed. Use 1½ cups crumbs. Add melted butter and process a few seconds longer to mix. Press mixture into the bottom and up the sides of a 9'' pie plate. Bake at 350°F for 8 to 10 minutes. Cool completely.

Grater: Grate chocolate, using firm pressure. Transfer to a small dish. Wash and dry the bowl, the cover and blade.

Combine marshmallows, milk and salt in the top of a double boiler. Cook over simmering water until marshmallows melt. Cool thoroughly.

Tip processor forward by placing a thick book underneath the base. Using the **Steel Knife,** process cream until stiff, about 45 seconds. Measure 2 cups of the whipped cream and fold into cooled marshmallow mixture with a rubber spatula. Fold in grated chocolate, reserving about 1 tbsp. to garnish pie. Pour mixture into cooled crust. Add icing sugar to remaining whipped cream in processor. Process for a few seconds to blend. Garnish pie. Sprinkle with reserved grated chocolate and maraschino cherries. Refrigerate overnight before serving.

Yield: 6 to 8 servings. May be frozen.

STRAWBERRY MARSHMALLOW PIE

Follow recipe for Chocolate Flecked Marshmallow Cream Pie (above), omitting chocolate and cherries. Substitute 1 cup hulled strawberries. Slice on **Slicer,** using very light pressure. Fold into marshmallow/whipped cream mixture. Assemble as directed. If desired, garnish with whole strawberries which have been dipped in icing sugar.

Yield: 6 to 8 servings.

CHOCOLATE CREAM PIE

Baked 9'' pie crust
Chocolate Pastry Cream (p. 317)
1½ c. whipping cream

2 tbsp. icing sugar
grated chocolate, to garnish

Prepare your favorite pie crust. Cool completely. Prepare Pastry Cream as directed; fold in dessert topping or whipped cream as directed in the **Note** for Crème Pâtissière on p. 317. Pour into pie shell. Cool completely.

Steel Knife: Tip the processor forward by placing a thick book underneath the base. Process whipping cream until it reaches the texture of sour cream, about 35 seconds. Add sugar and process about 10 seconds longer, until stiff.

Garnish pie with whipped cream and grated chocolate. Refrigerate 3 to 4 hours before serving. May be frozen. Thaw overnight in fridge.

Yield: 6 to 8 servings.

CHOCOLATE MARSHMALLOW PIE

8 oz. pkg. chocolate wafers	½ c. milk
⅓ c. melted butter or margarine	2 squares semi-sweet chocolate, halved
¼ c. walnuts, if desired	2 c. chilled whipping cream
20 marshmallows (about 2 cups)	3 tbsp. sugar

Steel Knife: Process wafers until coarse crumbs are formed, about 15 to 20 seconds. Add melted butter and process a few seconds longer to mix. Press mixture into the bottom and up the sides of a 9" or 10" pie plate. Bake at 350°F for 8 to 10 minutes. Cool completely.

Steel Knife: Process nuts with 5 or 6 quick on/off turns, until coarsely chopped. Set aside.

Heat marshmallows, milk and chocolate in the top of a double boiler over simmering water until melted, stirring to blend. Chill in ice water until mixture is cooled and mounds slightly when dropped from a spoon.

Whip cream. An electric mixer will give maximum volume and produce a lighter texture, but the processor may be used. Insert **Steel Knife.** Tip the processor forward by placing a thick book underneath the base. Process whipping cream until it reaches the texture of sour cream, about 35 seconds. Add sugar and process about 10 seconds longer, until stiff. (With an electric mixer, sugar should be added when cream is nearly stiff.) Measure 2 cups of whipped cream and fold with the chopped nuts into chocolate mixture. Pour into cooled crust. Place remaining whipped cream in a pastry bag, using a star tube, and garnish pie. Refrigerate overnight before serving.

Yield: 8 servings.

Note: This pie may be frozen most successfully. Let stand 5 to 10 minutes before serving. When frozen, the taste is similar to an ice cream pie, whereas when it is refrigerated, it becomes more like a chiffon pie. Try it both ways!

EASY FRUIT FLAN
(Any fruits in season may be used to top this pie.)

Almond Pat-A-Crust (p. 306)	¼ c. sour cream
⅓ c. whipping cream	fresh fruit (strawberries, green grapes, bananas, cantaloupe, blueberries, etc.)
1 pkg. (4 serving size) instant vanilla pudding	
1 c. milk	¼ c. warm apricot preserves

Prepare crust as directed. Bake and cool.

Steel Knife: Place a heavy book under the base of the processor so that the machine is tipped forward. Process cream until stiff, about 35 to 40 seconds. Do not insert pusher in feed tube. Empty bowl. Process pudding with milk and sour cream until smooth and blended, about 30 seconds, scraping down sides of bowl as necessary. Add whipped cream and blend a few seconds longer. Pour into pie shell and chill.

Prepare fruit. Strawberries and grapes should be cut in half lengthwise with a sharp knife. Bananas may be sliced on the **Slicer,** using light pressure. Cantaloupe should be thinly sliced by hand in attractive crescents. Arrange fruit attractively in a circular design over the chilled custard. Strawberries and grapes should be placed cut-side down. Brush with warm preserves. Chill before serving.

Yield: 8 servings. Do not freeze.

Note: If you have an attractive ceramic quiche dish, it may be used.

FRESH STRAWBERRY FLAN

½ recipe Standard Butter
  Pastry (p. 304)
Crème Pâtissière (p. 317) or 1
  pkg. vanilla pudding & pie
  filling (the kind you cook)

½ c. red currant jelly
1 pint strawberries, hulled &
  cut in half lengthwise

Prepare pastry as directed. Roll out chilled pastry on a floured pastry cloth into a 12" circle. Tranfer to an 11" flan pan with a removeable bottom. Roll the rolling pin over the edges of the pan and the excess dough will be cut away. Line with aluminum foil and fill with rice or peas to weigh down pastry. Bake at 400°F for 10 minutes. Remove foil and rice or peas. Bake about 5 minutes longer, until golden. Cool completely.

Prepare Crème Pâtissière as directed, or cook pudding according to the package directions. Let cool. Cover with waxed paper to prevent a skin from forming. (May be prepared in advance up to this point.)

Heat jelly on low heat in a saucepan until melted. Brush a little on the bottom of the pie shell. Let set for 5 minutes. Add Crème Pâtissière or pudding. Do not fill more than ½" thick. Arrange berries attractively over the pastry cream. Brush with jelly. Refrigerate for 2 to 3 hours before serving.

Yield: 8 servings.

Note: Do not assemble the flan more than 2 to 3 hours in advance, or results will not be satisfactory. Do not freeze assembled flan.

FRENCH FRUIT FLAN

Follow directions for Fresh Strawberry Flan (above) as directed, but substitute the following toppings:- (You may use a combination of several fruits, if you wish, arranged in a circular design.)

1) 28 oz. can peach slices, well drained, halved lengthwise and patted dry.
2) 3 tins mandarin orange segments, well-drained and patted dry.
3) 3 firm bananas (cut to fit feed tube and sliced with light pressure on the **Slicer**). Dip in lemon juice to prevent discoloration.
4) 2 - 14 oz. cans apricot halves, well-drained and patted dry.
5) fresh green grapes, halved lengthwise.
6) 2 cups blueberries

Glaze with melted red currant jelly (or apricot jam which has been put through a sieve after heating). If desired, add a little of your favorite liqueur while heating the jelly or jam.

Yield: 8 servings. Do not freeze.

FUDGE RIBBON ALASKA PIE

9" baked pie shell
peppermint candy (¼ c.
  crushed)
¾ c. sugar
½ c. evaporated milk
6 oz. pkg. chocolate chips
1 tsp. vanilla

1 litre or 1 quart peppermint
  or vanilla ice cream, slightly
  softened
3 egg whites
¼ tsp. cream of tartar
6 tbsp. sugar

Prepare pie crust, bake and cool completely.

Steel Knife: Drop peppermint stick candy through the feed tube while the machine is running. Process until crushed. Set aside.

Combine sugar and evaporated milk in a saucepan. Simmer until sugar is dissolved, stirring occasionally. Process the chocolate chips on the **Steel Knife** until finely chopped, about 30 seconds. Pour hot milk mixture and vanilla through the feed tube while the machine is running and process until chocolate is melted and mixture is blended. Cool completely.

Press half of the softened ice cream into the pie shell. Cover with half of the cooled sauce. Repeat with remaining ice cream and sauce. Wrap and freeze until firm.

15 Minutes Before Serving: Using electric mixer, beat egg whites with cream of tartar until soft peaks form. Gradually beat in sugar. Continue beating until whites are stiff and no sugar can be felt when you rub the meringue between your fingertips. Fold 3 tbsp. crushed candy into meringue. Spread over frozen filling, sealing edges well. Swirl meringue to make decorative peaks. Place on a baking sheet and bake at 475°F for 3 to 5 minutes, until golden. Sprinkle remaining candy over meringue. Serve immediately.

Yield: 8 servings.

Serving Hint: Dip knife into water before cutting pie to prevent meringue from sticking to knife. Repeat whenever meringue sticks.

MOUSSE PIE

Oatmeal Cookie Pie
  Crust (p. 306)
Strawberry Mousse (p. 229)

1 c. chilled whipping cream
  plus 2 tbsp. sugar (or 1
  envelope dessert topping
  mix plus ½ cup milk)

Prepare pie crust according to directions. Bake and cool.

Follow directions for Strawberry Mousse. Pour into cooled crust and refrigerate.

Steel Knife: Place a thick book underneath the base of the processor so that the machine is tipped forward. Do not insert pusher in feed tube. Process whipping cream with sugar (or dessert topping with milk) until stiff. Cream will be stiff in about 45 seconds, and dessert topping will take about 2 minutes. Garnish pie. Chill for 3 to 4 hours before serving.

Yield: 8 servings. Do not freeze.

Variations: Instead of Strawberry Mousse, use any of the following as fillings:-
Raspberry Mousse (p. 229), Orange Mousse (p. 229), Lemon Mousse (p. 229), Lemon Marshmallow Mousse (p. 230), Peach Mousse (p. 230), Frosty Lime Mousse (p. 230), Orange Sherbet Bavarian (p. 228).

LEMON MERINGUE PIE

2 lemons
9" baked pie shell
1 c. sugar
3 tbsp. flour
3 tbsp. cornstarch
dash salt

1½ c. boiling water
2 egg yolks
1 tbsp. butter or margarine
3 egg whites
¼ tsp. cream of tartar
6 tbsp. sugar

Using a potato peeler, peel the yellow portion of lemon rind, being careful not to include any of the bitter white pith. Squeeze juice from lemons and measure ⅓ cup juice. Prepare and bake pie shell.

Steel Knife: Process lemon rind with 1 cup sugar until finely minced, beginning with 4 quick on/off turns, then letting machine run about 30 seconds. Add flour, cornstarch and salt. While machine is running, add boiling water through feed tube. Process about 5 seconds. Transfer to a heavy saucepan and cook over medium heat, stirring constantly, until mixture thickens and boils. Boil 1 minute.

Steel Knife: Process egg yolks with lemon juice for a few seconds. Add about half of the hot mixture and process about 8 to 10 seconds. Return mixture to saucepan and boil 1 minute longer, stirring constantly. Remove from heat and stir in butter. Pour hot filling into pie shell.

Using electric mixer, beat egg whites with cream of tartar until foamy. Beat in sugar a tablespoon at a time. Continue beating until stiff and glossy and the meringue does not feel grainy when rubbed between your fingers. Pile meringue onto hot pie filling, sealing meringue onto edge of crust to prevent shrinking and weeping. Bake at 350°F for 8 to 10 minutes, until golden. Cool away from drafts.

Yield: 8 servings. Do not freeze.

PINE-APPLY PIE

Standard Butter Pastry (p. 304)
6 large apples, peeled, cored
    & halved
14 oz. can crushed pineapple,
    well drained

¾ c. sugar (or to taste)
1 tsp. cinnamon
¼ c. flour
2 tbsp. bread or cracker
    crumbs

Prepare pastry as directed. Chill dough while preparing filling.

Slicer: Slice apples. using medium pressure. Transfer to a mixing bowl and combine with drained pineapple, sugar, cinnamon and flour.

Roll out half of pastry on a floured pastry cloth, using a stocking cover for your rolling pin, or use a lightly floured board. Place in an ungreased 9" pie plate. Trim edges of pastry even with edges of pan. Sprinkle bread or cracker crumbs in pie shell. Add filling, mounding it slightly higher in the centre. Roll out remaining pastry and cut several slits in it. Carefully place over filling. Trim dough, leaving ½" overhang. Tuck top crust under bottom brust. Flute edges. Brush crust with a little water and sprinkle with about 1 tsp. sugar.

Bake at 425°F for 10 minutes; reduce heat to 350°F and bake 30 minutes longer, until golden.

Yield: 6 to 8 servings. Freezes well.

PECAN PIE

unbaked 9" pie shell	1 tsp. vanilla or rum extract
1 c. sugar	½ tsp. salt
4 eggs	1 c. pecans
1 c. dark corn syrup	

Prepare pastry and place in an ungreased 9" pie plate.

Steel Knife: Process remaining ingredients except pecans for 8 to 10 seconds, until blended. Add pecans and mix in with 1 or 2 very quick on/off turns. Pour mixture into pie shell.

Bake at 350°F for 55 to 60 minutes, or until a knife inserted in the centre of the pie comes out clean.

Yield: 8 servings. May be frozen. Best if served slightly warm. Reheat at 350°F for about 5 minutes just before serving. Delicious with ice cream or slightly sweetened whipped cream.

CHOC' FULL OF PECAN PIE

9" unbaked pie shell	1 c. pecans
2 squares unsweetened	3 eggs
chocolate	1¼ c. sugar
2 tbsp. butter or margarine	¾ c. flaked coconut, if desired

Prepare your favorite pastry and place in an ungreased 9" pie plate. Melt chocolate with butter over low heat. Let cool.

Steel Knife: Process nuts with 5 or 6 quick on/off turns, until coarsely chopped. Empty bowl and set aside. Process eggs with sugar for 3 or 4 seconds. Add melted chocolate mixture and process for a few seconds, until blended. Add nuts and coconut. Mix in with 1 or 2 very quick on/off turns. Pour mixture into unbaked pie shell. Bake at 375°F for 35 to 45 minutes, just until set. Pie will firm up when cooled. Delicious served with ice cream.

Yield: 6 to 8 servings. May be frozen.

PUDDING PARFAIT PIE

1 envelope dessert topping	1 pkg. (4 serving size) instant
mix	pudding (any flavor)
2 c. milk	Baked 9" graham wafer crust

Steel Knife: Place a thick book under the base of the processor so that the machine is tipped forward. Do not insert pusher in feed tube. Process dessert topping with ½ cup milk until stiff. Sprinkle instant pudding over whipped topping. Add remaining 1½ cups milk through the feed tube while the machine is running. Scrape down sides of bowl as necessary. Process until smooth and blended, about 20 to 30 seconds.

Pour mixture into baked and cooled graham wafer crust. Top with desired topping (see Note below). Chill for 3 to 4 hours, until firm.

Yield: 8 servings. Do not freeze.

Note: An easy topping is a 19 oz. can of your favorite pie filling (e.g. cherry, blueberry, pineapple, etc.). Use vanilla pudding. Another quick trick is to reserve about ¼ cup crumb mixture that you make for the crust, and sprinkle it over the filling.

CHOCOLATE PARFAIT PIE

Follow recipe for Pudding Parfait Pie (p. 315), using instant chocolate pudding and a baked 9'' Chocolate Wafer Crust (p. 306). As a garnish, prepare either an additional envelope of dessert topping mix with ½ cup milk, or 1 cup chilled whipping cream plus 2 tbsp. sugar. Process until stiff, using the **Steel Knife.**

Yield: 8 servings. Do not freeze.

CREAM PUFFS (PATE A CHOUX)

½ c. butter or margarine	½ tsp. sugar (increase to 1
1 c. water	tbsp. for sweet fillings)
½ tsp. salt	1 c. flour
	4 eggs

Combine butter, water, salt and sugar in a saucepan. Bring to a boil, stirring occasionally. As soon as butter is melted, remove from heat and dump in flour all at once. Stir vigorously with a wooden spoon until mixture pulls away from the sides of the pan and forms a ball. Cool 5 minutes.

Steel Knife: Transfer mixture from saucepan into the processor bowl. Process for 5 seconds. Drop eggs through feed tube one at a time while machine is running. Process about 25 to 30 seconds longer after you have added all the eggs. Mixture should be smooth and shiny.

Transfer dough into a pastry bag fitted with a ¼'' or ½'' plain tube and pipe mounds of dough onto a lightly greased cookie sheet. (If you don't have a pastry bag, drop mixture by rounded tablespoons onto baking sheet.) If desired, you may glaze the cream puffs with a little beaten egg before baking.

Bake at 425°F for 10 minutes, reduce heat to 375°F and bake 20 to 25 minutes longer, depending on size. Puffs should be golden. Remove from oven and cut a 1'' slit in each puff to allow steam to escape. Cool completely, cut off tops and remove any softened dough inside puffs. Delicious filled with sweetened whipped cream and iced with chocolate icing, or filled with ice cream, frozen and served with hot chocolate sauce. Also excellent filled with Crème Pâtissière (p. 317). Cream puffs freeze well.

Yield: 15 medium or 30 miniature puffs.

Note: Cream puffs are also delicious filled with sautéed vegetables or seafood. Use minimum amount of sugar. Excellent as an hors d'oeuvre for cocktail parties.

ECLAIRS

Follow recipe for Cream Puffs, but shape into 3'' fingers. Bake as directed. Freezes well.

RHUBARB PIE

Standard Butter Pastry (p. 304)
or your favorite pastry recipe
for a 2 crust pie
4 c. sliced rhubarb

1¼ c. sugar (or to taste)
⅓ c. flour
1 tbsp. butter or margarine

Prepare pastry as directed. Chill before rolling.

Slicer: Cut rhubarb to fit feed tube. Slice, using firm pressure. Measure about 4 cups sliced. Mix with sugar and flour.

Roll out half of pastry on a pastry cloth into a large circle about 2'' larger than pie plate. Transfer to a 9'' pie plate. Trim off any overhanging edges. Fill with rhubarb filling. Dot with butter. Roll out remaining pastry, cut slits in it and place over filling. Tuck top crust under bottom crust. Flute. Sprinkle with a little sugar.

Bake at 425°F for 40 to 50 minutes, until golden brown.

Yield: 8 servings. May be frozen.

STRAWBERRY RHUBARB PIE

Follow recipe for Rhubarb Pie (above), but substitute about 2 cups halved strawberries for half of the rhubarb.

PINEAPPLE RHUBARB PIE

Follow recipe for Rhubarb Pie (above), but substitute a 14 oz. can drained crushed pineapple for about 1 cup of the rhubarb.

CREME PATISSIERE

(French Pastry Cream)

1 c. milk
3 egg yolks
¼ c. sugar
¼ c. flour

1 tbsp. butter
1 tbsp. Grand Marnier or
Kirsch (or 1 tsp. vanilla
extract)

Heat milk in a heavy bottomed saucepan until steaming.

Steel Knife: Process egg yolks with sugar and flour until well mixed, about 15 to 20 seconds. Add hot milk through feed tube while machine is running. Process until smooth. Return mixture to saucepan and cook, whisking or stirring constantly, until very thick. Use medium heat to start, then reduce to low to prevent scorching. Remove from heat. Beat in butter and flavoring. Cool. Cover with plastic wrap to prevent a skin from forming. May be frozen or prepared 3 to 4 days in advance and refrigerated until needed.

Yield: About 1¼ cups. This amount is correct to fill an 11'' flan. Recipe may be doubled to fill tarts or cream puffs.

Note: Whipped cream or dessert topping may be folded into pastry cream as a filling for cream pies, or serve in individual dessert dishes. Whip 1 cup whipping cream or 1 envelope dessert topping mix (made according to package directions) for a single recipe.

CHOCOLATE PASTRY CREAM

Grater: Grate 2 or 3 squares semi-sweet chocolate, using firm pressure. Stir into hot milk for Crème Pâtissière. Proceed as directed above. Use a chocolate flavored liqueur instead of Grand Marnier as flavoring. May be frozen.

APPLE STRUDEL

Sour Cream Pastry (p. 305)   ½ c. walnuts, if desired
5 or 6 apples, peeled & cored   ½ c. raisins, if desired
½ c. sugar   2 tbsp. fine dry bread crumbs
1 tsp. cinnamon   sifted icing sugar
2 tbsp. flour

Prepare pastry as directed. Roll out half of dough into a large rectangle as thinly as possible (about 8'' x 15'').

Slicer or French Fry Blade: Cut apples to fit feed tube. Slice, using light pressure. Mix apples with sugar, cinnamon and flour.

Steel Knife: Chop nuts until fine, about 8 to 10 seconds. Add nuts and raisins to apples.

Sprinkle dough with about 1 tbsp. bread crumbs. Spread half the apple filling over the dough to within 1'' of the edges. Roll up, turning in ends. Place on a cookie sheet which has been lined with a piece of lightly greased tinfoil. Make sure that the strudel is placed seam-side down. Repeat with remaining ingredients.

Bake at 375°F for 35 to 45 minutes, until golden brown. Cool. Sprinkle with icing sugar.

Yield: 2 rolls. Will serve about 12, if cut in 2'' slices. May be frozen. Delicious served warm and topped with a scoop of ice cream.

Variation: Instead of using Sour Cream Pastry, use 3 sheets of filo dough (available in specialty food stores) for each apple strudel. Brush each sheet of dough lightly with a little oil and place one on top of the other. Prepare filling. Sprinkle 2 tbsp. crumbs over dough. Top with apples. Roll up and place seam-side down on foil. Bake as directed, reducing baking time slightly.

Yield: 1 large roll.

CHERRY STRUDEL

Sour Cream Pastry (p. 305)   ½ c. coconut
½ c. walnuts or pecans   1½ c. canned cherry pie filling

Prepare pastry as directed. Chill. Divide dough into 2 equal parts. Roll out one piece at a time into a rectangle about 15'' x 8'' on a floured board or pastry cloth.

Steel Knife: Process nuts until coarsely chopped, using about 6 or 8 quick on/off turns. Stir nuts, coconut and pie filling together to mix.

Spread half the filling along the 15'' edge to within ½'' of the sides. Roll up, turning in ends. Place seam-side down on a cookie sheet which has been lined with a piece of lightly greased foil. Repeat with remaining dough and filling.

Bake at 425°F about 25 minutes, or until golden. Cool. Sprinkle heavily with icing sugar and cut in 2'' slices.

Yield: 2 rolls (about 12 slices). May be frozen.

Note: Blueberry pie filling may be substituted.

Festive Holiday Favorites

Holiday Hints

- **Holiday time** is guest time, so prepare as much as possible well in advance and stock up your freezer so you will be able to spend time with your company.

- **Leftovers** can be transformed into delicious dishes quickly with the aid of your processor.

- **Dips** can be thinned with a little milk and used as salad dressings.

- **Fish, chicken, turkey and roasts** can be used in casseroles, crêpes, quiches and pâtés.

- **Hard cheeses** can be shredded on the **Grater** and stored in the freezer in a plastic bag. No need to thaw before using.

- **Bread** can be used for stuffings, to make bread crumbs or as a topping for casseroles. Whirl leftover chunks of bread on the **Steel Knife** with your favorite herbs (e.g. basil, oregano, rosemary, thyme, salt & pepper) plus a little butter or oil to moisten. Store in the freezer for an instant topping.

- **Leftover wine** can be refrigerated and used to add flavor to meats, poultry, gravies and sauces.

- **Veggies** are great to use in quick soups. Cooked vegetables can be puréed on the **Steel Knife,** added to broth and simmered for 15 minutes. Add rice or fine noodles to thicken.

- **Your processor** can help you whip up quick gifts from the kitchen. Nothing's as loving as something from **your** oven!

- **Use containers** that have a function for packaging your homemade gifts. Once the food has been enjoyed, the container remains to be used by the recipient of your gift.

- **Gobble-Up Gifts:** Miniature Fruitcakes, assorted cookies in various shapes, Chocolate Sauce, assorted Brownies, Chocolate Truffles, English Plum Pudding, Butter Tarts, assorted squares. Refer to Alphabetical Index for page numbers and Tabbed Index for general categories.

- **Bake cakes** in attractively shaped pans, unmold and wrap when cool with plastic wrap. Place cakes back in baking pans. Give the cake, cake pan and recipe as a gift!

- **Assorted cookies** can be placed in pretty paper cups and packed in foil containers covered with plastic wrap and decorated with a bow. Write out the recipes on recipe cards and place them in a recipe box, which you can also gift-wrap.

- **Fruitcakes** can be made in miniature loaf pans. Moisten cheesecloth with brandy or Grand Marnier or a mixture of the two, wrap fruitcakes in cheesecloth, then in foil. Let ripen in the refrigerator or in a cool place for at least 2 weeks. Freeze if desired.

- The **Steel Knife** is excellent to crush ice for all your drinks, or to whip up cocktails. Be sure to refer to your instruction booklet to make sure that your machine can process ice. Standard-size processors can hold about 3 cups liquid; large capacity machines can handle 6 cups.

- **Coffee** can be raised to a gourmet's delight with this quick trick. Prepare espresso coffee as usual. Heat milk until steaming, then process on the **Steel Knife** for 20 to 30 seconds, until foamy. Fill cups half full with hot coffee, then top with foaming milk. Sprinkle with a light dusting of cinnamon or grated chocolate. (My favorite version is with chocolate coffee.)

- **Another way with coffee:** Prepare freshly brewed coffee and fill cups ¾ full. Add 1 tbsp. brandy, Kahlúa or Grand Marnier to each cup. Top with whipped cream (prepared on the **Steel Knife**). Sprinkle with grated chocolate.

★★★★★★★★★★★★★★★★★★

SALMON MOUSSE

(This delicious mousse, with its pale orange color,
is a beautiful hors d'oeuvre for Thanksgiving,
Christmas or any festive occasion.)

1 **envelope unflavored gelatin**	¼ **c. fresh dill (or 1 tbsp.**
¼ **c. cold water**	**dried dill)**
½ **c. boiling water**	2 **- 7 ¾ oz. cans salmon,**
¾ **c. chilled whipping cream**	**drained & flaked (discard**
(35%)	**bones)**
½ **c. Mayonnaise (p. 65)**	1 **tbsp. lemon juice**
4 **green onions, cut in 2" pieces**	6 **drops Tabasco sauce**
(or ½ small onion)	¼ **tsp. paprika**
	¾ **tsp. salt**
	dash pepper

Sprinkle gelatin over cold water in measuring cup. Let stand 5 minutes to soften. Add boiling water and stir to dissolve gelatin. Cool slightly.

Steel Knife: Whip cream until stiff, about 45 seconds. Do not insert pusher in feed tube. Volume of cream will be increased if you place a heavy book under the base of the processor so that the machine is tipped forward. Transfer to a small bowl.

Prepare mayonnaise as directed. You will have 1 cup. Remove half from the bowl and reserve for another use. Drop green onions and dill through the feed tube while machine is running. Process until fine, about 10 seconds. Add dissolved gelatin and process just until blended. Add remaining ingredients and blend in with on/off turns, scraping down sides of processor bowl with a spatula. Pour into a lightly greased 6-cup mold. Cover and refrigerate until set, about 4 hours. (May be prepared ahead and frozen up to 2 weeks.)

To unmold, loosen edges with a knife, dip mold ¾ of the way into hot water, count to 3 and invert onto a lettuce-lined platter. Garnish with sliced lemon, cucumbers, pimiento strips and olives. Serve with black bread or crackers. Serves 12 to 16.

Note: Substitute 1½ to 2 cups fresh cooked salmon, halibut or even canned tuna. I use a fish-shaped mold, but it is equally attractive in a ring mold.

CREAM OF PUMPKIN SOUP
An excellent recipe to use up the leftover canned pumpkin
from my Pumpkin Pie. May be served hot or cold.

3 tbsp. butter
1 medium onion, halved
2¼ c. boiling water
2 c. canned or fresh pumpkin
   purée

2 tsp. instant chicken soup
   mix
¾ tsp. salt
freshly ground pepper
½ tsp. dill weed
1¼ c. milk
2 tsp. additional butter

Melt butter in a 2 quart saucepan. **Steel Knife:** Process onion with 2 or 3 on/off turns, until coarsely chopped. Sauté for 3 or 4 minutes on medium heat, until golden. Add water, pumpkin, soup mix and seasonings. Cover partially and simmer for 15 minutes. Process on **Steel Knife** about 30 seconds, or until smooth. Return mixture to saucepan. Pour milk into processor bowl and process for a few seconds to remove the remaining purée clinging to the bowl. Add to saucepan along with 2 tsp. butter. Taste to correct seasonings.

Yield: 4 servings. May be frozen.

Note: When reheating soup, use low heat. Do not boil.

MARINATED STUFFED ROAST TURKEY ✓

12- to 14-lb. turkey
2 cloves garlic
¾ c. oil
¼ c. wine vinegar or lemon
   juice

¼ tsp. pepper
½ tsp. dry mustard
1 tsp. paprika
¼ tsp. each basil, thyme,
   sage & savory
Turkey Stuffing (see below)
1 tsp. salt

Wipe turkey with a damp cloth and pat dry with paper towels. Remove excess fat and giblets from the cavity. Place in a large roasting pan.

Steel Knife: Drop garlic through the feed tube while the machine is running. Process until minced. Add oil, vinegar and seasonings; process 3 or 4 seconds to blend. Rub over the entire outside of the turkey. Cover turkey with foil and refrigerate overnight. Remove from refrigerator about an hour before cooking. Prepare stuffing. Stuff cavity and neck of turkey loosely to allow for expansion during cooking. Close with skewers and string. Fasten legs close to the body with string.

Place turkey on a greased rack, breast-side down. Roast uncovered at 325°F for 20 minutes to the pound, about 4½ to 5 hours. Turn turkey breast-side up halfway during cooking time. Baste occasionally. If turkey gets too brown, cover loosely with a tent of foil. Turkey is done when a drumstick moves easily in its socket, and if juices run clear when the thigh is pricked. If you wish to use a meat thermometer, insert it into the meaty portion of the thigh not touching the bone. Cook to 175°–180°F. Allow turkey to stand at least 20 minutes before carving.

Yield: 12 to 14 servings. Leftovers may be refrigerated or frozen, but be sure to remove all the stuffing and wrap it separately. Serve with Cranberry Relish (p. 000).

LET'S TALK TURKEY!

- Turkey leftovers can be a blessing in disguise. They can be transformed into a multitude of marvels with the help of your processor.

- Make Chicken Salad Spread (p. 29) or Chopped Chicken and Egg Appetizer (p. 30), substituting turkey for chicken. Both recipes are delicious—it just depends on the amount of leftovers you have on hand. Put into a pastry bag and pipe onto crackers for a quick hors d'oeuvre. Also great to stuff hollowed-out cherry tomatoes.

- Chop leftover turkey coarsely with on/off turns on the **Steel Knife** and add to quiches, crêpes, soufflés or omelets.

- Sauté chopped onions, mushrooms and celery (on/off turns on the **Steel Knife**). Add coarsely chopped turkey (on/off turns on the **Steel Knife**). Prepare 1 cup Sauce Velouté (p. 63) and combine with turkey and sautéed vegetables. Use to stuff miniature Cream Puffs (p. 316).

- Mandarin Chicken Balls (p. 147), using cooked turkey, is a delightful dish for your most discriminating guests. They'll never believe you made it from leftovers!

- Stir-fries are another excellent place to use leftover turkey.

- Save skin and bones from the turkey and use to make broth. Place in a large stockpot and cover with cold water. Bring to a boil. Remove any scum from the surface. Add 3 or 4 carrots, 1 onion or leek, celery leaves or stalks (3 or 4 will do) and salt & pepper. Simmer covered for 1½ to 2 hours. Delicious! I have even used the carcass from smoked turkey and added chopped vegetables for a delicious soup.

TURKEY STUFFING ✓

6 c. soft bread crumbs (see Note below)	2 eggs
½ c. parsley, loosely packed	¼ - ½ c. chicken broth or water
2 onions, quartered	1 tsp. salt
2 stalks celery, cut in chunks	1 tsp. paprika
¼ c. oil	½ tsp. each pepper, basil, thyme, savory & sage
1 apple, peeled, cored & quartered	

Steel Knife: Drop chunks of bread through the feed tube while the machine is running. Process until fine crumbs are formed. Measure 6 cups crumbs into a large mixing bowl. Process parsley until minced, about 8 to 10 seconds. Add to crumbs. Process onions with 3 or 4 on/off turns, until coarsely chopped. Empty bowl. Repeat with celery. Sauté celery and onions in oil on medium heat until golden, about 5 minutes. Add to crumbs.

Process apple until minced, about 10 seconds. Add eggs and process 2 or 3 seconds longer. Add with seasonings and enough broth to moisten crumb mixture. Mix well. (May be made in advance up to this point and refrigerated for 1 or 2 days, well-covered.) Stuff turkey loosely, filling no more than ¾ full to allow for expansion. Extra stuffing may be wrapped in greased aluminum foil and baked at 325°F for 1 hour.

Yield: for a 12 to 14 lb. turkey. Leftover stuffing may be frozen. Remove from turkey, cool, wrap well in foil and freeze up to 1 month.

Note: Save leftover ends and crusts of stale bread and store in a plastic bag in the freezer. Tear or break into chunks and process on the **Steel Knife**. Thawing is not necessary.

TURKEY GRAVY ✓

Pour pan juices from turkey into a container and freeze about 15 minutes, or until the fat rises to the top. Skim off fat. Measure 2 tbsp. fat back into roasting pan. Add 2 tbsp. flour and cook on low heat, stirring to loosen browned bits from the bottom of the pan. When golden brown, gradually blend in reserved pan juices from turkey plus enough chicken broth to make a total of 2 cups liquid. Add 1 tsp. Worcestershire sauce. Simmer for 5 minutes, scraping up any remaining browned bits from the bottom of the pan. Add salt & pepper to taste.

Yield: 2 cups thin gravy.

Note: For a thicker gravy, use 4 tbsp. fat and 4 tbsp. flour to 2 cups liquid.

CRANBERRY RELISH

3 c. cranberries	½ c. apricot jam
1 large orange, cut in chunks (discard seeds)	1 c. sugar
	1 tsp. lemon juice

Steel Knife: Process cranberries until finely ground, about 25 to 30 seconds, scraping down sides of bowl as necessary. Empty bowl. Process orange until fine, about 15 seconds. Place all ingredients in processor bowl and process until well mixed, about 10 seconds longer. Refrigerate for 1 to 2 days to blend flavors. May be frozen. Serve with chicken or turkey. Keeps about 1 month in refrigerator.

Yield: about 3½ cups.

Note: Delicious on toast, or over ice cream!

PUMPKIN PIE

½ recipe Standard Butter Pastry (p. 304)	½ tsp. ground ginger
1½ c. canned or fresh pumpkin purée	¼ tsp. nutmeg
	¼ tsp. ground cloves
¾ c. brown sugar, firmly packed	dash salt
2 eggs	1¼ c. whipping cream (35%)
1¼ tsp. cinnamon	¼ c. Grand Marnier
	12 pecan halves to garnish

Prepare pastry as directed. Roll out chilled dough on a floured pastry cloth about 2" larger than pie plate. Carefully transfer to a deep 9" pie plate. Trim off overhanging edges, leaving about ½" excess. Turn edges under and make a decorative fluted edge.

Steel Knife: Process pumpkin, brown sugar, eggs, spices and salt for 30 seconds, until well blended, scraping down sides of bowl as necessary. Add cream and Grand Marnier through the feed tube while the machine is running and process a few seconds longer to blend. Pour into unbaked pie shell. Bake at 425°F for 15 minutes, reduce heat to 325°F and bake 40 to 45 minutes longer, or until a knife inserted into the center comes out clean. Place 8 pecans in a circular design around the edge of warm pie and press lightly into filling. Arrange remaining 4 pecans to form a smaller circle.

Yield: 6 to 8 servings. May be frozen, but use within 6 weeks.

Note: Delicious with lightly sweetened whipped cream which has been flavored with 1 or 2 tbsp. Grand Marnier.

PUMPKIN PURÉE

Wash pumpkin and cut in several pieces. Remove the seeds and stringy portion. (The seeds can be roasted in a 200°F oven until dry and crisp, about 1 hour. If desired, dot with butter during roasting. Remove from oven and sprinkle with salt. Let cool on paper towelling to remove any excess moisture.)

Place pumpkin pieces in a pan skin side up, cover with boiling water and bake at 350°F for 1 hour, or until tender. Drain well and cool. Scrape out the pulp and process on the **Steel Knife** until smooth. May be frozen. When thawed, be sure to drain off any excess liquid.

Yield: about 2 to 3 cups, depending on size.

HERBED CHEESE LOG

An easy and elegant centerpiece for your Christmas
buffet table. Serve with assorted crackers
and/or pumpernickel bread.

1 c. pecans or walnuts	2 tbsp. sour cream or
2 bunches fresh parsley,	yoghurt
washed & very well dried	2 tsp. Worcestershire sauce
2 or 3 cloves garlic, peeled	½ tsp. oregano
4 green onions, cut in 2" pieces	½ tsp. basil
1½ lb. cream cheese, chilled &	pimiento strips for garnish
cut into chunks	

Steel Knife: Process nuts with 6 or 8 quick on/off turns, until finely chopped. Empty bowl. Process parsley until fine, about 12 to 15 seconds. Spread parsley on a piece of aluminum foil to make a 10" square. Reserve about 1 tbsp. parsley. Drop garlic and onion through the feed tube while the machine is running. Process until minced. Add cheese, sour cream, Worcestershire sauce, seasoning and 1 tbsp. parsley. Process until smooth, about 30 seconds, scraping down sides of bowl once or twice.

Spread cheese over parsley to within ½" of edges. Sprinkle with chopped nuts. Using foil to help you, roll up like a jelly roll, covering log completely with parsley. (If cheese mixture is too soft, you may chill it to facilitate rolling.) Seal foil so that there is an air pocket around the log. Refrigerate until firm. Carefully transfer to a long platter. Garnish with pimiento strips.

Yield: 12 to 15 servings. May be made 2 days in advance, but do not freeze.

Note: The herbed cheese mixture may be piped through a pastry tube onto crackers, celery stalks or used to fill tiny cream puffs. If desired, omit oregano and basil and substitute 2 tbsp. fresh dill. Truly dill-icious!

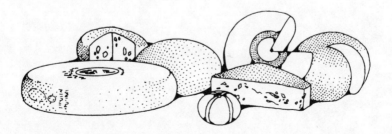

STOLLEN √

This is the traditional bread served in Germany
on Christmas Eve in place of fruitcake.

1 tsp. sugar	½ c. sugar
¼ c. lukewarm water (105° -	2 eggs
115°F)	¾ c. candied mixed fruit
2 pkgs. yeast	1 c. raisins &/or currants
½ c. milk	½ c. candied cherries, halved
½ c. butter	¾ c. sliced almonds
3¼ c. flour	

Dissolve sugar in warm water. Sprinkle yeast over and let stand for 8 to 10 minutes. Stir to dissolve. Meanwhile, heat milk until steaming. Remove from heat, add butter and stir to melt. Let cool.

Steel Knife: Place flour, sugar and dissolved yeast mixture in processor bowl. Process for 10 seconds to mix. Add milk, butter and eggs and process until dough forms a mass around the blades. (Have an additional ¼ cup flour ready in case the machine begins to slow down and dump in through the feed tube if necessary.) Process about 45 seconds; dough will be somewhat sticky.

Turn out onto a floured board and knead in fruit, raisins, cherries and almonds. Knead about 2 minutes, adding only enough flour to keep dough from sticking to your hands or the board. Make sure that fruit is evenly distributed throughout the dough.

Place in a large bowl that has been greased with about 2 tsp. of butter. Turn dough over so that all surfaces are lightly greased. Cover with foil or plastic wrap and let rise in a warm place until double in bulk. Punch down. Turn out onto a lightly floured board and divide in half. Roll or pat each piece of dough into a 12'' x 7'' oval. Fold in half the long way and press firmly to seal. Brush with melted butter.

Place on a greased baking sheet and form into a crescent shape. Cover with towels and let rise until double. Brush once again with melted butter. Bake at 375°F for about 30 minutes, until golden brown. Ice with White Glaze (p. 206), substituting almond extract for the vanilla. Decorate with red and green candied cherries and almonds to form flowers and leaves. Use half a red cherry for the center, almonds for the petals and strips of green cherries to form stems and leaves.

Yield: 2 Stollen. May be frozen.

CHOCOLATE YULE LOG √
(Bûche de Noël)

6 **eggs, separated**	¼ **tsp. salt**
1 **c. sugar**	¼ **cup icing sugar**
⅓ **c. cocoa**	1½ **c. whipping cream (35%)**
1 **tsp. baking powder**	12 **oz. pkg. chocolate chips**
1 **c. pecans or walnuts**	2 **tbsp. coffee liqueur, strong coffee or Grand Marnier**

Line a 12" x 18" jelly roll pan with aluminum foil, allowing it to extend slightly over the edges of the pan to help in removal. Butter and flour foil well. Set aside.

Steel Knife: Process egg yolks with ¾ cup sugar until pale yellow, about 1 minute. Add cocoa, baking powder and nuts; process about 15 seconds, until nuts are coarsely chopped. Transfer to a large mixing bowl.

Beat egg whites with salt until soft peaks form (use an electric mixer or a copper bowl with a whisk for maximum volume). Add remaining ¼ cup sugar and beat until stiff. Add about ¼ of the whites to the chocolate mixture to lighten it. Carefully fold in remaining whites just until blended. Spread evenly in pan. Bake at 350°F about 15 to 18 minutes, or until top springs back when lightly touched. Do not overbake. Cool 5 minutes.

Sprinkle a clean towel with icing sugar. Turn cake out onto towel and peel off paper. Roll cake and towel together lengthwise into a long roll. Cool completely.

While cake is baking, heat cream to boiling (about 3½ minutes on high power in the microwave). Process chocolate chips on the **Steel Knife** until finely chopped, about 30 seconds. Pour boiling cream through the feed tube. Chocolate will melt instantly. Add coffee liqueur. Place processor bowl with chocolate mixture in freezer for about 1 hour, until chilled. Stir occasionally. Process until thick and light, about 45 seconds. If not thick enough, chill 5 or 10 minutes longer.

Unroll cake and spread with half the chocolate. Reroll and transfer to a serving platter lined with strips of wax paper. Cut a small diagonal slice off each end of the roll and place them on top of the log to make stumps. Frost log completely and run the tines of a fork through the icing so that it resembles bark. Remove wax paper strips carefully and chill until firm. May be frozen.

Yield: 12 servings.

ENGLISH PLUM PUDDING
(A variation on the recipe taught in my cooking school.
Make it 2 to 3 weeks ahead so that it can mellow.)

4 or 5 slices white bread, torn
into 2" chunks
⅓ c. blanched almonds or
walnuts
1 c. currants
1½ c. Sultana raisins
½ c. mixed candied peel
½ c. flour
¾ c. brown sugar, firmly packed
1 tsp. cinnamon
½ tsp. nutmeg

⅛ tsp. Allspice
⅛ tsp. ground cloves
½ c. candied cherries
1 medium apple, peeled,
quartered & seeded
1 medium lemon,
quartered & seeded
2 eggs
⅓ c. oil
½ c. orange juice (part
brandy may be used)

Butter pudding molds very well. Use one 6 cup bowl or mold **or** two 3 cup bowls **or** four 1½ cup bowls. (Well-greased 1 lb. coffee cans may be used.)

Steel Knife: Process bread until fine crumbs are formed, about 20 seconds. Measure 2 cups crumbs into a large mixing bowl. Chop nuts coarsely, about 6 to 8 on/off turns. Add to bowl along with currants, raisins and candied peel. Process flour, sugar, spices and cherries with 3 or 4 quick on/off turns, until cherries are coarsely chopped. Stir into fruit mixture until fruit is well coated with flour. Process apple and lemon until fine, about 15 seconds. Add to bowl. Process eggs, oil, juice and brandy about 5 seconds. Add to bowl and mix well.

Pour into prepared bowls, filling no more than ⅔ full. Cover with a double layer of greased aluminum foil. Tie securely with string. Place on a rack in a steamer or Dutch oven. Add boiling water halfway up the sides of the bowls. Cover pot tightly. Simmer on top of the stove (a large pudding takes 6 hours and small puddings take 3 hours). Add additional boiling water as needed to maintain water level.

Remove from steamer and cool slightly. Unmold and cool completely. Wrap in foil and store in a cool, dry place or in the refrigerator. (May also be wrapped in cheesecloth that has been moistened with brandy, then overwrapped tightly with foil.)

To serve: Return pudding to greased bowl and cover tightly with greased foil. Steam 1 hour for small puddings and 1½ to 2 hours for large puddings. Serve with Brandy Hard Sauce (see below).

Yield: 8 to 10 servings. May be frozen. Thaw and steam as directed above before serving.

BRANDY HARD SAUCE

2" square lemon or orange rind
(remove with a potato peeler)
1½ c. icing sugar

½ c. butter, cut in chunks
3 tbsp. brandy
1 tsp. vanilla

Steel Knife: Process rind, sugar and butter for 15 seconds, until rind is finely grated. Add brandy and vanilla and process a few seconds longer, until smooth. Chill before serving. May be frozen.

Note: For a milder flavor, reduce brandy to 1 tbsp. and use 2 tbsp. milk. Add ½ tsp. nutmeg, if desired.

CHOCOLATE TRUFFLES
The ultimate in chocolate ecstasy. They make a wonderful
Christmas gift—if you can keep them hidden!

¼ c. cocoa
2 tbsp. icing sugar
1 c. whipping cream (35%)
8 oz. semisweet or bittersweet
chocolate (preferably Tobler)

1 tbsp. rum, cognac, Kahlúa,
Grand Marnier or Amaretto

Steel Knife: Process cocoa and icing sugar for 3 or 4 seconds to blend. Transfer to a 9'' plate. Heat cream to boiling. Break chocolate into chunks. Process with several on/off turns to start, then let machine run until chocolate is fine, about 30 seconds. Pour boiling cream through the feed tube while the machine is running and process just until smooth. Cool slightly. Blend in liqueur.

Remove **Steel Knife,** cover bowl and refrigerate until mixture is firm, about 3 hours or overnight. (You can speed up the time by placing the mixture in the freezer for about an hour, stirring several times.) Use 2 spoons and drop 1'' mounds of chocolate into the reserved cocoa mixture. Roll into balls, coating all surfaces with chocolate. Place in paper candy cups. Refrigerate or freeze until needed.

Yield: about 4 dozen.

Note: Truffles may also be coated with grated semi-sweet chocolate, or dipped in tempered semisweet chocolate or melted summer coating "chocolate" (available at shops that specialize in candy-making equipment). If you wish to dip the truffles, you must freeze them first to prevent them from melting.

CHRISTMAS COOKIES √
These thin, crisp cookies can be cut into stars,
wreaths, bells, trees, Santas, and other shapes. Great
for all-year round—just use your favorite cookie cutters
and have the kids help!

¾ c. chilled butter, cut into
chunks
1 c. sugar
2 eggs

1 tsp. vanilla or lemon juice
2½ c. flour
1 tsp. baking powder
¼ tsp. salt

Steel Knife: Process butter, sugar, eggs and flavoring for 2 minutes, until well creamed. Stop machine once or twice to scrape down sides of bowl. Add remaining ingredients and process with 3 or 4 on/off turns, just until mixed. Divide dough into 4 pieces, flour surface of dough lightly and wrap in plastic wrap. Chill until firm enough to roll, about 1 to 2 hours.

Roll out ⅛'' thick on a lightly floured surface. Cut into various shapes. Save all the scraps and reroll at the end in order to prevent the dough from becoming too tough. Place cookies on ungreased cookie sheets. Bake at 400°F about 6 to 8 minutes, until golden.

Yield: about 5 dozen. Freezes well.

Note: If desired, brush unbaked cookies with lightly beaten egg white and decorate with tiny colored sprinkles, finely chopped nuts or granulated sugar before baking.

CROWN ROAST OF LAMB

A dish fit for a king, this roast is perfect for Easter dinner.
Allow 2 to 3 ribs per person.

16- to 18-rib crown roast of lamb (about 4½ lb.)	2 tsp. salt
2 cloves of garlic, cut in thin slivers	½ tsp. pepper
	1 tsp. crushed rosemary
½ lemon	1 tsp. dried thyme

Preheat oven to 450°F. With the point of a sharp knife, insert slivers of garlic into the meaty portion of the lamb. Rub lemon all over lamb, then rub with combined seasonings. Cover the ends of the bones with aluminum foil to prevent them from burning. Stuff the center of the roast with crumpled foil to help retain its shape.

Place roast on a rack in a shallow roasting pan, place in oven and reduce heat to 350°F. Roast uncovered for about 1 hour and 15 minutes (about 140°F - 150°F on a meat thermometer). Roast will be medium. Remove foil about 1 hour before roast is done to allow for browning on the inside.

Place roast on a large round platter, remove foil from bones and let stand for 10 minutes to facilitate carving. Place paper frills on the bones and stuff the center with Nice Rice (below). Garnish platter with sprigs of fresh mint.

Yield: 8 servings.

NICE RICE

1 medium onion, cut in chunks	2 tsp. dried mint or 2 tbsp. fresh mint (see Note below)
1 stalk celery, cut in chunks	
2 tbsp. oil	dash salt & pepper
1 c. long-grained rice	¼ tsp. thyme
2 c. chicken broth	1½ c. fresh or frozen peas few drops fresh lemon juice

Steel Knife: Process onion and celery with 3 or 4 on/off turns, until coarsely chopped. Heat oil in a 2 quart saucepan. Add onion and celery and sauté on medium heat for 1 minute. Add rice, stir to coat with oil and cook 2 minutes longer, stirring often. Add broth and seasonings, bring to a boil and cook covered for 20 minutes. Remove from heat, stir in peas and lemon juice, cover and let stand 10 minutes longer.

Yield: 6 to 8 servings. May be frozen.

Note: Fresh mint should be washed and well dried on paper toweling before processing. Process on the **Steel Knife** until fine, about 10 seconds.

HOT CROSS BUNS

Traditional Easter fare. These are ever so easy to make
with the help of your food processor.

1 tsp. sugar	**¼ tsp. Allspice**
¼ c. lukewarm water (105° - 115°F)	**¼ tsp. cloves**
	¼ c. butter, cut in chunks
1 pkg. yeast	**¾ c. milk, scalded & cooled**
3¼ c. flour	**2 eggs**
¼ c. brown sugar, lightly packed	**¼ c. dried candied fruit, if desired**
½ tsp. salt	
1 tsp. cinnamon	**¾ c. raisins or currants**
¼ tsp. nutmeg	**1 egg yolk blended with 1 tbsp. water**
	white glaze (p. 206)

Dissolve sugar in lukewarm water. Sprinkle yeast over and let stand for 8 to 10 minutes, until foamy. Stir to dissolve.

Steel Knife: Place flour, brown sugar, salt, spices and butter in processor bowl. Process for 20 to 25 seconds, until no large pieces of butter remain. Add dissolved yeast mixture and process another 5 seconds. Add milk and eggs through feed tube while machine is running. If machine begins to slow down, dump in another 3 to 4 tbsp. flour through the feed tube. Process about 45 seconds. Dough will be somewhat sticky and quite elastic.

Empty bowl onto a lightly floured board. Knead in candied fruit and raisins by hand. Knead for 1 to 2 minutes, until smooth and elastic. Place in a large bowl that has been greased with about 2 tsp. butter. Turn dough over so that all surfaces are lightly greased. Cover with foil or plastic wrap and let rise until double in bulk, about 2 hours at room temperature. Punch down.

Divide dough into 15 equal pieces and roll into flattened rounds. Place rounds on a greased baking sheet barely touching each other. Cover and let rise until double in bulk, about 1 hour. Using a sharp knife, cut a fairly deep cross on the top of each bun. Brush with egg yolk mixture. Bake at 375° for 20 minutes until golden brown. Brush while hot with about ¾ of White Glaze (p. 206). Cool. Make cross on top of each bun by piping remaining glaze through a pastry bag using a #3 writing tube.

Yield: about 15 buns. May be frozen.

GINGERBREAD COOKIES

1 egg
½ c. cold butter, cut in
   chunks
½ c. light brown sugar, firmly
   packed
¼ c. molasses

2¼ c. flour
¼ tsp. salt
½ tsp. baking soda
½ tsp. ground cloves
1 tsp. powdered ginger
1 tsp. cinnamon

Steel Knife: Process egg, butter and brown sugar 1 minute. Add molasses and process 1 minute longer. (If you oil the measuring cup, molasses will slide right out!) Add half the flour along with remaining ingredients. Process with 3 on/off turns to blend. Add remaining flour and process 5 to 6 seconds longer, just until dough gathers together into a sticky mass. Remove from bowl and knead in a little extra flour to make a dough that is somewhat soft but firm enough to roll. Divide in two, wrap in waxed paper and refrigerate for 1 to 2 hours.

Roll out ⅛'' thick (see Note below). Cut into gingerbread boys and girls with floured cookie cutters. Bake at 375°F about 10 minutes. Cool. Ice with White Glaze (p. 266) and decorate with raisins and bits of candied cherries. If desired, omit icing and decorate with raisins and cherries before baking. Freezes well.

Yield: 1 to 2 dozen, depending on size.

Note: Dough may be rolled out between sheets of waxed paper on a cookie sheet, then frozen. Cut frozen dough into shapes and arrange on greased and floured cookie sheets.

Alternate Method: Roll the dough directly onto greased and floured cookie sheets without sides. Scraps can be lifted out with a floured spatula, gathered together and rerolled.

Passover

(Included in this index is a selection of recipes found in other sections of the cookbook that can be adapted easily for Passover with little or no adjustment. Refer to appropriate asterisk at bottom of this page.)

*1) Substitute matzo meal instead of crumbs.
*2) Substitute half the amount of potato starch for flour.
*3) Omit any spices &/or products not allowed for Passover.
*4) Substitute potato starch for corn starch.

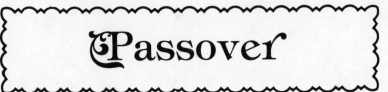

- **Your processor** will be an excellent time-saver for you during Passover when you are busy cooking for your family and guests. You will be able to do all your grating, chopping and slicing, and it will take no time for you to adapt your old favorites.

- **Some manufacturers** have separate bowls and blades available for purchase if you keep a Kosher kitchen and change all your dishes for Passover. Although this is quite expensive to do, many cooks have become so accustomed to using their machine daily that they just don't want to do without it.

- **Do not use** your processor to make sponge cakes for Passover. An electric mixer is far superior.

- **Many recipes** throughout this book can be easily used for Passover. Matzo meal can be used to bind hamburger mixtures and to bread fish, meat and poultry. Processor Passover rolls are quick to make and your children will be able to have their "sandwich". Mayonnaise can be whipped up in just a minute. Omit the mustard called for in the recipe; results will still be satisfactory. Make your own peanut butter!.

- **Potato starch** can be used to thicken gravies and sauces. Substitute 1 tbsp. potato starch for each tablespoon of cornstarch or each 2 tablespoons of flour.

- **Matzo Meal** is easy to make. Process 2 cups matzo farfel or 3 matzos, broken up, on the **Steel Knife** until fine. **Yield:** 1 cup meal.

- **Leftover chicken, turkey and roasts** are ideal to fill blintzes. The **Steel Knife** will grind them to the desired fineness in a matter of seconds. They are also good in **Shepherd's Pie:** Moisten ground meat with gravy, salt & pepper. If necessary, add an egg to bind the meat together. Top with mashed potatoes and bake at 350°F about 45 minutes, or until golden.

- **Chicken or Meat Patties:** Process an onion on the **Steel Knife** until fine. Add 2 cups of meat or poultry, cut in chunks, 2 eggs, ¼ c. matzo meal and salt & pepper. Process about 10 seconds longer, until well blended. Shape into patties and brown in hot oil for a few minutes on each side. Good hot or cold.

- **Omelets** are another quick meal idea. Vegetables can be chopped with on/off turns on the **Steel Knife.** Salami or cooked chicken or meat can be sliced with firm pressure on the **Slicer.** Process eggs on the **Steel Knife** for 2 or 3 seconds. Omelets are a great way to use up leftover vegetables.

- **Use stale sponge cake** to make **Passover Trifle:** Moisten cubes of sponge cake with a little wine. Arrange in layers with packaged pudding mix (prepared according to directions) and canned or fresh fruit. Crumble macaroons on the **Steel Knife** and use as a top layer. Garnish with chopped nuts and/or grated chocolate. Chill.

I find that Charoset is quick to process;
My machine does it with hardly a mess.
Chopped Liver and Eggplant are as easy as pie
And chopping those onions won't make me cry.

Grinding my fish is no longer a task
But grating horseradish still calls for a mask!
Matzo balls will be as light as a feather
(Add extra meal if you want them like leather!)

Carrots are sliced for the Tsimmis with ease,
And making my Stuffing is really a breeze.
Blintzes and Latkes, what a delight,
And making my salad won't take all night.

Passover rolls are so quick to turn out,
You'll make them quite often, without a doubt.
Apple Cake, Brownies, a Cheese Cake to treasure,
I give you my best, just process with pleasure!

★★★★★★★★★★★★★★★★★★★★★

CHAROSET

½ c. walnuts
3 large apples, peeled & cored
2 or 3 tbsp. sugar or honey

1 tsp. cinnamon
⅓ c. sweet red wine
dash of ginger, if desired

Steel Knife: Process nuts for 6 to 8 seconds, until coarsely chopped. Empty bowl. Add apples which have been cut in chunks. Process until minced. Add nuts back to processor bowl along with remaining ingredients. Blend mixture together with quick on/off turns, until mixed.

Yield: about 2½ cups. Refrigerate mixture until serving time.

KNAIDLACH FOR A CROWD
(Matzo Balls)

3¼ c. matzo meal
1½ tsp. salt
¼ tsp. pepper

9 extra-large eggs
(measure 2 cups eggs)
1 c. oil
1 c. water

Steel Knife: Place matzo meal and seasonings in processor bowl. Add eggs. Process for 10 to 15 seconds. Pour oil and water through the feed tube while the machine is running. Process for 20 to 30 seconds, until fairly smooth. Mixture will be quite loose.

Transfer to a large bowl and refrigerate for at least 4 hours or overnight. Mixture will thicken. Fill 2 large soup pots half full with water. Add ½ tsp. salt to each pot. Bring to a boil. Wet hands and shape mixture into 2'' balls. Drop into boiling liquid. Cover partially and simmer for 45 to 55 minutes, until light and puffed and cooked through.

Yield: about 2½ dozen matzo balls.

To Freeze: Add matzo balls to chicken soup and freeze in plastic containers or jars, leaving 2'' at the top for expansion during freezing.

MOM'S MATZO BALLS
Prepare as directed on p. 60, but omit baking powder for Passover.

MATZO BALLS LYONNAISE

8 matzo balls (p. 323)   salt and pepper, to taste
2 medium onions   ½ tsp. paprika
2 tbsp. oil

Slice matzo balls ¼" thick with a sharp knife. Insert **Slicer** in processor. Slice onions using light pressure. Sauté onions in oil on medium heat until golden. Add matzo ball slices and sprinkle with seasonings. Sauté on both sides about 3 or 4 minutes, until lightly browned.

Yield: 4 servings. Best served immediately. Serve as a side dish with chicken or roast.

PASSOVER CRANBERRY SWEET & SOUR MEATBALLS

2 lb. ground beef (or 2 lb. lean   Sauce:
 · beef, cut in 1½" chunks)   2 - 14 oz. cans cranberry
2 cloves garlic   sauce
1½ tsp. salt   ½ tsp. cinnamon
¼ tsp. pepper   2 - 8 oz. tins tomato sauce (or
1 egg   2 - 10 oz. tins
¼ c. matzo meal   tomato-mushroom sauce)

Steel Knife: If meat is not already ground, put about ⅓ of the beef chunks into the processor bowl and process until finely chopped, about 8 seconds. Do not overprocess. Transfer to a large mixing bowl. Repeat twice more with remaining beef chunks, adding each in turn to the mixing bowl. Drop garlic through feed tube while machine is running. Process until minced. Add egg and seasonings. Process a few seconds. Mix into meat along with matzo meal.

Wipe processor bowl clean with paper towels. Place cranberry sauce and cinnamon in processor. Add tomato sauce through feed tube while machine is running. Process 10 to 15 seconds. Immediately remove bowl from base of machine and pour sauce into a 3 quart saucepan. Heat to simmering.

Form meat mixture into tiny meatballs. Drop into simmering sauce. Cover and simmer slowly, about 1½ hours.

Yield: 10 servings as an appetizer or 6 as a main course. Freezes well.

PASSOVER WACKY FRANKS ✓
(Hot Dog and Bun, All Baked in One)

½ c. oil   1 tbsp. sugar
1 c. water   4 eggs
2 c. matzo or cake meal   12 hot dogs, frozen
1 tsp. salt

Combine oil and water in a saucepan and bring to a boil. Add dry ingredients and mix well, until mixture pulls away from the sides of the pan. Transfer mixture into the processor bowl.

Steel Knife: Process mixture for five seconds. Add eggs one at a time through feed tube while machine is running. Process 30 to 40 seconds longer, until smooth.

Mold mixture around frozen hot dogs, oiling hands slightly for easier handling. Place on a greased foil-lined baking sheet. Bake at 375°F for 50 minutes. Remove from oven and insert wooden skewers.

Yield: 12 servings. May be frozen.

STUFFED SHOULDER STEAK ROLLS

Stuffing:
2 onions, quartered
2 tbsp. oil
1 c. mushrooms, if desired
1 stalk celery
1 large carrot, scraped
1 c. matzo meal
2 eggs
2 tbsp. water
¾ tsp. salt
dash pepper

Meat Rolls:
4 shoulder steaks, ¼" thick
salt, pepper, paprika
¼ c. potato starch
3 tbsp. oil
¾ c. red wine (part chicken broth or consommé may be used)
10 oz. can whole mushrooms, drained, if desired

Steel Knife: Process onions with 3 or 4 quick on/off turns, until coarsely chopped. Heat oil in a large skillet. Add onions and sauté for 5 minutes. Process mushrooms with 3 or 4 quick on/off turns. Add to onions and cook 2 to 3 minutes longer.

Steel Knife: Cut celery and carrot in 1" chunks. Process until fine, about 8 to 10 seconds. Add sautéed vegetables along with remaining ingredients for stuffing and process just until mixed, using on/off turns.

Meat Rolls: Trim excess fat from meat. Pound to flatten slightly. Sprinkle lightly on both sides with salt, pepper and paprika. Spread stuffing evenly over meat to within ¼" from edges. Roll up like a jelly roll. Coat meat on all sides with potato starch. (**Note:** If you are very careful, it is not necessary to tie the meat rolls.)

Heat oil in skillet. Add meat rolls and brown on all sides. Remove to an ovenproof casserole. Add wine to skillet, and using a wooden spoon, scrape up any browned bits sticking to the pan. When mixture is reduced to about half, pour over meat rolls. (May be prepared in advance up until this point.) Add mushrooms, if desired.

Cover and bake at 350°F for 1½ to 2 hours, until tender.

Yield: 4 generous servings. May be frozen.

PASSOVER BLINTZES

3 eggs
½ tsp. salt
1 c. water
¼ c. potato starch
2 tbsp. cake meal
1 tbsp. oil

Steel Knife: Combine all ingredients in processor bowl and process until smooth, about 15 seconds.

Use a crêpe pan or Teflon skillet. Grease lightly for the first blintz. Pour about 3 tbsp. batter (just enough to cover the bottom of the pan) into the skillet and cook about 45 seconds on one side only, until the top surface is dry. Flip for 5 seconds on second side. Turn out onto a tea towel. Repeat with remaining batter. (May be prepared in advance up to this point and refrigerated or frozen until needed.)

Place about 3 tbsp. desired filling on blintz and roll up, turning in ends. Brown in hot butter or oil on all sides, until golden. (For a large quantity, you may bake blintzes. Heat about ½ c. butter or oil at 400°F in a 9" x 13" casserole. Add blintzes. Bake 10 minutes. Turn over and bake 10 minutes longer, or until golden.)

Yield: about 16 blintzes. May be frozen.

EGG ROLL BLINTZES

Passover Blintzes (p. 325)
2 onions, quartered
2 stalks celery, cut in chunks
1 pint mushrooms
oil for frying
½ medium-sized cabbage, cut
in wedges to fit feed tube

1 c. cooked chicken (discard
skin & bones)
2 cloves garlic, crushed
¼ tsp. ginger
salt & pepper, to taste

Prepare blintz leaves as directed and set aside while you prepare the filling.

Steel Knife: Process onions with 3 or 4 quick on/off turns, until coarsely chopped. Empty bowl. Repeat with celery, then with mushrooms, emptying bowl each time. Brown quickly in hot oil in a large skillet over high heat.

Grater: Grate cabbage, using firm pressure. Add to skillet and cook a few minutes longer, stirring.

Slicer: Slice chicken, using firm pressure. Add to skillet along with garlic, ginger and salt and pepper. Mixture should be fairly dry. Otherwise, sprinkle with 1 tbsp. potato starch to absorb excess moisture. Cool before filling blintz leaves.

Place about 3 tbsp. filling on each blintz leaf and roll up, turning in ends. (May be prepared in advance up to this point and refrigerated or frozen until needed.)

Either brown in hot oil until golden on both sides, **or** bake at 400°F in an oblong pan which has been preheated for about 5 minutes with oil to a depth of ⅛th inch. If baking, turn after 10 minutes and brown on second side.

Yield: about 16.

FARFEL, CHICKEN & VEGETABLE KUGEL

3 c. matzo farfel
2 c. chicken broth, heated
2 onions
2 stalks celery
1 c. mushrooms
½ green pepper

2 cooked chicken breasts,
skin & bones removed (or 2
c. cooked chicken)
3 tbsp. oil
3 eggs
salt, pepper, garlic powder &
paprika

Combine farfel and broth in a mixing bowl and let stand while you sauté the vegetables.

Slicer: Cut vegetables to fit feed tube. Slice onions and celery, using medium pressure. Slice mushrooms and green pepper, using light pressure. Make sure to remove all bones from chicken. Either slice by hand, or slice on the processor, using very heavy pressure. (If chicken is very cold, it will slice easier.)

Heat oil in a large skillet. Add vegetables and brown quickly over high heat. Add chicken and cook 1 or 2 minutes longer, stirring to mix well.

Steel Knife: Process eggs for 2 or 3 seconds. Add all ingredients to farfel and mix well. Season to taste. Place mixture in a well-greased 2 quart casserole. Bake at 350°F for 1 hour, until golden brown.

Yield: 8 generous servings. May be frozen.

FARFEL, CHICKEN & VEGETABLE MUFFINS

Follow recipe for Farfel, Chicken & Vegetable Kugel (p. 326), but place mixture in well-greased muffin tins. Bake at 350°F for 45 minutes, or until golden brown. These make a delicious lunch for the children.

Yield: about 15 muffins.

FARFEL APPLE PUDDING

3 c. matzo farfel	¼ c. walnuts
cold water to cover	3 apples, peeled, cored &
3 eggs	halved
½ tsp. salt	½ c. raisins
1 tsp. cinnamon	3 tbsp. oil
¾ c. sugar	

Combine farfel with cold water to cover. Drain immediately, pressing out excess moisture. Place in a large mixing bowl. Add eggs, salt, cinnamon and sugar and mix lightly.

Steel Knife: Chop nuts with several quick on/off turns. Add to farfel.

Grater: Grate apples, using medium pressure. Add with raisins and oil to farfel. Mix well. Turn mixture into a well-greased casserole. Bake at 375°F about 35 minutes, or until nicely browned.

Yield: 8 servings. May be frozen.

PASSOVER CARROT KUGEL

6 to 8 medium carrots, scraped	6 eggs
	2 tbsp. matzo meal
2 large apples, peeled, cored & halved (1 c. grated)	½ c. potato starch
	1 c. sugar
1 lemon, quartered, seeds discarded (do not peel)	½ c. sweet red wine

Grater: Cut carrots to fit feed tube crosswise. Grate, using firm pressure. Measure 2 cups firmly packed. Empty into a mixing bowl. Grate apple, using medium pressure. Add to carrots.

Steel Knife: Process lemon until fine. Add to mixing bowl. Process eggs for 3 to 4 seconds. Add with remaining ingredients to mixing bowl and mix well. Place in a well-greased 2 quart casserole. Bake at 375°F for about 50 to 60 minutes, until golden brown.

Yield: 6 to 8 servings. May be frozen.

PASSOVER CARROT TSIMMIS

2 lb. carrots, scraped &   ¼ c. sugar
   trimmed   3 tbsp. oil
2 c. boiling water   1 tbsp. potato starch
½ tsp. salt   ¼ c. cold water or orange juice
½ c. honey   dash of ginger, if desired

Slicer: Cut carrots to fit feed tube. Slice, using firm pressure. Transfer to a large saucepan and add boiling water and salt. Cover and simmer for about 20 minutes, or until fairly tender. Drain, reserving about ½ cup cooking liquid. Add honey, sugar and oil and mix well. Dissolve potato starch in cold water or juice and stir into carrots along with ginger. Adjust seasonings to taste.

Bake uncovered at 375°F for about 30 minutes, stirring occasionally.

Yield: 6 servings. May be frozen. Excellent!

Note: If desired, prepare your favorite recipe for matzo balls, and make tiny balls. Simmer in boiling water for about 20 minutes. Drain and add to boiled carrots. Bake as directed, stirring occasionally, being careful not to break the matzo balls.

MATZO MEAL LATKES

1½ c. matzo meal   ⅛ tsp. pepper
 4 eggs   ⅛ tsp. garlic powder
1¼ c. cold water   ⅛ tsp. onion powder
 1 tsp. salt   oil for frying

Steel Knife: Combine all ingredients in processor bowl and process until blended, about 8 to 10 seconds. Let mixture stand for a few minutes to thicken.

Heat oil to a depth of ⅛'' in a large skillet. Drop mixture from a large spoon into hot oil and flatten slightly with the back of the spoon. Fry on both sides until brown and crispy. Drain on paper towelling.

Yield: about 18 pancakes. May be frozen.

PASSOVER CHEESE LATKES

½ lb. dry cottage cheese   ½ tsp. cinnamon
3 eggs   ¼ c. sour cream
2 tbsp. sugar   ½ c. matzo meal or cake meal
1 tbsp. melted butter or oil   ¼ tsp. salt
                                  butter & oil for frying

Steel Knife: Combine all ingredients in processor bowl and process until smooth and blended, about 20 to 25 seconds. Scrape down sides of bowl as necessary.

Melt about 2 tbsp. butter and 2 tbsp. oil in a large skillet. When bubbling, drop cheese mixture from a large spoon into skillet. Brown on medium heat on both sides until golden. Repeat with remaining cheese mixture, adding more butter and oil to skillet as necessary. Serve hot with sour cream and berries, or with honey.

Yield: about 12 pancakes. May be frozen.

QUICK MATZO MEAL STUFFING

1 onion, quartered
1 stalk celery, cut in chunks
1 large carrot, scraped & cut
   in chunks
1¾ c. matzo meal

2 eggs
⅔ c. chicken broth or water
3 tbsp. oil
salt & pepper, to taste
¼ tsp. garlic powder

Steel Knife: Process onion, celery and carrot until minced, about 10 seconds. Add remaining ingredients and process until well mixed.

Yield: for a large veal brisket or capon. If you have extra stuffing, wrap in aluminum foil and bake separately for about 45 minutes.

MOCK MEAT KNISHES

4 potatoes, peeled & cut in 2"
   chunks
boiling salted water
2 tbsp. margarine or oil
1 egg
½ c. matzo meal
salt & pepper, to taste

Filling:
1¼ c. chopped liver, ground
cooked roast or chicken
(see directions below for
additional ingredients)

Cook potatoes in boiling salted water to cover until tender. Drain well. Return saucepan to high heat for about 30 to 40 seconds to dry excess moisture from potatoes.

Plastic Knife: Place potatoes with margarine and egg in processor bowl. Process with 4 or 5 quick on/off turns. Remove cover and cut through potatoes in several places with a rubber spatula, bringing up the mashed potato from the bottom of the bowl, and pushing the larger chunks downwards. Add matzo meal and seasonings. Process **just** until smooth and lump-free, about 20 seconds, stopping machine once or twice to scrape down sides of bowl with your spatula. Mixture will be quite sticky.

Line a baking sheet with tinfoil and grease generously with a little oil. Drop potato mixture from the spatula into about 8 or 10 mounds. Prepare filling. Any cooked leftover meat is ideal. Process on the **Steel Knife** until minced, about 10 seconds. If meat is dry, moisten with a little leftover gravy, broth, or an egg. Season to taste.

Oil the palms of your hands and shape potato mixture into flat patties. Place about 2 tbsp. filling in the centre of each patty and wrap the potato mixture around the filling. Shape like knishes. (The oiling of the potato mixture will help the knishes have a golden, crusty exterior.) Bake at 400°F for about 35 minutes, until golden brown.

Yield: 8 to 10 knishes. These reheat very well, or may be frozen.

PASSOVER PIE CRUST

1 c. matzo meal
3 tbsp. sugar
1 tsp. cinnamon

6 tbsp. butter or margarine,
cut in chunks

Steel Knife: Combine all ingredients in processor bowl. Process until well blended, about 20 to 25 seconds. Press into the bottom and up the sides of a greased 9" pie plate. Bake at 375°F for 18 to 20 minutes, until golden. Cool completely. Fill as desired.

PASSOVER CREAM PIE

Passover Pie Crust (p. 329)   **1 pkg. Passover pudding (instant or the kind you cook), vanilla or chocolate**

Prepare crust as directed, reserving about 2 or 3 tbsp. crumbs to use as a topping to garnish pie. Bake and cool crust completely.

Prepare pudding according to package directions. Fill crust. Sprinkle with crumbs. Refrigerate until well chilled and firm.

Yield: 8 servings. Do not freeze.

PASSOVER APPLE CRUMB PIE

(Easy and Sure to Please!)

Crust:
2 c. matzo meal
6 tbsp. sugar
2 tsp. cinnamon
¾ c. butter or margarine, cut in chunks

Filling:
5 or 6 apples, peeled & cored
¼ c. sugar
1 tsp. cinnamon (or to taste)

Steel Knife: Place all ingredients for crust in processor bowl. Process until well blended, about 20 to 25 seconds. Reserve about 1¼ cups crumbs for topping. Press remaining crumbs into the bottom and up the sides of a greased 9'' pie plate.

Slicer: Cut apples to fit feed tube. Slice, using firm pressure. Combine with remaining filling ingredients. Fill crust. Sprinkle reserved crumbs over apples. Bake at 400°F (or 375°F if using a pyrex pie plate) for 40 to 45 minutes.

Yield: 8 servings. May be frozen.

PASSOVER APPLE CAKE

Filling:
4 large apples, peeled, cored & halved
½ c. sugar (or to taste)
1 tsp. cinnamon
1 tbsp. potato starch

Batter:
3 eggs
¾ c. sugar
½ c. oil
¾ c. cake meal
¼ c. potato starch
1 tsp. cinnamon
¼ c. orange or lemon juice

Slicer: Slice apples, using firm pressure. Transfer to a large mixing bowl and mix with remaining filling ingredients.

Steel Knife: Process eggs with sugar for 1 minute, until light. Add oil through the feed tube while the machine is running and process another 30 to 40 seconds. Remove cover and add cake meal, potato starch and cinnamon. Drizzle juice over dry ingredients. Process with about 3 quick on/off turns, until smooth. Let batter stand for about 1 or 2 minutes to thicken slightly while you grease the baking pan.

Pour half the batter into a greased 8'' or 9'' square baking pan. Cover with apples. Top with remaining batter. Bake at 375°F about 45 to 50 minutes, until nicely browned.

Yield: 9 servings. May become soggy if frozen.

PASSOVER ROLLS

½ c. oil
2 c. water
1 tsp. salt

2 tsp. sugar
2 c. matzo meal or cake meal
4 eggs

Combine oil, water, salt and sugar in a saucepan. Bring to a boil. Remove from heat and add matzo or cake meal all at once. Stir vigorously until mixture pulls away from the sides of the pan. Cool for 5 minutes.

Steel Knife: Transfer mixture from saucepan into the processor bowl. Process for 5 seconds. Drop eggs through feed tube one at a time while the machine is running. Process about 20 seconds longer, until smooth.

Drop from a large spoon onto a lightly greased cookie sheet. Leave about 2'' between rolls for expansion during baking. Bake at 400°F for 50 to 60 minutes, until nicely browned.

Yield: about 10 to 12 rolls, depending on size. Delicious for sandwiches. Freezes well.

Note: As a treat for the children, shape into hot dog rolls. Bake as above.

PASSOVER CREAM PUFFS

½ c. orange juice
½ c. water
¼ c. butter or margarine
¼ tsp. salt

2 tbsp. sugar
1 c. cake meal
4 eggs

Combine juice, water, butter, salt and sugar in a saucepan. Bring to a boil, stirring occasionally. As soon as butter is melted, remove from heat and dump in cake meal all at once, stirring vigorously, until mixture pulls away from the sides of the pan. Cool 5 minutes.

Steel Knife: Transfer mixture from saucepan into processor bowl. Process for 5 seconds. Drop eggs through feed tube one at a time while machine is running. Process about 25 to 30 seconds longer after you have added all the eggs. Mixture should be smooth and shiny.

Drop rounded tablespoons of mixture onto a lightly greased cookie sheet, leaving about 2'' between puffs to allow for expansion during baking. (If desired, you may brush the puffs with a little beaten egg before baking for a shiny surface.)

Bake at 425°F for 10 minutes. Reduce heat to 375°F and bake 25 to 30 minutes longer. Remove from oven and cut a 1'' slit in each puff to allow steam to escape. Cool completely before filling.

Yield: about 15 medium or 30 miniature puffs. May be frozen. Delicious filled with vanilla pudding which has been flavored with grated orange rind. Substitute about ¼ cup orange juice for part of the milk when making the pudding. Do not freeze filling.

Note: If desired, pull out the soft insides of the puff before filling.

PASSOVER BANANA CAKE
(An electric mixer is needed for this recipe.)

½ c. nuts   1½ c. sugar
2 large, ripe bananas   1 tbsp. lemon juice
8 eggs, separated   ½ c. potato starch
¼ tsp. salt   ½ c. cake meal

Steel Knife: Process nuts for 8 seconds, until finely chopped. Empty bowl. Process bananas until puréed.

Beat egg yolks with salt for 1 minute in large bowl of the electric mixer. Add half of sugar gradually, and beat for 3 minutes, Add bananas and lemon juice slowly. Beat 3 minutes longer. Sift potato starch and cake meal together and fold in very carefully with a rubber spatula.

Wash beaters thoroughly and dry well. Beat whites in small bowl of electric mixer until foamy. Gradually add remaining sugar, continuing to beat until whites are stiff but not dry. Fold whites gently into yolk mixture. Fold in nuts. Bake at 350°F in an ungreased 10'' tube pan for 1 hour. Reduce heat to 300°F and bake 10 minutes longer. Invert immediately and cool completely. May be frozen.

MY MOTHER'S PASSOVER CAKE

(An electric mixer is needed for this cake, but your processor is excellent to "grate" the chocolate. You need 2 large mixing bowls for this recipe.)

3 oz. bittersweet chocolate bar   ½ c. cold water
½ c. almonds, if desired   ½ c. potato starch
9 eggs, separated   ½ c. cake meal
1½ c. sugar   ½ tsp. salt

Steel Knife: Break chocolate into 1'' chunks. Process until fine, about 30 seconds. Add nuts and process until finely chopped, about 12 to 15 seconds longer.

In large mixing bowl, beat egg yolks on electric mixer until light, about 3 to 4 minutes. Add sugar and water and beat on high speed for 8 to 10 minutes. Combine potato starch and cake meal. Sprinkle over yolk mixture a little at a time (a sifter or strainer will help) and fold in carefully. Then fold in grated chocolate and nuts. Wash beaters thoroughly and dry well.

In a large mixing bowl, beat whites with ½ tsp. salt until stiff, but not dry. Carefully fold into batter.

Pour gently into an ungreased 10'' tube pan. Bake at 350°F for 1 hour, then reduce heat to 300°F for 15 minutes. Invert immediately and let hang until cool.

Note: Batter should come to within 1½'' from top of pan. If necessary, make a 2'' collar of tinfoil around the top of the pan.

FARFEL MARSHMALLOW TREATS

¼ c. butter
3½ c. Passover marshmallows
  (with or without coconut
  coating)
1 c. nuts (walnuts or almonds)

5 c. matzo farfel
½ tsp. cinnamon
2 large (about 3 oz. each)
  Passover chocolate bars

Melt butter on low heat. Add marshmallows and stir until melted. Remove from heat.

Steel Knife: Chop nuts with quick on/off turns, until finely chopped. Add **half** the nuts to the marshmallows. Reserve remaining nuts for garnish. Stir in matzo farfel and cinnamon. Mix well. Spread evenly in a buttered 9'' x 13'' pan. Wet hands and pat down evenly.

Melt chocolate. Drizzle over farfel mixture. Sprinkle with reserved nuts. Cool until chocolate is set. Cut in squares. Guaranteed to please the kids.

Yield: about 4 dozen squares.

PASSOVER CHEESE CAKE

(Rich and Creamy)

Passover Pie Crust (p. 329)
1 lb. cream cheese, cut in
  chunks
2 eggs
½ c. sugar
1 tsp. vanilla or 1 tbsp. orange
  juice

Topping:
1 c. sour cream
2 tbsp. sugar
½ tsp. vanilla

Prepare crust as directed and press into the bottom and up the sides of a greased 9'' pie plate. Do not bake.

Steel Knife: Process cheese with eggs, sugar and vanilla for about 30 seconds, stopping machine once or twice to scrape down sides of bowl. Spread cheese mixture evenly over crust. Bake at 375°F for 25 to 30 minutes, until set. Cool slightly.

Steel Knife: Combine topping ingredients and process for a few seconds to blend. Spread evenly over cheese cake. Return to oven and bake at 375°F for 5 minutes longer. Cool; then chill before serving.

Yield: 6 to 8 servings. If desired, garnish with fresh strawberries.

Variation: Omit sour cream topping. Top cooled cheese cake with Fresh Strawberry Glaze (p. 219), using potato starch.

PASSOVER BROWNIES

1 c. walnuts	½ c. cocoa
4 eggs	1 c. cake meal
1½ c. sugar	1 tbsp. potato starch
²/₃ c. oil	1 tbsp. orange juice

Steel Knife: Chop nuts coarsely with 6 or 8 quick on/off turns. Empty bowl. Process eggs with sugar for 1 minute, until light. Add oil through the feed tube while the machine is running. Process 30 seconds longer. Remove cover and sprinkle cocoa, cake meal and potato starch over batter. Add orange juice. Process with 3 or 4 quick on/off turns. Add nuts and mix in quickly with 1 or 2 more on/off turns.

Pour batter into a greased 9'' x 13'' baking pan. Bake at 350°F about 25 minutes.

Either: Cool and cut into squares. (May be frosted with packaged Passover frosting.)

Or: Place chocolate covered mint patties over hot brownies and spread quickly to ice. The white peppermint filling will blend together with the melting chocolate and make a delicious icing.

Or: I sometimes cut marshmallows in half and place them cut-side down on top of the hot brownies. They are baked another 5 minutes and then cooled. Ice with packaged Passover frosting.

Additional Recipes

ALPHABETICAL INDEX